W.D. GANN TREASURE DISCOVERED

DISCOVERED

SIMPLE TRADING PLANS FOR STOCKS & COMMODITIES

W.D. GANN TREASURE DISCOVERED

SIMPLE TRADING
PLANS FOR
STOCKS &
COMMODITIES

ROBERT KRAUSZ,
MH.BCHE

MULTIPLE TIME FRAME APPLICATIONS
CHARTED BY THE FIBONACCI TRADER™
COMPUTER PROGRAM

Marketplace Books
Columbia, Maryland

ISBN 1-59280-227-3

Printed in the United States of America.

DISCLAIMER

GEOMETRIC TRADERS INSTITUTE, INC.
757 SE 17TH STREET, SUITE 272
FT. LAUDERDALE, FLORIDA 33316 USA

FOREWORD

Robert Krausz left a legacy of immeasurable value to the investment trading world. He was designated as a "market wizard" by Jack Schwager in his book <u>The New Market Wizards: Conversations with America's Top Traders</u>. He developed the first multiple timeframe analysis software available to the general public. He created over 20 custom indicators for market analysis. And probably most importantly, he was willing to share his knowledge about trading and market analysis with others.

Robert's life experiences were diverse and far-reaching. He grew up in Budapest and lived there until World War II when he escaped as he was being taken to a concentration camp. He subsequently lived in several orphanages until he eventually ended up in South Africa. As an adult he moved to England where he became a successful business owner, and eventually to the United States where he became a master trader. It was during his trading years that I first met Robert. I was invited to his home in Fort Lauderdale, FL to discuss some complementary trading methods we were developing independently. I will not forget the experience of entering Robert's trading room where an array of computer screens displayed data generated from indicators—most of which were new and previously unknown to me. The concepts were original and their use definitely not the pattern of "conventional trading." Most of the indicators Robert was using were his unique creations as shown in the table below:

Custom Market Analysis Indicators Developed by Robert Krausz

Arkay Swing Chart	Fibonacci Zones Channels
Balance Step	Fibonacci Zones
Double Hi-Lo Point	Flipit
Dynamic Balance Point	HiLo Activator
Dynamic BP Step	Hi-Lo Bands
Dynamic BPS Oscillator	Krausz Ratio Bands
Dynamic Fibonacci Channel	ROCO
Dynamic Fibonacci Range	TrendFinder
Dynamic FiboZone	TrendPoint Dynamic
Dynamic Range	TrendPoint
Dynamic Trio	Triple Switch
Fast Point Switch	

Robert's passion was to share his knowledge through teaching others the basis of his skill in trading. New software programs were required for computer application of these novel indicators. To accomplish that Robert hired his own personal programmer (a brilliant one!) to write the computer code that would make implementation of his ideas possible. A less magnanimous person could have kept these ideas and become a successful private trader; instead he chose to share them. As one of his family members related,

> "I was always impressed by Robert's generosity... I don't mean financial generosity... I mean the generosity of his time, his ideas, and his work, which he shared so freely. He didn't wait for someone he knew to be interested to ask for it, he just gave it to them. He knew he could do very well financially by keeping his ideas about trading and the software he developed to himself... or he could go out in the world, meet people, share ideas and be so much richer in spirit. And that's what he did!"

He made his market analysis program, the Fibonacci Trader, available to the general public. One of the unique features of Fibonacci Trader is the ability to chart, correlate and test trading indicators and algorithms in multiple time frames. Robert understood the power of interpretation from utilizing multiple time frames for market analysis. I recall the rules he understood so well and related to me often:

- Each time frame has its own Trend, Momentum, Volatility, Support and Resistance.

- Analysis in the longer time frame overrules analysis in the shorter time frame.

- The shorter time frame will manifest any changes more quickly than the longer time frame.

- The longer time frame is best used to determine the strength and direction of the trend.

- The shorter time frame is best used to determine specific support and resistance, and specific trade entry points.

- What appears to be chaos in one time frame can be orderly in another time frame.

Robert's method of analysis influenced my philosophies for trading. Over a decade of working together, he shared a number of concepts I have used everyday to guide my trading. He was familiar with global markets, global exchanges, and with traders on five continents. Through his association I became knowledgeable and comfortable with trading markets throughout the world.

Although my work with Robert primarily dealt with the futures markets, the same trading methodologies are equally applicable to the equity markets. This book, <u>A W.D. Gann Treasure Discovered</u>, gives the methodology that will permit traders to apply systematic trading plans to both futures and equity markets. The trading plans describe specific entry rules, exit rules, profit objectives, and overall risk management. To realize value in the application of the plans described in the book, each trader is admonished to understand the essential elements that Robert utilized to develop an effective trading plan: market direction, tradeable trend, support and resistance points, action points, and money management techniques.

Any successful plan must include the derivation of these core elements, each of which must be clearly defined and given specific trading rules. Furthermore, it is critical that the plan adopted be personally backtested. If your plan has not been backtested to your satisfaction, it should not be used in real-time trading. Even so, one must appreciate that a successful 10-year backtest does <u>not</u> guarantee similar results in the future. Experience has guaranteed, however, that failure of performance in a backtest assures that it will not work in a consistent manner in the future. Robert always encouraged readers to verify the results. "Backtest, backtest, backtest," he espoused. "There is no other way to proceed forward with confidence in a plan."

Any author who has presented a trading strategy knows there will always be the "nay-sayers." This never bothered Robert. He didn't listen to anyone telling him what couldn't be done; he did what he found could be done. Robert Krausz influenced my life and that of many others. He loved teaching people how to trade both in concept and practice. Sharing valuable knowledge with others is one of the most admirable legacies to which one can aspire. That is the legacy of Robert Krausz as carried on in this book.

John Jackson

MECHANICAL METHOD & TREND INDICATOR
FOR TRADING IN GRAINS

BY W. D. GANN

Press on. Nothing in the world can take the place of persistence. Talent will not; nothing is more common than unsuccessful people with talent. Genius will not; unrewarded genius is almost a proverb. Education alone will not; the world is full of educated derelicts. Persistence and determination alone are omnipotent.

Calvin Coolidge

The previous page is an exact copy of the front cover of W. D. Gann's original trading course.

TABLE OF CONTENTS

This book is dedicated to my wife Jeanne.
"The best trade I ever made"

THE REAL STORY

Who was the greatest market researcher of all time?

Before you answer, consider this: Do you know anyone who has researched in depth the following: price bar patterns, astronomy, multiple time frame relationships, swing chart trend definitions, support and resistance zones based on angles? Have you met any traders that have investigated numerology, ancient and modern geometry, mathematical relationships of numbers, squaring time and price? Or Western and Hindu astrology, pyramid technology, and the possible ties to the markets? Do you know of anyone doing this degree of research, and without a computer?

Such a trader was W.D. Gann.

W. D. Gann was an enigma. Much has been written about Gann's success, or lack of it. Questions still remain as to how great his techniques were, or how poor. Did he make fortunes or lose them? And more importantly, can any of his concepts stand up in today's fast moving computer driven markets?

Did you know that back in the 1950's he charged some $5,000 for his courses? At that time, that was the price of an average three bedroom house in the USA. Today, the equivalent cost would be over $50,000. So, back then you had to be pretty serious about trading to pay that amount of money. And yet, wouldn't that price be worth it if the techniques were genuine?

The answer to this question lies within each trader's perception of value. Some traders consider $39.95 too high of a price for a book describing a trading technique. To others, valid market knowledge is priceless.

THE ROAD AHEAD

I will show you what I consider to be valid market knowledge, based on W. D. Gann's original work. And what do I mean by valid market knowledge? The knowledge is a set of fixed rules to trade by. You will see that the rules are valid because they meet a number of requirements; conditions that my twenty years of trading have taught me are important. Before I discuss this plan, though, I want to share with you the story of how I came into possession of this technical concept of swing trading.

W. D. Gann has published a number of books, unfortunately, the majority of the time Gann wrote in the manner of the ancient mystics; hiding the real meaning behind the surface explanation. Having read his books many times, I found his directions to be vague and

1

convoluted. And not just me, others, both his followers as well as his detractors have tried to explain his concepts in an understandable and usable way. Nevertheless, very few authors have succeeded. And as I said, it is Gann's own fault. A small example of the challenge is his overuse of the word "square": squaring time and price; the square of nine; the square of 24; and on the square. Fortunately, while his books were obscure, his actual trading courses are more direct and straight to the point.

Some ten years ago, I put out the word here and in Europe that I was interested in purchasing original W.D. Gann material, especially his courses. You cannot believe the nuts that fell to the ground, from con-men to dreamers! All trails led to nowhere until a few months ago when the universe rewarded my persistence, right on my doorstep.

Some of you may know that Joe Rondinone was the last trader taught by Gann before he passed away to the "great trading room in the sky." You can imagine my astonishment when Rondinone asked me if I was interested in some original Gann courses that he bought from Gann back in 1955.

Rondinone explained that the courses were typed on W.D. Gann's letterhead, not in the usual printed format. Also, they were signed and dated by Gann in his purple ink. All five courses were in their original binding. After much haggling, we settled on the price of $1.00 (yes, you read that correctly, one dollar).

Mr. Rondinone's motives were clear, stating: "I want these manuscripts in the hands of a trader and researcher who appreciates their real value and will use them." Frankly, I was amazed at my good fortune and Joe's generosity. The entire treasure-trove consisted of five courses and two unfinished pages, dated April 18, 1955, and headed "Time Periods on the Master 7 Day Period for Soybeans". Obviously, these were a work in progress, as Gann passed away soon after that date.

One method though, caught my eye. It was the "Mechanical Method and Trend Indicator for Trading Grains" and it shouted to be studied first. Given my personal approach to trading, this method was given priority, and the results of that examination are what you will find in the following chapters. Before we continue the story, I want you to understand the importance of having a trading plan.

TRADING PLANS

After 20 years of trading, I find it almost impossible to trade without a plan that does not have fixed rules. Why? Why not just keep up to date with all the news, and trade as you see fit? Because, if you do not have a set of fixed rules, you cannot do a back test. Without a back test how do you know if your plan worked in the past? Yes, I know that just because the plan produces positive results in the past, this does not guarantee success in the future. But I do guarantee that if the plan does not produce positive mathematical expectations during the back test then it will never work in the future.

Let me ask you: Would you consider building a house without an architectural plan? Of course not! No plan would lead to chaos. The same thing applies to trading. So what constitutes a good trading plan? A valid trading plan must have some minimum components to earn the right to be called valid.

At the simplest level, a plan must define:
• Market direction (the general direction of the market; for example, the overall trend.)
• Tradable trend (the trade direction, in other words; the immediate swing.)
• Support and resistance points (exact zones.)
• Action points (entry-exit-pyramid rules.)
• Money management techniques. These should include at least:
    A) Capital required for your plan.
    B) Stop and Stop/Reversal rules.
    C) Profit protection rules.
    D) Percentage of capital per trade. (This varies according to the plan.)

With a trading plan that fits this description, you may be ready to trade. Now, back to my story of W. D.'s "mechanical method." Slowly, I worked my way through the well worn pages, making notes as I went along. Can you imagine my surprise when I came to his pages 11 and 12 (reproduced here on pages 5 and 6) and saw that Gann had altered some of his original calculations and signed these alterations in his usual purple ink?

These alterations were fitted in between the paragraphs. Although the original course is dated June 1933, the actual alterations were handwritten in early 1955. So I can presume that Gann thought it was important enough to insert and sign it before he sent the course to Mr. Rondinone. And what did Gann write? Very simply: "**Use 2 day charts and rules better than 3 day. Signed W. D. Gann**."

Does Mr. Gann changing a three day swing definition to a two day swing definition make it into a treasure? I could only come to a conclusion by doing a comparative back test on today's hyper markets using both daily charts and intra-day time periods, and that is exactly what I did!

Charting by hand, a back test of the T-Bond futures markets proved to me that W. D. Gann's new Two Day Swing Concept provided two pieces of vital information: First, the trend direction and second, the points of support and resistance. The manner was simple, yet brilliant.

Why the T-Bond market for the back test? The 30-year T-Bond contract was chosen for this test because this is my main trading vehicle, and my understanding of this market's rhythm is such that if the Two Day Swing did not work well enough, I would spot this quickly, and not waste any time on further research of this tool.

Besides my own working knowledge of this market, the T-Bond futures contract traded on the CBOT is currently the second largest futures contract in the world. Just yesterday, as I write this, the daily volume was over 400,000 contracts and the open interest was over 500,000 contracts. Not only is this a giant market, but I believe the most sophisticated traders are involved. There are hedgers, bank traders, scalpers, interest rate players, all trading for their own reasons and quantities.

Therefore, if a trading concept is going to work, then this is the place where I want to test it first. So, what were the results? Not only did I find that it held up nicely on the Daily Chart, but the Intra-day results were also acceptable. After satisfying myself on the Daily bars, by hand charting, I knew the acid test would be in computerizing the entire concept in "real time," on a Multiple Time Frame basis. Fortunately, I already had a real time computer program, the "Fibonacci Trader®", that functioned in Multiple Time Frame format, Real Time or End of Day.

Much excellent programming was done in the Fibonacci Trader® to bring the entire technique to the standard of clarity and user friendliness that I required from a trader's point of view. But the toughest part was still to come.

All of W.D.'s Swing concepts had to be pulled together and integrated with my approach to formulate a mechanical trading plan that was tradable and profitable. Those of you who have tried to do this will know exactly what I am talking about. This is not the time or place for a detailed discussion, but three points must be mentioned.

1. Any "valid" plan of this mechanical nature must have a simple philosophical basis. It can be geometric, mathematical, time oriented or any combination thereof.
2. Curve fitting or "over-optimizing" is the Kiss of Death to any mechanical trading plan. Unfortunately, there are programs out there that encourage system designers to do just that. Robustness is the key word.
3. Must be dynamic enough to change with the market.

The concepts and techniques embodied in these plans are similar to those I use in my personal trading, incorporating Multiple Time Frames, Fibonacci and Gann techniques. Always mechanical, always fixed rules, always with serious back testing.

NOTE: All rules work best in active fast-moving markets and the big profits are made trading in active markets. If you follow these rules, you will make money. Make up your mind to follow the rules before you start and success is assured.

SPACE CHARTS
RULES FOR ACTIVE MARKETS AT HIGH LEVELS

Many times in history Wheat has sold at $1.75 to $3.50 per bushel. These high prices will recur some day, so you need to know how to trade in markets that move 10 to 20¢ per bushel per day and how to get out near tops and bottoms because the moves will be so fast that you cannot wait for Trend Line bottoms to be broken in every case, and cannot wait for daily bottoms to be broken or daily tops to be crossed, especially where the range is 15¢ per bushel a day, or even where it is 7 to 10¢ per day.

When a market is having a rapid advance or a rapid decline of this kind, you should keep a space chart of 3 points. By this I mean, that during the day, when Wheat declines 3¢ per bushel from any top, then advances 3¢ per bushel from any bottom, you should record it. Then the first time that Wheat breaks under a bottom of a 3¢-move, consider that the trend has reversed temporarily. This may only be for one day or for one or two days, but it is a warning to get out.

You should also keep a chart of 1¢ movements if you are watching the tape. However, when the markets are very active at high prices, I consider that the best chart to keep is the 3¢ moves.

Do not try to Keep this up W.D.Gann

HOURLY CHART

In active, fast-moving markets, where you can get the prices every hour it is important to keep the Hourly high and low and also mark the opening of the hour and the closing of the hour.

Apply the same rules that you do to your Daily high and low chart. The first time that the market breaks a Trend Line bottom on the Hourly chart or crosses a Trend Line top, consider that the trend has changed temporarily.

If there are a series of hours with tops around the same level, or bottoms around the same level, for several hours, then when the market crosses 1¢ per bushel over an Hourly top, or breaks 1¢ under an Hourly bottom, consider that your trend has changed at least temporarily and trade accordingly.

Even in a narrow market or in a market that is moving 1 to 3¢ per day, if you keep an hourly high and low chart, you will see the value of it in getting a quick change in trend.

All of these rules are given you to protect your capital and protect your profits; to help you get out near the top as possible and as near the bottom as possible. Don't forget to always use stop loss orders. This is your "emergency brake" and your "safety valve" to protect you when the market reverses.

use 2 Day Chart and rules better than 3 Day W.D

3-DAY CHART OR MAIN TREND INDICATOR

The 3-day Chart should be kept on a separate sheet of chart paper from the

Daily high and low Chart and Trend Line. It is used in connection with the Minor Trend Indicator, or the Trend used with the Mechanical Method.

HOW TO MAKE UP 3-DAY CHART

For the 3-day Movement or Main Trend Indicator, the rules are as follows:

The 3-day Chart is made up of moves of 3 days or more. When an option starts to advance and makes higher bottoms and higher tops for 3 consecutive days, you move the line on the 3-day Chart up to the top of the 3rd day; then if it continues to move up, making higher tops without reacting as much as 3 days, you continue to move the line on the 3-day Chart up to the top of each day until the option reacts 3 days or makes lower bottoms for 3 consecutive days or more.

Then you move the line on the 3-day Chart down and continue to move it down to the lowest price as long as the option makes lower bottoms without rallying 3 days.

The first time that an option rallies 3 days from any bottom, that is, making higher tops for 3 consecutive days or more, you move the line up.

This chart is based on higher tops and lower bottoms and not on closing prices. An option may close lower on the 3rd day, but not make a lower bottom, in which case you make no change on the 3-day Chart. An option may close higher on the 3rd day from the bottom but not make a higher top on the 3rd day, and in that case, you do not move the line up on the 3-day Chart.

EXCEPTION TO RULE

There is an exception to the rule for making up the 3-day Chart. When an option is very active near the top or bottom, making a wide range, and crosses the top or bottom of a move made by the Trend Line Indicator in less time than 3 days, then you record the move on your 3-day Chart just the same as if there had been a move of 3 days in one direction.

INDICATIONS FOR CHANGE IN TREND

Rule 27 - CROSSING TOPS OR BREAKING BOTTOMS OF 3-DAY MOVES

The surest sign of a change in the main trend is when a move on the 3-day Chart is exceeded by 1 to 3¢. When an option breaks under a bottom made by the 3-day Chart, you consider that the main trend has turned down, and when a move crosses a top made by the 3-day Chart, consider that the main trend has turned up, at least temporarily.

Breaking 1¢ under the last 3-day bottom or crossing the last 3-day top by 1¢ in slow or semi-active markets is enough to show a change in the trend.

Rule 28 - FIRST 3-DAY REACTION OR RALLY

After a prolonged advance, watch the first time that there are 3-full days of lower prices or the first time that the 3-day Chart is moved down, as this will often be the first sign that the end of the move is near.

Next, watch the second move of 3 days down on the 3-day Chart and see if it is lower than the Trend Line bottom or the minor Trend Indicator or under

Two "REAL TIME" PLANS AND Two "END OF DAY" PLANS will be shown.

The Real Time Plans are:
A) BASIC PLAN with 10-year back test for the 30-Year T-Bonds.
B) PROFESSIONAL PLAN with a 6-year back test for the 30-Year T-Bonds contract.

The "End of Day" Plans are:
A) BASIC PLAN for five major stocks - IBM, Eli Lilly, Philip Morris, Intel, and J. P. Morgan. Each with its own 5-year back test.
B) BASIC PLAN for T-Bonds, with a 5-year back test.

This gives a total of 46 years of back testing.

Does this mean that the plans only work on these commodities and stocks? No. Perhaps you should check into some others.

Starting with the basics we will work up to advanced concepts and techniques. Whilst there are no Advanced Plans included, there is more than enough to get your teeth into. Perhaps in my next book I will cover "Advanced or Intra-day Plans".

Not only are the rules for each plan clearly presented, but the majority of this book is taken up with the "real meat", ie: the exact history of each and every back test, trade by trade, chart by chart, rule by rule. I have kept the fluff to a minimum and for that reason this book is not everyone's cup of tea.

The serious student who will take the time to check through the charts trade by trade will realize what I am sharing. You can use it as "stand alone" or blend it with your own plan and your tools.

Many thanks to all the people who made this book possible. Joe Rondinone, a friend, a teacher and a great trader, who provided the original Gann courses for this book. My editor, Thom Hartle, a true professional. Linda Long, who labored late into the night with super humor. Carlos Toscano de Almeida, our programmer, whose patience deserves a medal. Thomas Long's technical knowledge was of great help. Doug Shannon for his excellent help in back testing. There are many others to whom thanks are due for the kindness they have shown me. Tim Slater of Dow Jones and Co. Jack Schwager, who interviewed me for "New Market Wizards". Jon Lutsi and Mike Tedesco of Standard & Poors Comstock. Larry Jacobs of "Trader's World". To all my students on five continents for their trust and confidence.

Best wishes and super trading,

Robert Krausz, MH. BCHE

GANN SWING TRADING BASICS

> Simplicity is often the voice of God.
> Albert Einstein

NEW GANN SWING CHARTIST©

SWING TRADING BASICS AND TERMINOLOGY

Clear definitions of the terms used for this technical approach is required before the concept can be understood and trading rules applied.

You will find throughout this book that I am fond of definitions; fudging can only cause problems and losses in the end. Every definition is illustrated by a Chart.

1. SWING DIRECTION

a) What causes the swing direction to change?
b) What causes a pause in the swing direction and then to carry on in the original swing direction?

2. TREND

a) What causes the trend to change?
b) How does the trend go into Neutral?

3. SUPPORT AND RESISTANCE

a) Definition of Support and Resistance.
b) How does Support hold or fail?
c) How does Resistance hold or fail?

4. SLOPE

a) What is the Slope?
b) What is the difference between Slope and Trend?

All of these definitions are illustrated in the charts that follow. The explanations next to the charts will enable you to be aware of the concepts.

Please realize that in the beginning we are focusing on one time period only, the Daily Bars. As we progress, the interesting world of Multiple Time Frames will be covered and analyzed.

1. SWING DIRECTION

UPSWING   **CHART #1**

FROM DOWN TO UP

The Swing Direction can change to UP <u>ONLY</u> if you get TWO <u>CONSECUTIVE</u> HIGHER HIGHS.

(W. D. Gann also needed higher lows for his swings to change direction. But in today's fast computerized markets, I do not use that qualifier.)

DOWNSWING   **CHART #2**

FROM UP TO DOWN

The Swing Direction can change to DOWN <u>ONLY</u> if you get <u>TWO CONSECUTIVE LOWER LOWS</u>.

Both Swings are applicable to any time period. A "pause" in the Swing is covered in the Advanced Section (see page 387).

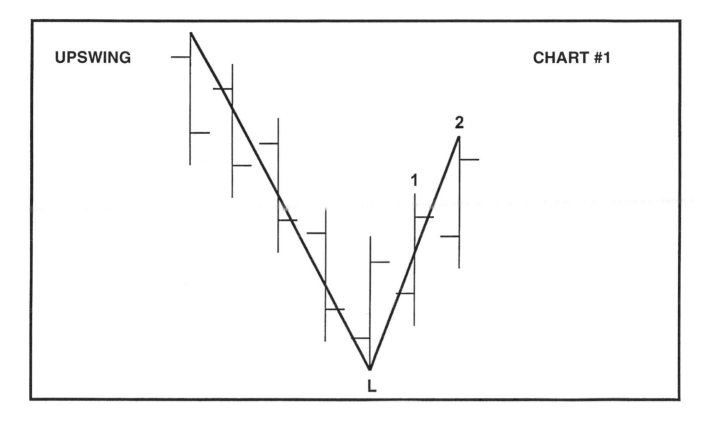

UPSWING   CHART #1

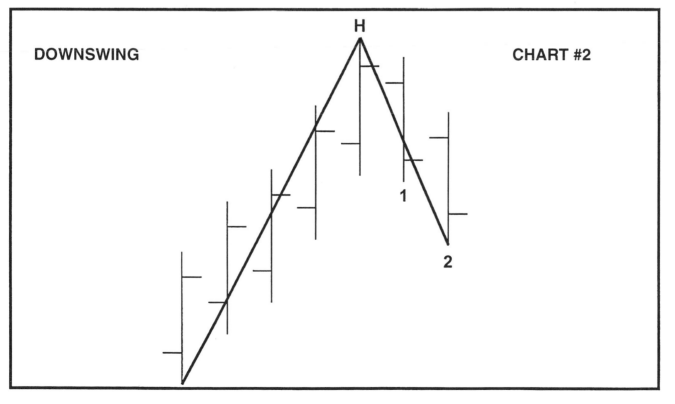

DOWNSWING   CHART #2

13

2. TREND

UPTREND **CHART #3**

<u>Trend change from DOWN to UP</u>

Prices must take out the nearest "Peak" <u>and</u> the Trend was previously Down (Uptrend is shown as a Solid Line).

DOWNTREND **CHART #4**

<u>Trend change from UP to DOWN</u>

Prices must take out the nearest "Valley" <u>and</u> the Trend was previously UP. Downtrend is shown as a Dashed Line. (The definition of Trend change is the same for any time period being analyzed.)

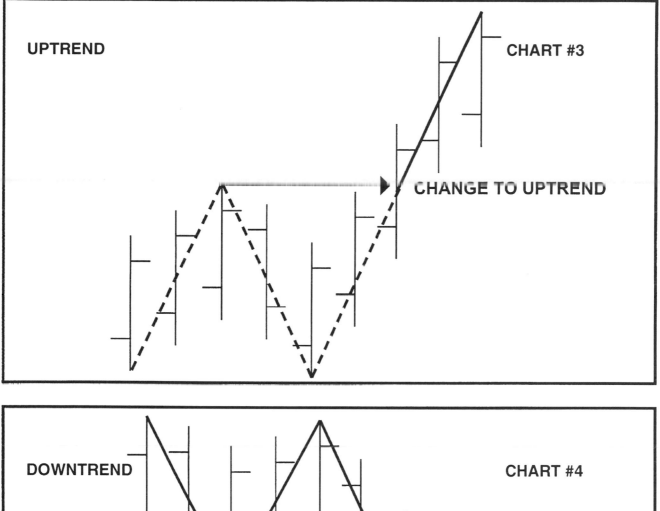

UPTREND   CHART #3

CHANGE TO UPTREND

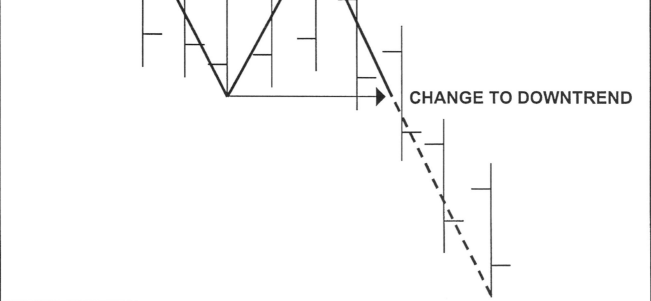

DOWNTREND   CHART #4

CHANGE TO DOWNTREND

3. SUPPORT AND RESISTANCE

SUPPORT   **CHART #5**

Support is the "Valley" of the previous clearly defined Swing. As long as prices do not penetrate <u>below</u> the "Valley" point then Support is holding. This "Valley" point is actually the Low of the previous Swing.

If prices penetrate BELOW the "Valley" then Support may be failing.

RESISTANCE   **CHART #6**

Resistance is the "Peak" of the previous clearly defined Swing. As long as prices do not rise <u>above</u> the "Peak" point then Resistance is holding. This "Peak" point is actually the High of the previous Swing.

If prices rise ABOVE the "Peak" point then Resistance may be failing.

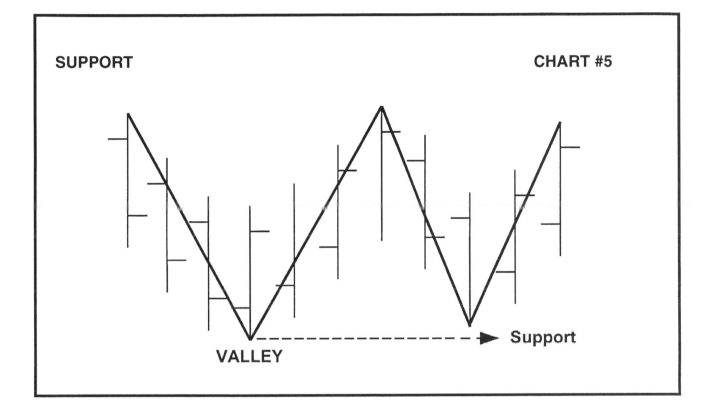

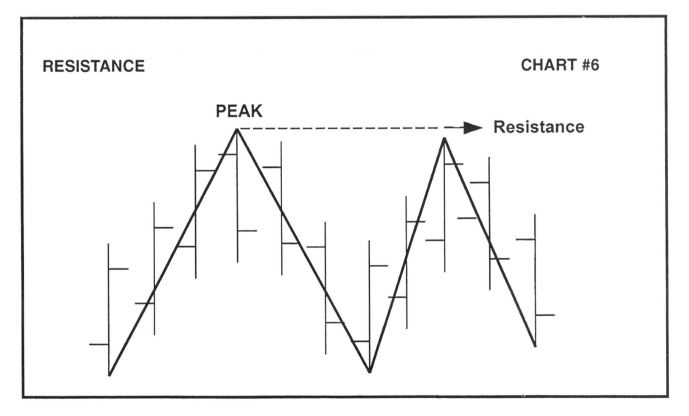

4. SLOPE

It is crucial that you understand the **difference** between TREND and SLOPE.

THE <u>TREND</u> IS DEFINED IN CHARTS 3 & 4.

THE <u>SLOPE</u> IS THE IMMEDIATE DIRECTION OF THE SWING.

UPSLOPE

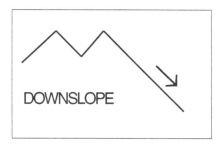
DOWNSLOPE

CHART #7 (Shows clearly Trend and Slope)

1) The **Trend** can be UP and the **Slope** is also UP. Please look at the Swing Ⓒ to Ⓓ .
   As you can see, the Trend is UP. (The Trend turned up at point X ----- X, that occurred
   during Swing Ⓐ to Ⓑ .)

2) The **Trend** can be UP **but** the **Slope** is DOWN. You can see this on the Down Swing Ⓓ
   to Ⓔ . The market is still in an uptrend, but from point X ----- X, at 730 changes to a
   Downtrend when the "Valley" point Ⓒ is passed to the Downside.

3) The **Trend** can be DOWN and the **Slope** is also DOWN. This occurs on the Downswing
   Ⓕ to Ⓖ . (The trend turned Down at point Ⓔ as prices dipped below the "Valley" point
   Ⓒ . at 730.00)

4) The **Trend** can be DOWN **but** the immediate direction of the swing, i.e. the **Slope**, can
   be UP as per UPswing Ⓔ to Ⓕ .

The importance of the Slope and the Trend being in tandem, ie: both in the <u>same</u> direction
will become obvious as we proceed.

Remember the Solid Line represents Trend Up and the Dashed Line represents Trend
Down. Please go to Chart 7A which explores Trend and Swing relationships further.

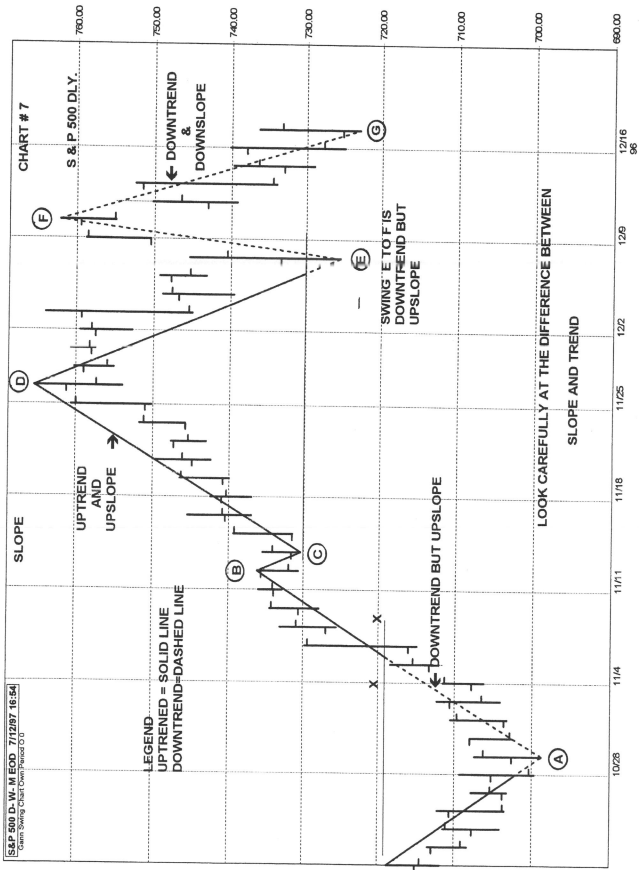

FIBONACCI TRADER (c) Robert Krausz

S&P 500 D- W- M EOD 7/12/97 16:54
Gann Swing Chart Own Period O 0

CHART # 7

S & P 500 DLY.

SLOPE

LEGEND
UPTRENED = SOLID LINE
DOWNTREND = DASHED LINE

UPTREND
AND
UPSLOPE

DOWNTREND
&
DOWNSLOPE

SWING 'E TO F IS
DOWNTREND BUT
UPSLOPE

DOWNTREND BUT UPSLOPE

LOOK CAREFULLY AT THE DIFFERENCE BETWEEN

SLOPE AND TREND

760.00
750.00
740.00
730.00
720.00
710.00
700.00
690.00

10/28   11/4   11/11   11/18   11/25   12/2   12/9   12/16
96

19

SLOPE VS. TREND

CHART #7A

As we saw in the previous chart (#7) you can have **only** four combinations.

1. UPTREND <u>AND</u> UPSLOPE.
2. UPTREND <u>BUT</u> DOWNSLOPE.

3. DOWNTREND <u>AND</u> DOWNSLOPE.
4. DOWNTREND BUT UPSLOPE.

(Combinations 1 and 3 are usually nice trading setups; more about this in the Advanced Concepts Section.)

This <u>Chart 7A</u> shows all 4 phases listed above. Please follow carefully.

1) UPTREND AND UPSLOPE.
   Clearly shown during Ⓚ to Ⓛ swing. The Trend and the Slope are both UP.
2) UPTREND <u>BUT</u> DOWNSLOPE.
   You can see this in two places: Swing Ⓛ - Ⓜ is a pretty clear Downslope.
   Now check out Ⓓ to Ⓔ . It started out as an Uptrend, BUT it <u>changed</u> to a Downtrend WHEN the "Valley" point Ⓒ was taken out at 109.13 (shown X ----- X). (As per our Trend Change Rule: Charts 3 & 4 which shows Trend change.)

From that point, it automatically turned into a DOWNTREND AND DOWNSLOPE. (You can see the result; there was a very short rally to Ⓕ and then the market collapsed.)

3) DOWNTREND <u>AND</u> DOWNSLOPE.
   Swing Ⓕ to Ⓖ is simple, both the Trend and the Slope is DOWN.
4) DOWNTREND BUT UPSLOPE.
   Ⓖ to Ⓗ is a clear illustration of a 3 day upswing in a Downtrend. So, here we had an Upslope even though the Trend was Down.

Now check out Ⓐ to Ⓑ carefully. It began as a Downtrend <u>BUT</u> Upslope and stayed like that until the previous "Peak" at 108.00 was surpassed upwards at X ----- X. At that moment our trend change rule kicks in and the Trend CHANGES to UP. So, now we have Uptrend and Upslope. Similar situation occurred at Swing Ⓘ to Ⓙ. The trend changed to UP at X ----- X 106.05 when the previous peak at Ⓗ was taken out to the upside. From that moment a Downtrend <u>BUT</u> Upslope <u>changed</u> to an Uptrend <u>AND</u> Upslope. (Please note the results.)

Also be aware that Ⓓ and Ⓕ are "Peaks". Ⓓ is the High Peak and Ⓕ drops. Ⓘ and Ⓚ are rising "Valley" points after Ⓖ. Both were part of a trend change.

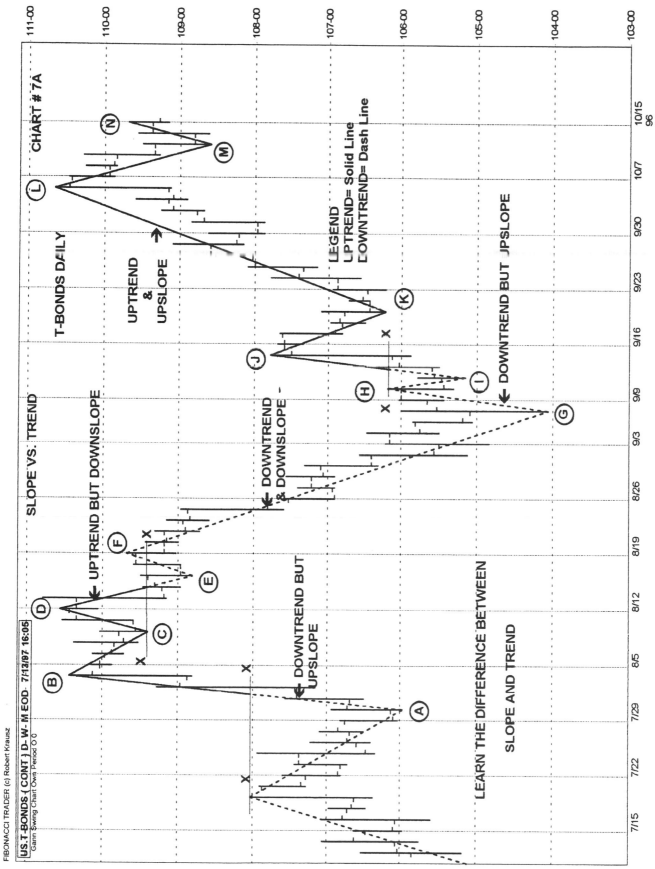

FIBONACCI TRADER (c) Robert Krausz

US. T-BONDS (CONT.) D- W- M EOD 7/13/97 16:05

Gann Swing Chart Own Period 0 0

SLOPE VS. TREND

T-BONDS DAILY

CHART # 7A

UPTREND & UPSLOPE

UPTREND BUT DOWNSLOPE

DOWNTREND & DOWNSLOPE

DOWNTREND BUT UPSLOPE

DOWNTREND BUT UPSLOPE

DOWNTREND BUT UPSLOPE

LEGEND
UPTREND= Solid Line
DOWNTREND= Dash Line

LEARN THE DIFFERENCE BETWEEN
SLOPE AND TREND

21

Let us look more carefully at these two areas. It is these setups of dropping *Peaks* and Rising *Valleys* that often end a trend run <u>and</u> the new trend may begin at these points.

DROPPING PEAKS   RISING VALLEYS

Dropping Peaks Ⓓ and Ⓕ
Please follow along. Ⓓ was the highest point of the up move. (It terminated there.) As prices took out the previous Valley at Ⓒ downwards, the Trend Definition <u>changed</u> to Downtrend.

A new Valley point was made at Ⓔ as prices made a quick 2 day retracement. The important point is to realize that the trend was <u>still</u> Down and could have changed to Up <u>ONLY</u> if Ⓓ was surpassed upwards. It was not!

Instead, the 2 day retracement stopped at Ⓕ and as prices went lower, this Ⓕ formed a LOWER Peak and as prices took out Ⓔ (previous Valley) they collapsed and went down for 11 days to Ⓖ.

Please realize, you can use the "mechanical" Basic Plan etc. without understanding the deeper Swing Trading concepts that are described throughout the book. But, I know that if you want to incorporate your own trading tools, a knowledge of these ideas will increase your confidence. Moreover, these two areas: Dropping Peaks and Rising Valleys may help you to anticipate potential turning points in the market when they occur at the end of a move.

Dropping Peaks like Ⓓ and Ⓕ gives you two pieces of useful information:
1) An attempted upwards retracement in a Downtrend failed, which kept the move in a Downtrend mode.
2) As soon as Peak Ⓕ formed, you can see it was LOWER than Ⓓ, a <u>NEW</u> resistance point was defined by the market at Ⓕ. Note that Ⓓ was the High of the entire previous up move.
These two pieces of information at the high of a move tells us that it has the potential to develop into a new trend in the opposite direction, Down.

In the Advanced Concept Section we will see how this can be used to "short" (sell) the market with a clearly defined stop point that gives us a picture of what our risk may be for that specific action.

Rising "Valleys" Ⓖ -Ⓘ- Ⓚ
This set up that happened at the end of a down move (Downslope Ⓕ to Ⓖ) is almost the mirror image of the top Ⓓ and Ⓕ.

In its simplest terms, we were in a Downtrend when Ⓖ occurred. A 3 day Upswing caused "Peak" Ⓗ. The market retreated to Ⓘ for 1 day only. Please realize that all of this time the market was in a Downtrend mode.

The next day, after Ⓘ; two things happened that rang the wake-up bell.
1) "Valley" Ⓘ was formed the moment "Peak" Ⓗ was taken out. We knew that we had a Rising Valley set up and we are ready.
2) The very next day the trend CHANGED to Uptrend at X ----- X and to an Upswing. We are potential buyers. This exact area will be examined in the Advanced Concepts section in detail
3) After Ⓙ formed, a 3 day down move provided us with "Valley" Ⓚ. Please note, the low of this "Valley" point Ⓚ checked out the failed "Peak" (Resistance) at Ⓗ (to the tick, by the way) to make sure that the failed resistance had become support. Which it had. Note the nice move up, ie. Uptrend and Upslope.

CHART 7B

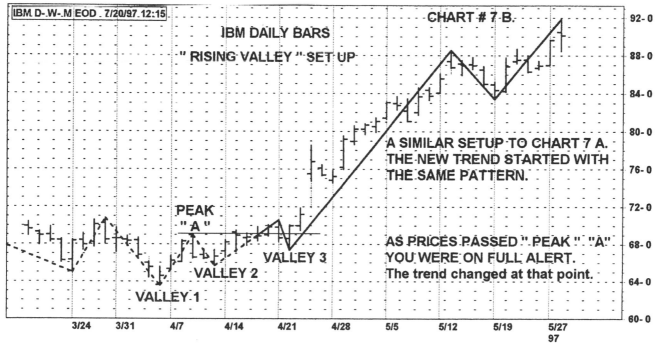

BASIC GANN SWING CHARTING TECHNIQUE

This is the first analytical concept that we will examine because the techniques used are relatively simple, and will lead us to the 'BASIC SWING PLAN'. Furthermore, it will lay the foundation for a deeper understanding of the markets and swing trading techniques in particular.

We can use the definitions just covered, in this case for 1 time period, the Daily Bars. By virtue of the fact that the Trend as well as Support and Resistance is so clearly defined, you could dovetail your own favorite tools with these concepts.

The charts show you the techniques faster than 10,000 words can. Nevertheless, if any of the points are not clear enough you can write to me at the address shown on the first page of this book or at the e-mail address given.

As we refer to each definition in greater depth, we can turn them into the simple rules that follow for our analysis.

By checking the terminology and matching it to the appropriate chart you can come to some simple conclusion. Such as: if the trend is UP and the Slope is also UP, then it may be more advisable to "look to buy" rather than to sell. Please note: I said "look to buy" - I did not say "Buy". To do that we need an Action Point (trigger) as well as a "Stop" or "Stop and Reverse" point. We never enter the market without placing a "Stop Loss" in case the trade goes against us. This way we protect our capital by knowing how much we are risking before we enter the market.

In the next few pages you will learn one of the simplest tools that I use. The "HiLo Activator". This functions not only as an Entry Action point but also as a Trailing Stop and as a "Stop Loss" point.

Before I detail the HiLo Activator, it is important to discuss the concept of "Energy Termination", because it is the termination of energy that sets up the Peaks and Valleys shown in Charts 7 and 7A. And it is those Peaks and Valleys that define the change in the Trend as well as defining Support and Resistance.

I tend to look at the movement of prices and the changes thereto as "vibrations". The vibration of prices can be called energy. Therefore, prices reach a "High" and then proceed downwards, which can only happen when the "Buying Energy" reached a Peak and then it "Terminated" (ie: the buying ceased). Thus, it can be called a "termination of energy"; the vibration stopped. At first glance this may appear theoretical and of no practical value, but it is this concept that will eventually set up the trading of Multiple Time Periods within the confines of Support/Resistance of "own" and the "Higher" time periods swings.

Quoting W. D. Gann from many years ago:
"After years of patient study I have proven to my entire satisfaction as well as demonstrated to others that vibration explains every possible phase and condition of the market."

So, we find at the extremes of moves (top or bottom) that vibrations are at their maximum within the confines of the price swings we are analyzing, especially the "time frame" we are trading. It is the extremes of the higher time periods that define the top or bottom of the major trend. This will be discussed in the "Advanced Concepts" section.

Let us now look at the Trigger we use for the Basic Swing Plan.

HiLo ACTIVATOR

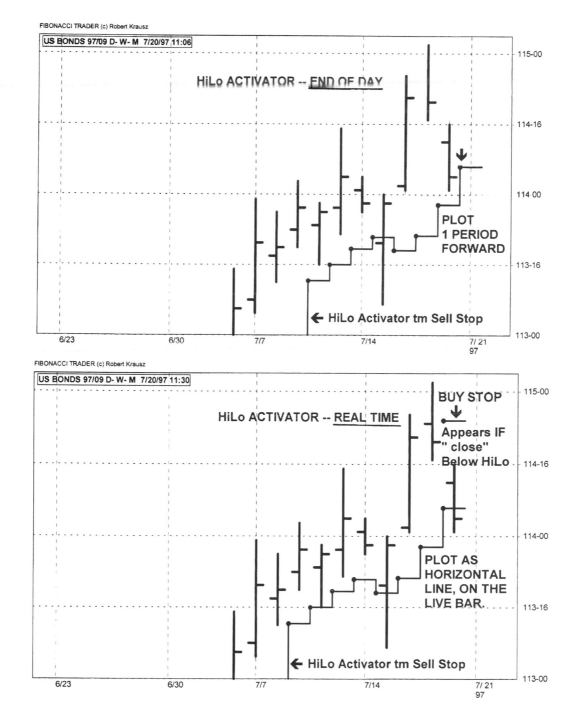

HiLo ACTIVATOR

This simple tool will act as our Entry Trigger as well as a Trailing Stop. You can see this in the Rules that follow for the Basic Swing Plan.

In reality, this is a simple moving average of the Highs and the Lows but plotted in an unusual manner. For this indicator we add the last three period's Highs (or Lows) and divide the sum by three. This <u>must</u> include the latest bar. The result is then plotted in such a way that, for Real Time action, we have a horizontal Live line to utilize. For End of Day it is plotted one period forward, so that you have a horizontal price point to act with tomorrow. Please see illustrations on previous page.

As a side note, of course I am aware that within 5 minutes of this book being published, all of the vultures out there will copy these ideas into their program. Especially the "gentlemen" who have never traded in their lives. So, what can I do about that? I quote Rudyard Kipling, the British poet from the 19th century:

> "And they asked me how I do it and
> I gave them the Scripture text,
>
> You keep your light so shining a
> little in front o' the next
>
> They copied all they could follow,
> but they could not copy my mind
>
> And I left 'em sweating and stealing
> a year and a half behind…"

All of the rules illustrated for the Basic Swing Plan and the charts that follow show clearly the effect of the "HiLo Activator". Once a "Buy" set up is activated, the HiLo Sell Stop follows the rising market plotted below the rising bars, and a "Sell" setup is exactly the opposite.

This step formation is visually easy to follow and once you get used to it then you know the market is up until you get a "Close" below the HiLo Activator Sell Stop, the Buy Stop will then appear. Of course, you can do this by hand, it's easy as I did it for years. The simplicity of it may deceive you to believe that it may be of little value. Check it out first before you make that judgement. At this stage, we are talking <u>only</u> about the Daily HiLo Activator on the Daily bars.

These four charts should help you to understand the HiLo calculation better. Please realize that in the Fibonacci Trader® program real-time, when, say, the HiLo Activator buy stop is penetrated by the price on the T-bonds by two ticks, the HiLo Activator sell stop comes up real time, but if the prices close back below the buy stop, then the sell stop disappears. This is like a warning sign – that is, the traffic light turning yellow.

Of course, none of this affects the results, the charts or the rules in the *Gann Treasure* book.

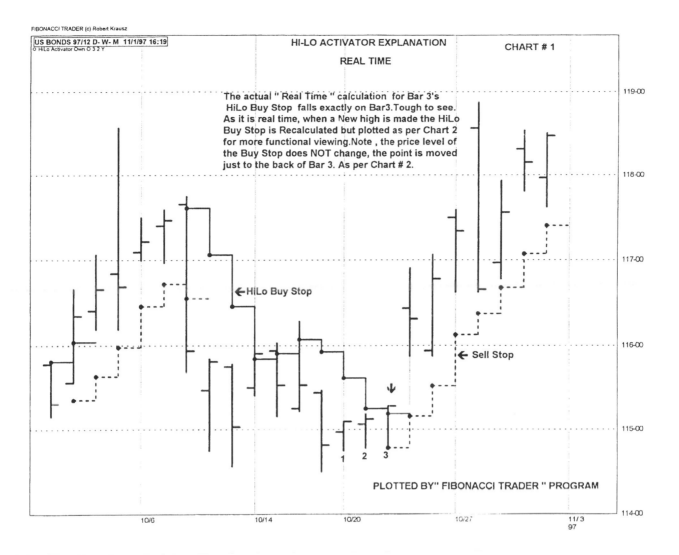

US BONDS 97/12 D-W-M 11/1/97 16:19
O HiLo Activator Own O 3 2 Y

HI-LO ACTIVATOR EXPLANATION

REAL TIME

CHART # 1

The actual " Real Time " calculation for Bar 3's
HiLo Buy Stop falls exactly on Bar3.Tough to see.
As it is real time, when a New high is made the HiLo
Buy Stop is Recalculated but plotted as per Chart 2
for more functional viewing.Note , the price level of
the Buy Stop does NOT change, the point is moved
just to the back of Bar 3. As per Chart # 2.

←HiLo Buy Stop

← Sell Stop

1   2   3

PLOTTED BY" FIBONACCI TRADER " PROGRAM

119-00
118-00
117-00
116-00
115-00
114-00

10/6   10/14   10/20   10/27   11/3
                                                    97

CHART 1: REAL-TIME MODE

Because the calculation includes the third period, that is, the "live" bar (in real-time mode), the actual HiLo point falls on this live bar, making it difficult to see. (As we want this indicator to be dynamic, we must include the live bar in the calculation; that's obvious.)

Many real-time charting programs have the facility to plot the moving average point back or forward as needed. The program used for this book, the Fibonacci Trader®, does this automatically.

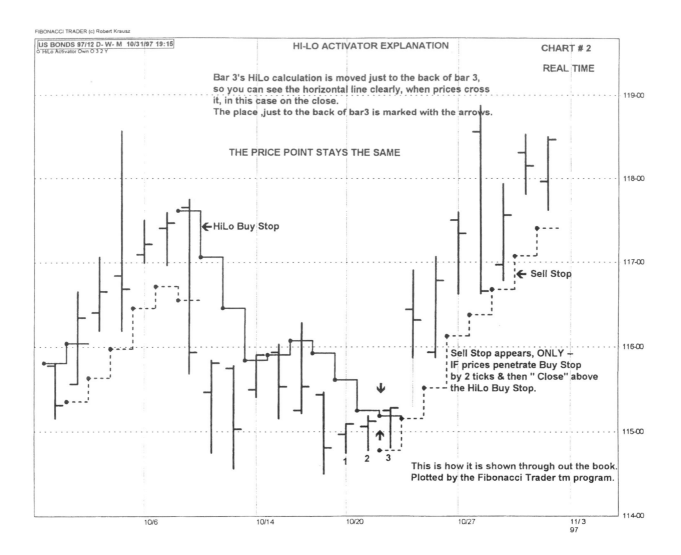

FIBONACCI TRADER (c) Robert Krausz

US BONDS 97/12 D- W- M 10/31/97 19:15
o HiLo Activator Own O 3 2 Y

HI-LO ACTIVATOR EXPLANATION

CHART # 2

REAL TIME

Bar 3's HiLo calculation is moved just to the back of bar 3,
so you can see the horizontal line clearly, when prices cross
it, in this case on the close.
The place ,just to the back of bar3 is marked with the arrows.

THE PRICE POINT STAYS THE SAME

←HiLo Buy Stop

← Sell Stop

Sell Stop appears, ONLY –
IF prices penetrate Buy Stop
by 2 ticks & then " Close" above
the HiLo Buy Stop.

1   2   3

This is how it is shown through out the book.
Plotted by the Fibonacci Trader tm program.

119-00
118-00
117-00
116-00
115-00
114-00

10/6   10/14   10/20   10/27   11/3
97

CHART 2: REAL-TIME MODE

This shows that the HiLo calculation that was on Bar 3 in the previous chart is now plotted just *behind* Bar 3, as a point with a short horizontal line that now lies across Bar 3.
Check it out.

Please note: The price level of the HiLo Activator buy stop does not change.

In this chart, Bar 3 closed above the buy stop, thus activating Buy Rule #1 (for the basic
plan, if the trend is up).

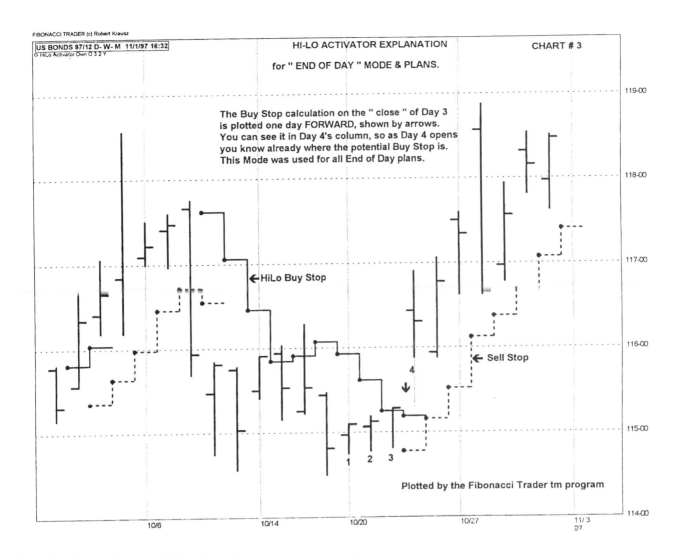

US BONDS 97/12 D- W- M 11/1/97 16:32
o HiLo Activator Own O 3 2 Y

HI-LO ACTIVATOR EXPLANATION

CHART # 3

for " END OF DAY " MODE & PLANS.

The Buy Stop calculation on the " close " of Day 3
is plotted one day FORWARD, shown by arrows.
You can see it in Day 4's column, so as Day 4 opens
you know already where the potential Buy Stop is.
This Mode was used for all End of Day plans.

← HiLo Buy Stop

← Sell Stop

Plotted by the Fibonacci Trader tm program

CHART 3: END-OF-DAY MODE

If you're using the end-of-day mode, you must move the HiLo Activator buy stop one day *forward*. Therefore, on the close of Day 3, the buy stop will be in Day 4's column. So you will be aware today where the buy stop is for tomorrow.

Please realize that you would be able to act only on the open of Day 4, as prices gapped, hitting the buy stop, as prices opened.

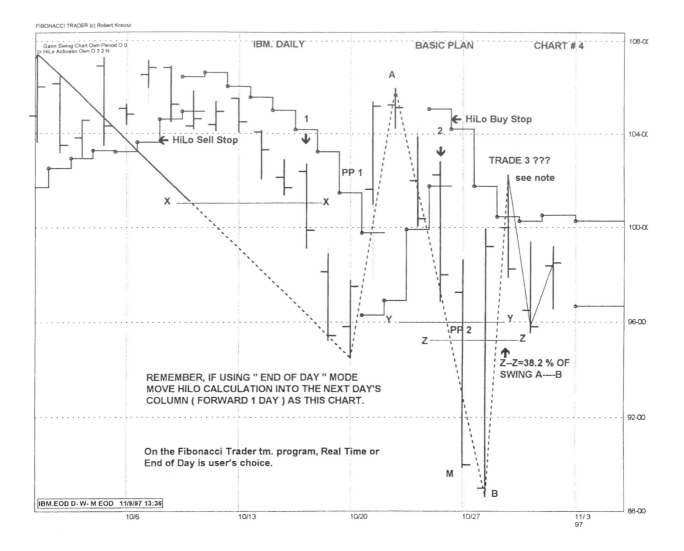

CHART 4: END-OF-DAY MODE FOR IBM

How did the Basic Plan survive Blue Monday's big drop on October 27, 1997?
See page 35 for the Basic Plan Rules. Trade 1 went short via trend change Rule 2, marked as "x—x" on the chart. This short was taken during the day, because you knew this price point – the point where the trend would be changing – for many days in advance. Thus, you could have given an order to your broker before the market opened. The price went down for two days.

But then, horror of horrors, prices gapped on the open above the buy stop and you closed out the trade on the open for a small loss.

Once again, you knew where the HiLo Activator was the day before your order could have been with the broker, an order such as, "if prices open above 100, etc."

An important point: Even though prices rose to point A, the trend was still down (dashed line), and with the Basic Plan, we can only act *with* the trend, so we are looking to sell.

30

Sell Rule #1 was hit on the close on Thursday, shown as trade 2.

Blue Monday, October 27, smashed the market down for the biggest one-day point drop on the DJIA, as we were smiling on the close. But on Tuesday, our smiles turned to frowns when the market made a new low at point B and then bounced like mad. So what to do? Two possibilities.

1) If you followed the market during the day, you would have known where point B (the low) was and you would have put in place PP Rule #3 (Profit Protection Rule 3, page 44) – a 38.2% retracement of swing A-B, and you could have exited the short trade at the point marked as "z—z" on the chart.

2) If you were not following the market during the day on Tuesday the 11th, then you could have used the low of Monday, M, to calculate the potential retracement of 38.2% of swing A-M (because M was the lowest low known to you).

    Profit Protection Rule #2 (PP#2) was hit on this basis, at Y-Y at a price of 96.00 on Tuesday. Your stop was a few ticks above this, and the order could have been with your broker. So a few dollars profit was gained on this trade, depending where you got filled.

Big moves down, big moves up. No miracles, but no disasters — the Basic Plan survived. Could you have taken trade 3 on Wednesday, October 12?

This type of trade is not included in the Basic Plan. But Friday, the 7th of November, gave the classic sell signal on the close in a downtrend. No chart for this yet.

This leads us into the Basic Swing Plan. Please remember, it is based on W. D. Gann's concepts, for the 30 Year T-Bonds. The 10 years results and trade by trade charts follow the illustrated rules.

I wish you good trading.

Robert Krausz, MH, BCHE

NEW GANN SWING CHARTIST©

BASIC SWING PLAN

"REAL TIME"

FOR U.S. T-BONDS
1987 - 1996

> ## All roads lead to Rome, but some are shorter than others.

INFORMATION FOR BASIC PLAN "REAL TIME"

1. This plan trades only with the trend.
2. The 10-year back test, with charts, rules and results are illustrated trade by trade for the entire period.
3. No deduction has been made for commission. Deduct what suits you.
4. All rules are clearly defined.
5. Please read the Disclaimer at the front of the book.
6. To get the most from this plan for T-Bonds, study the rules and work your way through the trades carefully. Check it out.
7. Can you change these rules? Can you dovetail your own ideas? I think you know the answer, but not without doing your own back track.
8. Each year we start with a capital of $30,000.
9. Each New Trade is 3 contracts.
10. There is no pyramiding with this plan.

SUGGESTED MINI-CHECKLIST FOR BASIC PLAN

After you have absorbed the simple rules for this plan and worked your way through the results day by day, trade by trade, you may want to consider setting up a Daily Checklist.

Example:

Direction of TREND	UP	❏	DOWN	❏
Position of HiLo Activator	ABOVE	❏	BELOW	❏

Price Point of previous VALLEY
Price Point of previous PEAK
Price Point of 38% Retracement

Also, have a place for the Date and the Number of Contracts. As there are basically only three rules and two qualifiers, a personalized checklist should be easy to prepare.

The importance of this is to establish your own frame of reference and set up a daily routine. Your planning should be done before and not when you enter the trade. I suggest that you write down the actual trade and read that to your broker. Less mistakes will be made if you follow this plan.

ROUTINE FOR CHECKING RESULTS AND BACKTEST

The Backtest results are divided into separate columns from Left to Right.
TRADE #1: This shows the trade number that matches the circled trade number on the actual charts. If you see PP, it means that a Profit Protection rule was hit.
DATE: Date of the Trade.
L/S: Long or Short.
PRICE: The price at which the tradewas exffected.
CTR: The number of contracts.
RULE: This is the Rule Number used to take action.
PROFIT: Shown in ticks (1 tick = $31.25).
LOSS: Shown in ticks (1 tick = $31.25).
ACCUM: Accumulated loss or profit.
MO. PROFIT (LOSS): Monthly Profit (Loss).
A/C EQUITY: Total money in the trading account.

- RULES -

BASIC GANN SWING PLAN

LONG ENTRY (BUYING)

QUALIFIERS (SET UP)

1. Gann Swing Chart must show an Uptrend (Solid Line).
2. Bar must close above HiLo Activator - Buy Stop by 2 ticks.

ENTRY RULES (ACTION POINTS) Use the one hit first.

RULE 1.   Buy when bar closes above HiLo Activator, "Buy Stop" line by 2 ticks (program default)
RULE 2.   Buy when Gann Swing Chart changes from Downtrend (Dashed Line) to Uptrend (Solid Line). Must have HiLo Activator "Sell Stop" below the bar.
RULE 3.   Buy when nearest "Peak" is passed upwards by 2 ticks. You must also have HiLo Activator "Sell Stop" below the bar.

SHORT ENTRY (SELLING)

QUALIFIERS (SET UP)

1. Gann Swing Chart must show a Downtrend (Dashed Line).
2. Bar must close below HiLo Activator - Sell Stop by 2 ticks.

ENTRY RULES (ACTION POINTS) Use the one hit first.

RULE 1.   Sell when bar closes below HiLo Activator "Sell Stop" line by 2 ticks (program default).
RULE 2.   Sell when Gann Swing Chart changes from Uptrend (Solid Line) to Downtrend (Dashed Line). You must have the HiLo Activator line "Buy Stop" above the bar.
RULE 3.   Sell when the nearest "Valley" is passed downwards by 2 ticks. You must also have the HiLo Activator "Buy Stop" line above the bar.

PROFIT PROTECTION RULES (for Longs or Shorts)

1. Take profit on all contracts if price closes above/below HiLo Activator.
2. 38% retracement rule. Take profits on all contracts on any 38% retracement of the current Gann Swing. Do not wait for the "close". Must be past the HiLo Activator before using this 38% retrace rule.

SEE ILLUSTRATED RULES

ENTRY RULES WITH THE TREND

UPTREND   **BUY RULE #1**

Buy on Bar Ⓐ Providing -------- The Gann Swing Chart shows an UPTREND (Solid Line). The BUY Signal occurs on Bar Ⓐ when prices "close" above the HiLo Activator - Long Stop.

DOWNTREND   **SELL RULE #1**

Sell on Bar Ⓐ Providing -------- The Gann Swing Chart shows a DOWNTREND (Dashed Line). The SELL Signal occurs on Bar Ⓐ when prices "close" below the HiLo Activator - Short Stop.

ENTRY RULES WITH THE TREND
TREND TRADING

Trend Trading Rule: Long Entry (Buy)

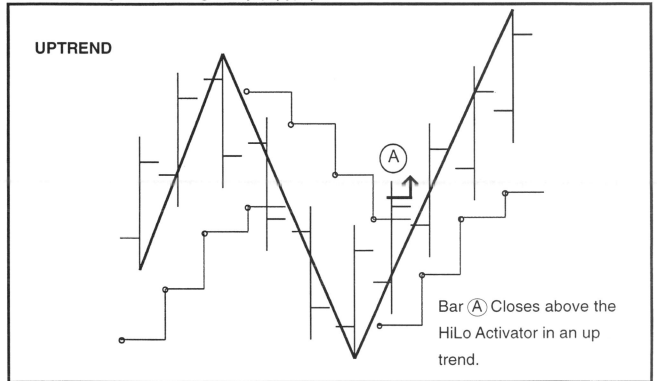

UPTREND

Bar (A) Closes above the HiLo Activator in an up trend.

Trend Trading Rule: Short Entry (Sell)

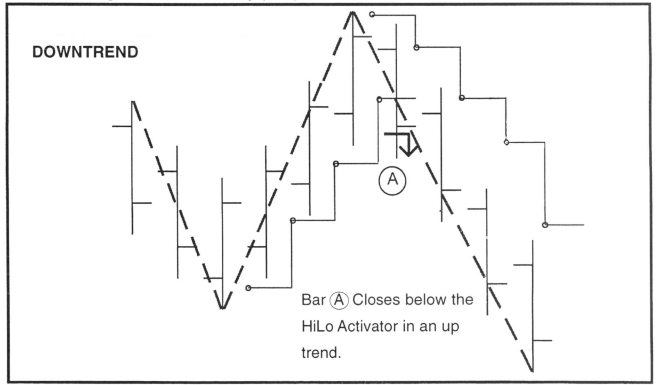

DOWNTREND

Bar (A) Closes below the HiLo Activator in an up trend.

ENTRY RULES VIA TREND CHANGE

TREND CHANGE   **BUY RULE #2**

Buy on Bar Ⓐ when prices surpass previous "Peak". Providing -------- The HiLo Activator <u>Sell Stop</u> is below the bars. (The Fibonacci Trader® program changes from Dashed to Solid line as the trend changes from Down to Up.) If using Real Time data the change occurs instantly.

TREND CHANGE   **SELL RULE #2**

Sell on Bar Ⓐ when prices drop below previous "Valley". Providing -------- The HiLo Activator <u>Buy Stop</u> is above the bars. (The Fibonacci Trader® program shows this change of trend, if using Real Time Data, instantly.)

ENTRY RULES VIA TREND CHANGE

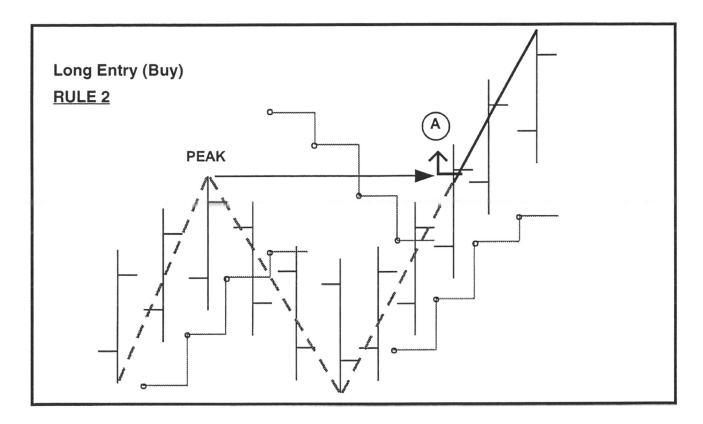

Long Entry (Buy)

RULE 2

PEAK

A

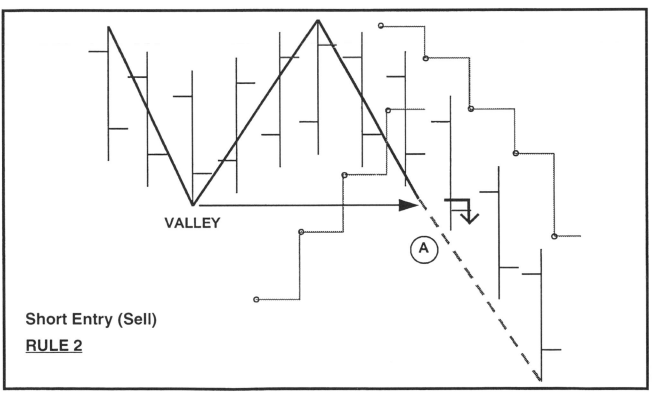

VALLEY

A

Short Entry (Sell)

RULE 2

ENTRY RULES IN DIRECTION OF TREND VIA PREVIOUS PEAK OR VALLEY

UPTREND - **VIA PREVIOUS PEAK** - **BUY RULE #3**

The Trend is UP (Swing Line is Solid). You can buy, when prices surpass the previous "Peak". Providing -------- The HiLo Activator Sell Stop is below the bars. Action is taken intraday. Buy signal occurs on Bar Ⓑ (use 2 ticks for T-Bonds).

DOWNTREND - **VIA PREVIOUS VALLEY** - **SELL RULE #3**

The Trend is DOWN (Swing Line is Dashed). You can sell, when prices drop below the previous "Valley". Providing -------- The HiLo Activator Buy Stop is above the bars. Action is taken intraday. Sell signal occurs on Bar Ⓑ (use 2 ticks for T-Bonds).

ENTRY RULES IN DIRECTION OF TREND VIA PREVIOUS PEAK OR VALLEY

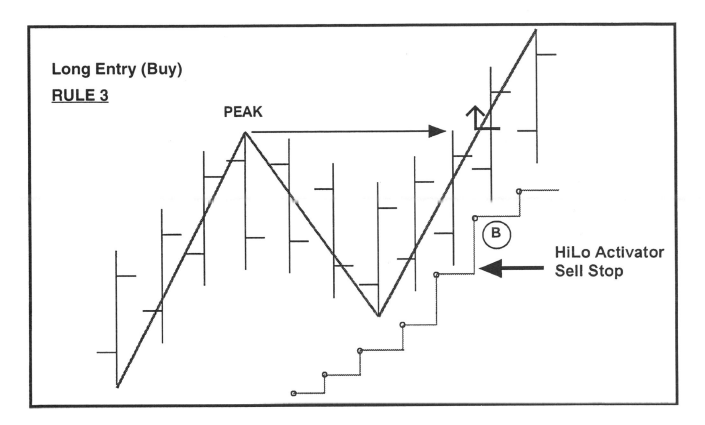

Long Entry (Buy)
RULE 3

PEAK

B

HiLo Activator
Sell Stop

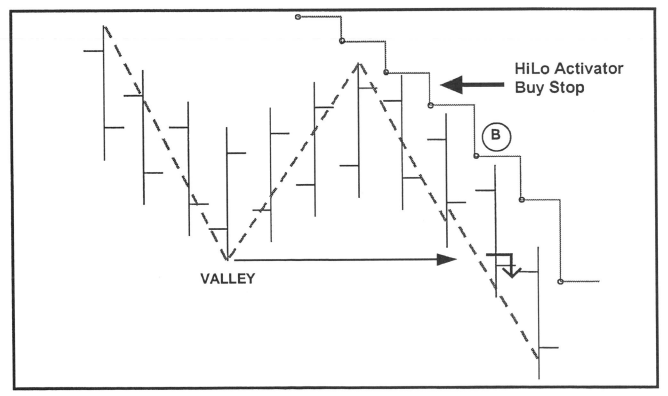

HiLo Activator
Buy Stop

B

VALLEY

PROFIT PROTECTION RULES
(PP)

PROFIT PROTECTION   **IF LONG**   **RULE #1**

If prices "close" below the HiLo Activator Sell Stop then close out all Long positions. This happens on Bar (A). This "close" must be at least 2 ticks below the HiLo Activator. Also the HiLo Activator must have "flipped", as shown on Bar (A). (ie: if the close is 2 ticks below the Sell Stop, then the buy stop will appear on the computer monitor screen.

PROFIT PROTECTION   **IF SHORT**   **RULE #1**

If prices "close" Above the HiLo Activator <u>Buy Stop</u> then close out all Short positions. This happens on Bar (A). This "close" must be at least 2 ticks above the HiLo Activator. Also the HiLo Activator must have "flipped", as shown on Bar (A). (ie: if the close is 2 ticks above the Buy Stop, then the sell stop will appear on the computer monitor screen.

PROFIT PROTECTION RULES
(PP)

Profit Protection Rule #1

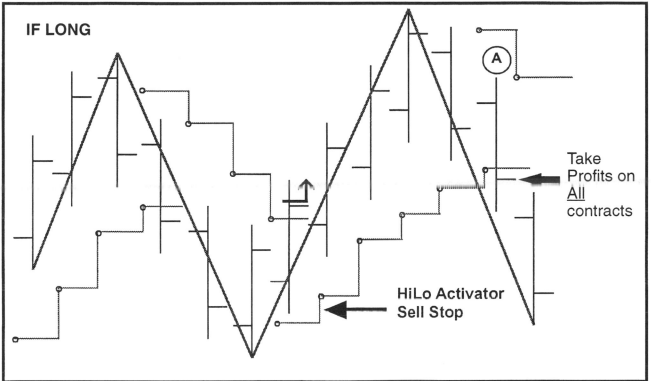

IF LONG

(A)

Take Profits on <u>All</u> contracts

HiLo Activator Sell Stop

Profit Protection Rule #1

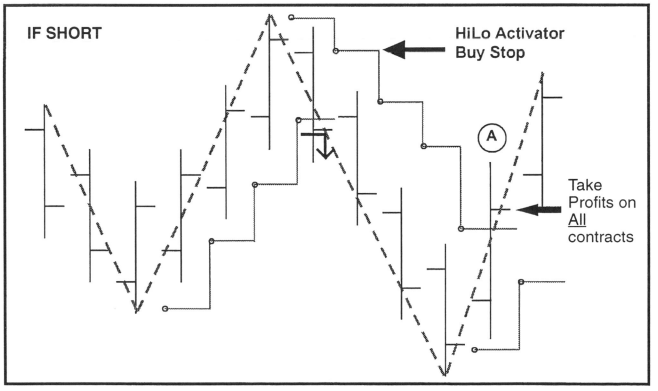

IF SHORT

HiLo Activator Buy Stop

(A)

Take Profits on <u>All</u> contracts

PROFIT PROTECTION RULES
(PP)

PROFIT PROTECTION   **IF LONG**   **RULE #2**

38% Retracement Rule

If prices Retrace 38% of Upswing Ⓐ - Ⓑ then close out all existing positions = Ⓒ.
Price must be past HiLo Activator <u>Sell Stop</u> by 2 ticks. Do not wait for the "close".

SEE GENERAL NOTES BEFORE USING THIS RULE (page 28).

PROFIT PROTECTION   **IF SHORT**   **RULE #2**

38% Retracement Rule

If prices Retrace 38% of Downswing Ⓐ - Ⓑ then close out all short positions = Ⓒ.
Price must be past HiLo Activator <u>Buy Stop</u> by 2 ticks. Do not wait for the "close".

SEE GENERAL NOTES BEFORE USING THIS RULE.

PROFIT PROTECTION RULES
(PP)

Profit Protection Rule #2

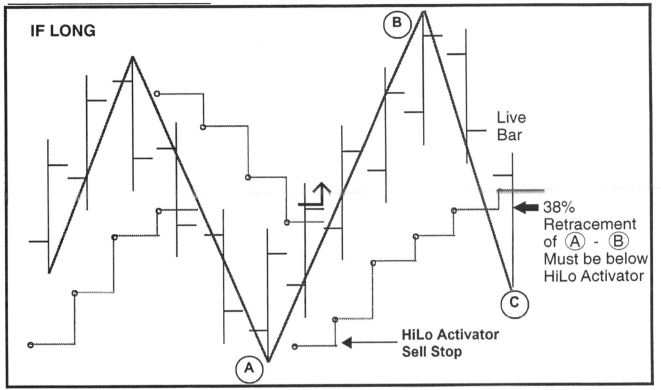

IF LONG

Live
Bar

38%
Retracement
of (A) - (B)
Must be below
HiLo Activator

HiLo Activator
Sell Stop

Profit Protection Rule #2

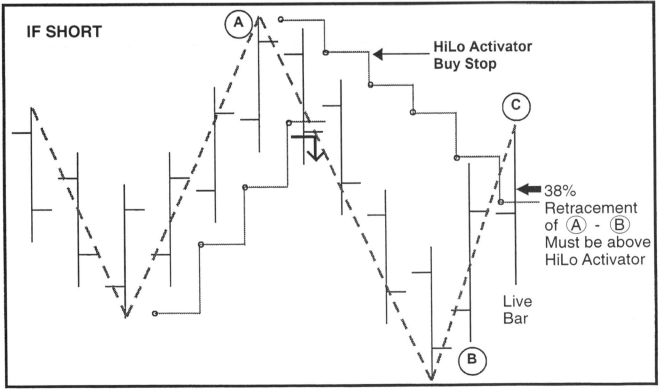

IF SHORT

HiLo Activator
Buy Stop

38%
Retracement
of (A) - (B)
Must be above
HiLo Activator

Live
Bar

Beginning Equity	$30,000.00	Ending Equity	$61,406.25
Total Net Profit	$31,406.25	Average Ticks/Mo.	
Gross Profit	$63,000.00	Gross Loss	($31,593.75)
Total No. Trades	30	Percentage Profitable	47%
No. Winning Trades	14	No. Losing Trades	16

Largest Winning Trade	$17,062.50	Largest Losing Trade	($8,062.50)
Average Winning Trade	$4,500.00	Average Losing Trade	($1,974.61)
Ratio Average Win/Loss	2.28	Average Trade	$1,046.88
Max. Consecutive Winners	3	Max. Consecutive Losses	5
Largest Consecutive Drawdown (%)	23.02%	Largest Consecutive Drawdown	($6,281.25)

Return on Account	105%
Profit/Drawdown Ratio	5.00

NOTES:
1) Initial A/C Size = $30,000

BASIC PLAN RESULTS

1987
US T-Bonds
New Gann Swing Chartist ©
BASIC TRADING PLAN

Fibonacci Trader (c):

TRADE#	DATE	L/S	PRICE	CTR.	RULE #	PROFIT	(LOSS)	ACCUM.	MO. PROFIT/(LOSS)	A/C EQUITY
1	1/2/87	L	72.22	3	Buy 1					$30,000.00
PP	1/14/87	S	73.00	3	PP2	30		30		$30,937.50
2	1/16/87	L	73.29	3	Buy 1					$30,750.00
PP	1/22/87	S	73.27	3	PP2		(6)	24		
3	1/26/87	S	72.19	3	Sell 2					$29,625.00
PP	1/28/87	L	72.31	3	PP1		(36)	(12)	(12)	
4	2/2/87	S	72.04	3	Sell 1					$28,781.25
PP	2/5/87	L	72.13	3	PP2		(27)	(39)		
5	2/6/87	L	73.13	3	Buy 2					$25,968.75
PP	2/7/87	S	72.15	3	PP2		(90)	(129)		
6	2/10/87	S	71.22	3	Sell 2					$24,656.25
PP	2/12/87	L	72.04	3	PP1		(42)	(171)		
7	2/24/87	L	73.18	3	Sell 2					
PP	3/3/87	S	74.01	3	PP1	45		(126)	(114)	$26,062.50
8	3/4/87	L	74.26	3	Buy 3					$24,000.00
PP	3/6/87	S	74.04	3	PP2		(66)	(192)		
9	3/9/87	S	73.28	3	Sell 2					$22,875.00
PP	3/13/87	L	74.08	3	PP2		(36)	(228)		
10	3/18/87	L	74.20	3	Buy 2					$21,468.75
PP	3/23/87	S	74.05	3	PP2		(45)	(273)		
11	3/24/87	S	73.26	3	Sell 2					$20,062.50
PP	3/26/87	L	74.09	3	PP2		(45)	(318)		
12	3/27/87	S	73.21	3	Sell 3					$37,125.00
PP	4/16/87	L	67.31	3	PP1	546		228	354	
13	4/20/87	S	66.10	3	Buy 1					$39,843.75
PP	4/28/87	L	65.13	3	PP2	87		315		
14	5/4/87	S	64.08	3	Sell 1					$44,156.25
PP	5/22/87	L	62.26	3	PP2	138		453		
15	5/26/87	L	65.14	3	Buy 2					$41,625.00
PP	6/2/87	S	64.19	3	PP2		(81)	372	144	
16	6/5/87	L	65.15	3	Buy 2					$47,250.00
PP	6/24/87	S	67.11	3	PP2	180		552		
17	6/26/87	S	66.13	3	Sell 2					

1987
US T-Bonds
New Gann Swing Chartist ©
BASIC TRADING PLAN

Fibonacci Trader

TRADE#	DATE	L/S	PRICE	CTR.	RULE #	PROFIT	(LOSS)	ACCUM.	MO. PROFIT/(LOSS)	A/C EQUITY
PP	7/2/87	L	66.29	3	PP2		(48)	504	132	$45,750.00
18	7/9/87	S	66.10	3	Sell 1			420		$43,125.00
PP	7/14/87	L	67.06	3	PP2		(84)			
19	7/21/87	S	65.14	3	Sell 1					$48,281.25
PP	8/5/87	L	63.23	3	PP2	165		585	81	
20	8/13/87	L	65.03	3	Buy 2					$46,593.75
PP	8/18/87	S	64.17	3	PP2		(54)	531		
21	8/28/87	S	62.16	3	Sell 2					$55,968.75
PP	9/11/87	L	59.12	3	PP1	300		831	246	
22	9/15/87	S	58.08	3	Sell 1					$54,468.75
PP	9/18/87	L	58.24	3	PP2		(48)	783		
23	9/24/87	S	58.04	3	Sell 1					$55,031.25
PP	10/2/87	L	57.30	3	PP2	18		801	(30)	
24	10/8/87	S	56.24	3	Sell 1					$46,968.75
25	10/21/87	L	59.14	6	Buy 2		(258)	543		$54,562.50
PP	10/28/87	S	61.31	3	PP1	243		786	(15)	
26	10/30/87	L	63.10	3	Buy 1					$56,812.50
PP	11/13/87	S	64.18	3	PP1	72		858		
27	11/20/87	L	65.09	3	Buy 1					$55,406.25
PP	11/24/87	S	64.26	3	PP2		(45)	813		
28	11/25/87	S	64.07	3	Sell 2					$57,187.50
PP	12/3/87	L	63.20	3	PP2	57		870	84	
29	12/7/87	S	62.15	3	Sell 1					$59,437.50
PP	12/15/87	L	61.23	3	PP2	72		942		
30	12/18/87	L	64.05	3	Buy 2					$61,406.25
PP	1/6/87	S	64.26	3	PP1	63		1005	135	

48

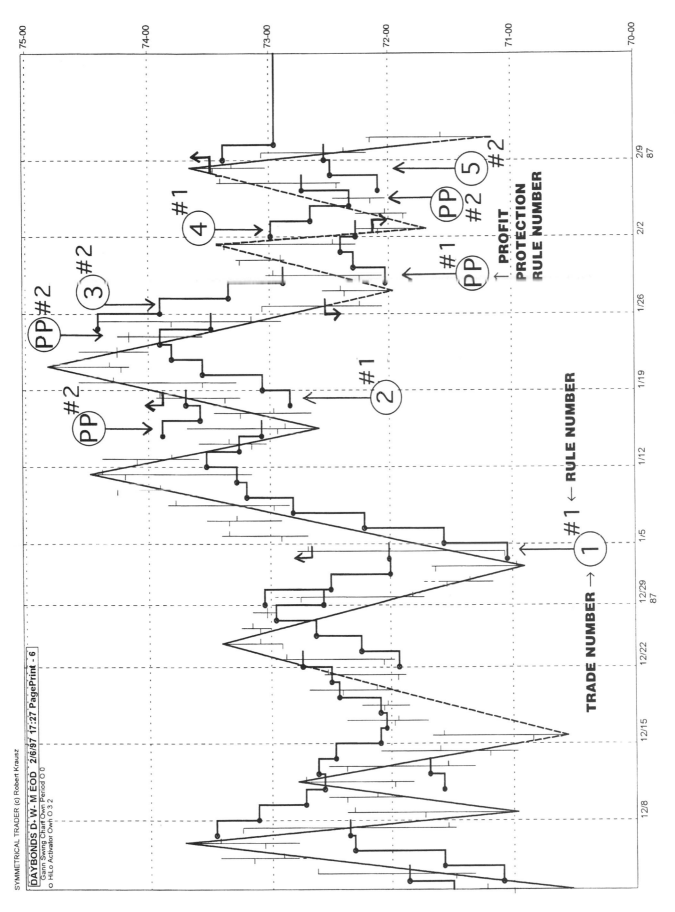

SYMMETRICAL TRADER (c) Robert Krausz

DAYBONDS D-W-M EOD 2/6/97 17:27 PagePrint - 6
Gann Swing Chart Own Period O 0
o HiLo Activator Own O 3 2

49

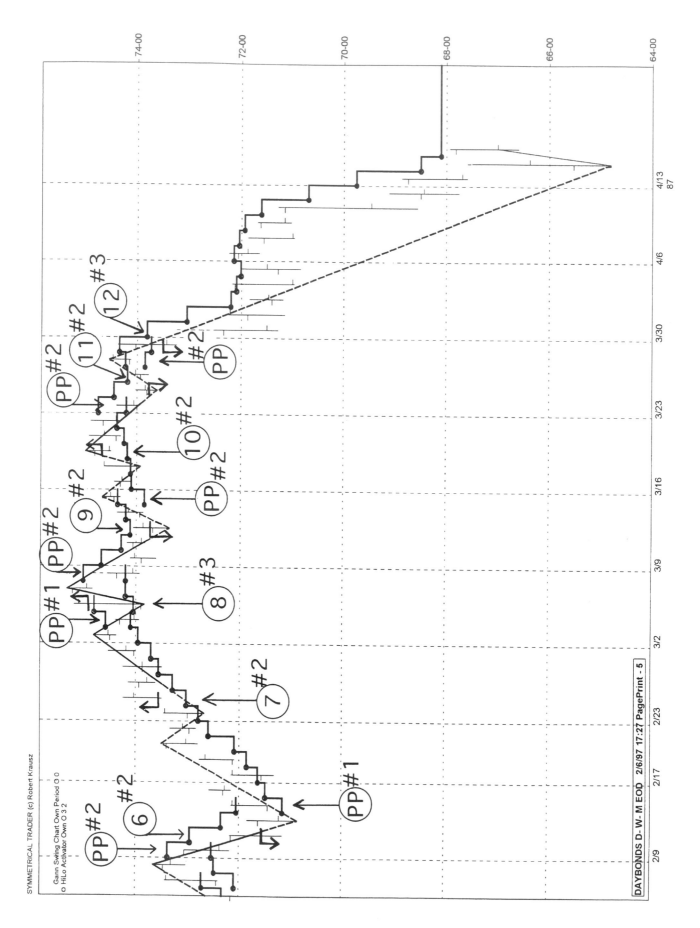

SYMMETRICAL TRADER (c) Robert Krausz

Gann Swing Chart Own Period O 0
o HiLo Activator Own O 3 2

DAYBONDS D- W- M EOD 2/6/97 17:27 PagePrint - 5

50

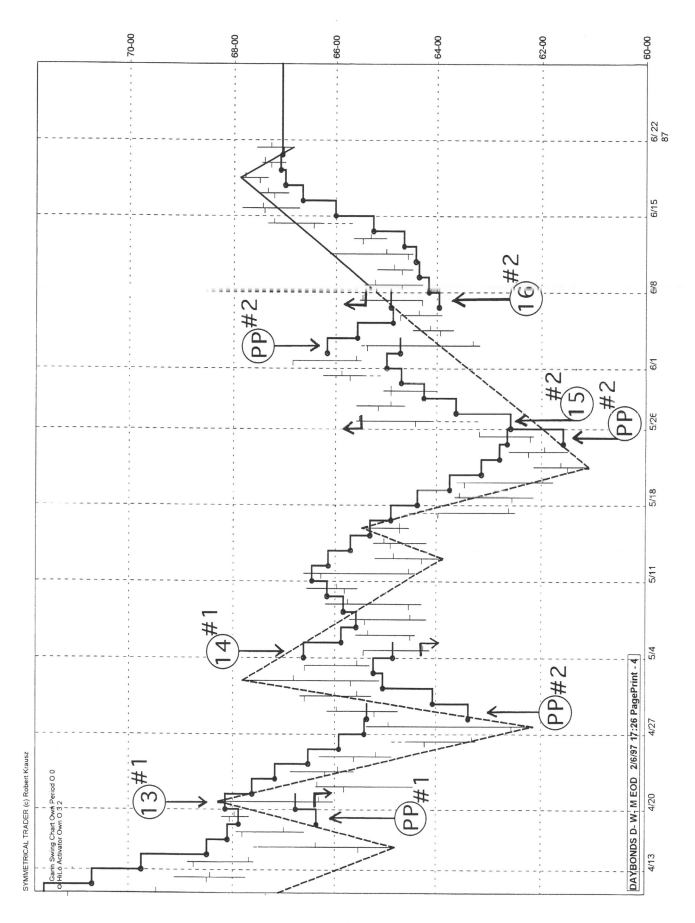

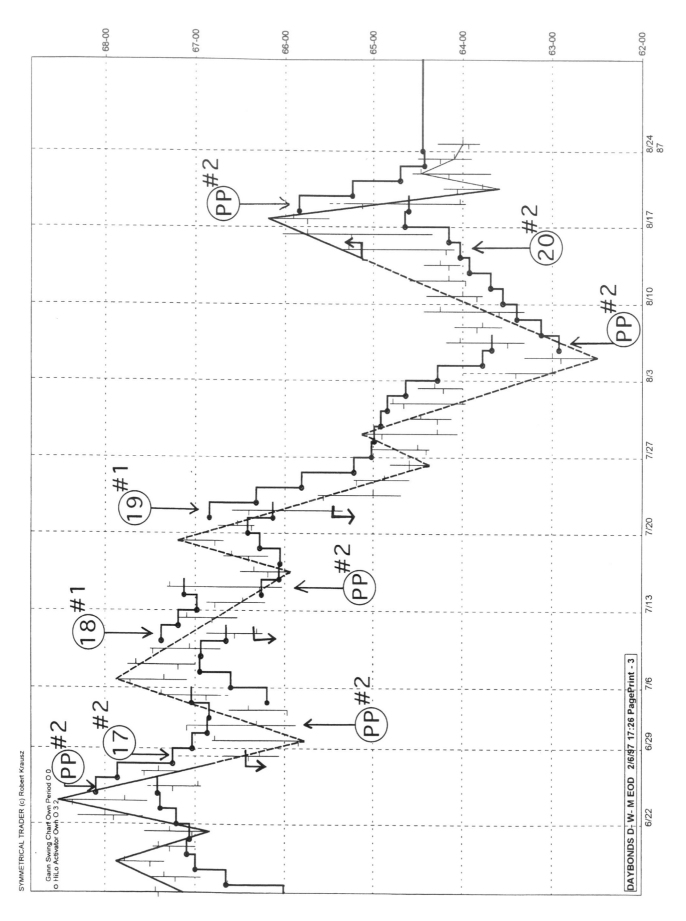

SYMMETRICAL TRADER (c) Robert Krausz

Gann Swing Chart Own Period O 0
o HiLo Activator Own O 3 2

DAYBONDS D: W- M EOD   2/6/97 17:26 PagePrint - 3

52

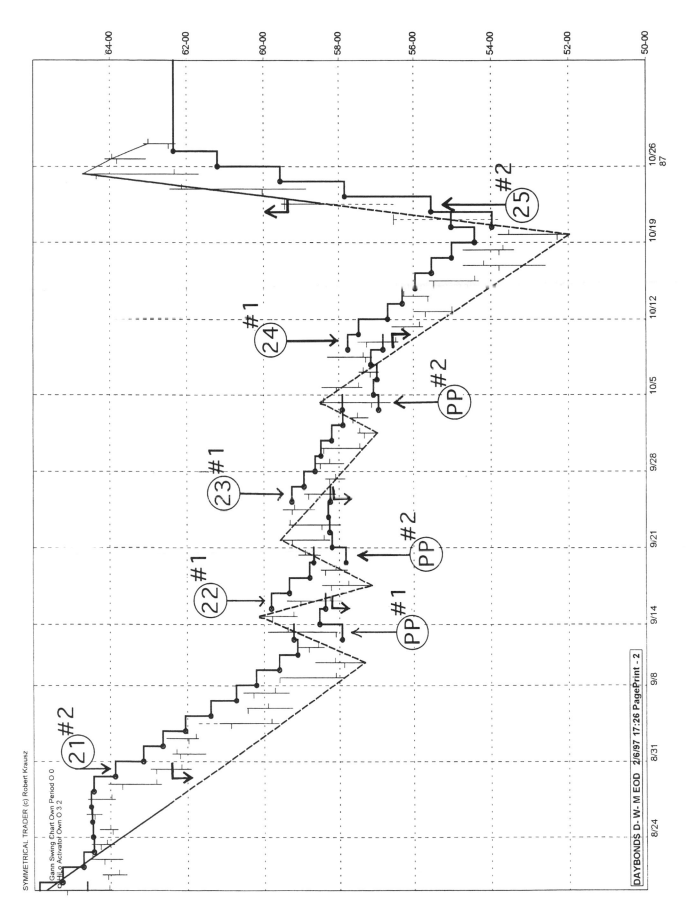

SYMMETRICAL TRADER (c) Robert Krausz

Gann Swing Chart Own Period O 0
Hi Lo Activator Own O 3 2

DAYBONDS D- W- M EOD 2/6/97 17:26 PagePrint - 2

53

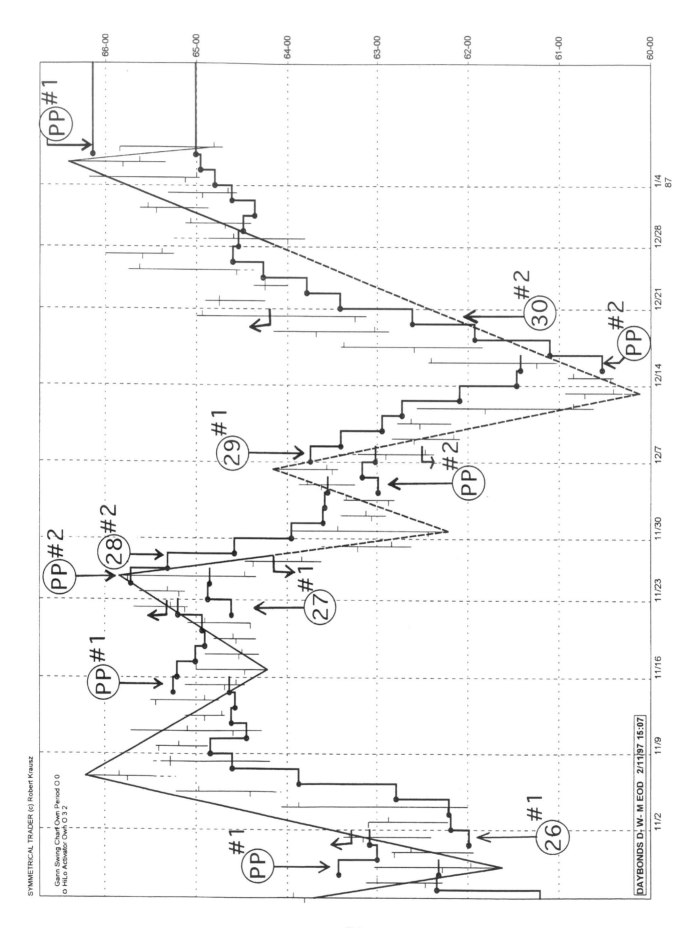

SYMMETRICAL TRADER (c) Robert Krausz

Gann Swing Chart Own Period O 0
o HiLo Activator Owh O 3 2

DAYBONDS D$_T$ W- M EOD 2/11/97 15:07

54

Beginning Equity	$30,000.00	Ending Equity	$45,093.75
Total Net Profit	$15,093.75	Average Ticks/Mo.	
Gross Profit	$31,106.25	Gross Loss	($19,312.50)
Total No. Trades	22	Percentage Profitable	50%
No. Winning Trades	11	No. Losing Trades	11

Largest Winning Trade	$ 9,468.75	Largest Losing Trade	($4,031.25)
Average Winning Trade	$3,127.84	Average Losing Trade	($1,755.68)
Ratio Average Win/Loss	1.78	Average Trade	$686.08
Max. Consecutive Winners	3	Max. Consecutive Losses	3
Largest Consecutive Drawdown (%)	14.13%	Largest Consecutive Drawdown	($8,625.00)

Return on Account	50%
Profit/Drawdown Ratio	1.75

1988
US T- Bonds
New Gann Swing Chartist© BASIC TRADING PLAN

Fibonacci Trader (c)

TRADE#	DATE	L/S	PRICE	CTR.	RULE #	PROFIT	(LOSS)	ACCUM.	MO. PROFIT/(LOSS)	A/C EQUITY
1	1/13/88	L	63.24	3	Buy 1					$30,000.00
PP	1/26/88	S	66.29	3	PP1	303		303	303	$39,468.75
2	1/27/88	L	68.19	3	Buy 3					$41,625.00
PP	2/12/88	S	69.10	3	PP1	69		372		$41,625.00
3	2/23/88	L	70.13	3	Buy 1					
PP	2/25/88	S	69.25	3	PP2		(60)	312	9	$39,750.00
4	3/18/88	S	68.11	3	Sell 2					
PP	4/6/88	L	66.31	3	PP1	129		441	129	$43,781.25
5	4/14/88	S	66.11	3	Sell 1					
PP	5/4/88	L	64.26	3	PP2	141		582	141	$48,187.50
6	5/12/88	S	64.02	3	Sell 3					
PP	5/13/88	L	64.16	3	PP2		(48)	534		$46,687.50
7	5/17/88	S	63.24	3	Sell 3					
8	6/1/88	L	63.15	6	Buy 2	27		561	(21)	$47,531.25
PP	6/16/88	S	65.18	3	PP1	201		762		$53,812.50
9	6/22/88	L	65.17	3	Buy 1					
PP	6/27/88	S	65.23	3	PP2		(18)	744	183	$53,250.00
10	6/30/88	L	66.15	3	Buy 1					
PP	7/5/88	S	66.04	3	PP2		(39)	705		$52,031.25
11	7/7/88	S	64.23	3	Sell 2					
PP	7/22/88	L	63.31	3	PP1	72		777		$54,281.25
12	7/27/88	S	63.17	3	Sell 1					
PP	7/29/88	L	64.02	3	PP2		(57)	720	(24)	$52,500.00
13	8/2/88	L	64.17	3	Buy 2					
PP	8/5/88	S	64.21	3	PP2	12		732		$52,875.00
14	8/10/88	S	63.07	3	Sell 2					
PP	8/16/88	L	62.21	3	PP1	54		786	66	$54,562.50
15	9/2/88	L	65.23	3	Buy 2					
PP	9/19/88	S	66.04	3	PP1	39		825		$55,781.25
16	9/23/88	S	65.25	3	Sell 2					
PP	9/29/88	L	66.03	3	PP1		(30)	795	9	$54,843.75

56

1988
US T- Bonds
New Gann Swing Chartist© BASIC TRADING PLAN   Fibonacci Trader (c)

TRADE#	DATE	L/S	PRICE	CTR.	RULE #	PROFIT	(LOSS)	ACCUM.	MO. PROFIT/(LOSS)	A/C EQUITY
17	10/7/88	L	68.07	3	Buy 2					
PP	10/12/88	S	67.15	3	PP1		(72)	723		$52,593.75
18	10/27/88	L	68.23	3	Buy 1					
PP	11/4/88	S	68.19	3	PP2		(18)	705	(120)	$52,031.25
19	11/15/88	S	66.29	3	Sell 2					
PP	11/29/88	L	66.11	3	PP1	54		759	54	$53,718.75
20	12/2/88	S	65.31	3	Sell 1					
PP	12/6/88	L	67.08	3	PP2		(129)	630		$49,687.50
21	12/14/88	S	66.31	3	Sell 1					
PP	12/20/88	L	67.24	3	PP2		(81)	549		$47,156.25
22	12/23/88	L	68.19	3	Buy 2					
PP	12/28/88	S	67.31	3	PP2		(66)	483	(276)	$45,093.75

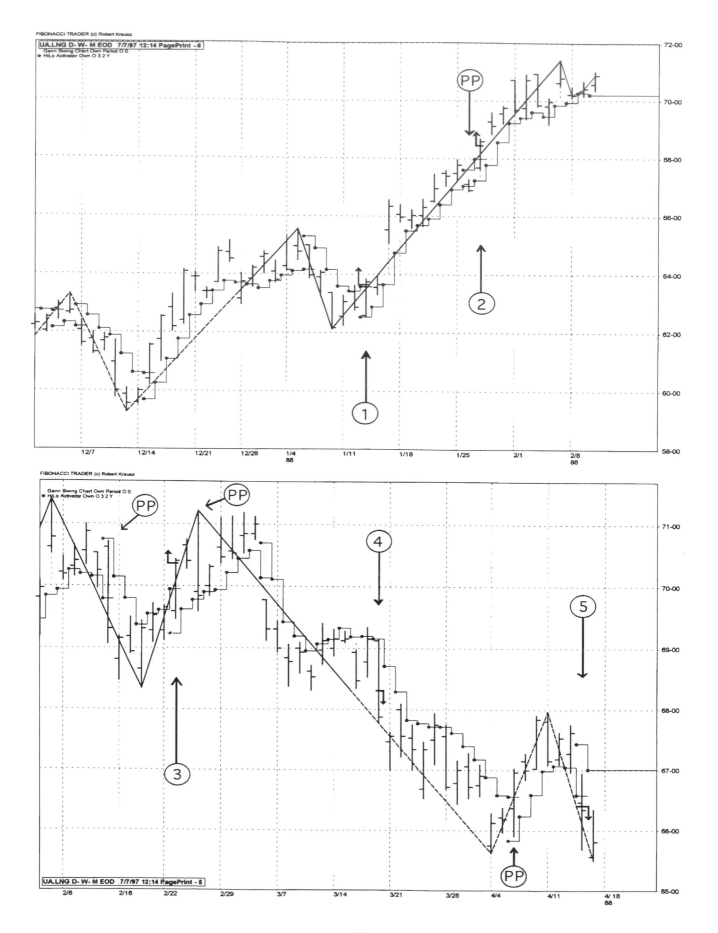

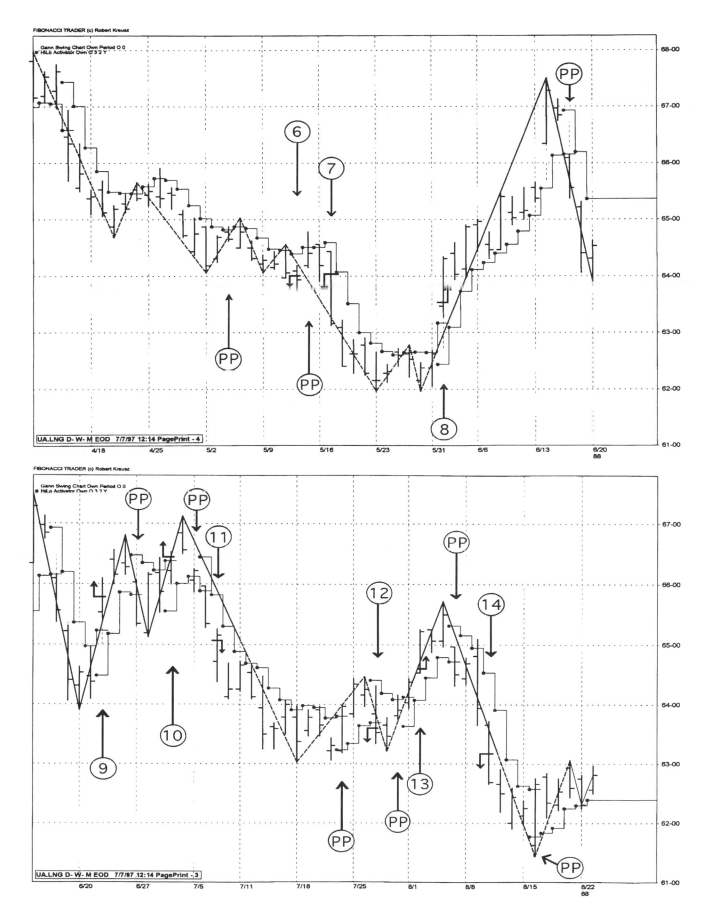

59

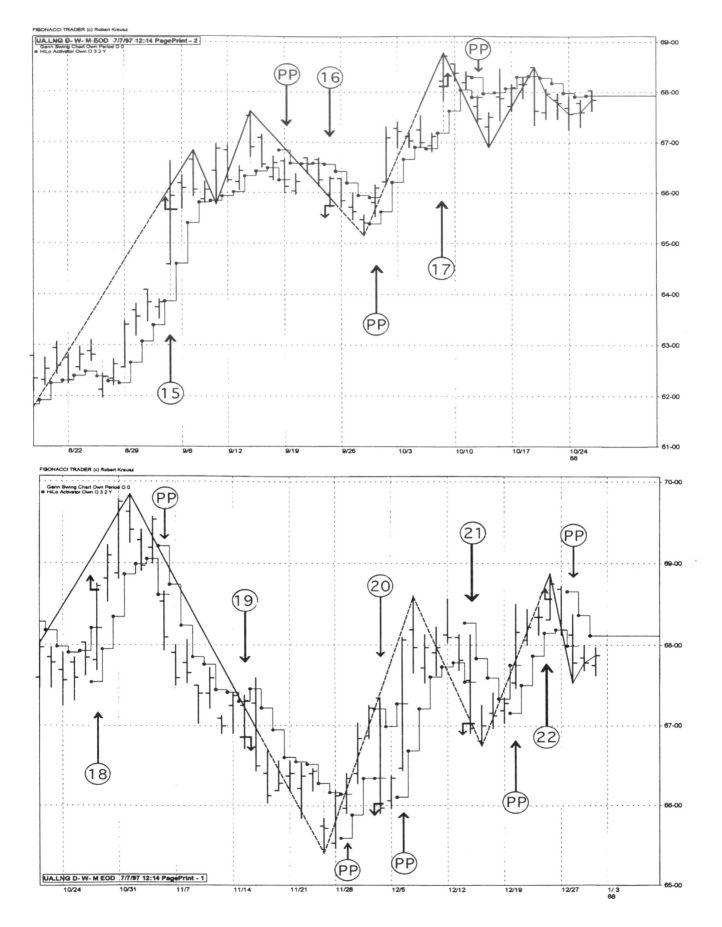

Beginning Equity	$30,000.00	Ending Equity	$52,187.50
Total Net Profit	$22,187.50	Average Ticks/Mo.	
Gross Profit	$47,218.75	Gross Loss	($25,031.25)
Total No. Trades	26	Percentage Profitable	46%
No. Winning Trades	12	No. Losing Trades	14

Largest Winning Trade	$15,062.50	Largest Losing Trade	($2,718.75)
Average Winning Trade	$3,934.90	Average Losing Trade	($1,787.95)
Ratio Average Win/Loss	2.20	Average Trade	$853.37
Max. Consecutive Winners	2	Max. Consecutive Losses	6
Largest Consecutive Drawdown (%)	24.13%	Largest Consecutive Drawdown	($11,281.25)

Return on Account	74%
Profit/Drawdown Ratio	1.97

NOTES:
1) Initial A/C Size = $30,000

1989
US T- Bonds
New Gann Swing Chartist© BASIC TRADING PLAN

Fibonacci Trader (c)

TRADE#	DATE	L/S	PRICE	CTR.	RULE #	PROFIT	(LOSS)	ACCUM.	MO. PROFIT/(LOSS)	A/C EQUITY
1	1/13/89	L	68.29	3	Buy 2					$30,000.00
PP	1/31/89	S	69.16	3	PP2	57		57	57	$31,781.25
2	2/9/89	S	68.12	3	Sell 2					
PP	3/6/89	L	67.11	3	PP1	99		156	99	$34,875.00
3	3/7/89	L	67.15	3	Buy 2					
PP	3/10/89	S	67.00	3	PP2		(45)	111		$33,468.75
4	3/17/89	S	66.18	3	Sell 2					
PP	3/22/89	L	66.00	3	PP1	54		165	9	$35,156.25
5	4/3/89	L	67.14	3	Buy 2					
PP	4/7/89	S	67.05	3	PP1		(51)	114		$33,562.50
6	4/14/89	L	67.27	3	Buy 1					
PP	5/1/89	S	68.08	3	PP2	39		153	(12)	$34,781.25
7	5/3/89	L	68.27	3	Buy 1					
PP	5/9/89	S	67.30	3	PP2		(87)	66		$32,062.50
8	5/12/89	L	69.14	3	Buy 3					
PP	6/15/89	S	74.14	3	PP1	482		548	395	$47,125.00
9	6/23/89	L	75.13	3	Buy 1					
PP	7/5/89	S	76.03	3	PP1	66		614	66	$49,187.50
10	7/7/89	L	76.31	3	Buy 1					
PP	7/14/89	S	76.03	3	PP2		(84)	530		$46,562.50
11	7/20/89	L	76.18	3	Buy 1					
PP	8/3/89	S	78.22	3	PP1	204		734	120	$52,937.50
12	8/11/89	S	76.02	3	Sell 2					
PP	8/16/89	L	76.05	3	PP1		(9)	725		$52,656.25
13	8/22/89	S	74.29	3	Sell 1					
PP	8/24/89	L	75.25	3	PP2		(84)	641		$50,031.25
14	8/29/89	S	74.24	3	Sell 3					
PP	8/31/89	L	75.19	3	PP2		(81)	560	(174)	$47,500.00
15	9/1/89	L	75.19	3	Buy 2					
PP	9/13/89	S	75.27	3	PP1	21		581		$48,156.25
16	9/25/89	S	74.19	3	Sell 2					

1989
US T- Bonds
New Gann Swing Chartist© BASIC TRADING PLAN   Fibonacci Trader (c)

TRADE#	DATE	L/S	PRICE	CTR.	RULE #	PROFIT	(LOSS)	ACCUM.	MO. PROFIT/(LOSS)	A/C EQUITY
PP	10/2/89	L	75.02	3	PP1		(45)	536	(24)	$46,750.00
17	10/6/89	L	76.21	3	Buy 2					
PP	10/11/89	S	76.29	3	PP1	21		557		$47,406.25
18	10/13/89	L	77.17	3	Buy 1					
PP	10/27/89	S	77.30	3	PP2	39		596	60	$48,625.00
19	11/1/89	L	78.22	3	Buy 1					
PP	11/3/89	S	78.04	3	PP2		(54)	542		$46,937.50
20	11/7/89	L	78.23	3	Buy 1					
PP	11/13/89	S	78.06	3	PP2		(51)	491		$45,343.75
21	11/16/89	L	79.03	3	Buy 3					
PP	11/17/89	S	78.09	3	PP2		(78)	413		$42,906.25
22	11/17/89	S	78.02	3	Sell 2					
PP	11/22/89	L	78.20	3	PP2		(54)	359		$41,218.75
23	11/27/89	S	78.09	3	Sell 1					
PP	11/30/89	L	78.17	3	PP2		(24)	335	(261)	$40,468.75
24	12/8/89	S	78.00	3	Sell 3					
PP	12/11/89	L	78.18	3	PP2		(54)	281		$38,781.25
25	12/14/89	L	78.24	3	Buy 2					
PP	12/22/89	S	78.27	3	PP2	9		290		$39,062.50
26	12/26/89	S	77.21	3	Sell 2					
PP	1/31/89	L	73.09	3	PP1	420		710	375	$52,187.50

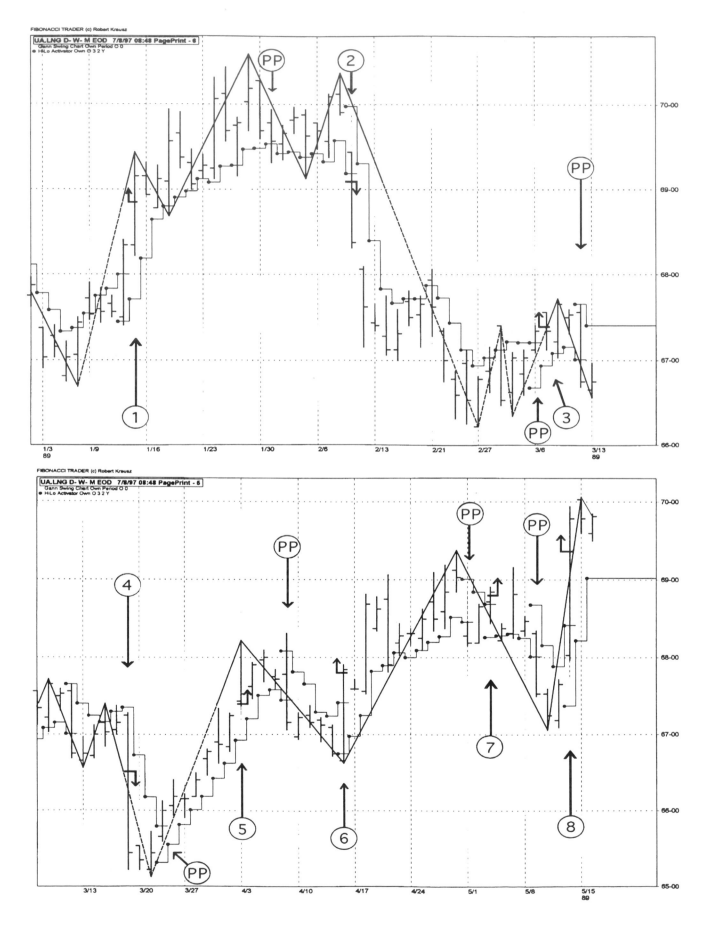
64

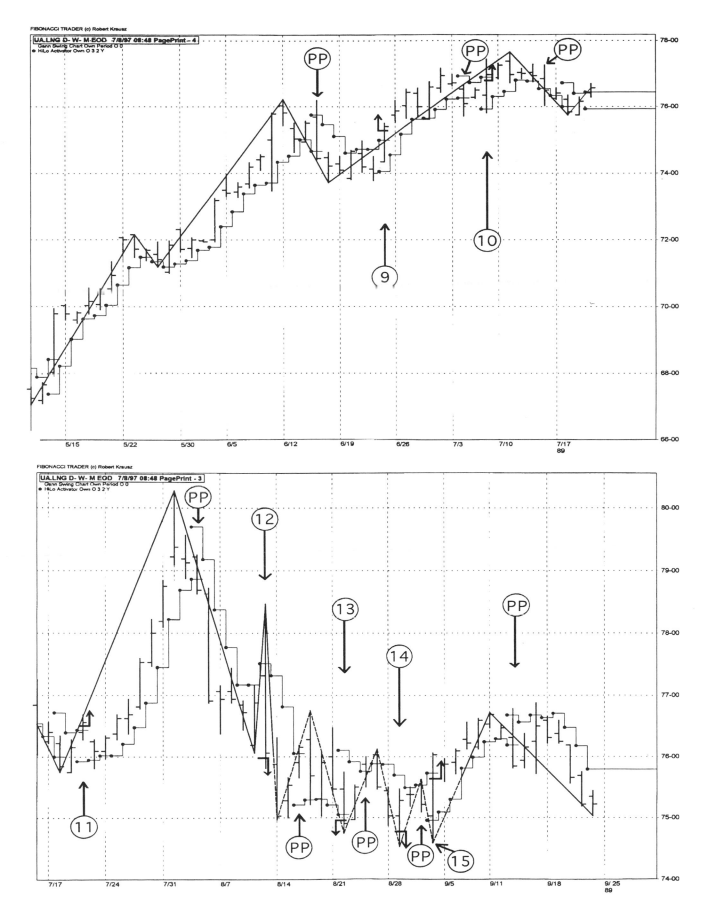

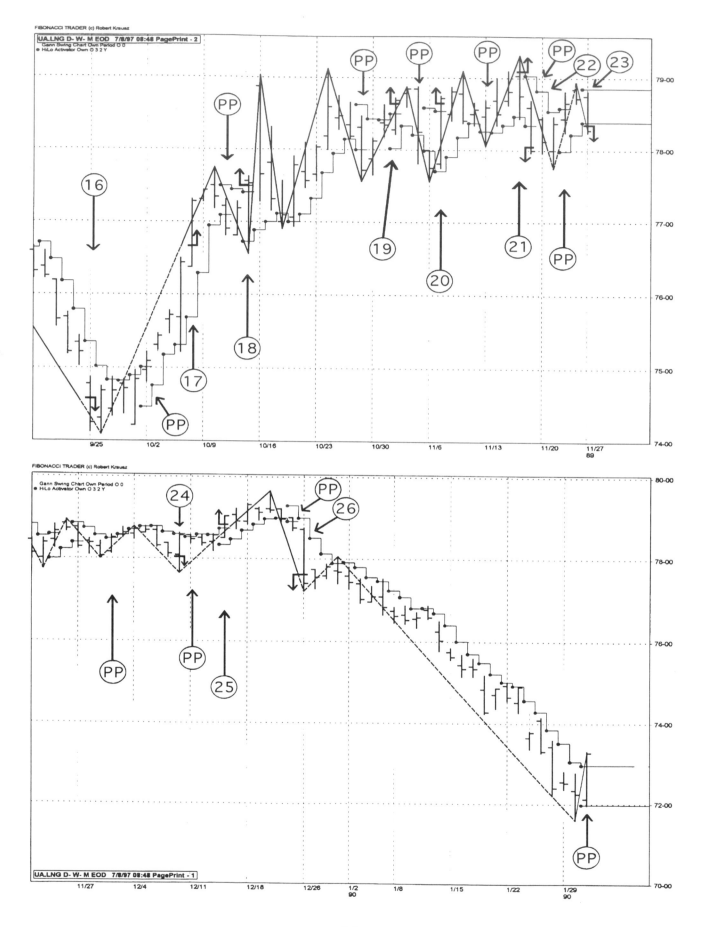

1990
US T- Bonds
New Gann Swing Chartist©
BASIC TRADING PLAN

Beginning Equity	$30,000.00	Ending Equity	$50,156.25
Total Net Profit	$20,156.25	Average Ticks/Mo.	
Gross Profit	$36,375.00	Gross Loss	($16,218.75)
Total No. Trades	23	Percentage Profitable	39%
No. Winning Trades	9	No. Losing Trades	14

Largest Winning Trade	$ 11,343.75	Largest Losing Trade	($2,250.00)
Average Winning Trade	$4,041.67	Average Losing Trade	($1,158.48)
Ratio Average Win/Loss	3.49	Average Trade	$876.36
Max. Consecutive Winners	3	Max. Consecutive Losses	3
Largest Consecutive Drawdown (%)	19.81%	Largest Consecutive Drawdown	($7,875.00)

Return on Account	67%
Profit/Drawdown Ratio	2.56

Notes:
1) Initial account size: $30,000

1990
US T- Bonds
New Gann Swing Chartist© BASIC TRADING PLAN

Fibonacci Trader (c)

TRADE#	DATE	L/S	PRICE	CTR.	RULE #	PROFIT	(LOSS)	ACCUM.	MO. PROFIT/(LOSS)	A/C EQUITY
1	2/5/90	S	72.20	3	Sell 1					$30,000.00
PP	2/8/90	L	72.24	3	PP2		(12)	(12)		
2	2/9/90	L	73.23	3	Buy 2					$29,625.00
PP	2/15/90	S	72.27	3	PP2		(60)	(72)		
3	2/20/90	S	71.19	3	Sell 2					$27,750.00
PP	2/22/90	L	72.00	3	PP2		(36)	(108)	(108)	
4	2/28/90	S	72.10	3	Sell 1					$26,625.00
PP	3/7/90	L	72.01	3	PP2	27		(81)		
5	3/13/90	S	70.19	3	Sell 3					$27,468.75
PP	3/14/90	L	71.12	3	PP2		(69)	(150)		
6	3/29/90	S	71.23	3	Sell 1					$25,312.50
PP	4/4/90	L	71.30	3	PP2		(21)	(171)	(63)	
7	4/16/90	S	71.07	3	Sell 1					$24,656.25
PP	5/4/90	L	69.21	3	PP2	150		(21)	150	
8	5/9/90	S	69.03	3	Sell 1					$29,343.75
PP	5/11/90	L	69.27	3	PP2		(72)	(93)		
9	5/18/90	S	70.26	3	Sell 1					$27,093.75
PP	5/22/90	L	71.11	3	PP2		(51)	(144)		
10	5/23/90	L	71.31	3	Buy 2					$25,500.00
PP	5/25/90	S	71.09	3	PP2		(63)	(207)	(186)	
11	5/30/90	L	71.25	3	Buy 1					$23,531.25
PP	6/15/90	S	73.06	3	PP2	135		(72)		
12	6/18/90	S	72.31	6	Sell 2					$27,750.00
PP	6/28/90	L	73.02	3	PP2		(9)	(81)	126	
13	7/6/90	S	72.20	3	Sell 1					$27,468.75
PP	7/12/90	L	72.25	3	PP1		(15)	(96)		
14	7/18/90	S	72.14	3	Sell 1					$27,000.00
PP	7/23/90	L	72.27	3	PP2		(39)	(135)		
15	7/30/90	L	73.05	3	Buy 2					$25,781.25
PP	8/2/90	S	73.17	3	PP2	6		(129)	(48)	
16	8/6/90	S	71.22	3	Sell 2					$25,968.75
PP	8/27/90	L	68.01	3	PP1	351		222	351	
17	9/14/90	S	68.07	3	Sell 1					$36,937.50

1990
US T - Bonds
New Gann Swing Chartist© BASIC TRADING PLAN

Fibonacci Trader (c)

TRADE#	DATE	L/S	PRICE	CTR.	RULE #	PROFIT	(LOSS)	ACCUM.	MO. PROFIT/(LOSS)	A/C EQUITY
PP	9/19/90	L	68.06	3	PP2	3		225		$37,031.25
18	9/21/90	S	67.08	3	Sell 3					
PP	9/27/90	L	67.21	3	PP2		(39)	186	(36)	$35,812.50
19	10/1/90	L	69.09	3	Buy 2					
PP	10/9/90	S	69.00	3	PP2		(24)	162		$35,062.50
20	10/15/90	L	69.04	3	Buy 1					
PP	10/29/90	S	70.06	3	PP1	102		264	78	$38,250.00
21	11/1/90	L	71.15	3	Buy 1					
PP	11/7/90	S	71.12	3	PP1		(9)	255		$37,968.75
22	11/12/90	L	73.01	3	Buy 1					
PP	12/13/90	S	76.26	3	PP1	363		618	354	$49,312.50
23	12/20/90	S	75.29	3	Sell 2					
PP	12/27/90	L	75.20	3	PP2	27		645	27	$50,156.25

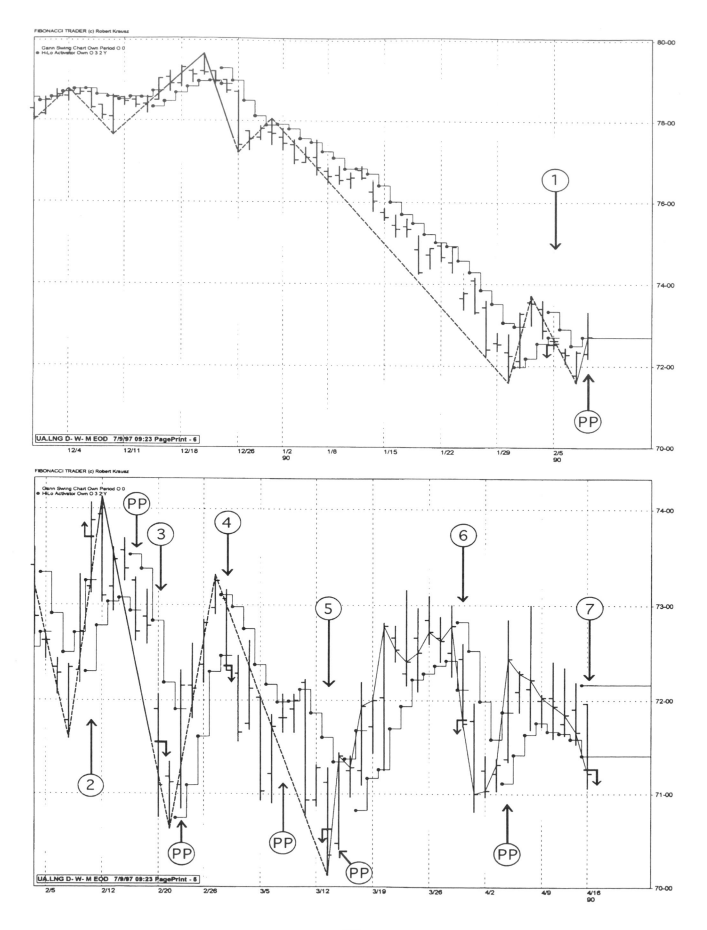

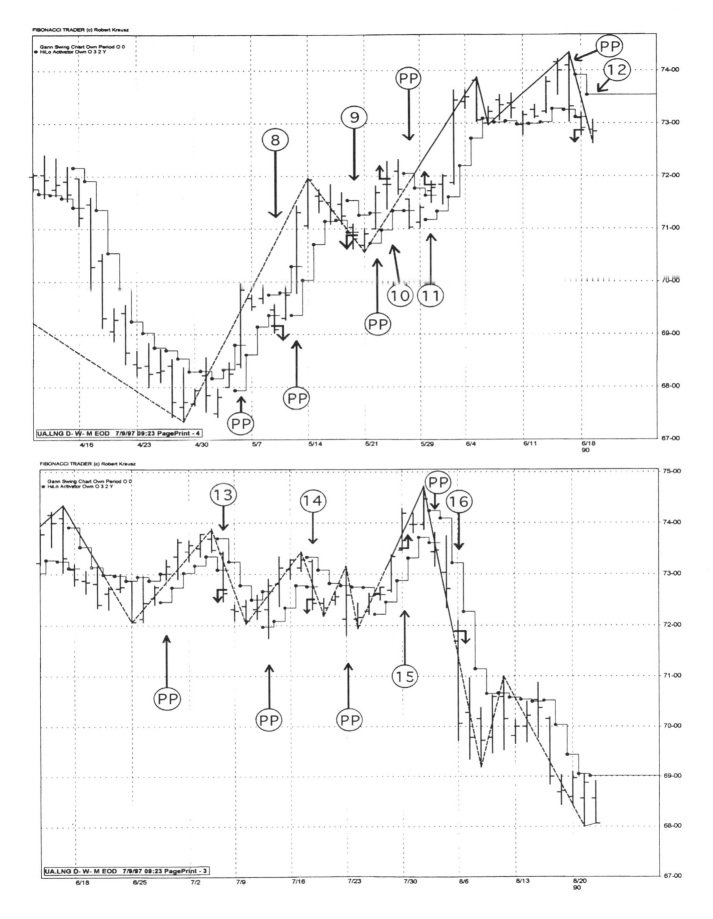

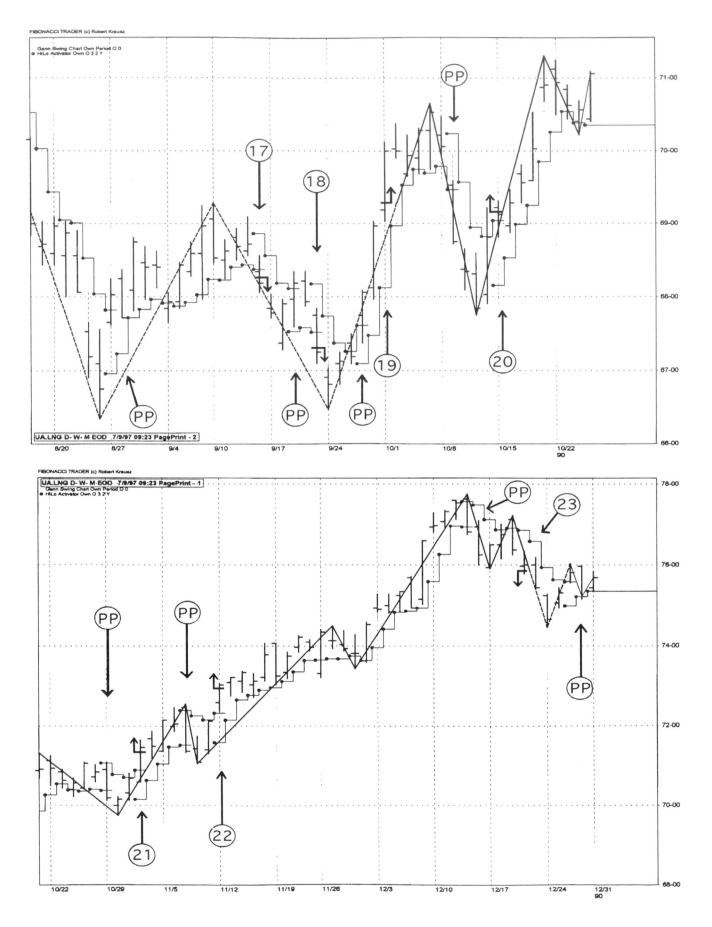

1991
US T- Bonds
New Gann Swing Chartist©
BASIC TRADING PLAN

Beginning Equity	$30,000.00	Ending Equity	$50,718.75
Total Net Profit	$20,718.75	Average Ticks/Mo.	
Gross Profit	$42,843.75	Gross Loss	($22,125.00)
Total No. Trades	23	Percentage Profitable	52%
No. Winning Trades	12	No. Losing Trades	11

Largest Winning Trade	$16,312.50	Largest Losing Trade	($5,250.00)
Average Winning Trade	$3,570.31	Average Losing Trade	($2,011.36)
Ratio Average Win/Loss	1.78	Average Trade	$900.82
Max. Consecutive Winners	2	Max. Consecutive Losses	3
Largest Consecutive Drawdown (%)	32.81%	Largest Consecutive Drawdown	($9,843.75)

Return on Account	69%
Profit/Drawdown Ratio	2.10

NOTES:
1) Initial A/C Size = $30,000

Fibonacci Trader (c)

TRADE#	DATE	L/S	PRICE	CTR.	RULE #	PROFIT	(LOSS)	ACCUM.	MO. PROFIT/(LOSS)	A/C EQUITY
1	1/3/91	L	77.07	3	Buy 2					$30,000.00
PP	1/4/91	S	76.06	3	PP2		(93)	(93)		$27,093.75
2	1/9/91	S	74.14	3	Sell 2					
PP	1/17/91	L	76.07	3	PP2		(168)	(261)		$21,843.75
3	1/25/91	S	75.29	3	Sell 1					
PP	1/30/91	L	76.15	3	PP2		(54)	(315)	(315)	$20,156.25
4	2/1/91	L	77.16	3	Buy 1					
PP	2/7/91	S	77.22	3	PP2	18		(297)		$20,718.75
5	2/20/91	S	77.21	3	Sell 2					
PP	3/7/91	L	75.27	3	PP1	174		(123)	192	$26,156.25
6	3/8/91	S	74.31	3	Sell 1					
PP	3/13/91	L	76.02	3	PP2		(102)	(225)		$22,968.75
7	3/15/91	S	75.05	3	Sell 1					
PP	3/21/91	L	74.30	3	PP2	18		(207)		$23,531.25
8	4/4/91	L	76.07	3	Buy 2					
PP	4/9/91	S	76.13	3	PP1	21		(186)	(63)	$24,187.50
9	4/12/91	L	76.30	3	Buy 1					
PP	4/18/91	S	76.28	3	PP2		(6)	(192)		$24,000.00
10	4/24/91	L	76.20	3	Buy 1					
PP	5/3/91	S	76.24	3	PP2	9		(183)	3	$24,281.25
11	5/10/91	S	75.20	3	Sell 2					
PP	5/17/91	L	76.03	3	PP1		(45)	(228)		$22,875.00
12	5/30/91	L	76.16	3	Buy 2					
PP	6/3/91	S	75.24	3	PP2		(69)	(297)	(114)	$20,718.75
13	6/3/91	S	75.17	3	Sell 2					
PP	6/14/91	L	74.10	3	PP1	117		(180)		$24,375.00
14	6/28/91	L	74.17	3	Buy 2					
PP	7/5/91	S	74.10	3	PP2		(21)	(201)	96	$23,718.75
15	7/11/91	L	74.21	3	Buy 1					
PP	7/17/91	S	74.21	3	PP1	0		(201)	0	$23,718.75
16	7/24/91	L	75.15	3	Buy 1					
PP	8/23/91	S	78.18	3	PP1	312		111		$33,468.75
17	8/28/91	L	79.15	3	Buy 1					
PP	9/5/91	S	79.04	3	PP2		(33)	78	279	$32,437.50
18	9/9/91	L	80.04	3	Buy 3					
19	10/9/91	S	81.26	6	Sell 2	159		237	159	$37,406.25

74

1991
US T- Bonds
New Gann Swing Chartist© BASIC TRADING PLAN

Fibonacci Trader (c)

TRADE#	DATE	L/S	PRICE	CTR.	RULE #	PROFIT	(LOSS)	ACCUM.	MO. PROFIT/(LOSS)	A/C EQUITY
PP	10/11/91	L	81.26	3	PP2	0		237		$37,406.25
20	10/17/91	S	80.24	3	Sell 1					
PP	10/24/91	L	80.16	3	PP1	21		258	21	$38,062.50
21	11/5/91	S	80.26	3	Sell 1					
PP	11/7/91	L	81.23	3	PP2		(87)	171		$35,343.75
22	11/8/91	L	82.14	3	Buy 2					
PP	11/13/91	S	82.04	3	PP2		(30)	141	(117)	$34,406.25
23	11/29/91	L	81.28	3	Buy 1					
PP	1/9/92	S	87.17	3	PP2	522		663	522	$50,718.75

75

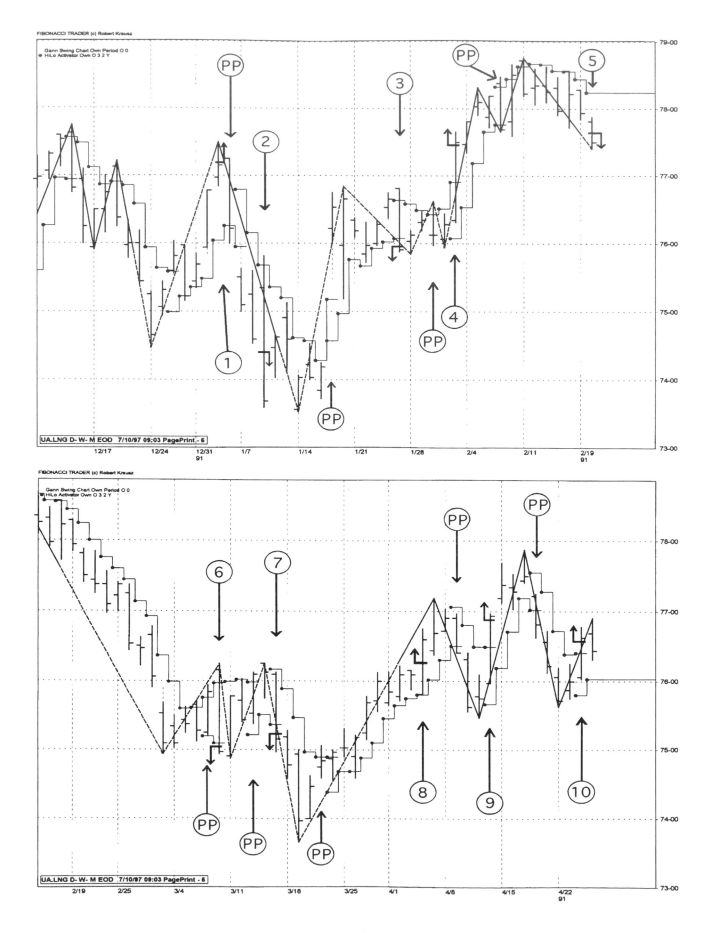

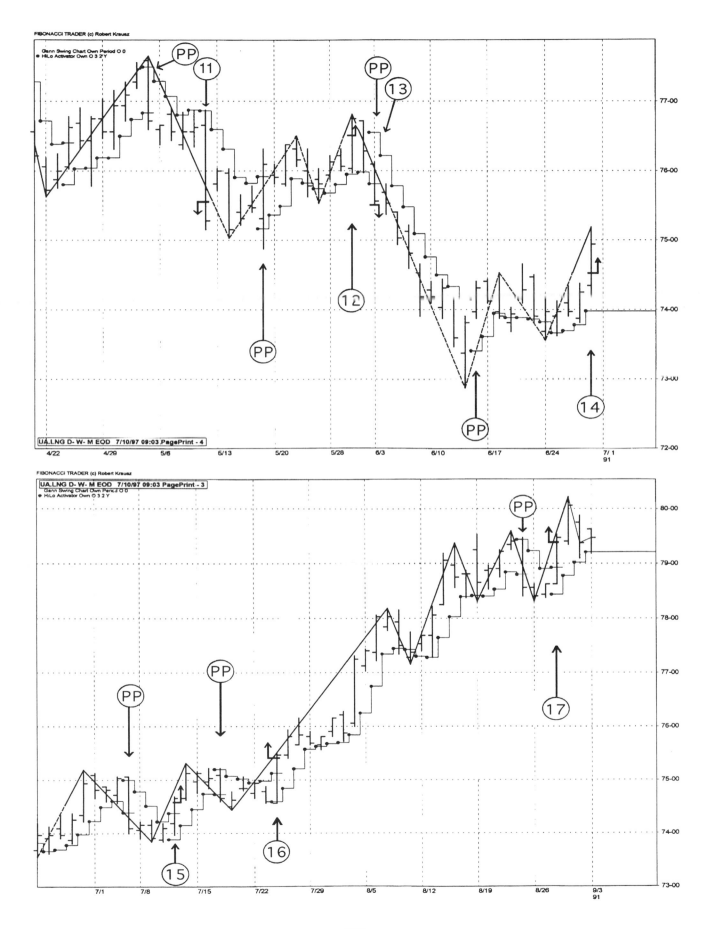

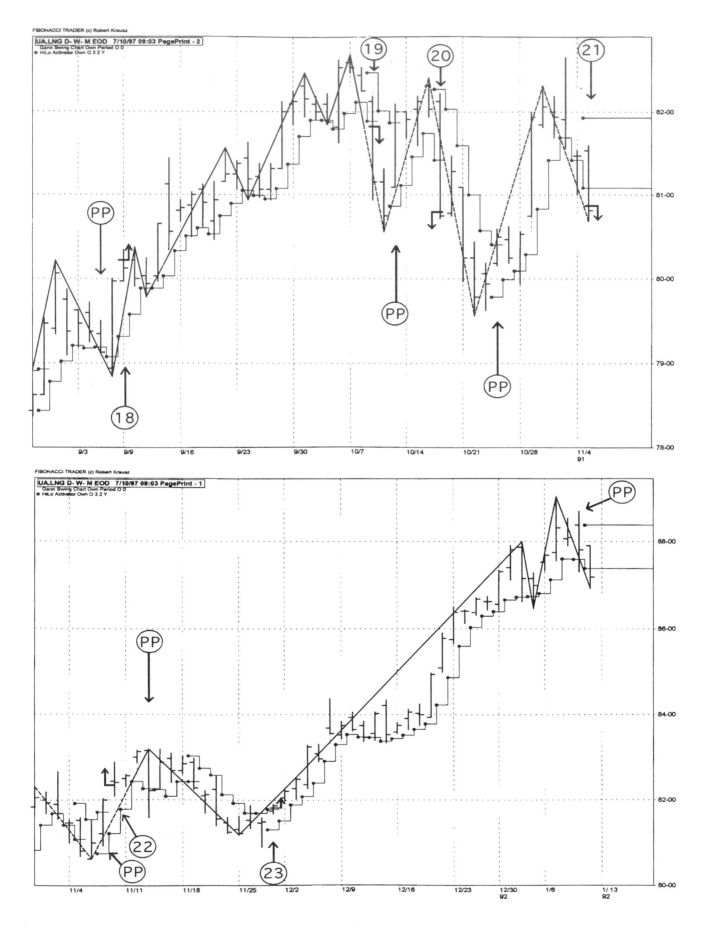

Beginning Equity	$30,000.00	Ending Equity	$41,906.25
Total Net Profit	$11,906.25		
Gross Profit	$26,718.75	Gross Loss	($14,812.50)
Total No. Trades	24	Percentage Profitable	42%
No. Winning Trades	10	No. Losing Trades	14

Largest Winning Trade	$10,031.25	Largest Losing Trade	($2,718.75)
Average Winning Trade	$2,671.88	Average Losing Trade	($1,058.04)
Ratio Average Win/Loss	2.53	Average Trade	$496.09
Max. Consecutive Winners	3	Max. Consecutive Losses	4
Largest Consecutive Drawdown (%)	19.88%	Largest Consecutive Drawdown	($6,093.75)

Return on Account	40%
Profit/Drawdown Ratio	1.95

NOTES:
1) Initial A/C Size = $30,000

79

1992
US T- Bonds: Gann Swing Chartist®
Basic Swing Plan (End of Day)

Fibonacci Trader®

Trade#	Date	L/S	Price	Ctr.	Rule #	Profit	(Loss)	Accum.	A/C Equity
1	1/14/92	S	86.15	3	Sell 2				$30,000.00
PP	1/21/92	L	86.08	3	PP1	21		21	$30,656.25
2	1/23/92	S	84.21	3	Sell 1				
PP	1/28/92	L	85.07	3	PP2		(54)	(33)	$28,968.75
3	1/29/92	S	84.04	3	Sell 1				
PP	2/5/92	L	84.09	3	PP2		(15)	(48)	$28,500.00
4	2/13/92	S	83.05	3	Sell 3				
PP	2/26/92	L	83.07	3	PP2		(6)	(54)	$28,312.50
5	3/3/92	S	83.01	3	Sell 1				
PP	3/9/92	L	83.05	3	PP2		(12)	(66)	$27,937.50
6	3/11/92	S	82.18	3	Sell 1				
PP	3/18/92	L	82.05	3	PP2	39		(27)	$29,156.25
7	4/1/92	L	83.11	3	Buy 2				
PP	4/8/92	S	83.11	3	PP1	0		(27)	$29,156.25
8	4/9/92	L	84.11	3	Buy 1				
PP	4/16/92	S	83.20	3	PP1		(69)	(96)	$27,000.00
9	4/20/92	S	83.09	3	Sell 2				
PP	5/1/92	L	82.21	3	PP2	60		(36)	$28,875.00
10	5/12/92	L	84.16	3	Buy 2				
PP	5/21/92	S	84.21	3	PP1	15		(21)	$29,343.75
11	5/29/92	L	84.30	3	Buy 1				
PP	6/1/92	S	84.01	3	PP2		(87)	(108)	$26,625.00
12	6/5/92	L	85.03	3	Buy 3				
PP	6/10/92	S	84.13	3	PP2		(66)	(174)	$24,562.50
13	6/12/92	L	84.27	3	Buy 1				
PP	6/23/92	S	85.02	3	PP1	21		(153)	$25,218.75
14	6/25/92	L	85.30	3	Buy 1				
PP	7/10/92	S	87.19	3	PP1	159		6	$30,187.50
15	7/16/92	L	88.00	3	Buy 1				
PP	8/13/92	S	91.11	3	PP2	321		168	$40,218.75
16	8/19/92	L	91.10	3	Buy 1				
PP	8/21/92	S	90.28	3	PP2		(42)	126	$38,906.25
17	8/25/92	S	89.27	3	Sell 2				

1992
US T- Bonds: Gann Swing Chartist®
Basic Swing Plan (End of Day)

Fibonacci Trader®

Trade#	Date	L/S	Price	Ctr.	Rule #	Profit	(_oss)	Accum.	A/C Equity
PP	9/1/92	L	90.13	3	PP2		(54)	72	$37,218.75
18	9/4/92	L	92.15	3	Buy 2				
PP	9/11/92	S	92.11	3	PP1		(12)	60	$36,843.75
19	9/25/92	L	91.30	3	Buy 1				
PP	10/6/92	S	91.22	3	PP2		(24)	36	$36,093.75
20	10/9/92	S	90.05	3	Sell 2				
PP	10/22/92	L	89.18	3	PP2	57		93	$37,875.00
21	11/2/92	S	88.30	3	Sell 1				
PP	11/10/92	L	88.25	3	PP2	15		108	$38,343.75
22	11/12/92	L	89.25	3	Buy 2				
23	11/27/92	S	89.21	6	Sell 2		(12)	96	$37,968.75
PP	12/3/92	L	89.28	3	PP2		(21)	75	$37,312.50
24	12/4/92	L	90.22	6	Buy 1				
PP	12/28/92	S	92.07	3	PP1	147		222	$41,906.25

81

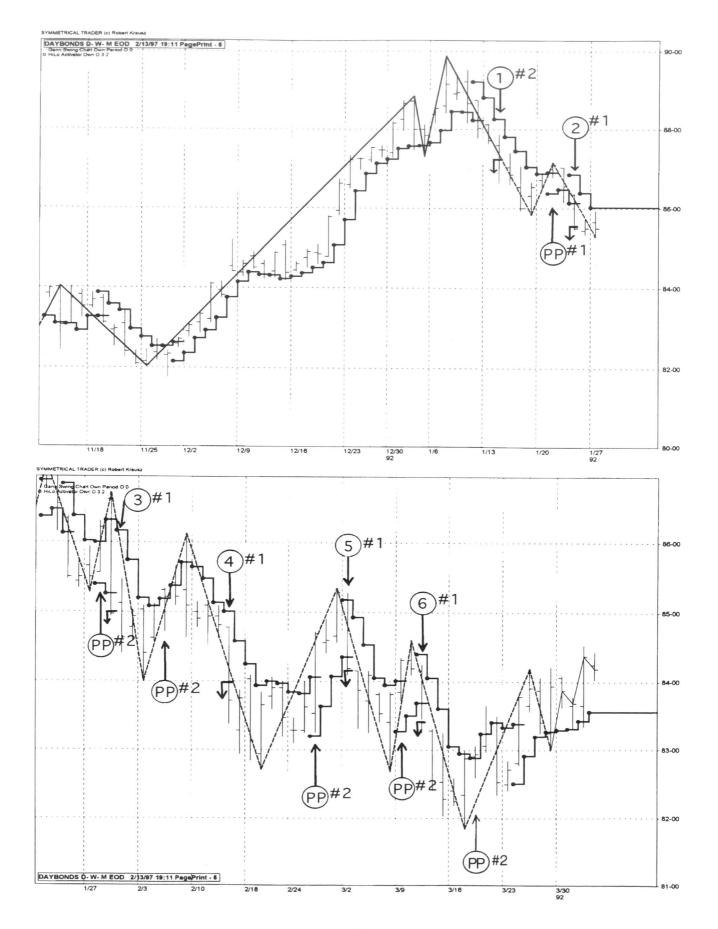

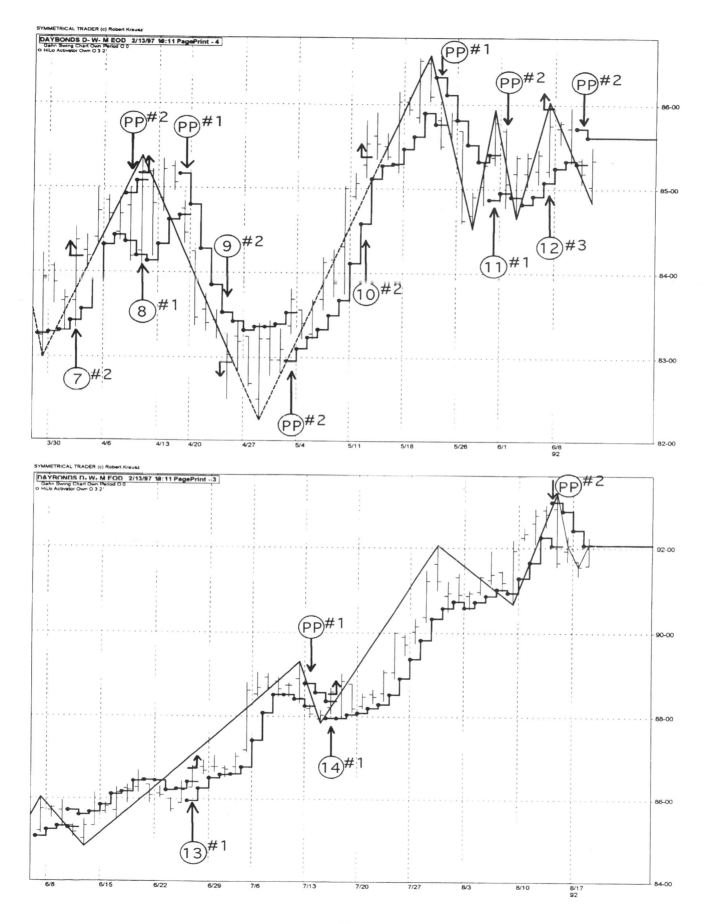

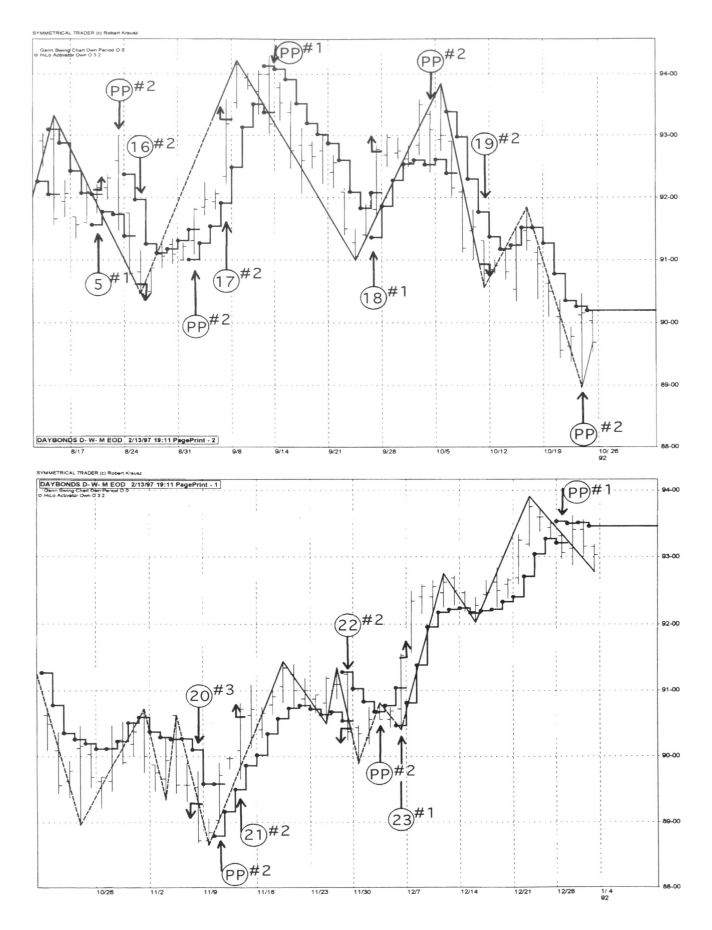

84

US T-BONDS: 1993
BASIC SWING PLAN
GANN SWING CHARTIST - FIBONACCI TRADER ®

Beginning Equity	$30,000.00	Ending Equity	$53,158.25
Total Net Profit	$23,156.25	Average Ticks/Mo.	
Gross Profit	$45,468.75	Gross Loss	($22,312.50)
Total No. Trades	21	Percentage Profitable	38%
No. Winning Trades	8	No. Losing Trades	13

Largest Winning Trade	$ 10,968.75	Largest Losing Trade	($4,218.75)
Average Winning Trade	$5,683.59	Average Losing Trade	($1,718.35)
Ratio Average Win/Loss	3.31	Average Trade	$ 1,102.68
Max. Consecutive Winners	2	Max. Consecutive Losses	3
Largest Consecutive Drawdown (%)	11.88%	Largest Consecutive Drawdown	($4,500.00)

Return on Account	77%
Profit/Drawdown Ratio	5.15

Notes:
1) Initial account size: $30,000

1993
US T- Bonds: Gann Swing Chartist®
Basic Swing Plan (End of Day)

Fibonacci Trader®

Trade#	Date	L/S	Price	Ctr.	Rule #	Profit	(Loss)	Accum.	A/C Equity
1	1/4/93	L	93.02	3	Buy 1				$30,000.00
PP	1/7/93	S	92.09	3	PP2		(75)	(75)	$27,656.25
2	1/8/93	S	91.14	3	Sell 2				
PP	1/14/93	L	91.27	3	PP2		(39)	(114)	$26,437.50
3	1/19/93	L	93.01	3	Buy 2				
PP	2/10/93	S	94.20	3	PP1	153		39	$31,218.75
4	2/18/93	L	96.28	3	Buy 1				
PP	3/5/93	S	99.14	3	PP2	246		285	$38,906.25
5	3/15/93	S	98.08	3	Sell 2				
PP	3/18/93	L	99.06	3	PP2		(90)	195	$36,093.75
6	3/26/93	S	97.29	3	Sell 1				
PP	4/7/93	L	98.06	3	PP2		(27)	168	$35,250.00
7	4/12/93	L	100.20	3	Buy 2				
PP	4/23/93	S	100.16	3	Sell 1		(12)	156	$34,875.00
8	5/3/93	L	100.06	3	Buy 1				
PP	5/7/93	S	100.10	3	PP2	12		168	$35,250.00
9	5/13/93	S	99.02	3	Sell 2				
PP	5/20/93	L	99.11	3	PP2		(27)	141	$34,406.25
10	6/11/93	L	101.14	3	Buy 2				
PP	7/21/93	S	105.03	3	PP2	351		492	$45,375.00
11	7/29/93	L	105.19	3	Buy 1				
PP	8/6/93	S	105.00	3	PP2		(57)	492	$43,593.75
12	8/9/93	L	105.31	3	Buy 3				
PP	8/13/93	S	105.27	3	PP2		(12)	480	$43,218.75
13	8/20/93	L	106.29	3	Buy 3				
PP	9/9/93	S	110.13	3	PP1	336		816	$53,718.75
14	9/21/93	S	109.04	3	Sell 2				
PP	9/23/93	L	110.01	3	PP2		(87)	729	$51,000.00
15	9/27/93	L	110.26	3	Buy 2				
PP	9/30/93	S	110.14	3	PP2		(36)	693	$49,875.00
16	10/8/93	L	111.31	3	Buy 1				
PP	10/19/93	S	112.01	3	PP2	6		699	$50,062.50
17	10/21/93	S	111.18	6	Sell 2				

1993
US T- Bonds: Gann Swing Chartist®
Basic Swing Plan (End of Day)

Fibonacci Trader®

Trade#	Date	L/S	Price	Ctr.	Rule #	Profit	(Loss)	Accum.	A/C Equity
PP	11/9/93	L	108.06	3	PP1	324		1023	$60,187.50
18	11/11/93	S	107.03	3	Sell 1				
PP	11/16/93	L	108.16	3	PP1		(135)	888	$55,968.75
19	11/18/93	S	107.16	3	Sell 1				
PP	11/24/93	L	107.07	3	PP1	27		915	$56,812.50
20	11/30/93	S	106.26	3	Sell 1				
PP	12/3/93	L	107.17	3	PP1		(69)	846	$54,656.25
21	12/22/93	L	108.13	3	Buy 1				
PP	12/30/93	S	107.29	3	PP2		(48)	798	$53,156.25

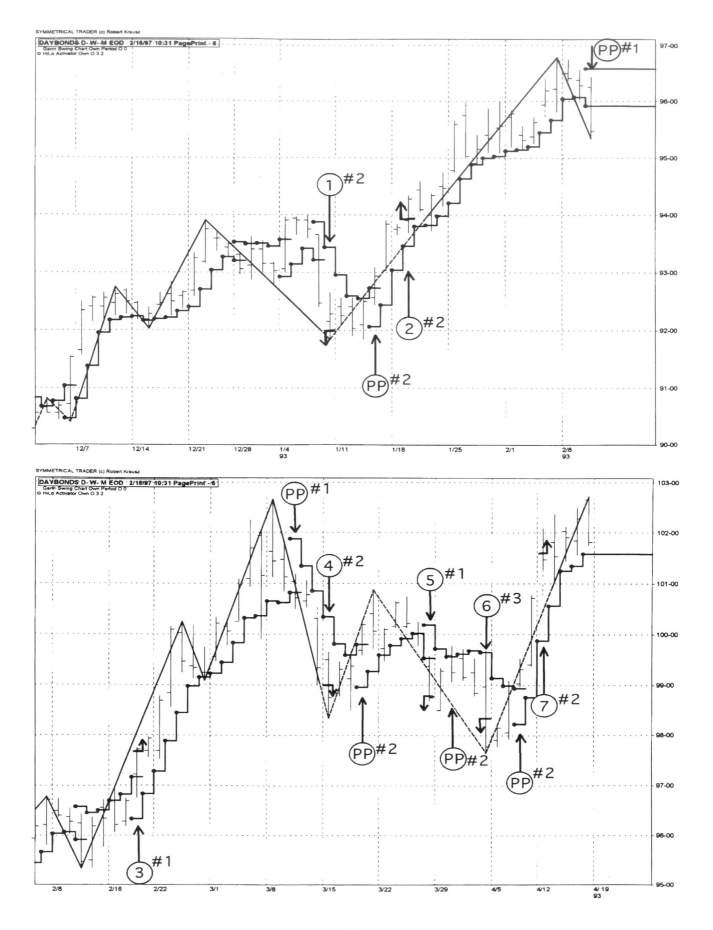

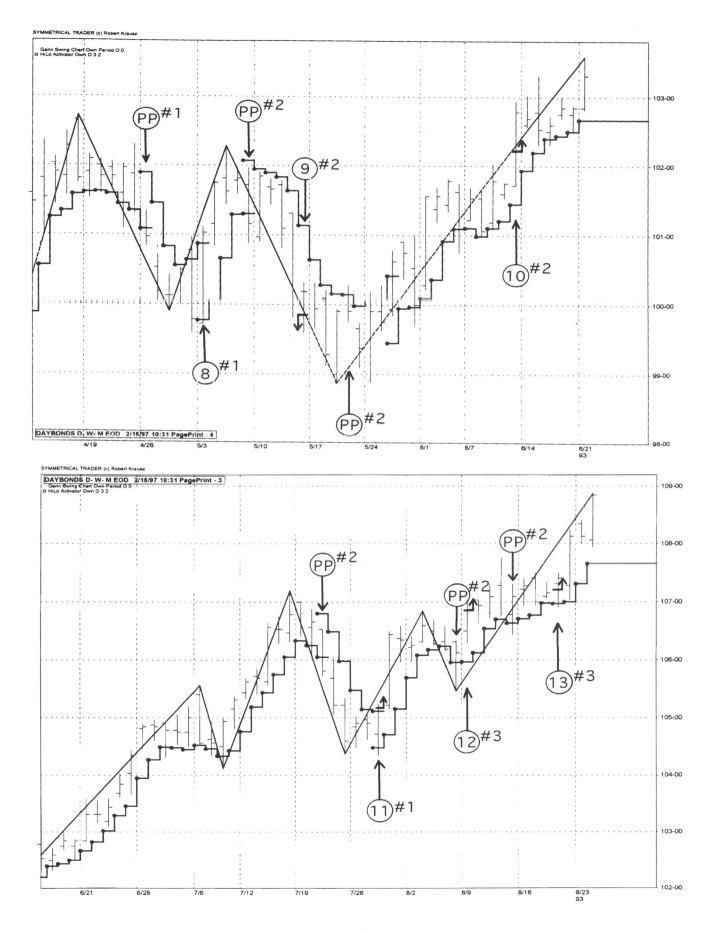

SYMMETRICAL TRADER (c) Robert Krausz

Gann Swing Chart Own Period O 0
O HiLo Activator Own O 3 2

DAYBONDS D. W. M EOD 2/16/97 10:31 PagePrint - 4

SYMMETRICAL TRADER (c) Robert Krausz

DAYBONDS D- W- M EOD 2/16/97 10:31 PagePrint - 3
Gann Swing Chart Own Period O 0
O HiLo Activator Own O 3 2

89

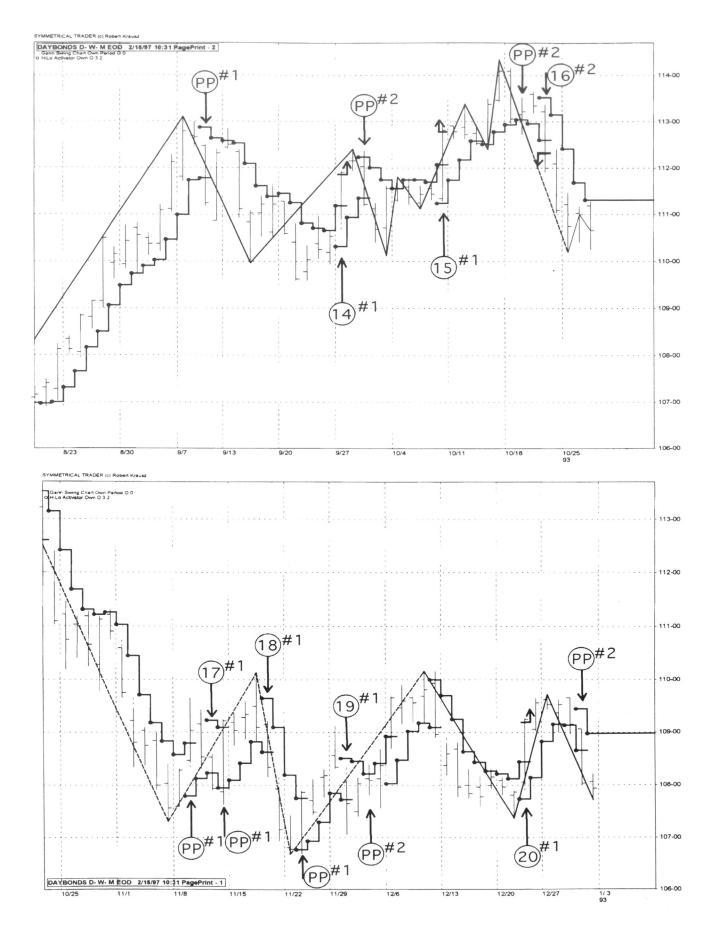

1994
US T- Bonds
New Gann Swing Chartist©
BASIC TRADING PLAN

Beginning Equity	$30,000.00	Ending Equity	$31,125.00
Total Net Profit	$1,125.00	Average Ticks/Mo.	
Gross Profit	$32,343.75	Gross Loss	($31,218.75)
Total No. Trades	26	Percentage Profitable	35%
No. Winning Trades	9	No. Losing Trades	17

Largest Winning Trade	$13,218.75	Largest Losing Trade	($4,312.50)
Average Winning Trade	$3,593.75	Average Losing Trade	($1,836.40)
Ratio Average Win/Loss	1.96	Average Trade	$43.27
Max. Consecutive Winners	4	Max. Consecutive Losses	5
Largest Consecutive Drawdown (%)	25.72%	Largest Consecutive Drawdown	($11,718.75)

Return on Account	4%
Profit/Drawdown Ratio	0.10

Notes:
1) Initial account size: $30,000

1994
US T- Bonds
New Gann Swing Chartist© BASIC TRADING PLAN

Fibonacci Trader (c)

TRADE#	DATE	L/S	PRICE	CTR.	RULE #	PROFIT	(LOSS)	ACCUM.	MO. PROFIT/(LOSS)	A/C EQUITY
1	1/3/94	S	107.12	3	Sell 2					$30,000.00
PP	1/7/94	L	108.00	3	PP2		(60)	(60)		$28,125.00
2	1/10/94	L	109.23	3	Buy 2					
PP	1/13/94	S	109.13	3	PP1		(30)	(90)		$27,187.50
3	1/18/94	L	109.13	3	Buy 1					
PP	1/25/94	S	109.06	3	PP2		(21)	(111)		$26,531.25
4	1/27/94	L	110.07	3	Buy 1					
PP	2/1/94	S	109.31	3	PP2		(24)	(135)	(135)	$25,781.25
5	2/4/94	S	108.26	3	Sell 2					
PP	3/16/94	L	104.13	3	PP1	423		288	423	$39,000.00
6	3/18/94	S	103.06	3	Sell 1					
PP	3/22/94	L	103.21	3	PP2		(45)	243		$37,593.75
7	3/24/94	S	102.14	3	Sell 1					
PP	4/7/94	L	99.30	3	PP1	240		483	195	$45,093.75
8	4/14/94	S	99.04	3	Sell 1					
PP	4/20/94	L	98.31	3	PP1	15		498		$45,562.50
9	4/25/94	L	100.21	3	Buy 2					
PP	4/28/94	S	99.21	3	PP2		(96)	402	(81)	$42,562.50
10	5/6/94	S	97.15	3	Sell 2					
PP	5/16/94	L	98.05	3	PP2		(66)	336		$40,500.00
11	5/23/94	S	98.04	3	Sell 1					
PP	6/2/94	L	98.27	3	PP2		(69)	267	(135)	$38,343.75
12	6/6/94	L	100.16	3	Buy 2					
PP	6/8/94	S	100.02	3	PP1		(42)	225		$37,031.25
13	6/22/94	L	99.01	3	Buy 1					
PP	6/24/94	S	97.31	3	PP2		(102)	123	(144)	$33,843.75
14	6/27/94	S	97.16	3	Sell 2					
PP	7/14/94	L	97.06	3	PP2	30		153		$34,781.25
15	7/29/94	L	98.17	3	Buy 2					
PP	8/5/94	S	99.06	3	PP2	63		216	93	$36,750.00
16	8/11/94	S	97.10	3	Sell 2					
PP	8/16/94	L	98.24	3	PP2		(138)	78		$32,437.50
17	8/18/94	S	98.04	3	Sell 1					

1994
US T- Bonds
New Gann Swing Chartist© BASIC TRADING PLAN

Fibonacci Trader (c)

TRADE#	DATE	L/S	PRICE	CTR.	RULE #	PROFIT	(LOSS)	ACCUM.	MO. PROFIT/(LOSS)	A/C EQUITY
PP	8/24/94	L	98.14	3	PP2		(30)	48	(168)	$31,500.00
18	9/9/94	S	97.16	3	Sell 2					$34,406.25
PP	9/14/94	L	96.17	3	PP1	93		141		
19	9/16/94	S	95.21	3	Sell 3					$37,500.00
PP	10/10/94	L	94.20	3	PP1	99		240	192	
20	10/19/94	S	94.27	3	Sell 1					$39,468.75
PP	10/28/94	L	94.06	3	PP2	63		303	63	
21	11/1/94	S	93.15	3	Sell 1					$39,750.00
PP	11/9/94	L	93.12	3	PP1	9		312		
22	11/11/94	S	92.08	3	Sell 1					$36,187.50
PP	11/15/94	L	93.14	3	PP2		(114)	198		
23	11/15/94	L	94.02	3	Buy 1					$32,531.25
PP	11/17/94	S	92.27	3	PP2		(117)	81		
24	11/23/94	L	94.07	3	Buy 2					$32,437.50
PP	11/29/94	S	94.06	3	PP1		(3)	78	(225)	
25	12/2/94	L	95.20	3	Buy 1					$31,781.25
PP	12/13/94	S	95.13	3	PP2		(21)	57		
26	12/14/94	L	96.16	3	Buy 3					$31,125.00
PP	12/29/94	S	96.09	3	PP2		(21)	36	(42)	

93

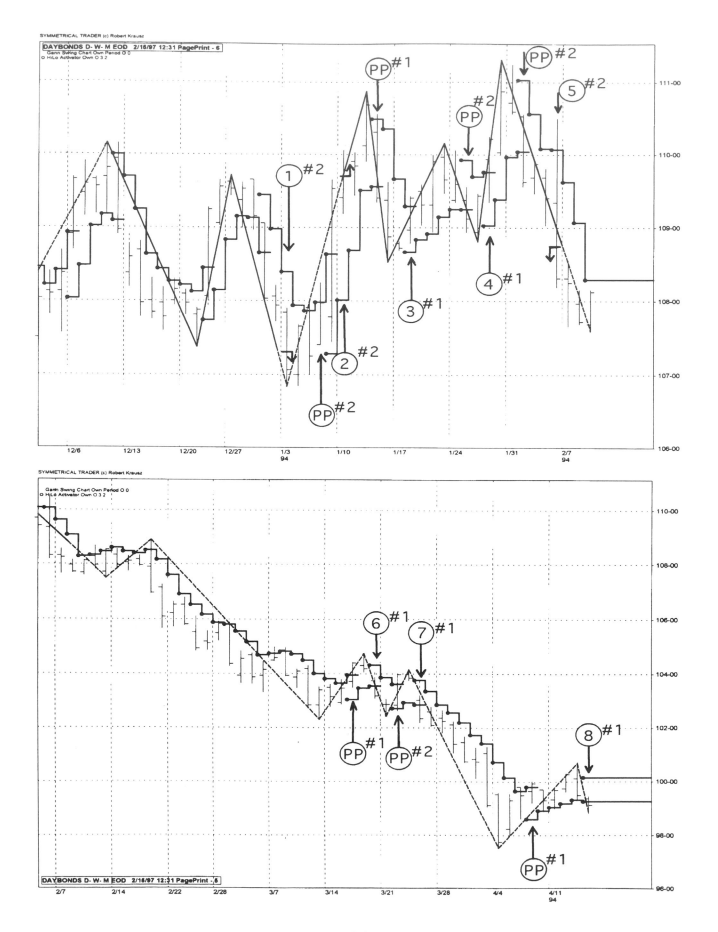

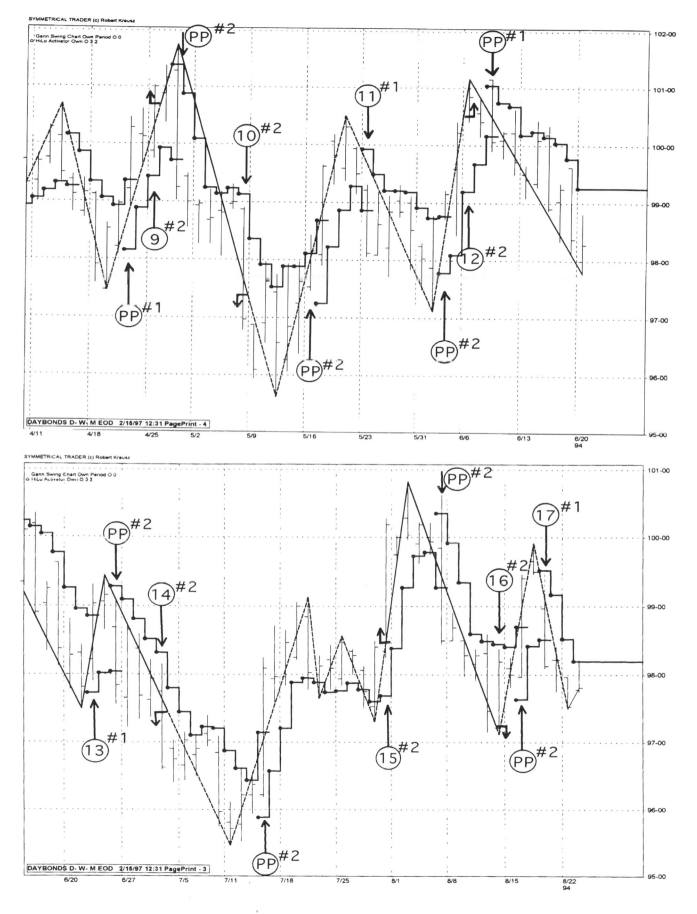

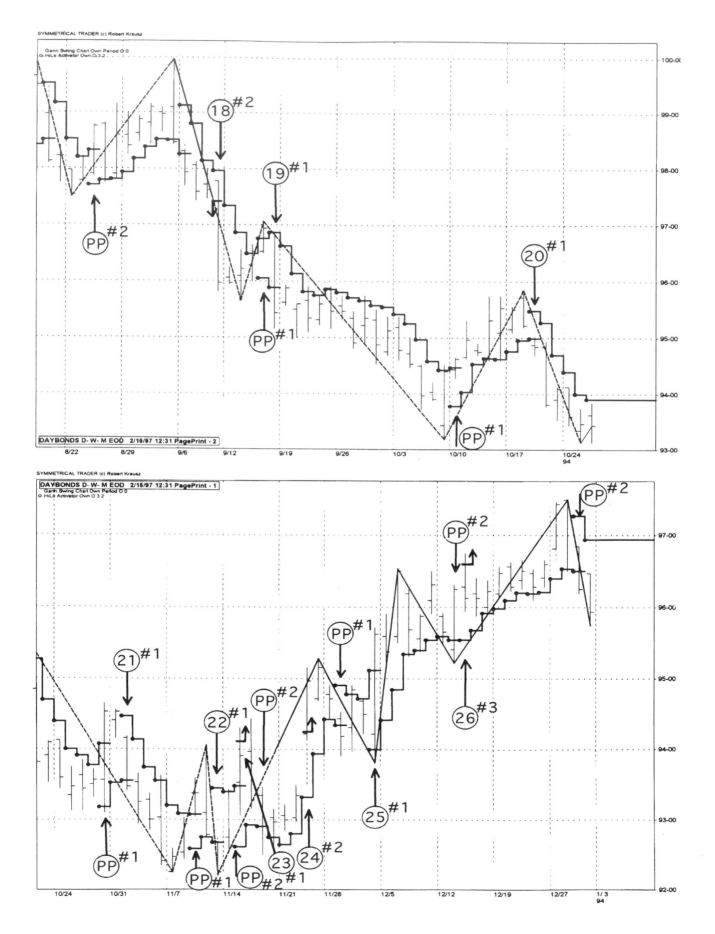

US T-BONDS: 1995
BASIC SWING PLAN
GANN SWING CHARTIST - FIBONACCI TRADER ®

Beginning Equity	$30,000.00	Ending Equity	$49,500.00
Total Net Profit	$19,500.00	Average Ticks/Mo.	
Gross Profit	$53,437.50	Gross Loss	($33,937.50)
Total No. Trades	27	Percentage Profitable	33%
No. Winning Trades	9	No. Losing Trades	18

Largest Winning Trade	$24,468.75	Largest Losing Trade	($3,468.75)
Average Winning Trade	$5,937.50	Average Losing Trade	($1,885.42)
Ratio Average Win/Loss	3.15	Average Trade	$722.22
Max. Consecutive Winners	2	Max. Consecutive Losses	5
Largest Consecutive Drawdown (%)	22.48%	Largest Consecutive Drawdown	($12,562.50)

Return on Account	65%
Profit/Drawdown Ratio	1.55

Notes:
1) Initial account size: $30,000

1995

US T- Bonds: Gann Swing Chartist®

Basic Swing Plan (End of Day)

Fibonacci Trader®

Trade#	Date	L/S	Price	Ctr.	Rule #	Profit	(Loss)	Accum.	A/C Equity
1	1/13/95	L	96.02	3	Buy 1				$30,000.00
PP	1/20/95	S	95.22	3	PP2		(36)	(36)	$28,875.00
2	1/25/95	L	95.20	3	Buy 1				
PP	2/9/95	S	97.25	3	PP1	111		75	$32,343.75
3	2/15/95	L	98.20	3	Buy 1				
PP	3/3/95	S	99.05	3	PP2	51		126	$33,937.50
4	3/6/95	S	98.01	3	Sell 2				
PP	3/8/95	L	98.24	3	PP2		(69)	57	$31,781.25
5	3/14/95	L	100.08	3	Buy 2				
PP	3/21/95	S	100.04	3	PP2		(12)	45	$31,406.25
6	3/24/95	L	100.26	3	Buy 1				
PP	3/29/95	S	100.11	3	PP2		(45)	0	$30,000.00
7	4/5/95	L	101.00	3	Buy 1				
PP	4/7/95	S	100.27	3	PP2		(15)	(15)	$29,531.25
8	4/13/95	L	101.19	3	Buy 1				
PP	4/19/95	S	100.30	3	PP2		(63)	(78)	$27,562.50
9	5/3/95	L	102.24	3	Buy 3				
PP	6/8/95	S	110.29	3	PP1	783		705	$52,031.25
10	6/13/95	L	111.04	3	Buy 1				
PP	6/27/95	S	111.09	3	PP1	15		720	$52,500.00
11	7/6/95	L	112.12	3	Buy 1			720	$49,687.50
PP	7/12/95	S	111.14	3	PP2		(90)		
12	7/18/95	S	109.24	3	Sell 2				
PP	7/25/95	L	108.10	3	PP1	138		858	$54,000.00
13	8/1/95	S	107.11	3	Sell 1			858	$51,093.75
PP	8/8/95	L	108.02	3	PP2		(93)		
14	8/11/95	S	106.15	3	Sell 3				
PP	8/16/95	L	106.30	3	PP2		(45)	813	$49,687.50
15	8/23/95	S	106.25	3	Sell 1				
PP	8/24/95	L	107.15	3	PP2		(66)	747	$47,625.00
16	8/24/95	L	107.25	6	Buy 1				
PP	9/8/95	S	110.12	3	PP2	249		996	$55,406.25
17	9/12/95	L	111.08	3	Buy 3				

1995
US T- Bonds: Gann Swing Chartist®
Basic Swing Plan (End of Day)

Fibonacci Trader®

Trade#	Date	L/S	Price	Ctr.	Rule #	Profit	(Loss)	Accum.	A/C Equity
PP	9/18/95	S	111.05	3	PP2		(9)	987	$55,125.00
18	9/20/95	L	112.02	3	Buy 1				
PP	9/21/95	S	111.00	3	PP2		102)	885	$51,937.50
19	9/22/95	S	110.09	3	Sell 2				
PP	9/29/95	L	110.22	3	PP2		(39)	846	$50,718.75
20	10/3/95	L	112.08	3	Buy 2				
PP	10/20/95	S	113.31	3	PP2	165		1011	$55,875.00
21	10/24/95	L	114.19	3	Buy 1				
PP	10/26/95	S	113.24	3	PP2		(75)	936	$53,531.25
22	10/27/95	S	113.12	3	Sell 2				
PP	10/31/95	L	114.17	3	PP2		111)	825	$50,062.50
23	11/1/95	L	114.31	3	Buy 1				
PP	11/7/95	S	114.24	3	PP1		(21)	804	$49,406.25
24	11/8/95	L	115.18	3	Buy 1				
PP	11/10/95	S	114.14	6	Sell 2		108)	696	$46,031.25
25	11/14/95	L	115.11	3	PP2		87)	609	$43,312.50
26	11/29/95	L	115.24	3	Buy 2				
PP	12/8/95	S	117.06	3	PP2	138		747	$47,625.00
27	12/22/95	L	117.21	3	Buy 1				
PP	1/4/96	S	118.09	3	PP1	60		807	$49,500.00

99

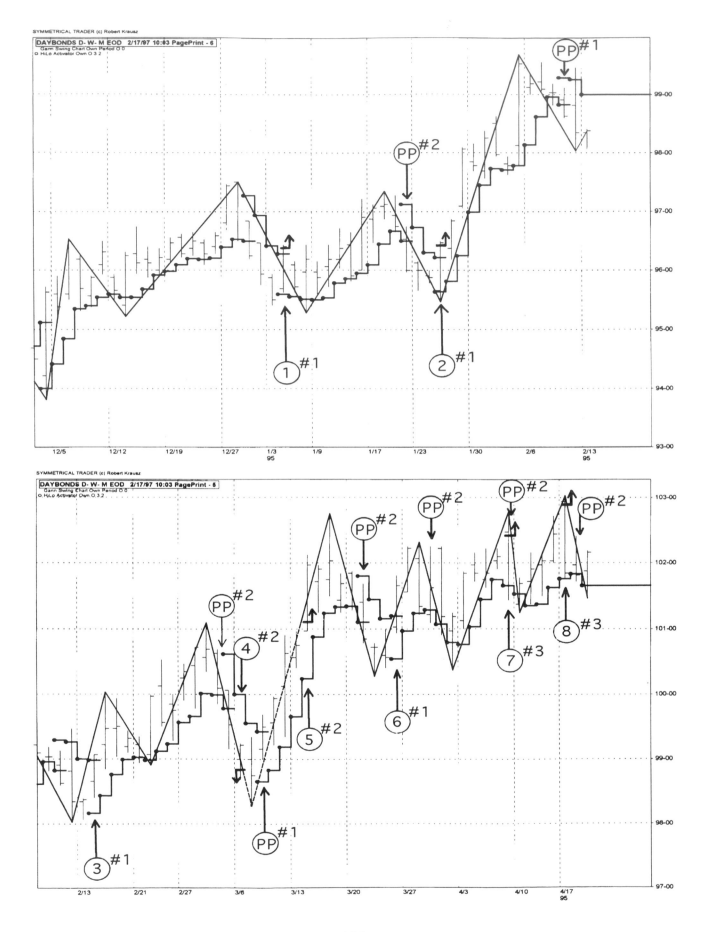

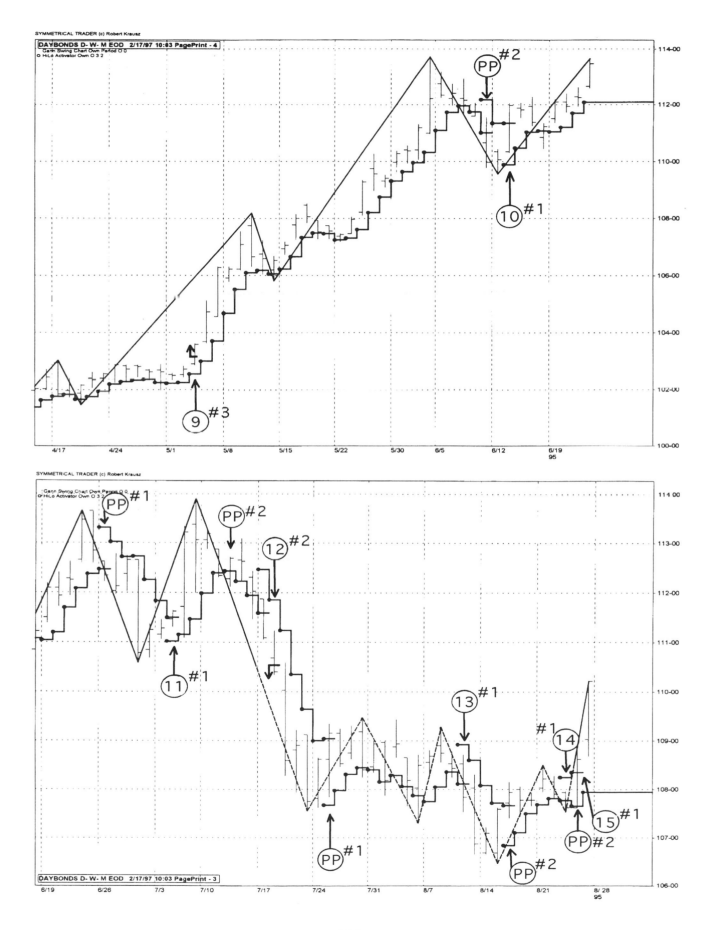

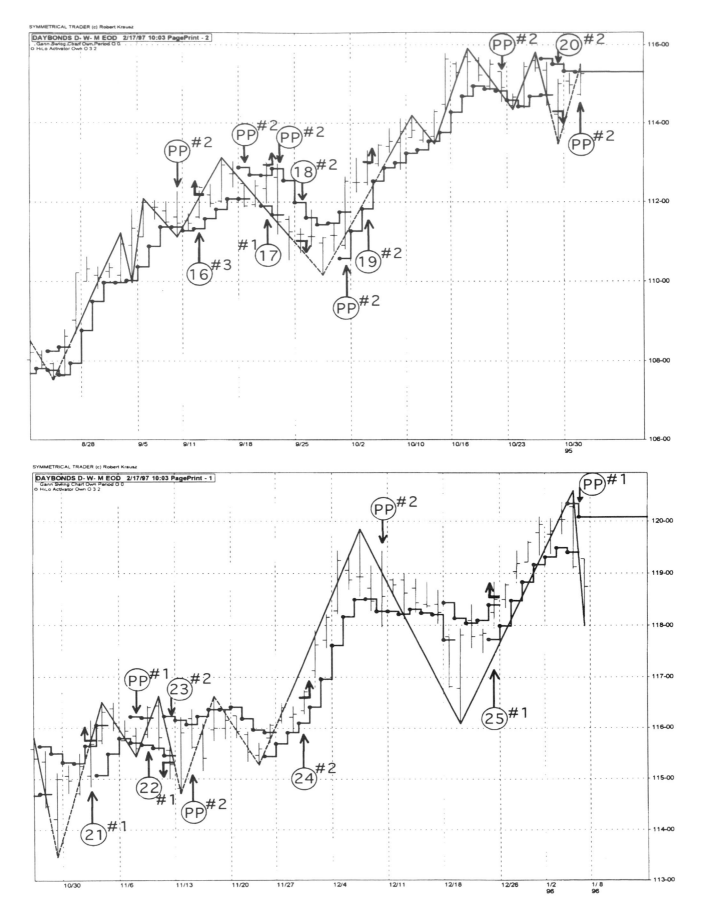

1996
US T-Bonds
New Gann Swing Chartist©
BASIC TRADING PLAN

Beginning Equity	$30,000.00	Ending Equity	$67,781.25
Total Net Profit	$37,781.25	Average Ticks/Mo.	
Gross Profit	$58,968.75	Gross Loss	($21,187.50)
Total No. Trades	26	Percentage Profitable	62%
No. Winning Trades	18	No. Losing Trades	10

Largest Winning Trade	$9,843.75	Largest Losing Trade	($3,750.00)
Average Winning Trade	$3,685.55	Average Losing Trade	($2,118.75)
Ratio Average Win/Loss	1.74	Average Trade	$1,453.13
Max. Consecutive Winners	4	Max. Consecutive Losses	2
Largest Consecutive Drawdown (%)	16.07%	Largest Consecutive Drawdown	($5,062.50)

Return on Account	126%
Profit/Drawdown Ratio	7.46

Notes:
1) Initial account size: $30,000

1996
US T- Bonds
New Gann Swing Chartist© BASIC TRADING PLAN

Fibonacci Trader (c)

TRADE#	DATE	L/S	PRICE	CTR.	RULE #	PROFIT	(LOSS)	ACCUM.	MO. PROFIT/(LOSS)	A/C EQUITY
1	1/16/96	L	118.16	3	Buy 1					$30,000.00
PP	1/22/96	S	119.00	3	PP1	48		48		$31,500.00
2	1/26/96	S	118.11	3	Sell 2					
PP	1/30/96	L	119.08	3	PP2		(87)	(39)	(39)	$28,781.25
3	2/12/96	L	119.02	6	Buy 1					
PP	2/15/96	S	118.09	3	PP2		(75)	(114)		$26,437.50
4	2/16/96	S	117.13	3	Sell 2					
PP	3/1/96	L	114.04	3	PP2	315		201	240	$36,281.25
5	3/1/96	L	114.15	6	Buy 1					
PP	3/6/96	S	113.30	3	PP2		(51)	150		$34,687.50
6	3/8/96	S	112.12	3	Sell 2					
PP	3/20/96	L	110.26	3	PP1	150		300		$39,375.00
7	3/27/96	S	110.08	3	Sell 1					
PP	4/1/96	L	110.20	3	PP1		(36)	264	264	$38,250.00
8	4/4/96	S	110.18	3	Sell 1					
PP	4/12/96	L	108.15	3	PP2	201		465		$44,531.25
9	4/18/96	S	108.12	3	Sell 1					
PP	4/22/96	L	109.14	3	PP1		(102)	363		$41,343.75
10	4/24/96	S	108.22	3	Sell 1					
PP	5/8/96	L	106.28	3	PP1	174		537	273	$46,781.25
11	5/16/96	S	107.28	3	Sell 1					
PP	5/23/96	L	109.04	3	PP2		(120)	417		$43,031.25
12	5/29/96	S	108.03	3	Sell 2					
PP	6/5/96	L	107.21	3	PP1	42		459		$44,343.75
13	6/7/96	S	106.16	3	Sell 1					
PP	6/14/96	L	106.15	3	PP2	3		462		$44,437.50
14	6/25/96	L	107.04	3	Buy 2					
PP	7/5/96	S	107.14	3	PP2	30		492	(45)	$45,375.00
15	7/5/96	S	105.29	3	Sell 1,2					
PP	7/10/96	L	106.29	3	PP2		(96)	396		$42,375.00
16	7/24/96	S	107.22	3	Sell 1					
PP	7/30/96	L	108.04	3	PP2		(48)	348	(144)	$40,875.00
17	8/1/96	L	109.08	3	Buy 2					

1996
US T - Bonds
New Gann Swing Chartist© BASIC TRADING PLAN

TRADE#	DATE	L/S	PRICE	CTR.	RULE #	PROFIT	(LOSS)	ACCUM.	MO. PROFIT/(LOSS)	A/C EQUITY
PP	8/13/96	S	110.26	3	PP2	150		498		$30,000.00
18	8/13/96	S	110.13	6	Sell 2					
PP	8/16/96	L	110.25	3	PP1		(36)	462		$44,437.50
19	8/23/96	S	109.01	3	Sell 1					
PP	9/9/96	L	107.07	3	PP1	174		636	288	$49,875.00
20	9/12/96	L	107.13	3	Buy 2	63				
PP	9/18/96	S	108.02	3	PP2			699		$51,843.75
21	9/24/96	L	108.20	3	Buy 1					
PP	9/30/96	S	109.04	3	PP2	48		747		$53,343.75
22	10/2/96	L	110.12	3	Buy 3					
PP	10/9/96	S	110.18	3	PP1	18		765	129	$53,906.25
23	10/17/96	L	111.04	3	Buy 1					
PP	10/22/96	S	110.27	3	PP2		(27)	738	(27)	$53,062.50
24	10/29/96	L	112.19	3	Buy 1					
PP	12/4/96	S	115.11	3	PP2	264		1002		$61,312.50
25	12/5/96	S	114.03	6	Sell 2				(738)	
PP	12/19/96	L	113.05	3	PP1	90		1092		$64,125.00
26	12/31/96	S	112.20	3	Sell 1					
PP	1/14/97	L	111.13	3	PP1	117		1209	1209	$67,781.25

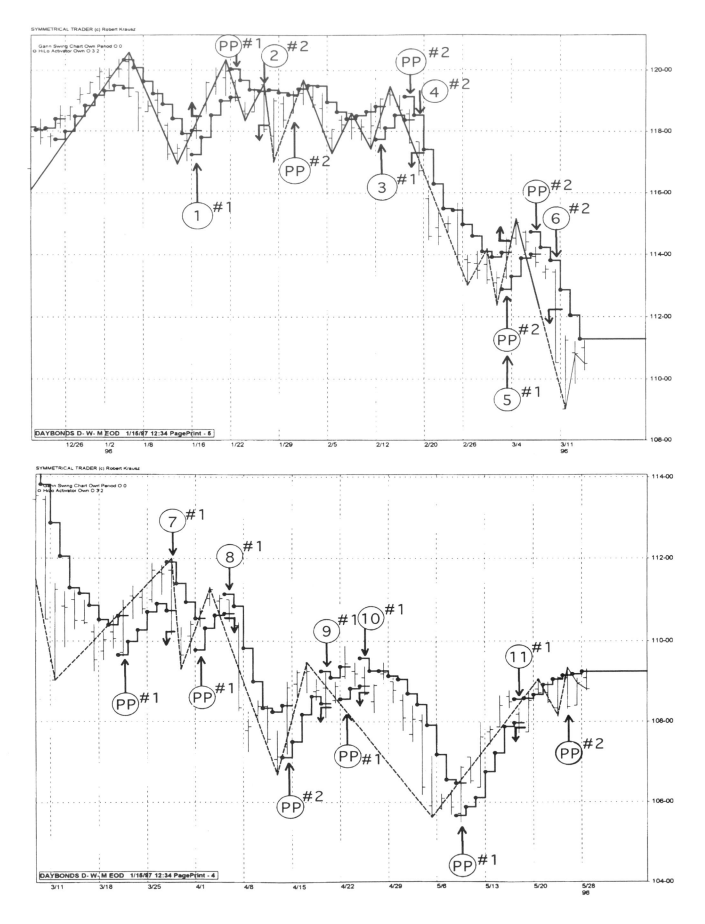

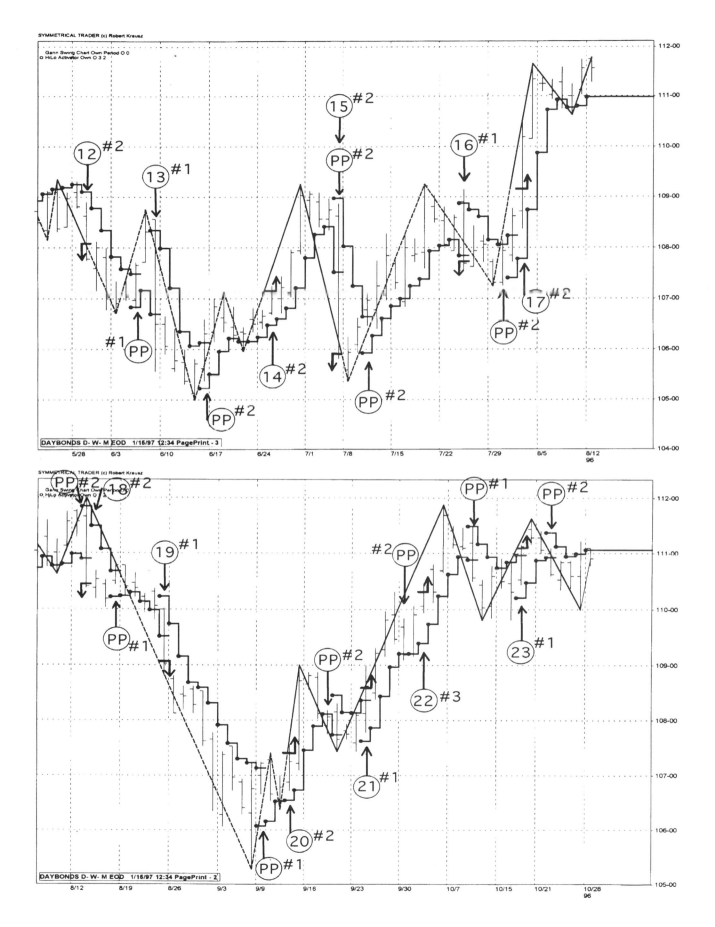

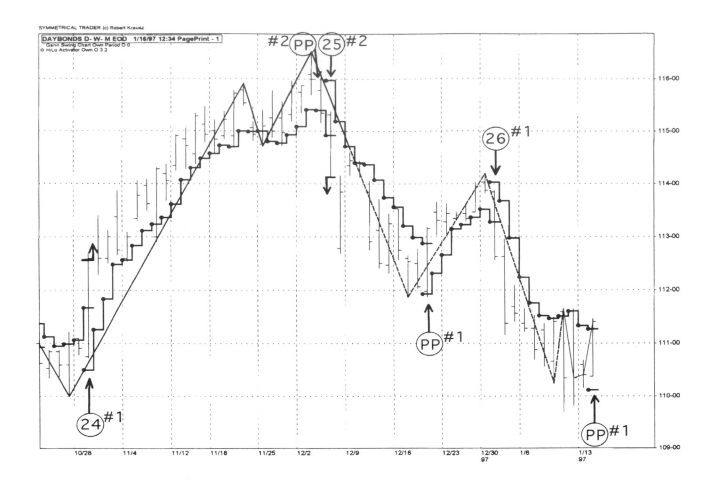

NEW GANN SWING CHARTIST©

BASIC SWING PLAN

FOR STOCKS & SHARES

REAL TIME: ELI LILLY, IBM, PHILIP MORRIS

END OF DAY: J. P. MORGAN, INTEL

BASIC SWING PLAN FOR STOCKS & SHARES

GENERAL NOTES

The Rules for trading STOCKS for this Basic Plan is the SAME as for the T-Bonds. The EXCEPTION is Rule #4. Please read it carefully.

1. This plan trades only with the Trend.

2. Each new trade is based on a 1000 share lot. BUT SAME RULES & PERCENTAGES apply for more or less shares.

3. A commission of 12 cents round trip has been deducted per share.

4. For Stocks and Shares, do not use Profit Protection Rule #2 (.382 Retracement Rule) UNLESS the swing is approximately 8-10% of the current stock price.

5. Normally, a 50% margin is used, but 100% margin cover is also shown in the Composite and the Annual Report.

6. The Composite is shown as most investors want to see this.

7. The initial Capital is set at the cost of 1000 shares.

8. Both "Real Time" and "End of Day" is shown for stocks. The plan has potential for both.

9. **For <u>End of Day</u> format you must move the HiLo Activator 1 day <u>forward</u>.**

10. Interest charges for margin and dividends are not included.

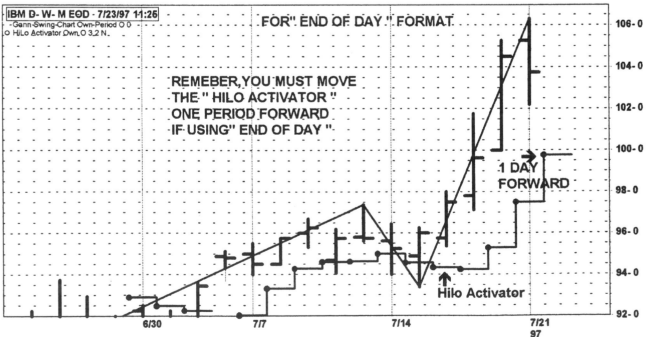

FIBONACCI TRADER (c) Robert Krausz

ELI LILLY CO. - 1992-1996 (5 YRS.) RT.
BASIC SWING PLAN - <u>COMPOSITE</u>
GANN SWING CHARTIST - FIBONACCI TRADER ®

<u>With 100% Margin</u>

Beginning Equity	$38,750.00	Ending Equity	$78,935.00
Total Net Profit	$47,625.00	Gross Loss	($35,875.00)
Gross Profit	$83,500.00	Total Commissions	$7,440.00
Total No. Trades	62	Percentage Profitable	56%
No. Winning Trades	35	No. Losing Trades	27

Largest Winning Trade	$9,500.00	Largest Losing Trade	($3,750.00)
Average Winning Trade	$2,385.71	Average Losing Trade	($1,328.70)
Max. Consecutive Winners	4	Max. Consecutive Losses	3
Average Drawdown (%)	10.38%	Average Drawdown ($)	($3,388.96)

Average Return on Account	23%
Profit/Drawdown Ratio	14.05

<u>With 50% Margin</u>

Beginning Equity	$19,375.00	Ending Equity	$59,560.00
Total Net Profit	$47,625.00	Gross Loss	($35,875.00)
Gross Profit	$83,500.00	Total Commissions	$7,440.00
Total No. Trades	62	Percentage Profitable	56%
No. Winning Trades	35	No. Losing Trades	10

Largest Winning Trade	$9,500.00	Largest Losing Trade	($3,750.00)
Average Winning Trade	$2,385.71	Average Losing Trade	($3,587.50)
Max. Consecutive Winners	4	Max. Consecutive Losses	3
Average Drawdown (%)	15.63%	Average Drawdown ($)	($3,388.96)

Average Return on Account	45%
Profit/Drawdown Ratio	14.05

Notes:
1) Each trade is equal to 1,000 shares.
2) Initial account is equal to what it would cost
   to trade 1,000 shares at a price/share at that time.
3) Commission is equal to 12 cents per round turn per share.
4) Plan handles less or more shares, percentages are the same.

111

ELI LILLY CO. - 1992
BASIC SWING PLAN
GANN SWING CHARTIST - FIBONACCI TRADER®

With 100% Margin

Beginning Equity	$38,750.00	Ending Equity	$50,055.00
Total Net Profit	$12,625.00	Gross Loss	($875.00)
Gross Profit	$13,500.00	Total Commissions	$1,320.00
Total No. Trades	11	Percentage Profitable	82%
No. Winning Trades	9	No. Losing Trades	2

Largest Winning Trade	$3,500.00	Largest Losing Trade	($500.00)
Average Winning Trade	$1,500.00	Average Losing Trade	($107.50)
Ratio Average Win/Loss	3.43	Average Trade	$1,147.73
Max. Consecutive Winners	4	Max. Consecutive Losses	1
Largest Consecutive Drawdown (%)	1.38%	Largest Consecutive Drawdown	($620.00)

Return on Account	29%
Profit/Drawdown Ratio	20.36

With 50% Margin

Beginning Equity	$19,375.00	Ending Equity	$30,680.00
Total Net Profit	$12,625.00	Gross Loss	($875.00)
Gross Profit	$13,500.00	Total Commissions	$1,320.00
Total No. Trades	11	Percentage Profitable	82%
No. Winning Trades	9	No. Losing Trades	2

Largest Winning Trade	$3,500.00	Largest Losing Trade	($500.00)
Average Winning Trade	$1,500.00	Average Losing Trade	($437.50)
Ratio Average Win/Loss	3.43	Average Trade	$1,147.73
Max. Consecutive Winners	4	Max. Consecutive Losses	1
Largest Consecutive Drawdown (%)	2.44%	Largest Consecutive Drawdown	($620.00)

Return on Account	58%
Profit/Drawdown Ratio	20.36

Notes:
1) Each trade is equal to 1,000 shares.
2) Initial account is equal to what it would cost
   to trade 1,000 shares at a price/share at that time.
3) Commission is equal to 12 cents per round turn.
4) Plan handles less or more shares.

1992
Eli Lilly Co. - Gann Swing Chartist®
Basic Swing Plan (Real Time)

Fibonacci Trader®

Trade #	Date	L/S	Price	Rule #	Profit	(Loss)	Accum.	A/C Equity	50% Margin
1	12/20/92	L	38 3/4	Buy 2				$38,750.00	$19,375.00
PP	1/15/92	S	42 1/4	PP1	3 4/8		$ 3,380.00	$42,130.00	$22,755.00
2	1/16/92	S	41 1/4	Sell 2					$24,260.00
PP	2/10/92	L	39 5/8	PP1	1 5/8		$ 4,885.00	$43,635.00	
3	2/13/92	S	37 7/8	Sell 1					$24,390.00
PP	2/26/92	L	37 5/8	PP1	2/8		$ 5,015.00	$43,765.00	
4	3/2/92	S	36 1/2	Sell 1					$25,145.00
PP	3/31/92	L	35 5/8	PP1	7/8		$ 5,770.00	$44,520.00	
5	4/1/92	L	36	Buy 2					$24,650.00
PP	4/16/92	S	35 5/8	PP1		- 3/8	$ 5,275.00	$44,025.00	
6	4/20/92	S	34 3/4	Sell 2					$25,405.00
PP	5/19/92	L	33 7/8	PP1	7/8		$ 6,030.00	$44,780.00	
7	6/2/92	S	32 3/8	Sell 1					$24,785.00
PP	6/29/92	L	32 7/8	PP1		- 4/8	$ 5,410.00	$44,160.00	
8	7/1/92	L	33	Buy 2					$26,540.00
PP	8/10/92	S	34 7/8	PP1	1 7/8		$ 7,165.00	$45,915.00	
9	8/19/92	S	34 1/2	Sell 2					$27,545.00
PP	9/1/92	L	33 3/8	PP1	1 1/8		$ 8,170.00	$46,920.00	
10	9/18/92	S	33 3/8	Sell 1					$30,300.00
PP	10/29/92	L	30 1/2	PP1	2 7/8		$10,925.00	$49,675.00	
11	11/3/92	L	31 1/2	Buy 2					$30,680.00
PP	12/11/92	S	32	PP1	4/8		$11,305.00	$50,055.00	

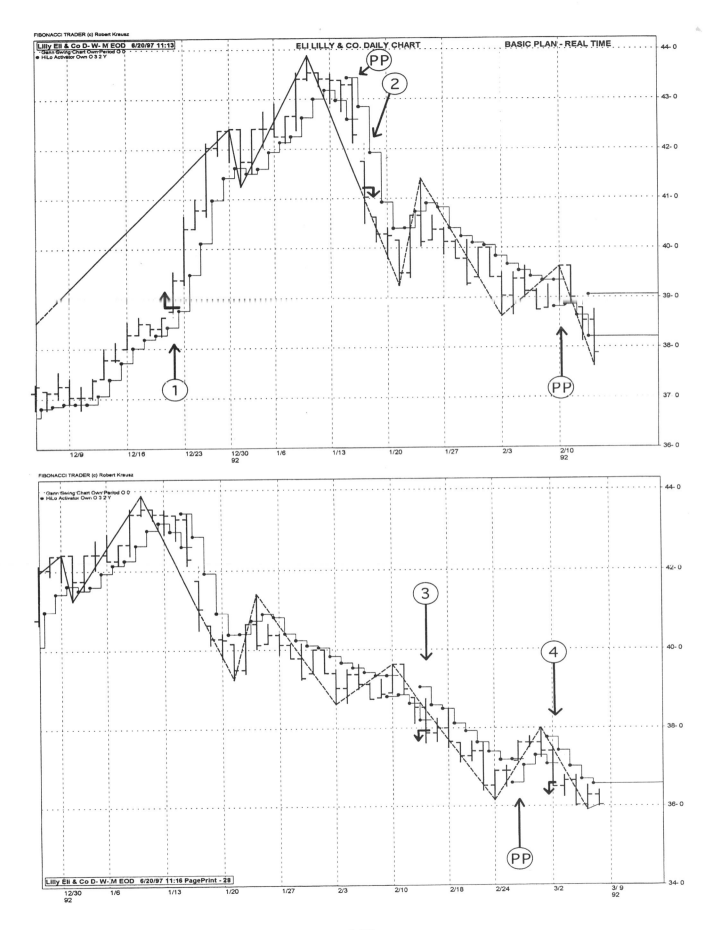

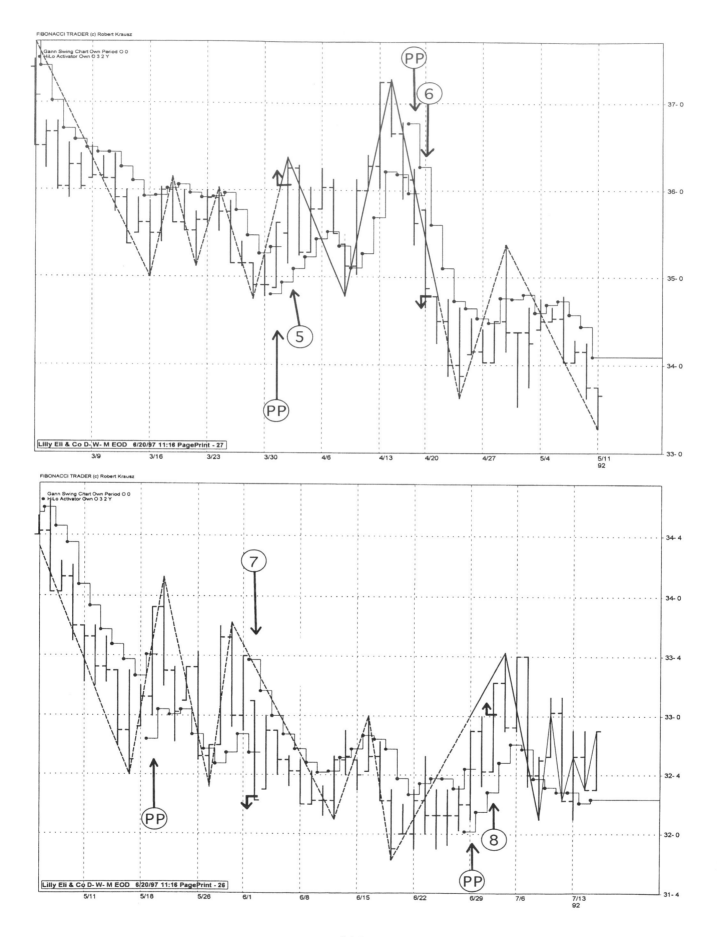

FIBONACCI TRADER (c) Robert Krausz

Gann Swing Chart Own Period O 0
HiLo Activator Own O 3 2 Y

Lilly Eli & Co D- W- M EOD   6/20/97 11:16 PagePrint - 27

3/9   3/16   3/23   3/30   4/6   4/13   4/20   4/27   5/4   5/11
92

FIBONACCI TRADER (c) Robert Krausz

Gann Swing Chart Own Period O 0
HiLo Activator Own O 3 2 Y

Lilly Eli & Co D- W- M EOD   6/20/97 11:16 PagePrint - 26

5/11   5/18   5/26   6/1   6/8   6/15   6/22   6/29   7/6   7/13
92

116

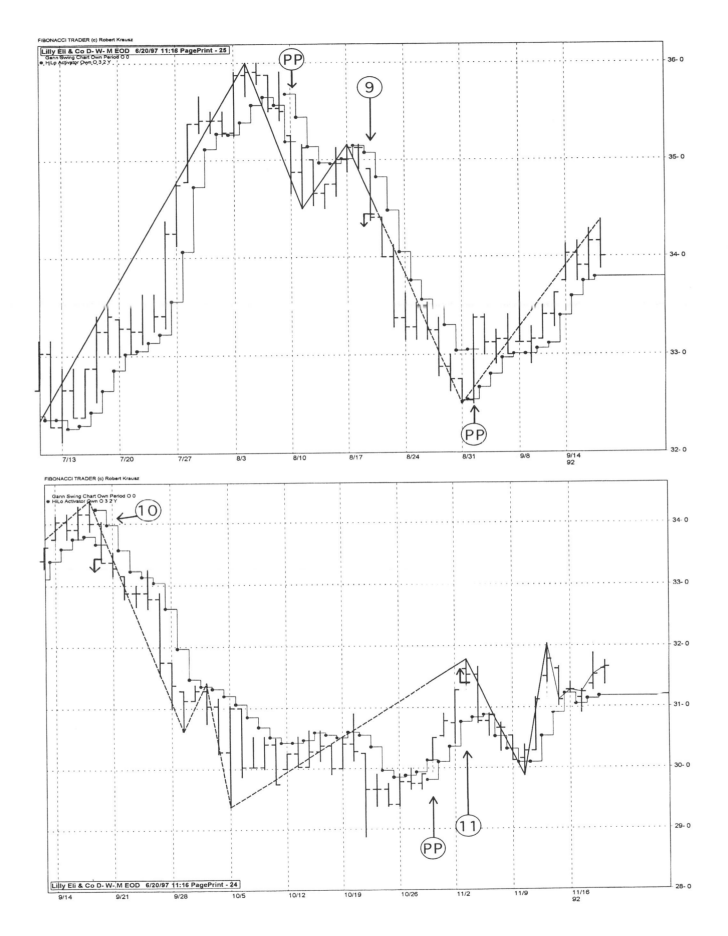

ELI LILLY CO. - 1993
BASIC SWING PLAN
GANN SWING CHARTIST - FIBONACCI TRADER®

With 100% Margin

Beginning Equity	$31,125.00	Ending Equity	$38,050.00
Total Net Profit	$8,125.00	Gross Loss	($2,875.00)
Gross Profit	$11,000.00	Total Commissions	$1,200.00
Total No. Trades	10	Percentage Profitable	60%
No. Winning Trades	6	No. Losing Trades	4

Largest Winning Trade	$4,250.00	Largest Losing Trade	($875.00)
Average Winning Trade	$1,833.33	Average Losing Trade	($718.75)
Ratio Average Win/Loss	2.55	Average Trade	$812.50
Max. Consecutive Winners	4	Max. Consecutive Losses	3
Largest Consecutive Drawdown (%)	8.68%	Largest Consecutive Drawdown	($3,225.00)

Return on Account	22%
Profit/Drawdown Ratio	2.52

With 50% Margin

Beginning Equity	$15,562.50	Ending Equity	$22,487.50
Total Net Profit	$8,125.00	Gross Loss	($2,875.00)
Gross Profit	$11,000.00	Total Commissions	$1,200.00
Total No. Trades	10	Percentage Profitable	60%
No. Winning Trades	6	No. Losing Trades	4

Largest Winning Trade	$4,250.00	Largest Losing Trade	($875.00)
Average Winning Trade	$1,833.33	Average Losing Trade	($718.75)
Ratio Average Win/Loss	2.55	Average Trade	$812.50
Max. Consecutive Winners	4	Max. Consecutive Losses	3
Largest Consecutive Drawdown (%)	14.94%	Largest Consecutive Drawdown	($3,225.00)

Return on Account	44%
Profit/Drawdown Ratio	2.52

Notes:
1) Each trade is equal to 1,000 shares.
2) Initial account is equal to what it would cost
   to trade 1,000 shares at a price/share at that time.
3) Commission is equal to 12 cents per round turn.
4) Plan handles less or more shares.

1993

Eli Lilly Co. - Gann Swing Chartist®
Basic Swing Plan (Real Time)

Fibonacci Trader®

Trade #	Date	L/S	Price	Rule #	Profit	(Loss)	Accum.	A/C Equity	50% Margin
1	12/28/92	S	31 1/8	Sell 2				$31,125.00	$15,562.50
PP	2/11/93	L	28 1/8	PP1	3		$ 2,880.00	$34,005.00	$18,442.50
2	2/16/93	S	26 1/2	Sell 1					
PP	2/24/93	L	25 3/8	PP1	1 1/8		$ 3,885.00	$35,010.00	$19,447.50
3	3/12/93	S	25 3/4	Sell 1					
PP	3/29/93	L	23 5/8	PP1	2 1/8		$ 5,890.00	$37,015.00	$21,452.50
4	4/29/93	L	24 1/4	Buy 2					
5	6/4/93	S	24 1/2	Sell 2	2/8		$ 6,020.00	$37,145.00	$21,582.50
PP	6/24/93	L	24 3/4	PP1		- 2/8	$ 5,650.00	$36,775.00	$21,212.50
6	7/1/93	S	23 1/2	Sell 3					
7	7/20/93	L	24 1/4	Buy 2		- 6/8	$ 4,780.00	$35,905.00	$20,342.50
PP	7/30/93	S	23 1/4	PP1		-1	$ 3,660.00	$34,785.00	$19,222.50
8	8/6/93	S	22 3/4	Sell 2					
PP	8/16/93	L	22 1/2	PP1	2/8		$ 3,790.00	$34,915.00	$19,352.50
9	8/23/93	S	23	Sell 1					
PP	8/26/93	L	23 7/8	PP1		- 7/8	$ 2,795.00	$33,920.00	$18,357.50
10	9/2/93	L	24 1/2	Buy 2					
PP	2/9/94	S	28 3/4	PP1	4 2/8		$ 6,925.00	$38,050.00	$22,487.50

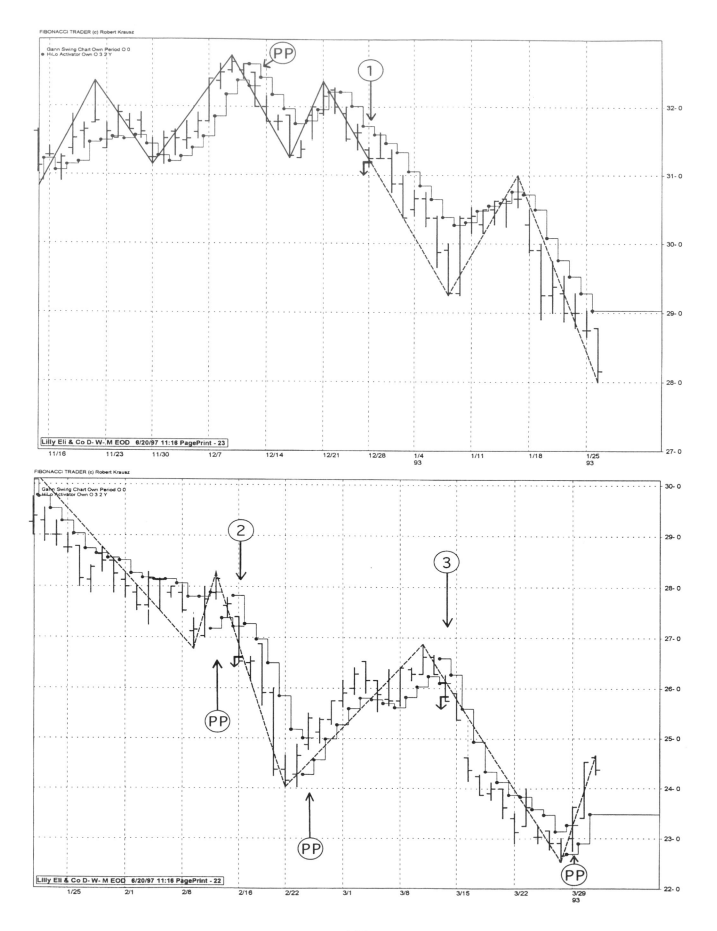

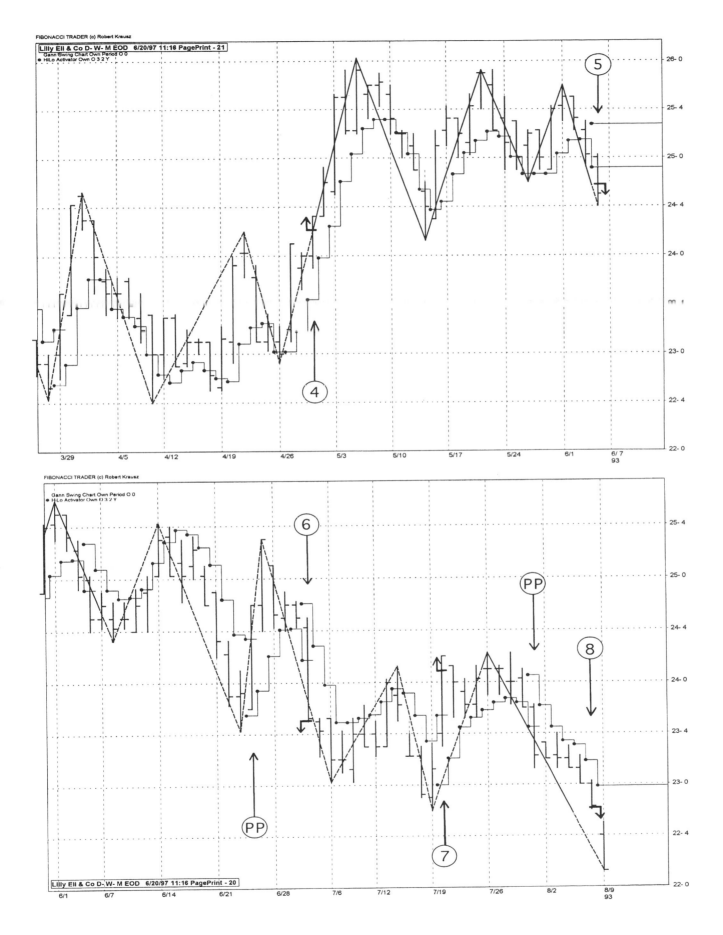

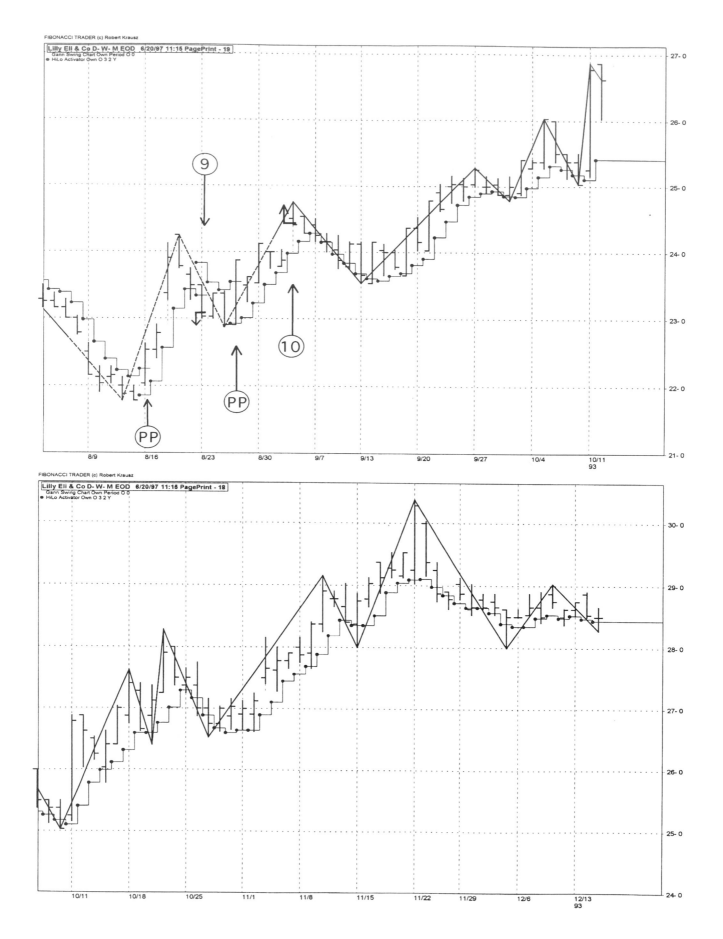

ELI LILLY CO. - 1994
BASIC SWING PLAN
GANN SWING CHARTIST - FIBONACCI TRADER®

With 100% Margin

Beginning Equity	$28,750.00	Ending Equity	$33,165.00
Total Net Profit	$5,375.00	Gross Loss	($2,875.00)
Gross Profit	$8,250.00	Total Commissions	$960.00
Total No. Trades	8	Percentage Profitable	75%
No. Winning Trades	6	No. Losing Trades	2

Largest Winning Trade	$5,125.00	Largest Losing Trade	($1,625.00)
Average Winning Trade	$1,375.00	Average Losing Trade	($1,437.50)
Ratio Average Win/Loss	0.96	Average Trade	$671.88
Max. Consecutive Winners	4	Max. Consecutive Losses	1
Largest Consecutive Drawdown (%)	5.94%	Largest Consecutive Drawdown	($1,865.00)

Return on Account	15%
Profit/Drawdown Ratio	2.88

With 50% Margin

Beginning Equity	$14,375.00	Ending Equity	$18,790.00
Total Net Profit	$5,375.00	Gross Loss	($2,875.00)
Gross Profit	$8,250.00	Total Commissions	$960.00
Total No. Trades	8	Percentage Profitable	75%
No. Winning Trades	6	No. Losing Trades	2

Largest Winning Trade	$5,125.00	Largest Losing Trade	($1,625.00)
Average Winning Trade	$1,375.00	Average Losing Trade	($1,437.50)
Ratio Average Win/Loss	0.96	Average Trade	$671.88
Max. Consecutive Winners	4	Max. Consecutive Losses	1
Largest Consecutive Drawdown (%)	10.96%	Largest Consecutive Drawdown	($1,865.00)

Return on Account	31%
Profit/Drawdown Ratio	2.88

Notes:
1) Each trade is equal to 1,000 shares.
2) Initial account is equal to what it would cost
   to trade 1,000 shares at a price/share at that time.
3) Commission is equal to 12 cents per round turn.
4) Plan handles less or more shares.

1994
Eli Lilly Co. - Gann Swing Chartist®
Basic Swing Plan (Real Time)

Fibonacci Trader®

Trade #	Date	L/S	Price	Rule #	Profit	(Loss)	Accum.	A/C Equity	50% Margin
1	2/10/94	S	28 3/4	Sell 2				$28,750.00	$14,375.00
PP	2/23/94	L	28 5/8	PP1	1/8		$ 5.00	$28,755.00	$14,380.00
2	3/7/94	S	27	Sell 1					
PP	3/18/94	L	26 3/4	PP1	2/8		$ 135.00	$28,885.00	$14,510.00
3	3/30/94	S	24 7/8	Sell 1					
PP	4/18/94	L	24 1/2	PP1	3/8		$ 390.00	$29,140.00	$14,765.00
4	5/2/94	L	25 3/8	Buy 1					
PP	6/6/94	S	27 3/4	PP1	2 3/8		$ 2,645.00	$31,395.00	$17,020.00
5	6/9/94	L	28 1/2	Buy 1					
PP	7/11/94	S	26 7/8	PP2		-1 5/8	$ 900.00	$29,650.00	$15,275.00
6	7/11/94	S	25	Sell 2					
7	8/2/94	L	25	Buy 2	0		$ 780.00	$29,530.00	$15,155.00
PP	11/22/94	S	30 1/8	PP1	5 1/8		$ 5,785.00	$34,535.00	$20,160.00
8	11/23/94	S	29 1/4	Sell 2					
PP	11/29/94	L	30 1/2	PP1		-1 2/8	$ 4,415.00	$33,165.00	$18,790.00

124

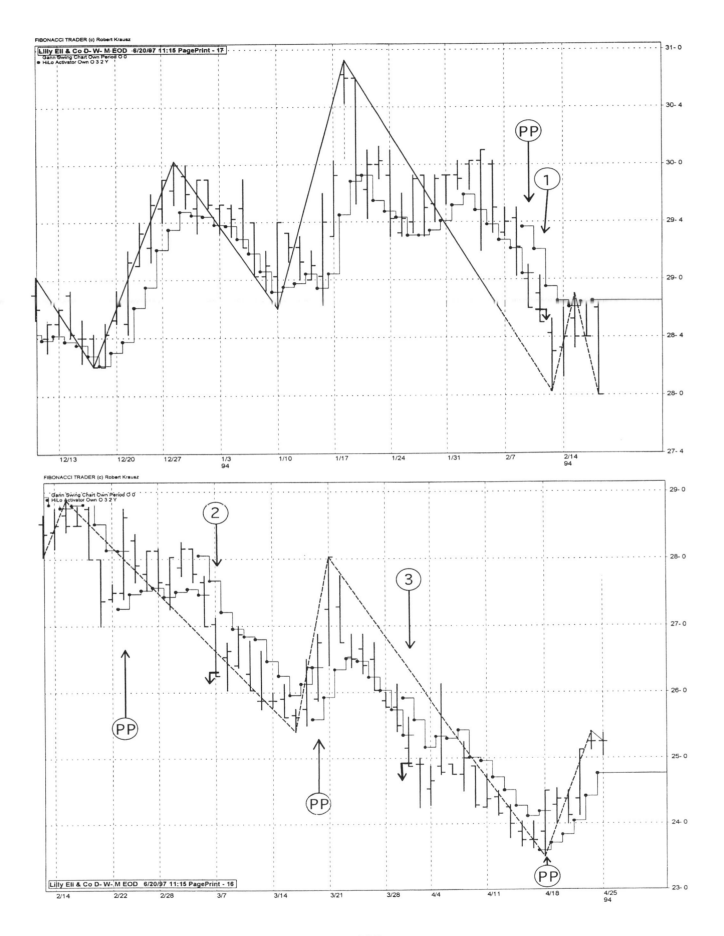

125

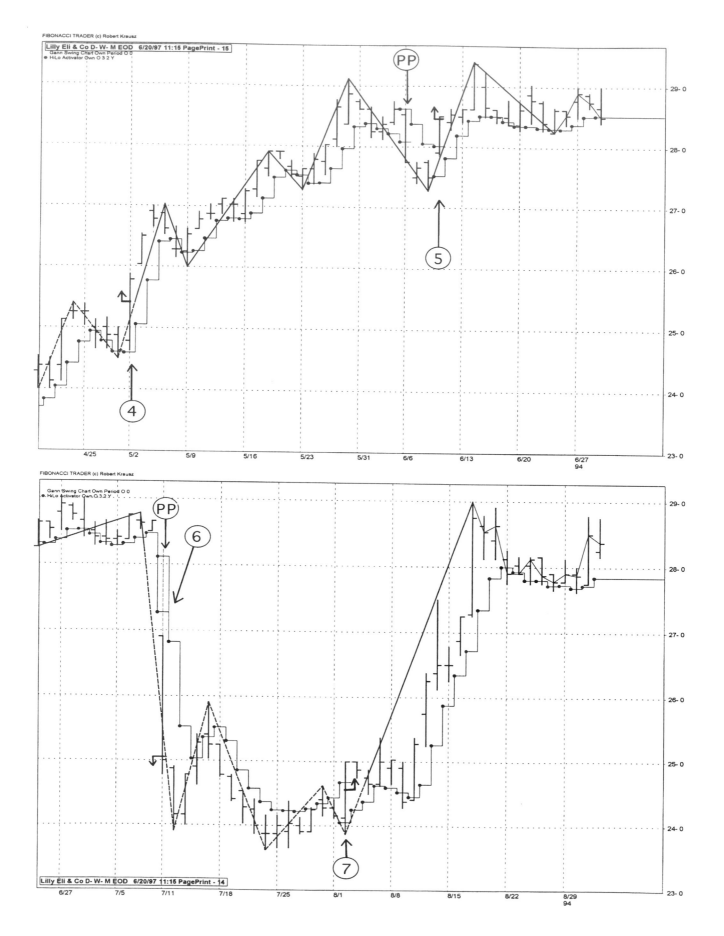

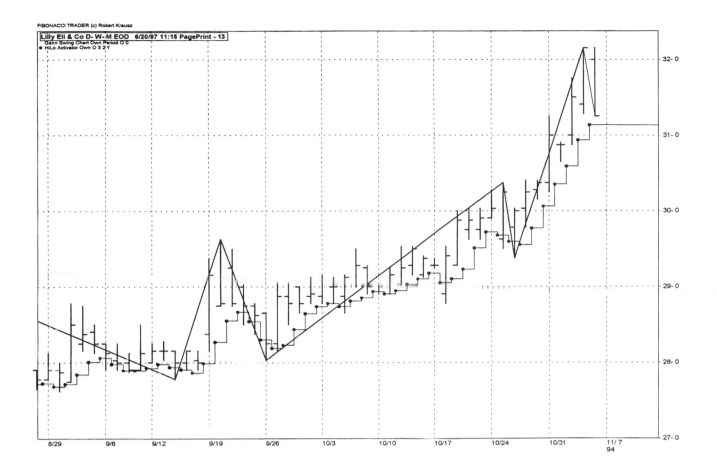

Lilly Eli & Co D- W- M EOD   6/20/97 11:15 PagePrint - 13
Gann Swing Chart Own Period O 0
● HiLo Activator Own O 3 2 Y

127

ELI LILLY CO. - 1995
BASIC SWING PLAN
GANN SWING CHARTIST - FIBONACCI TRADER®

With 100% Margin

Beginning Equity	$32,125.00	Ending Equity	$42,695.00
Total Net Profit	$12,250.00	Gross Loss	($3,750.00)
Gross Profit	$16,000.00	Total Commissions	$1,680.00
Total No. Trades	14	Percentage Profitable	57%
No. Winning Trades	8	No. Losing Trades	6

Largest Winning Trade	$5,500.00	Largest Losing Trade	($1,375.00)
Average Winning Trade	$2,000.00	Average Losing Trade	($625.00)
Ratio Average Win/Loss	3.20	Average Trade	$875.00
Max. Consecutive Winners	3	Max. Consecutive Losses	3
Largest Consecutive Drawdown (%)	12.05%	Largest Consecutive Drawdown	($4,340.00)

Return on Account	33%
Profit/Drawdown Ratio	2.82

With 50% Margin

Beginning Equity	$16,062.50	Ending Equity	$26,632.50
Total Net Profit	$12,250.00	Gross Loss	($3,750.00)
Gross Profit	$16,000.00	Total Commissions	$1,680.00
Total No. Trades	14	Percentage Profitable	57%
No. Winning Trades	8	No. Losing Trades	6

Largest Winning Trade	$5,500.00	Largest Losing Trade	($1,375.00)
Average Winning Trade	$2,000.00	Average Losing Trade	($625.00)
Ratio Average Win/Loss	3.20	Average Trade	$875.00
Max. Consecutive Winners	3	Max. Consecutive Losses	3
Largest Consecutive Drawdown (%)	21.75%	Largest Consecutive Drawdown	($4,340.00)

Return on Account	66%
Profit/Drawdown Ratio	2.82

Notes:
1) Each trade is equal to 1,000 shares.
2) Initial account is equal to what it would cost
   to trade 1,000 shares at a price/share at that time.
3) Commission is equal to 12 cents per round turn.
4) Plan handles less or more shares.

1995
Eli Lilly Co. - Gann Swing Chartist®   Fibonacci Trader®
Basic Swing Plan (Real Time)

Trade #	Date	L/S	Price	Rule #	Profit	(Loss)	Accum.	A/C Equity	50% Margin
1	12/20/95	L	32 1/8	Buy 2				$32,125.00	$16,062.50
PP	1/10/95	S	31 7/8	PP1		- 2/8	$ (370.00)	$31,755.00	$15,692.50
2	1/16/95	L	32 1/8	Buy 1					$16,072.50
PP	2/9/95	S	32 5/8	PP1	4/8		$ 10.00	$32,135.00	
3	2/22/95	L	32 3/4	Buy 1					
PP	3/30/95	S	36 3/4	PP1	4		$ 3,890.00	$36,015.00	$19,952.50
4	4/4/95	L	37 7/8	Buy 1					
PP	4/18/95	S	37 7/8	PP1	0		$ 3,770.00	$35,895.00	$19,832.50
5	4/24/95	L	38	Buy 1					
6	4/25/95	S	36 5/8	Sell 2		-1 3/8	$ 2,275.00	$34,400.00	$18,337.50
PP	4/28/95	L	37 3/8	PP1		- 6/8	$ 1,405.00	$33,530.00	$17,467.50
7	5/12/95	S	35 3/8	Sell 2					
PP	5/17/95	L	35 7/8	PP1		- 4/8	$ 785.00	$32,910.00	$16,847.50
8	6/1/95	L	37 3/8	Buy 2					
PP	6/20/95	S	37 3/8	PP1	0		$ 665.00	$32,790.00	$16,727.50
9	6/21/95	L	38 3/8	Buy 1					
10	7/7/95	S	38	Sell 2		- 3/8	$ 170.00	$32,295.00	$16,232.50
PP	7/12/95	L	38 1/2	PP1		- 4/8	$ (450.00)	$31,675.00	$15,612.50
11	8/24/95	L	39	Buy 2					
PP	10/2/95	S	44 1/2	PP1	5 4/8		$ 4,930.00	$37,055.00	$20,992.50
12	10/4/95	L	45 7/8	Buy 1					
PP	11/2/95	S	47 3/4	PP1	1 7/8		$ 6,685.00	$38,810.00	$22,747.50
13	11/8/95	L	48 3/4	Buy 1					
PP	11/22/95	S	49 1/4	PP1	4/8		$ 7,065.00	$39,190.00	$23,127.50
14	12/5/95	L	50 3/8	Buy 1					
PP	1/3/96	S	54	PP2	3 5/8		$10,570.00	$42,695.00	$26,632.50

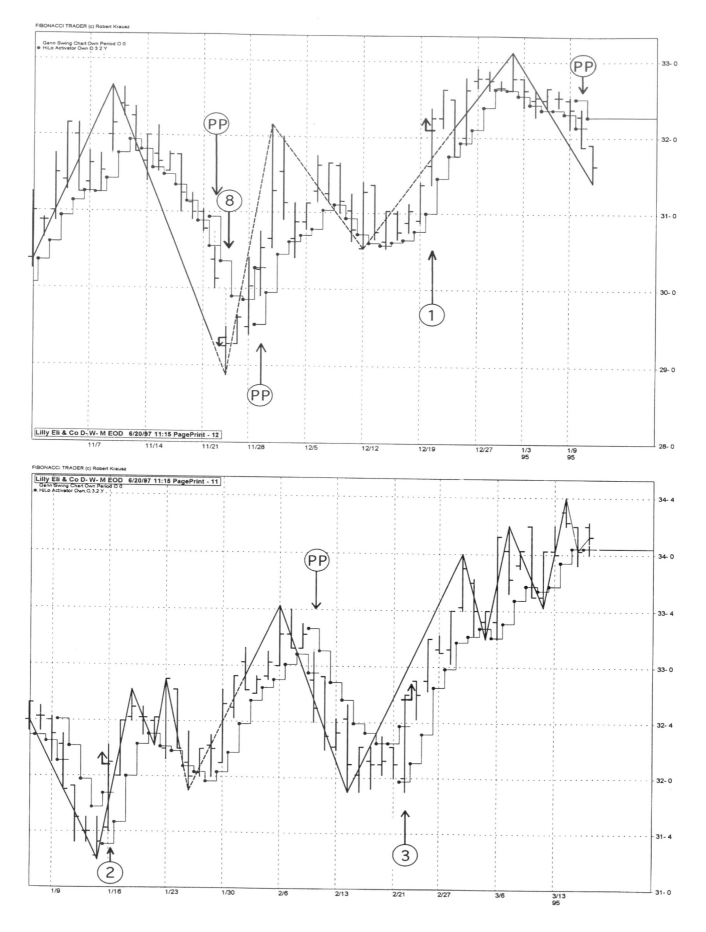

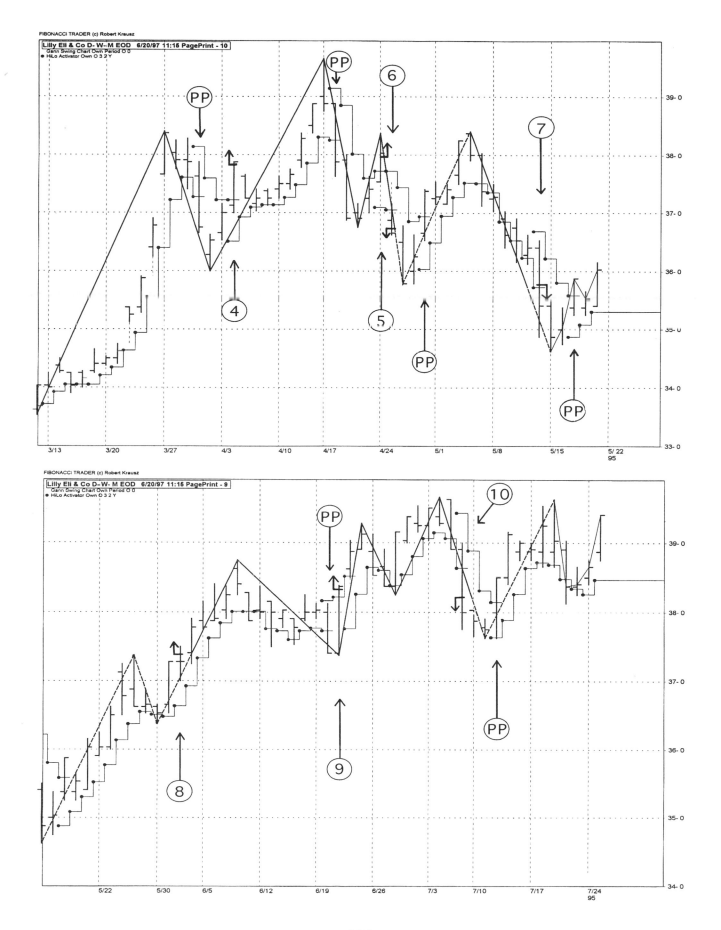

131

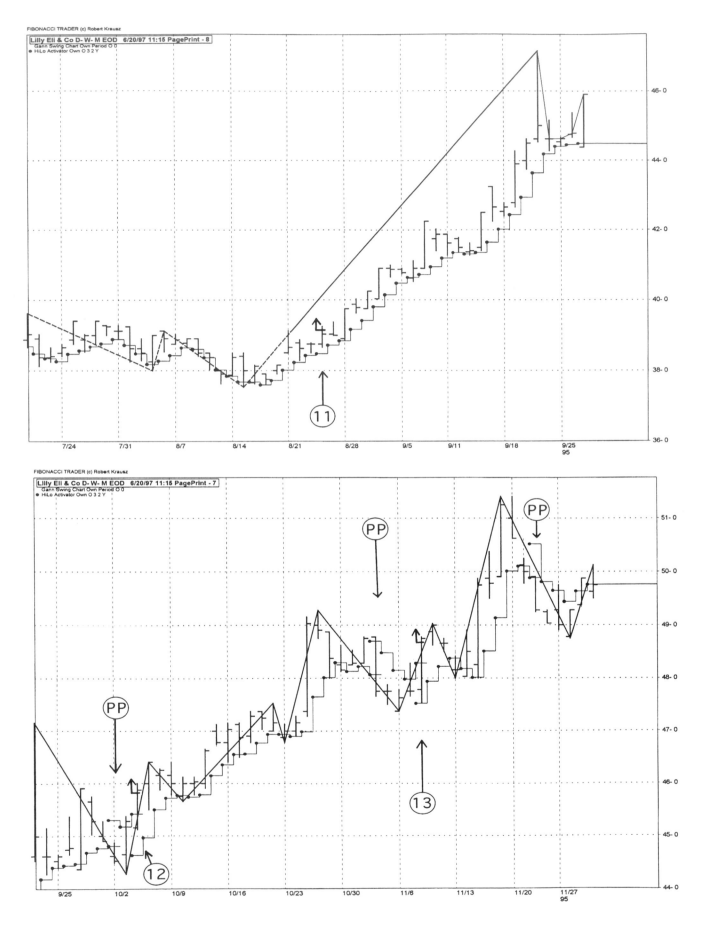

ELI LILLY CO. - 1996
BASIC SWING PLAN
GANN SWING CHARTIST - FIBONACCI TRADER®

With 100% Margin

Beginning Equity	$50,750.00	Ending Equity	$57,720.00
Total Net Profit	$9,250.00	Gross Loss	($25,500.00)
Gross Profit	$34,750.00	Total Commissions	$2,280.00
Total No. Trades	19	Percentage Profitable	32%
No. Winning Trades	6	No. Losing Trades	13

Largest Winning Trade	$9,500.00	Largest Losing Trade	($3,750.00)
Average Winning Trade	$5,791.67	Average Losing Trade	($1,961.54)
Ratio Average Win/Loss	2.95	Average Trade	$486.84
Max. Consecutive Winners	3	Max. Consecutive Losses	3
Largest Consecutive Drawdown (%)	17.92%	Largest Consecutive Drawdown	($12,605.00)

Return on Account	14%
Profit/Drawdown Ratio	0.73

With 50% Margin

Beginning Equity	$25,375.00	Ending Equity	$32,345.00
Total Net Profit	$9,250.00	Gross Loss	($25,500.00)
Gross Profit	$34,750.00	Total Commissions	$2,280.00
Total No. Trades	19	Percentage Profitable	32%
No. Winning Trades	6	No. Losing Trades	13

Largest Winning Trade	$9,500.00	Largest Losing Trade	($3,750.00)
Average Winning Trade	$5,791.67	Average Losing Trade	($1,961.54)
Ratio Average Win/Loss	2.95	Average Trade	$486.84
Max. Consecutive Winners	3	Max. Consecutive Losses	3
Largest Consecutive Drawdown (%)	28.04%	Largest Consecutive Drawdown	($12,605.00)

Return on Account	27%
Profit/Drawdown Ratio	0.73

Notes:
1) Each trade is equal to 1,000 shares.
2) Initial account is equal to what it would cost
   to trade 1,000 shares at a price/share at that time.
3) Commission is equal to 12 cents per round turn.
4) Plan handles less or more shares.

1996

Eli Lilly Co. - Gann Swing Chartist®

Basic Swing Plan (Real Time)

Fibonacci Trader®

Trade #	Date	L/S	Price	Rule #	Profit	(Loss)	Accum.	A/C Equity	50% Margin
1	1/10/96	S	50 7/8	Sell 2				$50,750.00	$25,375.00
2	1/29/96	L	53 5/8	Buy 2		-2 6/8	$ (2,870.00)	$47,880.00	$22,505.00
PP	2/16/96	S	62 1/4	PP1	8 5/8		$ 5,635.00	$56,385.00	$31,010.00
3	2/22/96	L	63 3/8	Buy 1					
PP	2/26/96	S	62 1/4	PP1		-1 1/8	$ 4,390.00	$55,140.00	$29,765.00
4	2/28/96	S	60 3/8	Sell 2					
PP	3/4/96	L	64 1/8	PP1		-3 6/8	$ 520.00	$51,270.00	$25,895.00
5	3/6/96	L	64 3/4	Buy 2					
PP	3/8/96	S	63 5/8	PP2		-1 1/8	$ (725.00)	$50,025.00	$24,650.00
6	3/18/96	S	59 5/8	Sell 2					
PP	3/20/96	L	62	PP1		-2 3/8	$ (3,220.00)	$47,530.00	$22,155.00
7	3/27/96	S	65 3/8	Sell 1					
PP	4/19/96	L	60 1/8	PP2	5 2/8		$ 1,910.00	$52,660.00	$27,285.00
8	4/23/96	S	57 3/8	Sell 1					
PP	4/26/96	L	58	PP2		- 5/8	$ 1,165.00	$51,915.00	$26,540.00
9	5/1/96	S	56	Sell 1					
PP	5/8/96	L	56 1/4	PP2		- 2/8	$ 795.00	$51,545.00	$26,170.00
10	5/17/96	L	60	Buy 2					
PP	6/12/96	S	64 1/4	PP1	4 2/8		$ 4,925.00	$55,675.00	$30,300.00
11	6/20/96	L	64 1/4	Buy 1					
PP	7/5/96	S	63 1/2	PP1		- 6/8	$ 4,055.00	$54,805.00	$29,430.00
12	7/10/96	S	61 5/8	Sell 2					
PP	7/18/96	L	58 1/4	PP2	3 3/8		$ 7,310.00	$58,060.00	$32,685.00
13	8/6/96	L	58 7/8	Buy 2					
PP	8/29/96	S	58 1/4	PP1		- 5/8	$ 6,565.00	$57,315.00	$31,940.00
14	9/3/96	L	59 3/4	Buy 1					
PP	10/28/96	S	69 1/4	PP2	9 4/8		$15,945.00	$66,695.00	$41,320.00
15	11/4/96	L	71 5/8	Buy 1					
PP	11/12/96	S	75 3/8	PP1	3 6/8		$19,575.00	$70,325.00	$44,950.00
16	11/19/96	S	74 3/8	Sell 2					
17	11/25/96	L	78	Buy 2		-3 5/8	$15,830.00	$66,580.00	$41,205.00
PP	12/2/96	S	74 5/8	PP1		-3 3/8	$12,335.00	$63,085.00	$37,710.00
18	12/4/96	S	73 3/8	Sell 2					

1996

Eli Lilly Co. - Gann Swing Chartist®

Basic Swing Plan (Real Time)

Fibonacci Trader®

Trade #	Date	L/S	Price	Rule #	Profit	(Loss)	Accum.	A/C Equity	50% Margin
PP	12/9/96	L	74 3/4	PP2		-1 3/8	$ 10,840.00	$61,590.00	$36,215.00
19	12/19/96	L	79 1/4	Buy 2					
PP	12/23/96	S	75 1/2	PP2		-3 6/8	$ 6,970.00	$57,720.00	$32,345.00

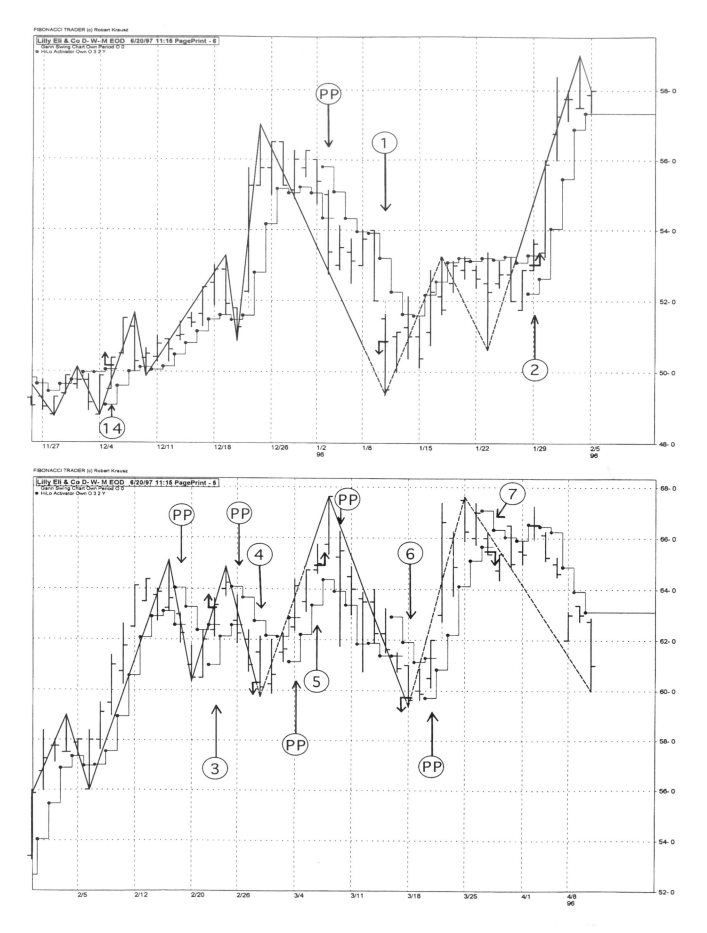

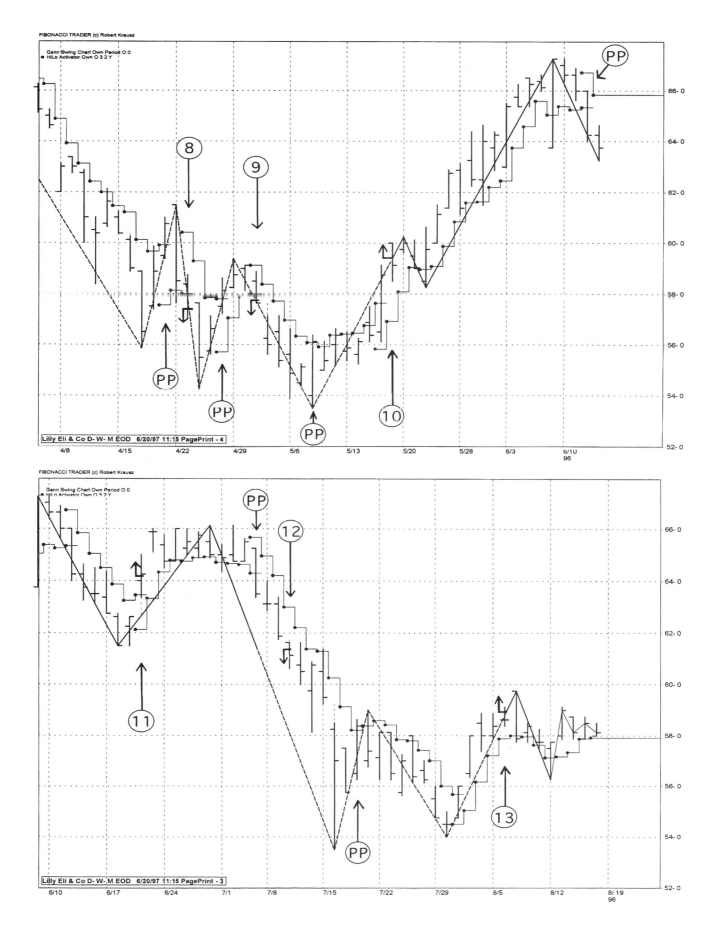

137

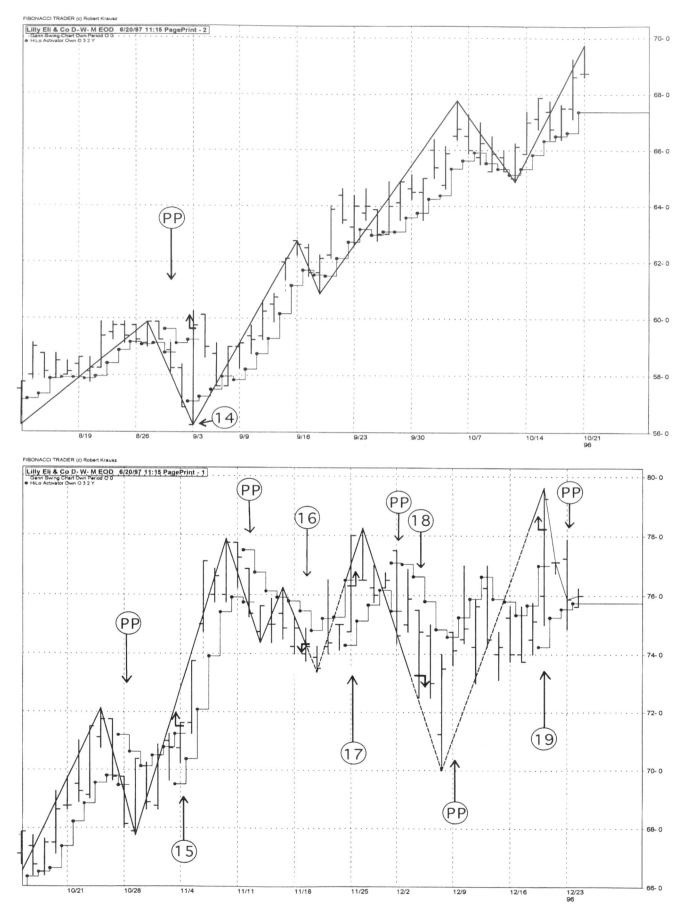

138

IBM - 1992-1996 (5 YRS.) RT.
BASIC SWING PLAN - COMPOSITE
GANN SWING CHARTIST - FIBONACCI TRADER ®

With 100% Margin

Beginning Equity	$89,125.00	Ending Equity	$185,860.00
Total Net Profit	$108,375.00	Gross Loss	($100,250.00)
Gross Profit	$208,625.00	Total Commissions	$11,640.00
Total No. Trades	97	Percentage Profitable	44%
No. Winning Trades	43	No. Losing Trades	10

Largest Winning Trade	$30,500.00	Largest Losing Trade	($4,500.00)
Average Winning Trade	$4,851.74	Average Losing Trade	($10,025.00)
Max. Consecutive Winners	3	Max. Consecutive Losses	3
Average Drawdown (%)	11.06%	Average Drawdown ($)	($9,419.00)

Average Return on Account	27%
Profit/Drawdown Ratio	11.51

With 50% Margin

Beginning Equity	$44,562.50	Ending Equity	$141,297.50
Total Net Profit	$108,375.00	Gross Loss	($100,250.00)
Gross Profit	$208,625.00	Total Commissions	$11,640.00
Total No. Trades	97	Percentage Profitable	44%
No. Winning Trades	43	No. Losing Trades	10

Largest Winning Trade	$30,500.00	Largest Losing Trade	($4,500.00)
Average Winning Trade	$4,851.74	Average Losing Trade	($10,025.00)
Max. Consecutive Winners	3	Max. Consecutive Losses	3
Average Drawdown (%)	19.48%	Average Drawdown ($)	($9,419.00)

Average Return on Account	48%
Profit/Drawdown Ratio	11.51

Notes:
1) Each trade is equal to 1,000 shares.
2) Initial account is equal to what it would cost
   to trade 1,000 shares at a price/share at that time.
3) Commission is equal to 12 cents per round turn per share.
4) Plan handles less or more shares, percentages are the same.

IBM - 1992
BASIC SWING PLAN
GANN SWING CHARTIST- FIBONACCI TRADER ®

With 100% Margin

Beginning Equity	$89,125.00	Ending Equity	$91,485.00
Total Net Profit	$5,000.00	Gross Loss	($24,500.00)
Gross Profit	$29,500.00	Total Commissions	$2,640.00
Total No. Trades	22	Percentage Profitable	41%
No. Winning Trades	9	No. Losing Trades	10

Largest Winning Trade	$13,625.00	Largest Losing Trade	($2,750.00)
Average Winning Trade	$3,277.78	Average Losing Trade	($2,450.00)
Ratio Average Win/Loss	1.34	Average Trade	$227.27
Max. Consecutive Winners	2	Max. Consecutive Losses	4
Largest Consecutive Drawdown (%)	13.61%	Largest Consecutive Drawdown	($12,455.00)

Return on Account	3%
Profit/Drawdown Ratio	0.40

With 50% Margin

Beginning Equity	$44,562.50	Ending Equity	$46,922.50
Total Net Profit	$5,000.00	Gross Loss	($24,500.00)
Gross Profit	$29,500.00	Total Commissions	$2,640.00
Total No. Trades	22	Percentage Profitable	41%
No. Winning Trades	9	No. Losing Trades	10

Largest Winning Trade	$13,625.00	Largest Losing Trade	($2,750.00)
Average Winning Trade	$3,277.78	Average Losing Trade	($2,450.00)
Ratio Average Win/Loss	1.34	Average Trade	$227.27
Max. Consecutive Winners	2	Max. Consecutive Losses	4
Largest Consecutive Drawdown (%)	26.53%	Largest Consecutive Drawdown	($12,455.00)

Return on Account	5%
Profit/Drawdown Ratio	0.40

Notes:
1) Each trade is equal to 1,000 shares.
2) Initial account is equal to what it would cost
   to trade 1,000 shares at a price/share at that time.
3) Commission is equal to 12 cents per round turn.
4) Plan handles less or more shares.

1992

IBM - Gann Swing Chartist®
Basic Swing Plan (Real Time)

Fibonacci Trader®

Trade #	Date	L/S	Price	Rule #	Profit	(Loss)	Accum.	A/C Equity	50% Margin
1	12/24/91	L	89 1/8	Buy 2				$89,125.00	$44,562.50
PP	1/9/92	S	91 1/4	PP1	2 1/8		$ 2,005.00	$91,130.00	$46,567.50
2	1/14/92	L	92 3/8	Buy 1					$46,947.50
PP	1/21/92	S	92 7/8	PP1	4/8		$ 2,385.00	$91,510.00	
3	2/3/92	S	89 3/4	Sell 2					
PP	2/4/92	L	92 1/4	PP1		-2 4/8	$ (235.00)	$88,890.00	$44,327.50
4	2/6/92	S	89 7/8	Sell 1					
PP	2/12/92	L	92 1/8	PP1		-2 2/8	$ (2,605.00)	$86,520.00	$41,957.50
5	2/25/92	S	88 1/4	Sell 1					
PP	3/12/92	L	89 1/8	PP1		- 7/8	$ (3,600.00)	$85,525.00	$40,962.50
6	3/13/92	L	89 5/8	Sell 2					
PP	3/17/92	S	87 5/8	PP1		-2	$ (5,720.00)	$83,405.00	$38,842.50
7	3/24/92	S	85 1/8	Sell 2					
8	4/8/92	L	84 7/8	Buy 2	2/8		$ (5,590.00)	$83,535.00	$38,972.50
PP	4/21/92	S	89 3/4	PP1		-1 5/8	$ (7,335.00)	$81,790.00	$37,227.50
9	4/24/92	L	88 1/8	Buy 1					
PP	4/30/92	S	90 3/4	PP1	1 5/8		$ (5,830.00)	$83,295.00	$38,732.50
10	5/13/92	L	92 3/8	Buy 1					
PP	5/19/92	S	92 1/2	PP1		-2 6/8	$ (8,700.00)	$80,425.00	$35,862.50
11	6/3/92	S	89 3/4	Sell 1					
PP	6/8/92	L	91	PP1		-1 2/8	$ (10,070.00)	$79,055.00	$34,492.50
12	6/11/92	L	92	Sell 2					
PP	7/2/92	S	96 7/8	PP1	4 7/8		$ (5,315.00)	$83,810.00	$39,247.50
13	7/15/92	L	99 1/4	Buy 1					
PP	7/17/92	S	95 3/4	PP2		-3 4/8	$ (8,935.00)	$80,190.00	$35,627.50
14	7/29/92	L	94 3/8	Buy 1					
PP	8/4/92	S	94	PP1		- 3/8	$ (9,430.00)	$79,695.00	$35,132.50
15	8/5/92	S	92 3/8	Sell 2					
PP	8/25/92	L	87 1/8	PP1	5 2/8		$ (4,300.00)	$84,825.00	$40,262.50
16	9/4/92	S	86	Sell 1					
PP	9/10/92	L	87 1/2	PP1		-1 4/8	$ (5,920.00)	$83,205.00	$38,642.50
17	9/11/92	L	87 5/8	Buy 2					
18	9/15/92	S	85 1/2	Sell 2		-2 1/8	$ (8,165.00)	$80,960.00	$36,397.50

1992
IBM - Gann Swing Chartist®
Basic Swing Plan (Real Time)   **Fibonacci Trader®**

PP	9/21/92	L	84 3/8	PP1	1 1/8		$ (7,160.00)	$81,965.00	$37,402.50
19	9/24/92	S	82 1/2	Sell 1					
PP	11/2/92	L	68 7/8	PP1	13 5/8		$ 6,345.00	$95,470.00	$50,907.50
20	11/5/92	S	65 7/8	Sell 1					
PP	11/9/92	L	67 1/2	PP1		-1 5/8	$ 4,600.00	$93,725.00	$49,162.50
21	11/11/92	S	65	Sell 1					
PP	11/24/92	L	64 7/8	PP1	1/8		$ 4,605.00	$93,730.00	$49,167.50
22	11/30/92	L	68	Buy 2					
PP	12/7/92	S	65 7/8	PP1		-2 1/8	$ 2,360.00	$91,485.00	$46,922.50

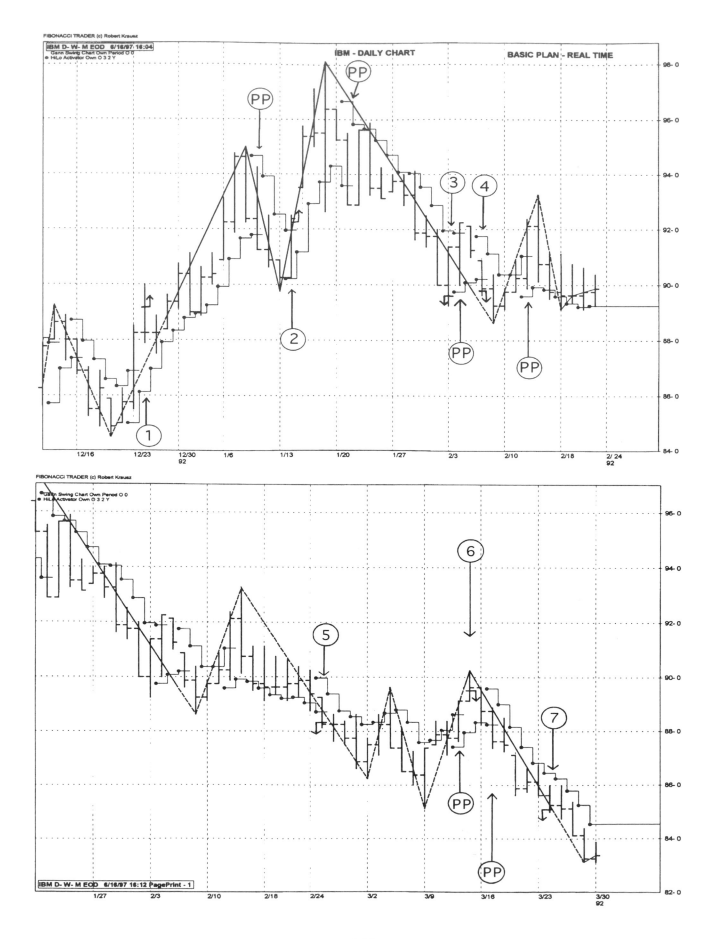

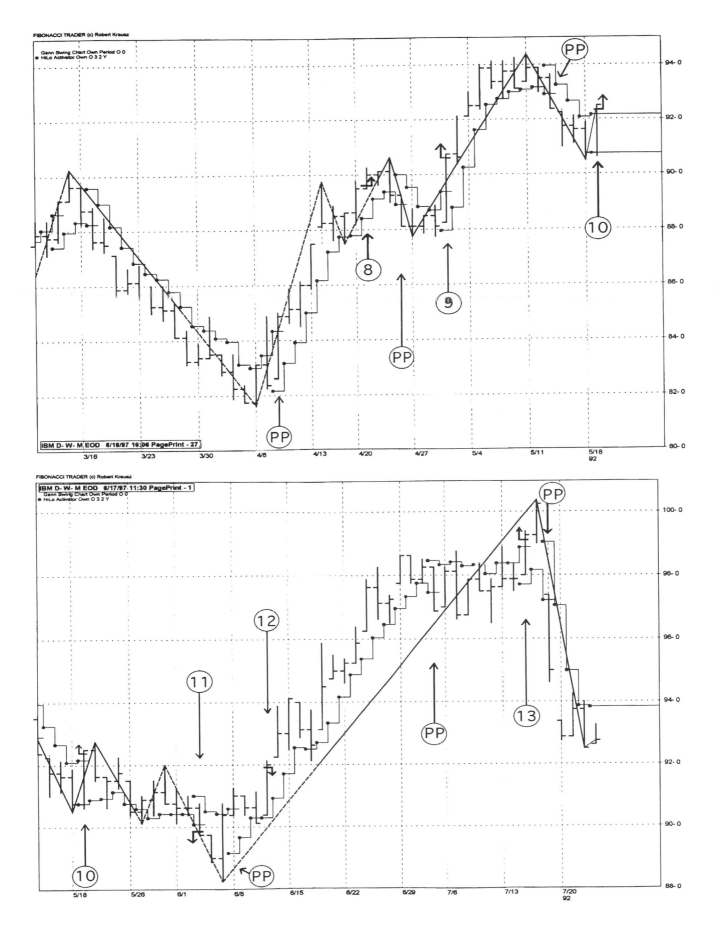

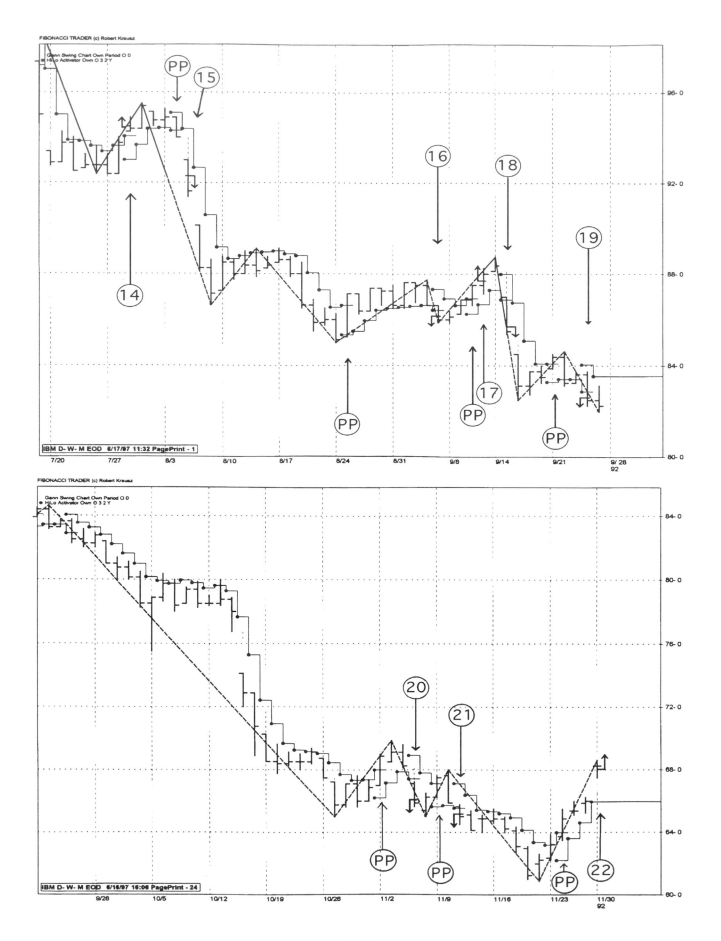

IBM - 1993
BASIC SWING PLAN
GANN SWING CHARTIST- FIBONACCI TRADER ®

With 100% Margin

Beginning Equity	$59,875.00	Ending Equity	$74,105.00
Total Net Profit	$8,375.00	Gross Loss	($16,875.00)
Gross Profit	$25,250.00	Total Commissions	($5,855.00)
Total No. Trades	21	Percentage Profitable	43%
No. Winning Trades	9	No. Losing Trades	12

Largest Winning Trade	$11,250.00	Largest Losing Trade	($2,750.00)
Average Winning Trade	$2,805.56	Average Losing Trade	($1,406.25)
Ratio Average Win/Loss	2.00	Average Trade	$398.81
Max. Consecutive Winners	3	Max. Consecutive Losses	5
Largest Consecutive Drawdown (%)	18.54%	Largest Consecutive Drawdown	($13,165.00)

Return on Account	24%
Profit/Drawdown Ratio	0.64

With 50% Margin

Beginning Equity	$29,937.50	Ending Equity	$35,792.50
Total Net Profit	$8,375.00	Gross Loss	($16,875.00)
Gross Profit	$25,250.00	Total Commissions	$2,520.00
Total No. Trades	21	Percentage Profitable	43%
No. Winning Trades	9	No. Losing Trades	12

Largest Winning Trade	$11,250.00	Largest Losing Trade	($2,750.00)
Average Winning Trade	$2,805.56	Average Losing Trade	($1,406.25)
Ratio Average Win/Loss	2.00	Average Trade	$398.81
Max. Consecutive Winners	3	Max. Consecutive Losses	5
Largest Consecutive Drawdown (%)	32.06%	Largest Consecutive Drawdown	($13,165.00)

Return on Account	20%
Profit/Drawdown Ratio	0.64

Notes:
1) Each trade is equal to 1,000 shares.
2) Initial account is equal to what it would cost
   to trade 1,000 shares at a price/share at that time.
3) Commission is equal to 12 cents per round turn.
4) Plan handles less or more shares.

1993
IBM - Gann Swing Chartist®
Basic Swing Plan (Real Time)

Fibonacci Trader®

Trade #	Date	L/S	Price	Rule #	Profit	(Loss)	Accum.	A/C Equity	50% Margin
1	12/15/92	S	59 7/8	Sell 2				$59,875.00	$29,937.50
PP	1/22/93	L	48 5/8	PP1	11 2/8		$11,130.00	$71,005.00	$41,067.50
2	1/26/93	L	52 7/8	Buy 2					
PP	2/3/93	S	51 1/8	PP1		-1 6/8	$9,260.00	$69,135.00	$39,197.50
3	2/8/93	L	52 7/8	Buy 1					
4	2/11/93	S	51 1/8	Sell 1		-1 6/8	$7,390.00	$67,265.00	$37,327.50
PP	2/25/93	L	53 3/4	PP1		-2 5/8	$4,645.00	$64,520.00	$34,582.50
5	2/26/93	L	54 3/8	Buy 2					
PP	3/11/93	S	54 7/8	PP1	4/8		$5,025.00	$64,900.00	$34,962.50
6	3/22/93	S	53 5/8	Sell 2					
7	4/2/93	L	52 5/8	Buy 2	1		$5,905.00	$65,780.00	$35,842.50
8	4/13/93	S	49 7/8	Sell 2		-2 6/8	$3,035.00	$62,910.00	$32,972.50
PP	4/20/93	L	50 5/8	PP1		-6/8	$2,165.00	$62,040.00	$32,102.50
9	4/22/93	S	48 1/2	Sell 1					
PP	4/28/93	L	49 7/8	PP1		-1 3/8	$670.00	$60,545.00	$30,607.50
10	5/6/93	S	48 1/4	Sell 1					
PP	5/18/93	L	49	PP1		-6/8	$(200.00)	$59,675.00	$29,737.50
11	5/27/93	L	53 1/8	Buy 2					
PP	6/7/93	S	52 1/4	PP1		-7/8	$(1,195.00)	$58,680.00	$28,742.50
12	6/8/93	S	51 7/8	Sell 2					
PP	6/25/93	L	49 3/4	PP1	2 1/8		$810.00	$60,685.00	$30,747.50
13	7/2/93	S	48 1/2	Sell 3					
PP	7/12/93	L	48 1/8	PP1	3/8		$1,065.00	$60,940.00	$31,002.50
14	7/16/93	S	46 3/8	Sell 3					
15	7/27/93	L	44 5/8	Buy 2	1 6/8		$2,695.00	$62,570.00	$32,632.50
16	8/11/93	S	42 1/4	Sell 1		-2 3/8	$200.00	$60,075.00	$30,137.50
PP	8/17/93	L	43	PP1		-6/8	$(670.00)	$59,205.00	$29,267.50
17	8/31/93	L	44 3/4	Buy 2					
PP	9/8/93	S	44 3/8	PP1		-3/8	$(1,165.00)	$58,710.00	$28,772.50
18	10/1/93	L	43 7/8	Buy 1					
PP	10/13/93	S	43 1/8	PP1		-6/8	$(2,035.00)	$57,840.00	$27,902.50
19	10/15/93	L	44 1/2	Buy 1					
PP	11/9/93	S	49 1/8	PP1	4 5/8		$2,470.00	$62,345.00	$32,407.50

148

1993
IBM - Gann Swing Chartist®   **Fibonacci Trader®**
Basic Swing Plan (Real Time)

20	11/11/93	L	52	Buy 1			$34,162.50
PP	11/30/93	S	53 7/8	PP1	1 7/8	$ 4,225.00	$64,100.00
21	12/10/93	L	55 1/4	Buy 1			$35,792.50
PP	12/30/93	S	57	PP1	1 6/8	$ 5,855.00	$65,730.00

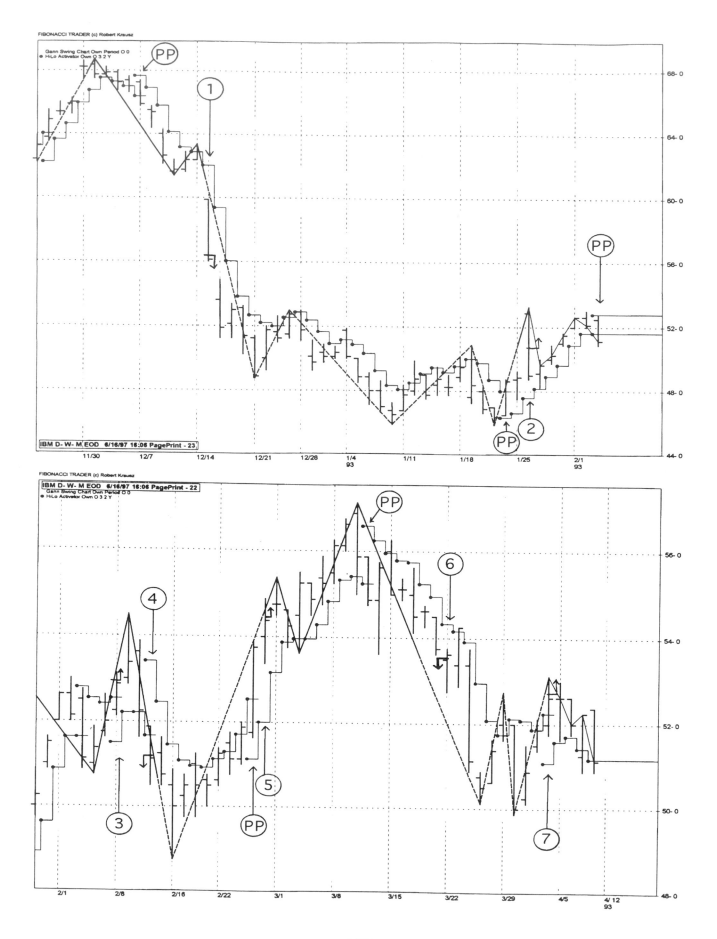

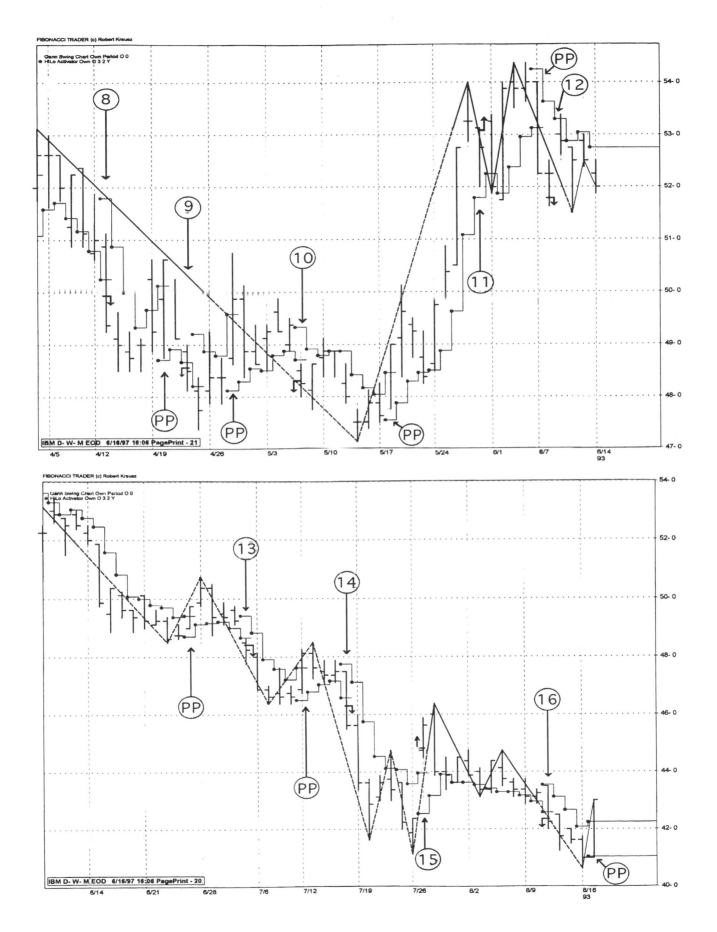

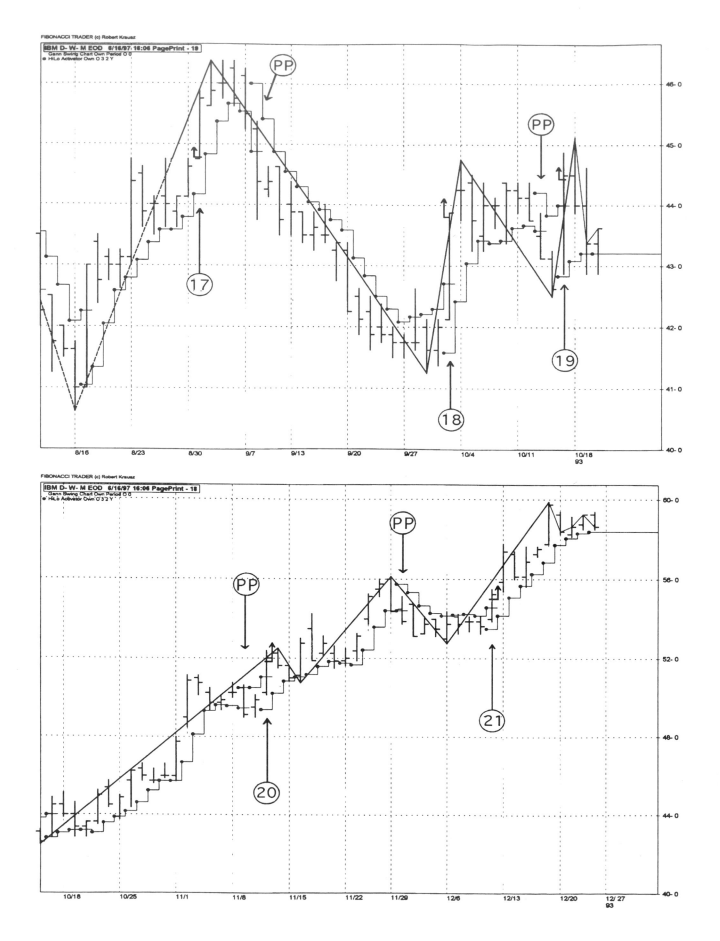

IBM - 1994
BASIC SWING PLAN
GANN SWING CHARTIST- FIBONACCI TRADER ®

With 100% Margin

Beginning Equity	$59,000.00	Ending Equity	$63,580.00
Total Net Profit	$6,500.00	Gross Loss	($17,875.00)
Gross Profit	$24,375.00	Total Commissions	$1,920.00
Total No. Trades	16	Percentage Profitable	38%
No. Winning Trades	6	No. Losing Trades	10

Largest Winning Trade	$9,500.00	Largest Losing Trade	($4,125.00)
Average Winning Trade	$4,062.50	Average Losing Trade	($1,787.50)
Ratio Average Win/Loss	2.27	Average Trade	$406.25
Max. Consecutive Winners	2	Max. Consecutive Losses	3
Largest Consecutive Drawdown (%)	8.93%	Largest Consecutive Drawdown	($6,235.00)

Return on Account	8%
Profit/Drawdown Ratio	1.04

With 50% Margin

Beginning Equity	$29,500.00	Ending Equity	$34,080.00
Total Net Profit	$6,500.00	Gross Loss	($17,875.00)
Gross Profit	$24,375.00	Total Commissions	$1,920.00
Total No. Trades	16	Percentage Profitable	38%
No. Winning Trades	6	No. Losing Trades	10

Largest Winning Trade	$9,500.00	Largest Losing Trade	($4,125.00)
Average Winning Trade	$4,062.50	Average Losing Trade	($1,787.50)
Ratio Average Win/Loss	2.27	Average Trade	$406.25
Max. Consecutive Winners	2	Max. Consecutive Losses	3
Largest Consecutive Drawdown (%)	15.47%	Largest Consecutive Drawdown	($6,235.00)

Return on Account	16%
Profit/Drawdown Ratio	1.04

Notes:
1) Each trade is equal to 1,000 shares.
2) Initial account is equal to what it would cost
   to trade 1,000 shares at a price/share at that time.
3) Commission is equal to 12 cents per round turn.
4) Plan handles less or more shares.

1994
IBM - Gann Swing Chartist®
Basic Swing Plan (Real Time)

Fibonacci Trader®

Trade #	Date	L/S	Price	Rule #	Profit	(Loss)	Accum.	A/C Equity	50% Margin
1	1/4/94	L	59	Buy 1				$59,000.00	$29,500.00
PP	1/17/94	S	57 1/2	PP1		-1 4/8	$ (1,620.00)	$57,380.00	$27,880.00
2	1/19/94	S	56 3/8	Sell 2					$27,135.00
PP	1/24/94	L	57	PP2	'	- 5/8	$ (2,365.00)	$56,635.00	
3	1/31/94	S	56 1/2	Sell 1					
PP	2/14/94	L	54	PP1	2 4/8		$ 15.00	$59,015.00	$29,515.00
4	2/17/94	S	52 3/4	Sell 1					
5	3/8/94	L	54 1/8	Buy 2		-1 3/8	$ (1,480.00)	$57,520.00	$28,020.00
PP	3/24/94	S	56 3/8	PP1	2 2/8		$ 650.00	$59,650.00	$30,150.00
6	4/21/94	L	58 3/8	Buy 1					
PP	4/28/94	S	57 1/8	PP1		-1 2/8	$ (720.00)	$58,280.00	$28,780.00
7	5/16/94	L	58 1/2	Buy 1					
PP	6/2/94	S	62	PP1	3 4/8		$ 2,660.00	$61,660.00	$32,160.00
8	6/13/94	L	63 3/4	Buy 1					
PP	6/16/94	S	62 7/8	PP1		- 7/8	$ 1,665.00	$60,665.00	$31,165.00
9	6/21/94	S	60 3/4	Sell 2					
10	7/14/94	L	57 7/8	Buy 2	2 7/8		$ 4,420.00	$63,420.00	$33,920.00
PP	7/19/94	S	55 5/8	PP1		-2 2/8	$ 2,050.00	$61,050.00	$31,550.00
11	7/20/94	S	54 7/8	Sell 2					
12	7/21/94	L	59	Buy 2		-4 1/8	$ (2,195.00)	$56,805.00	$27,305.00
PP	8/31/94	S	68 1/2	PP1	9 4/8		$ 7,185.00	$66,185.00	$36,685.00
13	9/13/94	L	69 1/4	Buy 1					
PP	10/24/94	S	73	PP1	3 6/8		$10,815.00	$69,815.00	$40,315.00
14	10/28/94	L	75 7/8	Buy 1					
15	11/4/94	S	72 1/2	Sell 2		-3 3/8	$ 7,320.00	$66,320.00	$36,820.00
PP	11/9/94	L	74	PP1		-1 4/8	$ 5,700.00	$64,700.00	$35,200.00
16	11/22/94	S	70 5/8	Sell 3					
1	12/19/94	L	71 5/8	Buy 1		-1	$ 4,580.00	$63,580.00	$34,080.00

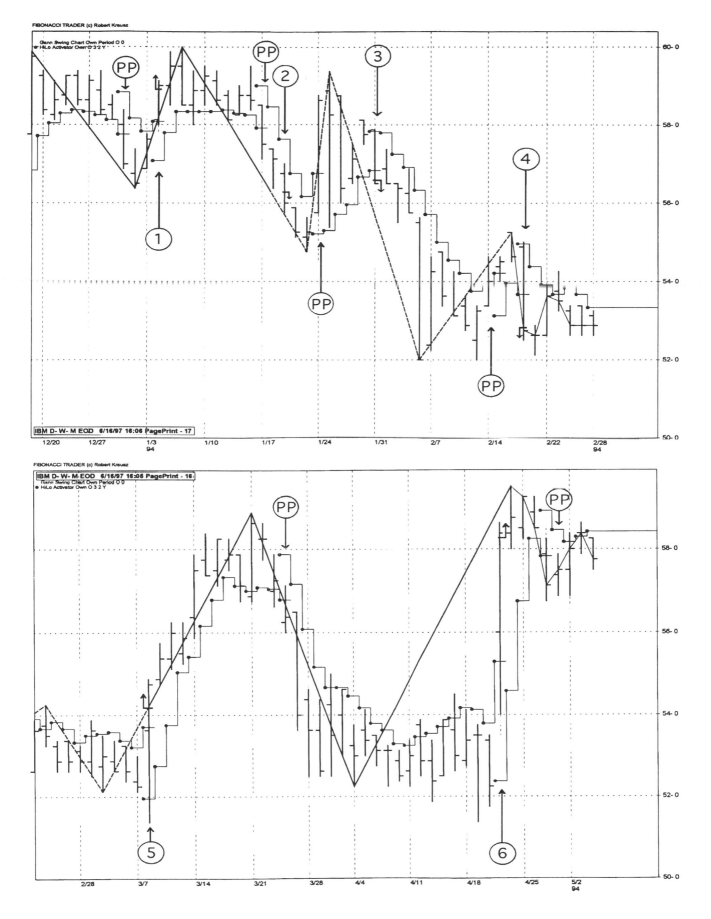

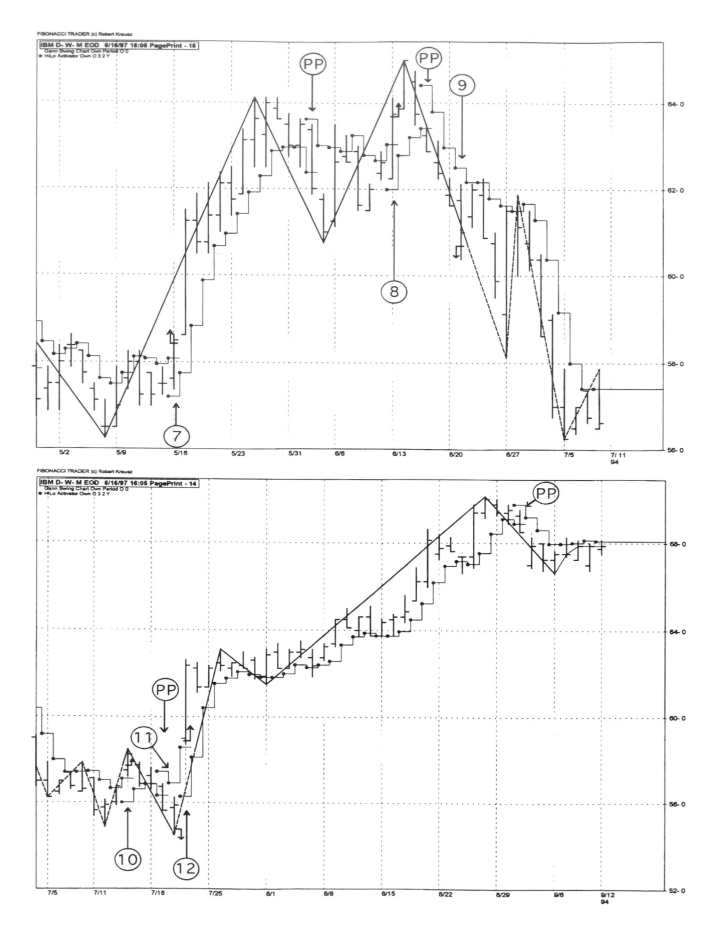

FIBONACCI TRADER (c) Robert Krausz

IBM D- W- M EOD 6/16/97 16:06 PagePrint - 15
Gann Swing Chart Own Period O 0
● HiLo Activator Own O 3 2 Y

FIBONACCI TRADER (c) Robert Krausz

IBM D- W- M EOD 6/16/97 16:06 PagePrint - 14
Gann Swing Chart Own Period O 0
● HiLo Activator Own O 3 2 Y

156

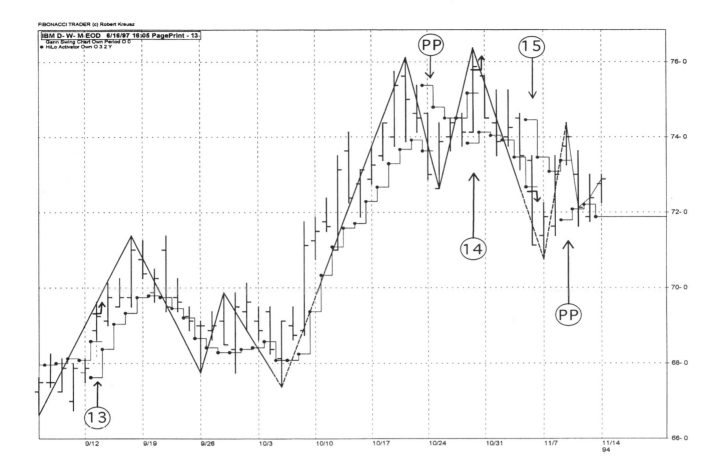

IBM D- W- M EOD 6/16/97 16:05 PagePrint - 13.
Gann Swing Chart Own Period O 0
● HiLo Activator Own O 3 2 Y

IBM - 1995
BASIC SWING PLAN
GANN SWING CHARTIST- FIBONACCI TRADER ®

With 100% Margin

Beginning Equity	$71,625.00	Ending Equity	$91,975.00
Total Net Profit	$22,750.00	Gross Loss	($14,625.00)
Gross Profit	$37,375.00	Total Commissions	$2,400.00
Total No. Trades	20	Percentage Profitable	55%
No. Winning Trades	11	No. Losing Trades	9

Largest Winning Trade	$13,375.00	Largest Losing Trade	($3,625.00)
Average Winning Trade	$3,397.73	Average Losing Trade	($1,625.00)
Ratio Average Win/Loss	2.09	Average Trade	$1,137.50
Max. Consecutive Winners	2	Max. Consecutive Losses	3
Largest Consecutive Drawdown (%)	6.03%	Largest Consecutive Drawdown	($5,115.00)

Return on Account	28%
Profit/Drawdown Ratio	4.45

With 50% Margin

Beginning Equity	$35,812.50	Ending Equity	$56,162.50
Total Net Profit	$22,750.00	Gross Loss	($14,625.00)
Gross Profit	$37,375.00	Total Commissions	$2,400.00
Total No. Trades	20	Percentage Profitable	55%
No. Winning Trades	11	No. Losing Trades	9

Largest Winning Trade	$13,375.00	Largest Losing Trade	($3,625.00)
Average Winning Trade	$3,397.73	Average Losing Trade	($1,625.00)
Ratio Average Win/Loss	2.09	Average Trade	$1,137.50
Max. Consecutive Winners	2	Max. Consecutive Losses	3
Largest Consecutive Drawdown (%)	10.45%	Largest Consecutive Drawdown	($5,115.00)

Return on Account	57%
Profit/Drawdown Ratio	4.45

Notes:
1) Each trade is equal to 1,000 shares.
2) Initial account is equal to what it would cost
   to trade 1,000 shares at a price/share at that time.
3) Commission is equal to 12 cents per round turn.
4) Plan handles less or more shares.

1995
IBM - Gann Swing Chartist®
Basic Swing Plan (Real Time)   Fibonacci Trader®

Trade #	Date	L/S	Price	Rule #	Profit	(Loss)	Accum.	A/C Equity	50% Margin
1	12/19/94	L	71 5/8	Buy 1				$71,625.00	$35,812.50
PP	1/20/95	S	75 3/8	PP1	3 6/8		$3,630.00	$75,255.00	$39,442.50
2	2/1/95	L	73 5/8	Buy 1				$76,135.00	$40,322.50
3	2/21/95	S	74 5/8	Sell 2	1		$4,510.00	$74,765.00	$38,952.50
PP	3/1/95	L	75 7/8	PP2		-1 2/8	$3,140.00		
4	3/2/95	L	76 1/4	Buy 2					
PP	3/22/95	S	81 5/8	PP1	5 3/8		$8,395.00	$80,020.00	$44,207.50
5	3/27/95	L	84	Buy 3					
PP	3/29/95	S	83	PP1		-2	$6,275.00	$77,900.00	$42,087.50
6	4/10/95	L	85	Buy 3					
PP	5/1/95	S	92	PP1	7		$13,155.00	$84,780.00	$48,967.50
7	5/3/95	L	94 3/8	Buy 1					
PP	5/18/95	S	93 1/8	PP1		-1 2/8	$11,785.00	$83,410.00	$47,597.50
8	5/23/95	L	96 1/8	Buy 2					
9	5/30/95	S	92 1/2	Sell 2		-3 5/8	$8,040.00	$79,665.00	$43,852.50
PP	6/13/95	L	91 3/4	PP1	6/8		$8,670.00	$80,295.00	$44,482.50
10	6/20/95	L	95 3/8	Buy 2					
PP	6/27/95	S	94 7/8	PP2		-4/8	$8,050.00	$79,675.00	$43,862.50
11	7/6/95	L	98 7/8	Buy 1					
PP	7/19/95	S	101 1/4	PP2	2 3/8		$10,305.00	$81,930.00	$46,117.50
12	7/25/95	L	108 5/8	Buy 3					
PP	7/31/95	S	108 7/8	PP1	2/8		$10,435.00	$82,060.00	$46,247.50
13	8/14/95	L	110 3/4	Buy 1					
PP	8/21/95	S	109 5/8	PP2		-1 1/8	$9,190.00	$80,815.00	$45,002.50
14	8/21/95	S	108 1/4	Sell 2					
PP	9/19/95	L	94 7/8	PP2	13 3/8		$22,445.00	$94,070.00	$58,257.50
15	9/22/95	S	93 7/8	Sell 1					
PP	10/12/95	L	93	PP1	7/8		$23,200.00	$94,825.00	$59,012.50
16	10/17/95	L	95 3/8	Buy 2					
PP	10/20/95	S	95 3/8	PP1	0		$23,080.00	$94,705.00	$58,892.50
17	10/23/95	L	99	Buy 1					
PP	10/26/95	S	95 1/8	PP2		-3 7/8	$19,085.00	$90,710.00	$54,897.50
18	11/2/95	L	99 1/8	Buy 3					

1995
IBM - Gann Swing Chartist®
Basic Swing Plan (Real Time)

Fibonacci Trader®

Trade #	Date	L/S	Price	Rule #	Profit	(Loss)	Accum.	A/C Equity	50% Margin
PP	11/7/95	S	98 3/4	PP1		- 3/8	$ 18,590.00	$90,215.00	$54,402.50
19	11/14/95	S	96 3/8	Sell 2					
PP	11/27/95	L	97	PP2		- 5/8	$ 17,845.00	$89,470.00	$53,657.50
20	12/13/95	S	94 1/2	Sell 1					
PP	12/19/95	L	91 7/8	PP1	2 5/8		$ 20,350.00	$91,975.00	$56,162.50

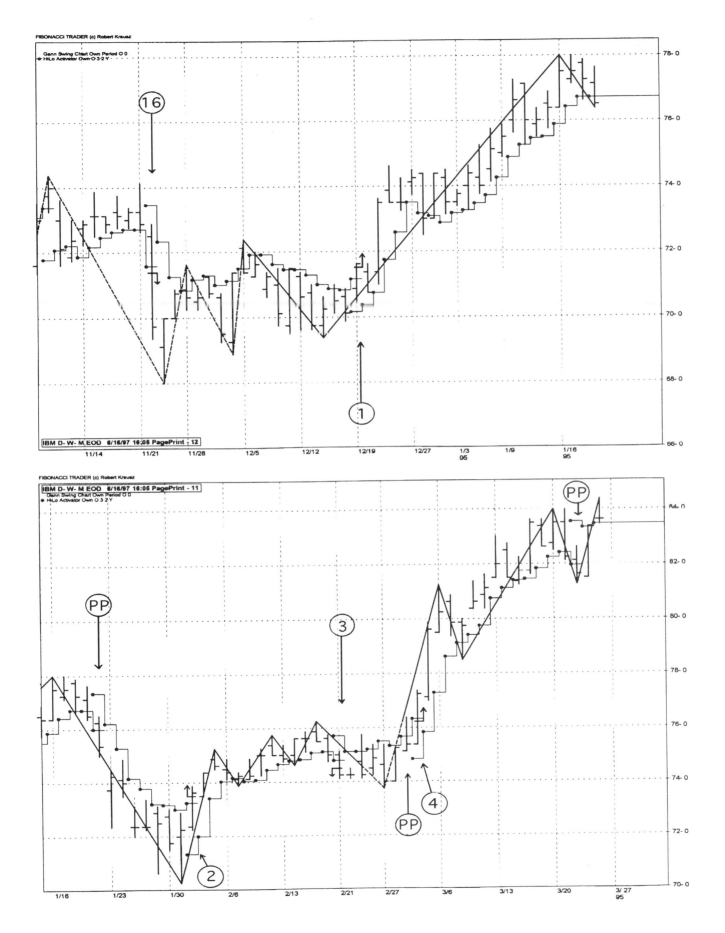

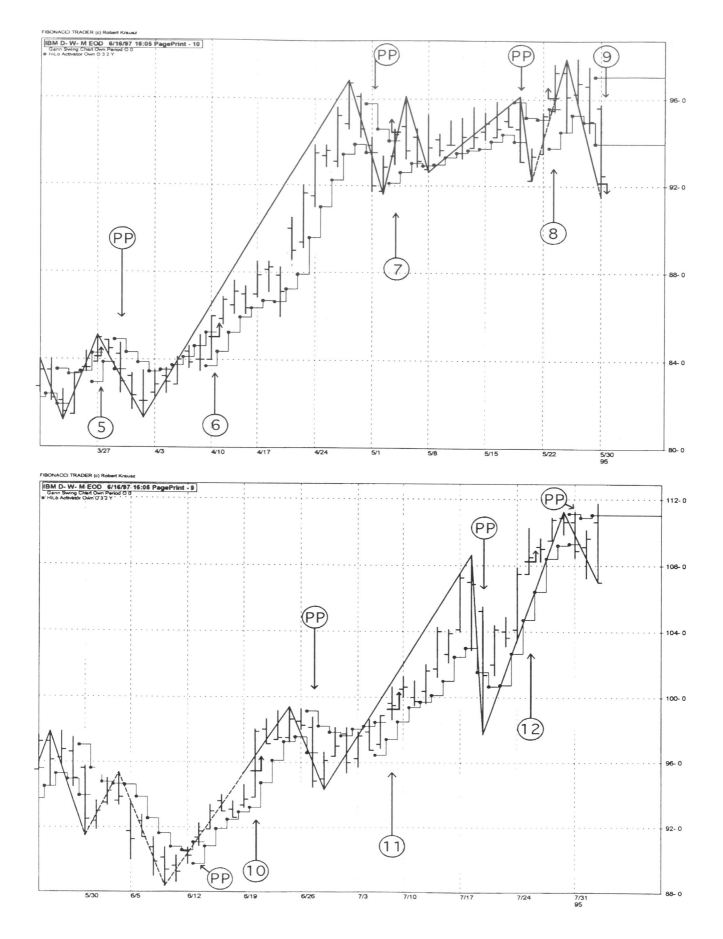

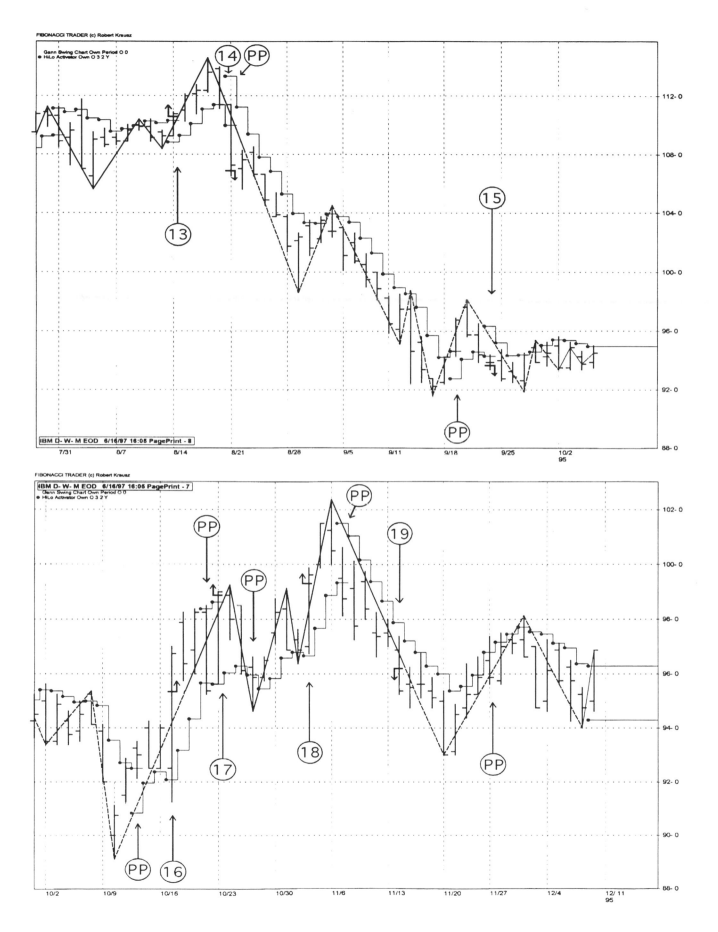

163

IBM - 1996
BASIC SWING PLAN
GANN SWING CHARTIST- FIBONACCI TRADER ®

With 100% Margin

Beginning Equity	$90,250.00	Ending Equity	$153,840.00
Total Net Profit	$65,750.00	Gross Loss	($26,375.00)
Gross Profit	$92,125.00	Total Commissions	$2,160.00
Total No. Trades	18	Percentage Profitable	44%
No. Winning Trades	8	No. Losing Trades	10

Largest Winning Trade	$30,500.00	Largest Losing Trade	($4,500.00)
Average Winning Trade	$11,515.63	Average Losing Trade	($2,637.50)
Ratio Average Win/Loss	4.37	Average Trade	$3,652.78
Max. Consecutive Winners	3	Max. Consecutive Losses	3
Largest Consecutive Drawdown (%)	8.20%	Largest Consecutive Drawdown	($10,125.00)

Return on Account	70%
Profit/Drawdown Ratio	6.49

With 50% Margin

Beginning Equity	$45,125.00	Ending Equity	$108,715.00
Total Net Profit	$65,750.00	Gross Loss	($26,375.00)
Gross Profit	$92,125.00	Total Commissions	$2,160.00
Total No. Trades	18	Percentage Profitable	44%
No. Winning Trades	8	No. Losing Trades	10

Largest Winning Trade	$30,500.00	Largest Losing Trade	($4,500.00)
Average Winning Trade	$11,515.63	Average Losing Trade	($2,637.50)
Ratio Average Win/Loss	4.37	Average Trade	$3,652.78
Max. Consecutive Winners	3	Max. Consecutive Losses	3
Largest Consecutive Drawdown (%)	12.92%	Largest Consecutive Drawdown	($10,125.00)

Return on Account	141%
Profit/Drawdown Ratio	6.49

Notes:
1) Each trade is equal to 1,000 shares.
2) Initial account is equal to what it would cost
   to trade 1,000 shares at a price/share at that time.
3) Commission is equal to 12 cents per round turn.
4) Plan handles less or more shares.

1996

IBM - Gann Swing Chartist®

Basic Swing Plan (Real Time)

Fibonacci Trader®

Trade #	Date	L/S	Price	Rule #	Profit	(Loss)	Accum.	A/C Equity	50% Margin
1	12/28/95	S	90 1/4	Sell 1				$90,250.00	$45,125.00
PP	1/16/96	L	87 3/8	PP2	2 7/8		$ 2,875.00	$93,005.00	$47,880.00
2	1/18/96	L	92 1/8	Buy 2					
PP	2/29/96	S	122 5/8	PP1	30 4/8		$ 33,375.00	$123,505.00	$78,380.00
3	3/15/96	L	119 7/8	Buy 1					
PP	3/20/96	S	118 1/2	PP2		-1 3/8	$ 32,000.00	$122,130.00	$77,005.00
4	3/25/96	S	112 1/4	Sell 2					
PP	4/2/96	L	115 1/8	PP2		-3 1/8	$ 28,875.00	$119,005.00	$73,880.00
5	4/12/96	S	111 1/2	Sell 1					
PP	4/16/96	L	115 5/8	PP2		-4 1/8	$ 24,750.00	$114,880.00	$69,755.00
6	4/17/96	S	109 7/8	Sell 3					
PP	4/25/96	L	108 3/8	PP1	1 4/8		$ 26,250.00	$116,380.00	$71,255.00
7	5/1/96	S	107	Sell 1					
PP	5/9/96	L	107 1/4	PP2		-2/8	$ 26,000.00	$116,130.00	$71,005.00
8	5/17/96	L	111	Buy 1					
PP	5/23/96	S	109 1/4	PP1		-1 6/8	$ 24,250.00	$114,380.00	$69,255.00
9	6/6/96	S	103 5/8	Sell 3					
PP	6/11/96	L	103 3/8	PP2	2/8		$ 24,500.00	$114,630.00	$69,505.00
10	7/3/96	S	98 1/2	Sell 1					
PP	7/9/96	L	99 3/4	PP2		-1 2/8	$ 23,250.00	$113,380.00	$68,255.00
11	7/11/96	S	97 1/2	Sell 3					
PP	7/16/96	L	95 3/4	PP2	1 6/8		$ 25,000.00	$115,130.00	$70,005.00
12	7/25/96	L	97 7/8	Buy 2					
PP	8/13/96	S	109 1/4	PP1	11 5/8		$ 36,625.00	$126,755.00	$81,630.00
13	8/21/96	L	112 1/4	Buy 1					
PP	10/9/96	S	126 3/8	PP1	14 1/8		$ 50,750.00	$140,880.00	$95,755.00
14	10/11/96	L	129 7/8	Buy 1					
PP	10/17/96	S	125 5/8	PP1		-4 2/8	$ 46,500.00	$136,630.00	$91,505.00
15	10/18/96	S	125 1/2	Sell 2					
16	10/31/96	L	129	Buy 1		-3 4/8	$ 43,000.00	$133,130.00	$88,005.00
PP	12/5/96	S	158 1/2	PP1	29 4/8		$ 72,500.00	$162,630.00	$117,505.00
17	12/16/96	S	151	Sell 2					
PP	12/18/96	L	155 1/2	PP2		-4 4/8	$ 68,000.00	$158,130.00	$113,005.00

165

1996
IBM - Gann Swing Chartist®
Basic Swing Plan (Real Time)

Fibonacci Trader®

Trade #	Date	L/S	Price	Rule #	Profit	(Loss)	Accum.	A/C Equity	50% Margin
18	12/23/96	S	154 1/4	Sell 1					
PP	1/3/97	L	156 1/2	PP2		-2 2/8	$ 65,750.00	$155,880.00	$110,755.00

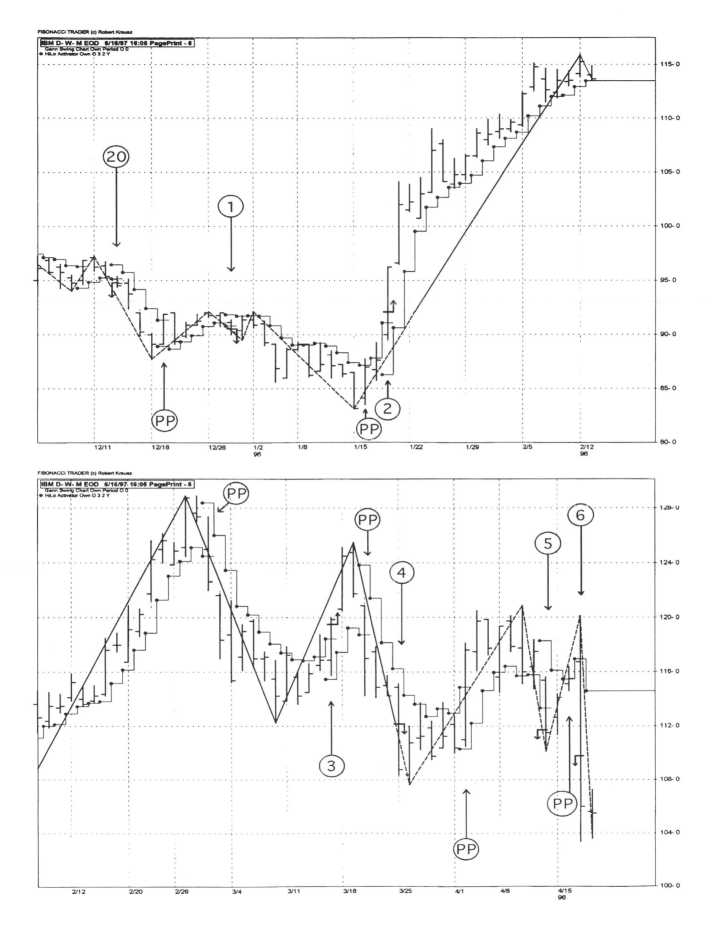

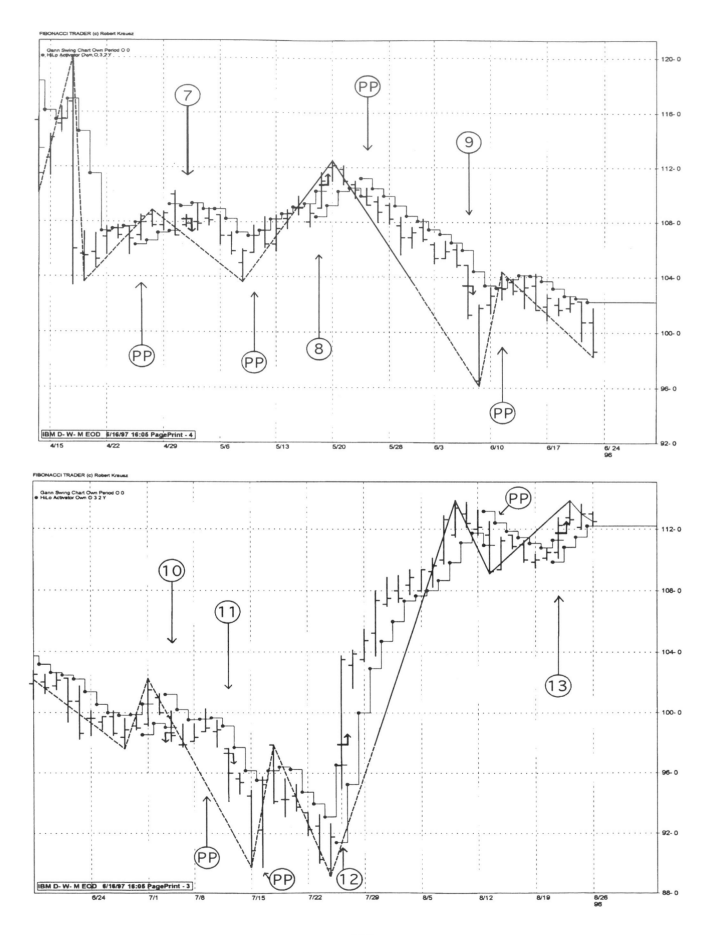

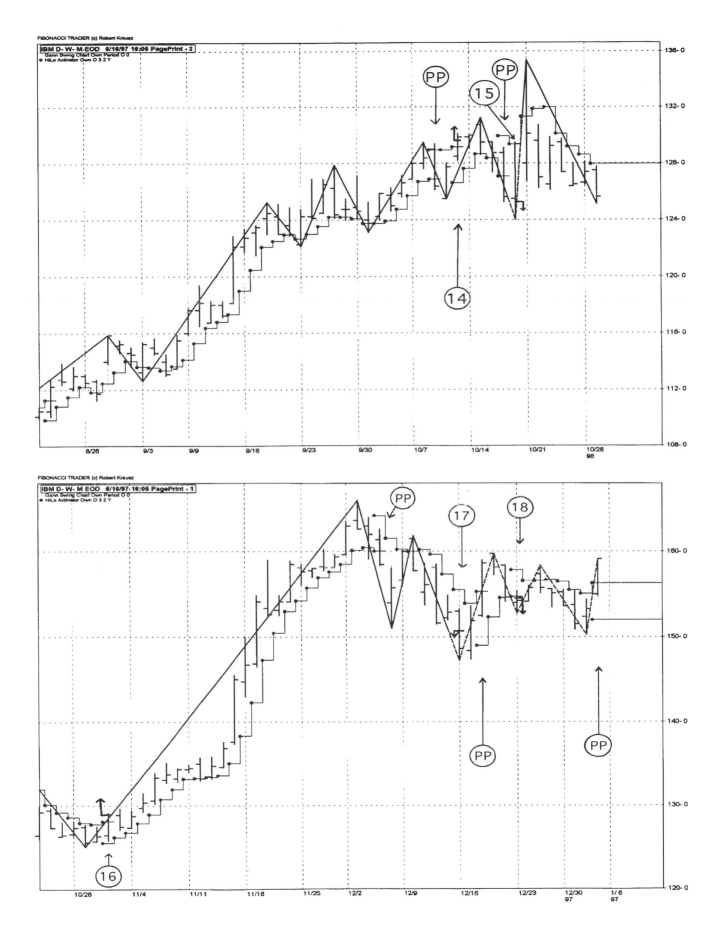

169

PHILIP MORRIS - 1992-1996 (5 YRS.) RT.
BASIC SWING PLAN - COMPOSITE
GANN SWING CHARTIST - FIBONACCI TRADER ®

With 100% Margin

Beginning Equity	$69,375.00	Ending Equity	$158,160.00
Total Net Profit	$98,625.00	Gross Loss	($42,875.00)
Gross Profit	$141,500.00	Total Commissions	$9,840.00
Total No. Trades	82	Percentage Profitable	56%
No. Winning Trades	46	No. Losing Trades	36

Largest Winning Trade	$13,875.00	Largest Losing Trade	($3,250.00)
Average Winning Trade	$3,076.09	Average Losing Trade	($1,190.97)
Max. Consecutive Winners	7	Max. Consecutive Losses	4
Average Drawdown (%)	5.34%	Average Drawdown ($)	($4,208.00)

Average Return on Account	26%
Profit/Drawdown Ratio	23.44

With 50% Margin

Beginning Equity	$34,687.50	Ending Equity	$123,472.50
Total Net Profit	$98,625.00	Gross Loss	($42,875.00)
Gross Profit	$141,500.00	Total Commissions	$9,840.00
Total No. Trades	82	Percentage Profitable	56%
No. Winning Trades	46	No. Losing Trades	10

Largest Winning Trade	$13,875.00	Largest Losing Trade	($3,250.00)
Average Winning Trade	$3,076.09	Average Losing Trade	($4,287.50)
Max. Consecutive Winners	7	Max. Consecutive Losses	4
Average Drawdown (%)	9.67%	Average Drawdown ($)	($4,208.00)

Average Return on Account	52%
Profit/Drawdown Ratio	23.44

Notes:
1) Each trade is equal to 1,000 shares.
2) Initial account is equal to what it would cost
   to trade 1,000 shares at a price/share at that time.
3) Commission is equal to 12 cents per round turn per share.
4) Plan handles less or more shares, percentages are the same.

171

PHILIP MORRIS - 1992
BASIC SWING PLAN
GANN SWING PLAN - FIBONACCI TRADER®

With 100% Margin

Beginning Equity	$69,375.00	Ending Equity	$87,950.00
Total Net Profit	$20,375.00	Gross Loss	($6,250.00)
Gross Profit	$26,625.00	Total Commissions	$1,800.00
Total No. Trades	15	Percentage Profitable	67%
No. Winning Trades	10	No. Losing Trades	5

Largest Winning Trade	$9,625.00	Largest Losing Trade	($2,500.00)
Average Winning Trade	$2,662.50	Average Losing Trade	($1,250.00)
Ratio Average Win/Loss	2.13	Average Trade	$1,358.33
Max. Consecutive Winners	7	Max. Consecutive Losses	4
Largest Consecutive Drawdown (%)	7.34%	Largest Consecutive Drawdown	($5,980.00)

Return on Account	27%
Profit/Drawdown Ratio	3.41

With 50% Margin

Beginning Equity	$34,687.50	Ending Equity	$53,262.50
Total Net Profit	$20,375.00	Gross Loss	($6,250.00)
Gross Profit	$26,625.00	Total Commissions	$1,800.00
Total No. Trades	15	Percentage Profitable	67%
No. Winning Trades	10	No. Losing Trades	5

Largest Winning Trade	$9,625.00	Largest Losing Trade	($2,500.00)
Average Winning Trade	$2,662.50	Average Losing Trade	($1,250.00)
Ratio Average Win/Loss	2.13	Average Trade	$1,358.33
Max. Consecutive Winners	7	Max. Consecutive Losses	4
Largest Consecutive Drawdown (%)	12.77%	Largest Consecutive Drawdown	($5,980.00)

Return on Account	54%
Profit/Drawdown Ratio	3.41

Notes:
1) Each trade is equal to 1,000 shares.
2) Initial account is equal to what it would cost
   to trade 1,000 shares at a price/share at that time.
3) Commission is equal to 12 cents per round turn.
4) Plan handles less or more shares.

1992
J.P. Morgan - Gann Swing Chartist®
Basic Swing Plan (End of Day)

Fibonacci Trader®

Trade #	Date	L/S	Price	Rule #	Profit	(Loss)	Accum.	A/C Equity	50% Margin
1	12/20/91	L	63 1/2	Buy 1				$63,500.00	$31,750.00
PP	1/2/92	S	67 7/8	PP1	4 3/8		$ 4,255.00	$67,755.00	$36,005.00
2	1/7/92	L	69	Buy 1				$66,135.00	$34,385.00
PP	1/9/92	S	67 1/2	PP1		-1 4/8	$ 2,635.00	$66,135.00	$34,385.00
3	1/13/92	S	66 1/2	Sell 2					
PP	2/4/92	L	62 1/8	PP1	4 3/8		$ 6,890.00	$70,390.00	$38,640.00
4	2/7/92	S	61 3/8	Sell 1					
PP	2/20/92	L	60 1/2	PP1	7/8		$ 7,645.00	$71,145.00	$39,395.00
5	2/25/92	L	60 7/8	Buy 2					
PP	2/28/92	S	60 1/8	PP1		- 6/8	$ 6,775.00	$70,275.00	$38,525.00
6	3/6/92	S	57 5/8	Sell 2					
PP	4/22/92	L	54 1/4	PP2	3 3/8		$10,030.00	$73,530.00	$41,780.00
7	4/22/92	L	55 5/8	Buy 1					
PP	5/13/92	S	56 1/4	PP1	5/8		$10,535.00	$74,035.00	$42,285.00
8	5/20/92	L	56 7/8	Buy 1					
PP	5/26/92	S	55	PP1		-1 7/8	$ 8,540.00	$72,040.00	$40,290.00
9	5/29/92	L	57 3/8	Buy 1					
PP	6/10/92	S	55 1/2	PP1		-1 7/8	$ 6,545.00	$70,045.00	$38,295.00
10	6/17/92	S	54	Sell 2					
PP	6/23/92	L	54 1/4	PP1		- 2/8	$ 6,175.00	$69,675.00	$37,925.00
11	7/2/92	L	57 3/4	Buy 1					
PP	7/15/92	S	60 1/4	PP1	2 4/8		$ 8,555.00	$72,055.00	$40,305.00
12	7/28/92	L	60 1/4	Buy 1					
13	8/19/92	S	59 3/8	Sell 2		- 7/8	$ 7,560.00	$71,060.00	$39,310.00
PP	8/27/92	L	59 3/4	PP1		- 3/8	$ 7,065.00	$70,565.00	$38,815.00
14	9/4/92	L	60 1/8	Buy 2					
PP	10/5/92	S	61	PP1	7/8		$ 7,820.00	$71,320.00	$39,570.00
15	10/15/92	L	61 7/8	Buy 1					
PP	10/22/92	S	61 7/8	PP1	0		$ 7,700.00	$71,200.00	$39,450.00
16	10/30/92	L	63	Buy 1					
PP	11/12/92	S	63 3/8	PP1	3/8		$ 7,955.00	$71,455.00	$39,705.00
17	11/13/92	S	63 1/4	Sell 2					
PP	11/25/92	L	62 3/8	PP1		- 7/8	$ 6,960.00	$70,460.00	$38,710.00

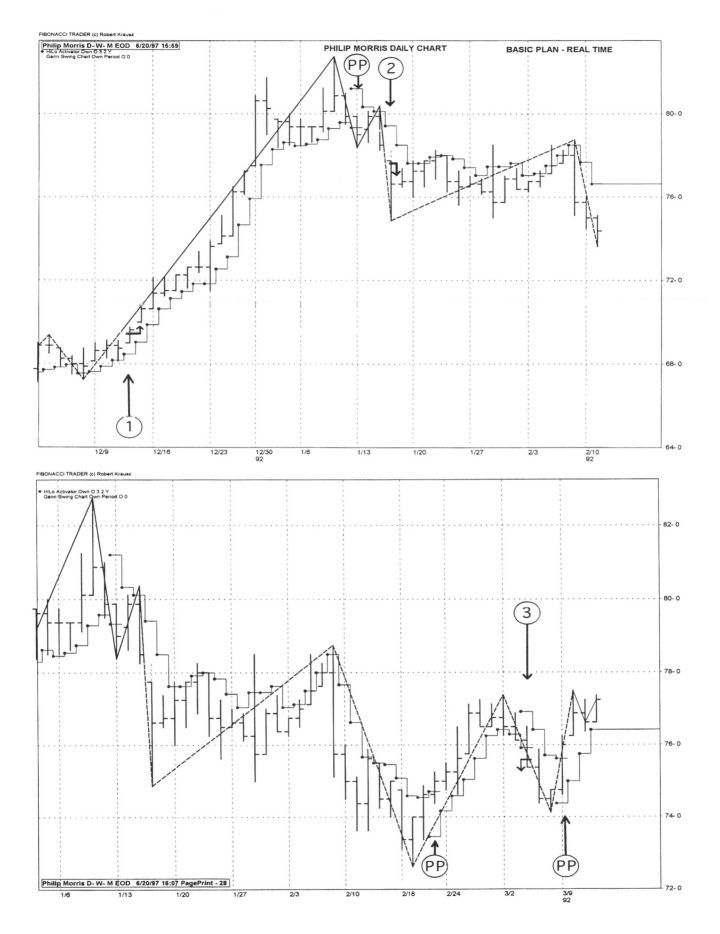

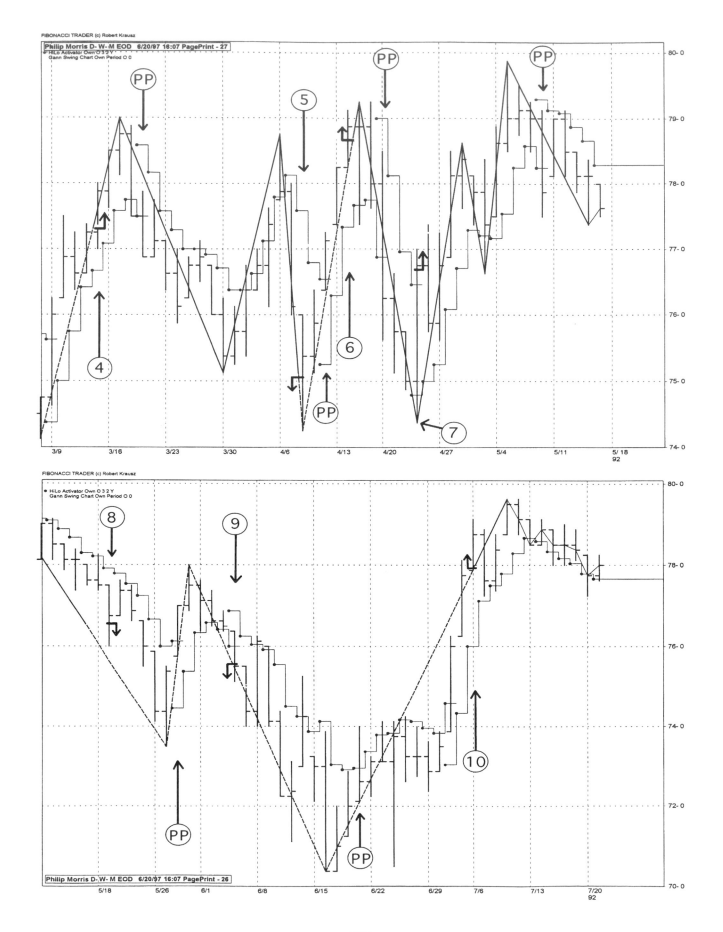

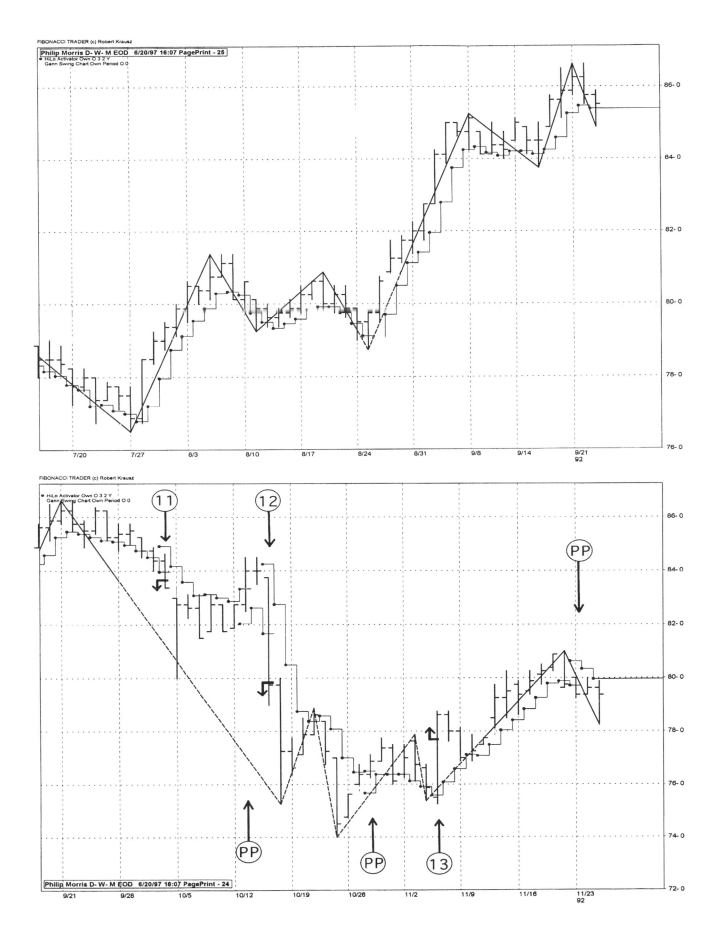

PHILIP MORRIS - 1993
BASIC SWING PLAN
GANN SWING PLAN - FIBONACCI TRADER®

With 100% Margin

Beginning Equity	$77,125.00	Ending Equity	$91,845.00
Total Net Profit	$17,000.00	Gross Loss	($7,500.00)
Gross Profit	$24,500.00	Total Commissions	$2,280.00
Total No. Trades	19	Percentage Profitable	53%
No. Winning Trades	10	No. Losing Trades	9

Largest Winning Trade	$10,250.00	Largest Losing Trade	($1,875.00)
Average Winning Trade	$2,450.00	Average Losing Trade	($833.33)
Ratio Average Win/Loss	2.94	Average Trade	$894.74
Max. Consecutive Winners	3	Max. Consecutive Losses	2
Largest Consecutive Drawdown (%)	4.61%	Largest Consecutive Drawdown	($3,720.00)

Return on Account	19%
Profit/Drawdown Ratio	4.57

With 50% Margin

Beginning Equity	$38,562.50	Ending Equity	$53,282.50
Total Net Profit	$17,000.00	Gross Loss	($7,500.00)
Gross Profit	$24,500.00	Total Commissions	$2,280.00
Total No. Trades	19	Percentage Profitable	53%
No. Winning Trades	10	No. Losing Trades	9

Largest Winning Trade	$10,250.00	Largest Losing Trade	($1,875.00)
Average Winning Trade	$2,450.00	Average Losing Trade	($833.33)
Ratio Average Win/Loss	2.94	Average Trade	$894.74
Max. Consecutive Winners	3	Max. Consecutive Losses	2
Largest Consecutive Drawdown (%)	8.82%	Largest Consecutive Drawdown	($3,720.00)

Return on Account	38%
Profit/Drawdown Ratio	4.57

Notes:
1) Each trade is equal to 1,000 shares.
2) Initial account is equal to what it would cost
   to trade 1,000 shares at a price/share at that time.
3) Commission is equal to 12 cents per round turn.
4) Plan handles less or more shares.

Philip Morris - Gann Swing Chartist®

Basic Swing Plan (Real Time)

Fibonacci Trader®

Trade #	Date	L/S	Price	Rule #	Profit	(Loss)	Accum.	A/C Equity	50% Margin
1	12/31/92	S	77 1/8	Sell 1				$77,125.00	$38,562.50
PP	1/8/93	L	73 7/8	PP2	3 2/8		$ 3,130.00	$80,255.00	$41,692.50
2	1/13/93	S	73	Sell 1					$42,197.50
PP	1/21/93	L	72 3/8	PP1	5/8		$ 3,635.00	$80,760.00	$42,197.50
3	1/29/93	L	75 1/8	Buy 1					
PP	2/9/93	S	73 5/8	PP2		-1 4/8	$ 2,015.00	$79,140.00	$40,577.50
4	2/17/93	S	70 1/4	Sell 2					
PP	2/26/93	L	67 1/4	PP2	3		$ 4,895.00	$82,020.00	$43,457.50
5	3/22/93	S	63	Sell 3					
PP	3/30/93	L	64	PP1		-1	$ 3,775.00	$80,900.00	$42,337.50
6	4/2/93	S	58 3/8	Sell 2					
PP	4/13/93	L	48 1/8	PP1	10 2/8		$13,905.00	$91,030.00	$52,467.50
7	4/23/93	S	47	Sell 1					
PP	4/29/93	L	47 1/4	PP1		- 2/8	$13,535.00	$90,660.00	$52,097.50
8	5/6/93	L	49 1/8	Buy 2					
PP	5/12/93	S	50	PP1	7/8		$14,290.00	$91,415.00	$52,852.50
9	5/25/93	L	51 1/4	Buy 1					
PP	5/28/93	S	50 1/8	PP1		-1 1/8	$13,045.00	$90,170.00	$51,607.50
10	6/8/93	S	49 5/8	Sell 2					
PP	6/11/93	L	49 5/8	PP1	0		$12,925.00	$90,050.00	$51,487.50
11	6/30/93	S	48 1/4	Sell 1					
PP	7/8/93	L	48 3/4	PP1		- 4/8	$12,305.00	$89,430.00	$50,867.50
12	7/9/93	L	49 1/2	Buy 2					
PP	7/16/93	S	47 3/4	PP1	1 6/8		$13,935.00	$91,060.00	$52,497.50
13	7/23/93	S	47 1/8	Sell 2					
PP	8/17/93	L	48 3/8	PP1		-1 2/8	$12,565.00	$89,690.00	$51,127.50
14	8/19/93	L	50 1/2	Buy 2					
PP	8/25/93	S	48 5/8	PP1		-1 7/8	$10,570.00	$87,695.00	$49,132.50
15	9/9/93	S	47 5/8	Sell 2					
PP	10/6/93	L	47	PP1	5/8		$11,075.00	$88,200.00	$49,637.50
16	10/11/93	L	48 3/4	Buy 2					
PP	11/4/93	S	52 5/8	PP1	3 7/8		$14,830.00	$91,955.00	$53,392.50
17	11/5/93	L	55 1/2	Buy 1					

1993

Philip Morris - Gann Swing Chartist®
Basic Swing Plan (Real Time)

Fibonacci Trader®

					1/4				
PP	11/17/93	S	55 3/4	PP1			$14,960.00	$92,085.00	$53,522.50
18	12/7/93	L	56 1/8	Buy 1					
PP	12/10/93	S	54 7/8	PP1		-1 1/4	$13,590.00	$90,715.00	$52,152.50
19	12/15/93	S	54 3/4	Sell 2					
PP	12/22/93	L	56	PP1		1 1/4	$14,720.00	$91,845.00	$53,282.50

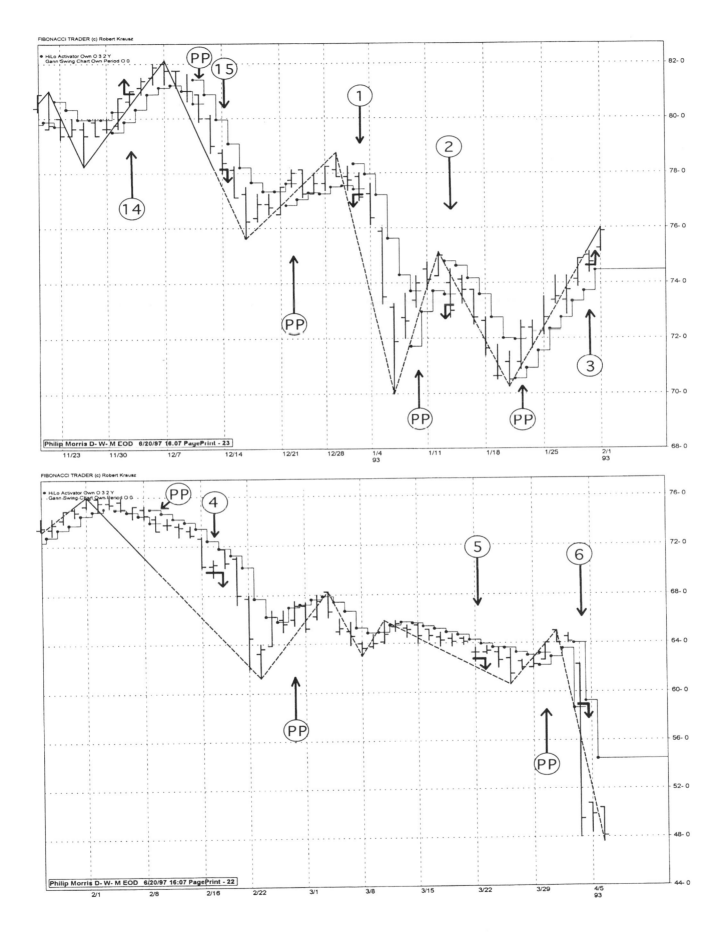

181

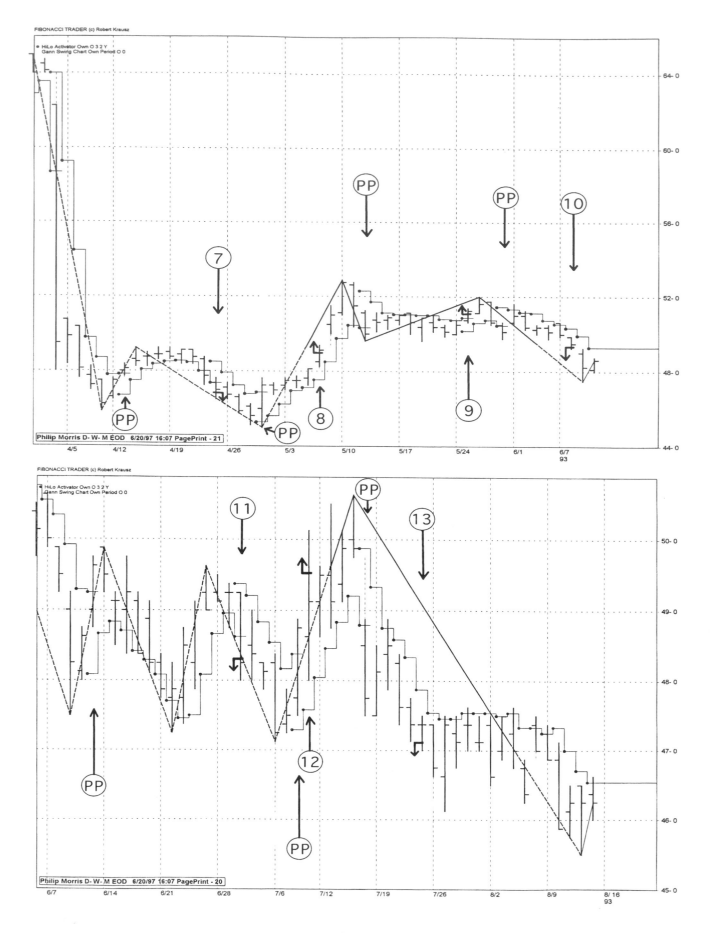

FIBONACCI TRADER (c) Robert Krausz

• HiLo Activator Own O 3 2 Y
Gann Swing Chart Own Period O 0

Philip Morris D- W- M EOD   6/20/97 16:07 PagePrint - 21

4/5   4/12   4/19   4/26   5/3   5/10   5/17   5/24   6/1   6/7
93

FIBONACCI TRADER (c) Robert Krausz

• HiLo Activator Own O 3 2 Y
Gann Swing Chart Own Period O 0

Philip Morris D- W- M EOD   6/20/97 16:07 PagePrint - 20

6/7   6/14   6/21   6/28   7/6   7/12   7/19   7/26   8/2   8/9   8/ 16
93

182

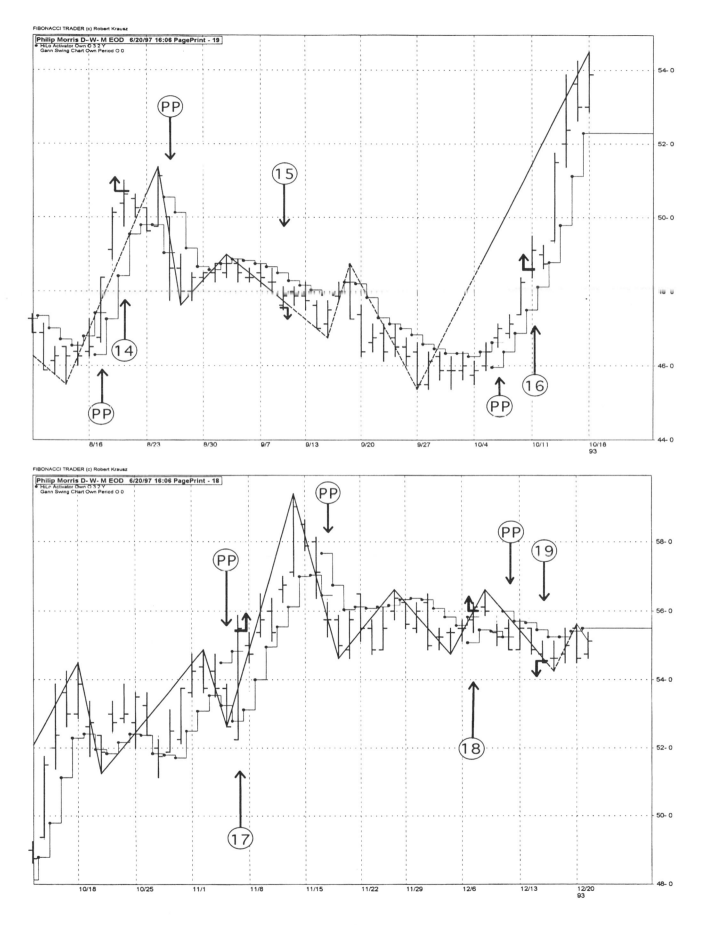

PHILIP MORRIS - 1994
BASIC SWING PLAN
GANN SWING PLAN - FIBONACCI TRADER®

With 100% Margin

Beginning Equity	$56,500.00	Ending Equity	$74,440.00
Total Net Profit	$19,500.00	Gross Loss	($3,500.00)
Gross Profit	$23,000.00	Total Commissions	$1,560.00
Total No. Trades	13	Percentage Profitable	69%
No. Winning Trades	9	No. Losing Trades	4

Largest Winning Trade	$9,000.00	Largest Losing Trade	($1,500.00)
Average Winning Trade	$2,555.56	Average Losing Trade	($875.00)
Ratio Average Win/Loss	2.92	Average Trade	$1,500.00
Max. Consecutive Winners	4	Max. Consecutive Losses	2
Largest Consecutive Drawdown (%)	2.72%	Largest Consecutive Drawdown	($1,620.00)

Return on Account	32%
Profit/Drawdown Ratio	12.04

With 50% Margin

Beginning Equity	$28,250.00	Ending Equity	$46,190.00
Total Net Profit	$19,500.00	Gross Loss	($3,500.00)
Gross Profit	$23,000.00	Total Commissions	$1,560.00
Total No. Trades	13	Percentage Profitable	69%
No. Winning Trades	9	No. Losing Trades	4

Largest Winning Trade	$9,000.00	Largest Losing Trade	($1,500.00)
Average Winning Trade	$2,555.56	Average Losing Trade	($875.00)
Ratio Average Win/Loss	2.92	Average Trade	$1,500.00
Max. Consecutive Winners	4	Max. Consecutive Losses	2
Largest Consecutive Drawdown (%)	5.16%	Largest Consecutive Drawdown	($1,620.00)

Return on Account	64%
Profit/Drawdown Ratio	12.04

Notes:
1) Each trade is equal to 1,000 shares.
2) Initial account is equal to what it would cost
   to trade 1,000 shares at a price/share at that time.
3) Commission is equal to 12 cents per round turn.
4) Plan handles less or more shares.

1994
Philip Morris - Gann Swing Chartist®
Basic Swing Plan (Real Time)

Fibonacci Trader®

Trade #	Date	L/S	Price	Rule #	Profit	(Loss)	Accum.	A/C Equity	50% Margin
1	12/30/93	L	56 1/2	Buy 2				$56,500.00	$28,250.00
PP	1/17/94	S	56 5/8	PP1	1/8		$ 5.00	$56,505.00	$28,255.00
2	1/26/94	L	59 1/4	Buy 1					$28,260.00
PP	2/2/94	S	59 3/8	PP1	1/8		$ 10.00	$56,510.00	
3	2/8/94	S	59 1/4	Sell 2					$28,015.00
PP	2/15/94	L	59 3/8	PP1		- 1/8	$ (235.00)	$56,265.00	
4	2/17/94	S	58 1/8	Sell 1					$27,145.00
PP	2/23/94	L	58 7/8	PP1		- 6/8	$ (1,105.00)	$55,395.00	
5	2/28/94	S	57	Sell 3					$27,150.00
PP	3/7/94	L	56 7/8	PP1	1/8		$ (1,100.00)	$55,400.00	
6	3/17/94	S	54 7/8	Sell 1					$31,405.00
PP	4/7/94	L	50 1/2	PP1	4 3/8		$ 3,155.00	$59,655.00	
7	4/11/94	S	48 1/8	Sell 1					$29,785.00
PP	4/14/94	L	49 5/8	PP1		-1 4/8	$ 1,535.00	$58,035.00	
8	5/4/94	S	52 1/2	Sell 1					$31,665.00
PP	5/12/94	L	50 1/2	PP1	2		$ 3,415.00	$59,915.00	
9	5/23/94	S	55 1/4	Buy 2					$36,170.00
PP	5/26/94	L	50 5/8	PP1	4 5/8		$ 7,920.00	$64,420.00	
10	6/6/94	L	50 7/8	Buy 1					$45,050.00
PP	9/9/94	S	59 7/8	PP1	9		$ 16,800.00	$73,300.00	
11	10/11/94	L	61 1/8	Buy 1					$45,930.00
PP	10/31/94	S	62 1/8	PP2	1		$ 17,680.00	$74,180.00	
12	11/14/94	L	62 5/8	Buy 1					$44,685.00
PP	11/21/94	S	61 1/2	PP1		-1 1/8	$ 16,435.00	$72,935.00	
13	12/1/94	S	59 3/8	Sell 2					$46,190.00
PP	12/13/94	L	57 3/4	PP1	1 5/8		$ 17,940.00	$74,440.00	

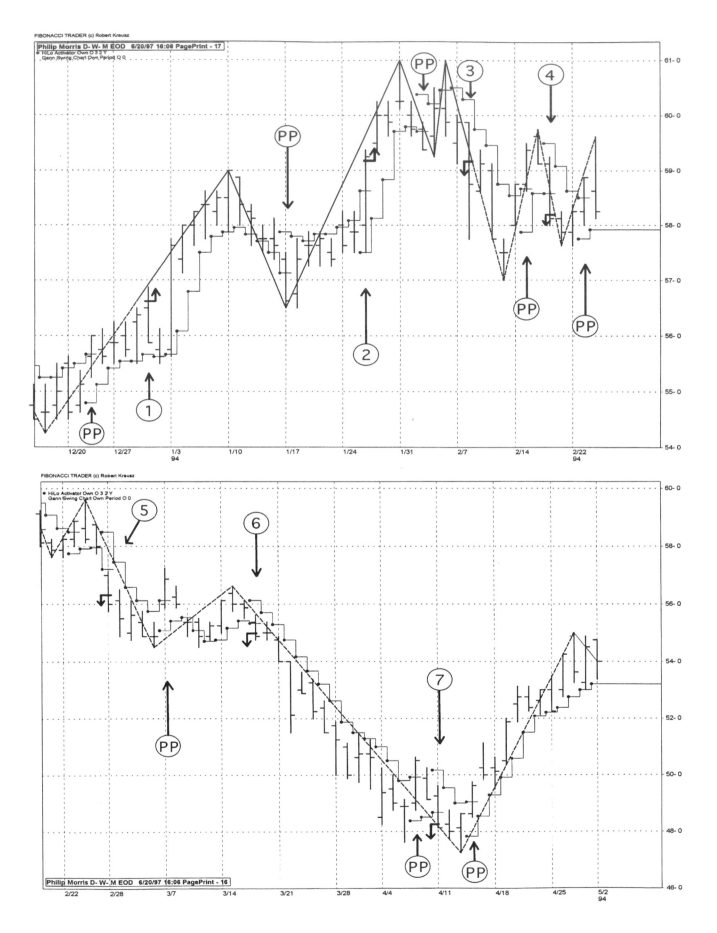

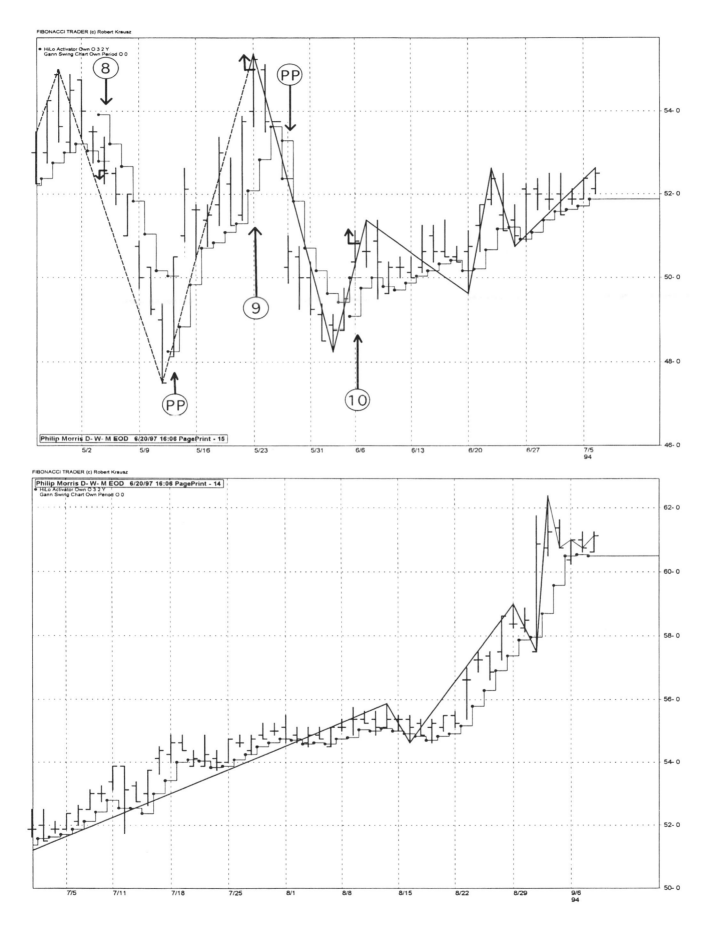

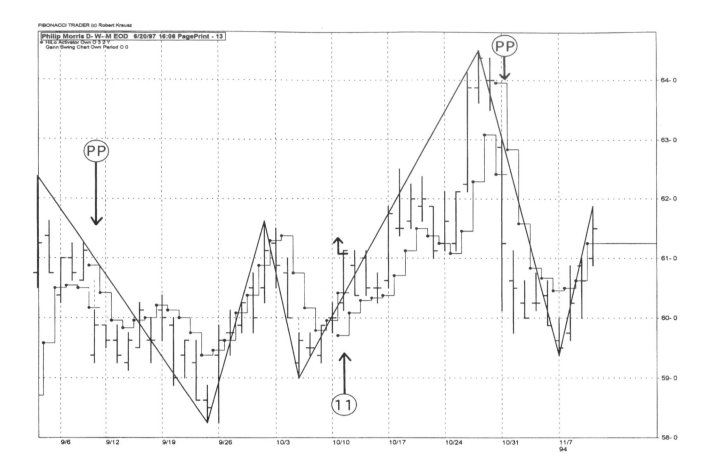

PHILIP MORRIS - 1995
BASIC SWING PLAN
GANN SWING PLAN - FIBONACCI TRADER®

With 100% Margin

Beginning Equity	$58,750.00	Ending Equity	$75,820.00
Total Net Profit	$18,750.00	Gross Loss	($8,500.00)
Gross Profit	$27,250.00	Total Commissions	$1,680.00
Total No. Trades	14	Percentage Profitable	50%
No. Winning Trades	7	No. Losing Trades	7

Largest Winning Trade	$13,875.00	Largest Losing Trade	($1,875.00)
Average Winning Trade	$3,892.86	Average Losing Trade	($1,214.29)
Ratio Average Win/Loss	3.21	Average Trade	$1,339.29
Max. Consecutive Winners	2	Max. Consecutive Losses	3
Largest Consecutive Drawdown (%)	7.05%	Largest Consecutive Drawdown	($4,610.00)

Return on Account	29%
Profit/Drawdown Ratio	4.07

With 50% Margin

Beginning Equity	$29,375.00	Ending Equity	$46,445.00
Total Net Profit	$18,750.00	Gross Loss	($8,500.00)
Gross Profit	$27,250.00	Total Commissions	$1,680.00
Total No. Trades	14	Percentage Profitable	50%
No. Winning Trades	7	No. Losing Trades	7

Largest Winning Trade	$13,875.00	Largest Losing Trade	($1,875.00)
Average Winning Trade	$3,892.86	Average Losing Trade	($1,214.29)
Ratio Average Win/Loss	3.21	Average Trade	$1,339.29
Max. Consecutive Winners	2	Max. Consecutive Losses	3
Largest Consecutive Drawdown (%)	12.79%	Largest Consecutive Drawdown	($4,610.00)

Return on Account	58%
Profit/Drawdown Ratio	4.07

Notes:
1) Each trade is equal to 1,000 shares.
2) Initial account is equal to what it would cost
   to trade 1,000 shares at a price/share at that time.
3) Commission is equal to 12 cents per round turn.
4) Plan handles less or more shares.

Philip Morris - Gann Swing Chartist®
Basic Swing Plan (Real Time)

Fibonacci Trader®

Trade #	Date	L/S	Price	Rule #	Profit	(Loss)	Accum.	A/C Equity	50% Margin
1	1/4/95	L	58 7/8	Buy 2				$58,750.00	$29,375.00
PP	2/9/95	S	60 5/8	PP1	1 6/8		$ 1,630.00	$60,380.00	$31,005.00
2	2/14/95	L	62	Buy 1				$58,385.00	$29,010.00
PP	2/17/95	S	60 1/8	PP1		-1 7/8	$ (365.00)		
3	2/24/95	L	60 3/4	Buy 1					
PP	3/30/95	S	66	PP1	5 2/8		$ 4,765.00	$63,515.00	$34,140.00
4	4/4/95	L	67 1/8	Buy 1					
PP	5/12/95	S	70 1/4	PP1	3 1/8		$ 7,770.00	$66,520.00	$37,145.00
5	5/23/95	L	70 3/4	Buy 1					
PP	5/26/95	S	69 7/8	PP1		- 7/8	$ 6,775.00	$65,525.00	$36,150.00
6	5/31/95	L	72 7/8	Buy 1					
PP	6/7/95	S	72 7/8	PP1	0		$ 6,655.00	$65,405.00	$36,030.00
7	6/15/95	L	72 3/4	Buy 1					
PP	7/13/95	S	75 1/2	PP1	2 6/8		$ 9,285.00	$68,035.00	$38,660.00
8	7/14/95	S	73 3/4	Sell 2					
PP	7/26/95	L	75 1/8	PP1		-1 3/8	$ 7,790.00	$66,540.00	$37,165.00
9	7/31/95	S	71 5/8	Sell 1					
PP	8/2/95	L	73 1/8	PP1		-1 4/8	$ 6,170.00	$64,920.00	$35,545.00
10	8/11/95	S	72	Sell 1					
PP	8/16/95	L	73 3/8	PP1		-1 3/8	$ 4,675.00	$63,425.00	$34,050.00
11	8/28/95	L	75 1/8	Buy 2					
PP	11/24/95	S	89	PP1	13 7/8		$ 18,430.00	$77,180.00	$47,805.00
12	12/4/95	L	90	Buy 1					
PP	12/8/95	S	89 1/4	PP1		- 6/8	$ 17,560.00	$76,310.00	$46,935.00
13	12/12/95	L	90 3/4	Buy 1					
PP	12/18/92	L	91 1/4	PP1	4/8		$ 17,940.00	$76,690.00	$47,315.00
14	12/19/95	S	88 7/8	Sell 2					
PP	12/26/95	L	89 5/8	PP1		- 3/4	$ 17,070.00	$75,820.00	$46,445.00

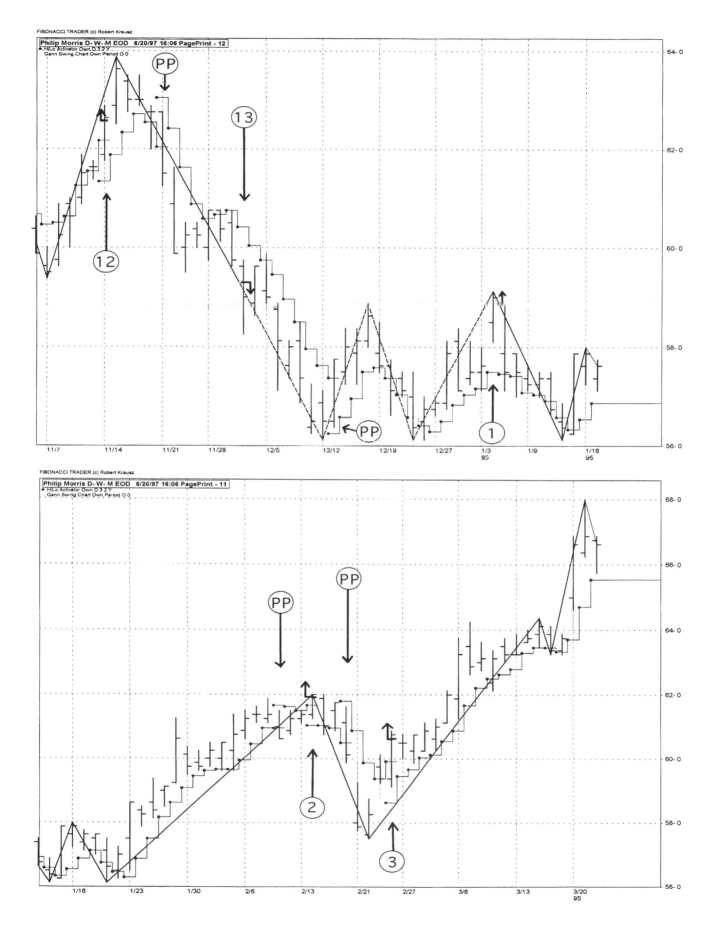

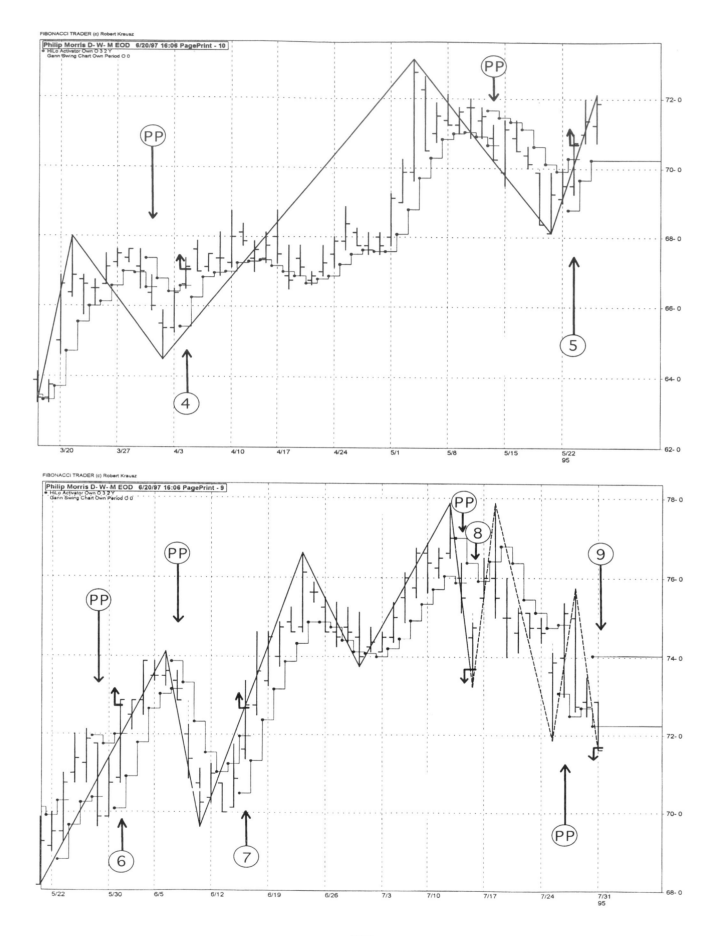

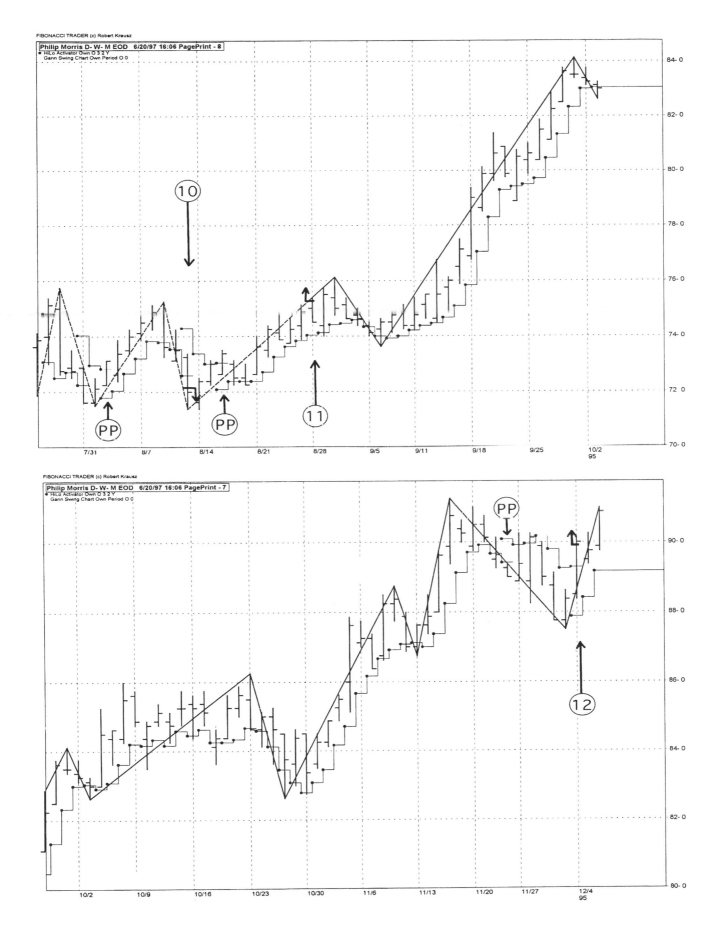

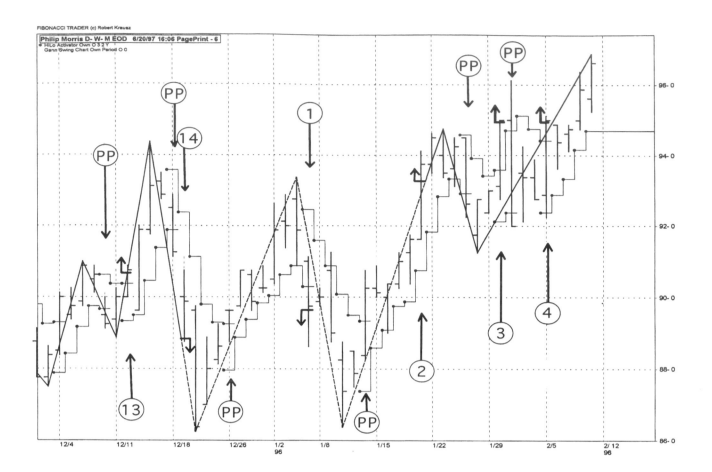

Philip Morris D- W- M EOD 6/20/97 16:06 PagePrint - 6
HiLo Activator Own O 3 2 Y
Gann Swing Chart Own Period O 0

194

PHILIP MORRIS - 1996
BASIC SWING PLAN
GANN SWING PLAN - FIBONACCI TRADER®

With 100% Margin

Beginning Equity	$89,750.00	Ending Equity	$110,230.00
Total Net Profit	$23,000.00	Gross Loss	($17,125.00)
Gross Profit	$40,125.00	Total Commissions	$2,520.00
Total No. Trades	21	Percentage Profitable	48%
No. Winning Trades	10	No. Losing Trades	11

Largest Winning Trade	$8,625.00	Largest Losing Trade	($3,250.00)
Average Winning Trade	$4,012.50	Average Losing Trade	($1,556.82)
Ratio Average Win/Loss	2.58	Average Trade	$1,095.24
Max. Consecutive Winners	3	Max. Consecutive Losses	3
Largest Consecutive Drawdown (%)	4.97%	Largest Consecutive Drawdown	($5,110.00)

Return on Account	23%
Profit/Drawdown Ratio	4.50

With 50% Margin

Beginning Equity	$44,875.00	Ending Equity	$65,355.00
Total Net Profit	$23,000.00	Gross Loss	($17,125.00)
Gross Profit	$40,125.00	Total Commissions	$2,520.00
Total No. Trades	21	Percentage Profitable	48%
No. Winning Trades	10	No. Losing Trades	11

Largest Winning Trade	$8,625.00	Largest Losing Trade	($3,250.00)
Average Winning Trade	$4,012.50	Average Losing Trade	($1,556.82)
Ratio Average Win/Loss	2.58	Average Trade	$1,095.24
Max. Consecutive Winners	3	Max. Consecutive Losses	3
Largest Consecutive Drawdown (%)	8.82%	Largest Consecutive Drawdown	($5,110.00)

Return on Account	46%
Profit/Drawdown Ratio	4.50

Notes:
1) Each trade is equal to 1,000 shares.
2) Initial account is equal to what it would cost
   to trade 1,000 shares at a price/share at that time.
3) Commission is equal to 12 cents per round turn.
4) Plan handles less or more shares.

1996

Philip Morris - Gann Swing Chartist®
Basic Swing Plan (Real Time)

Fibonacci Trader®

Trade #	Date	L/S	Price	Rule #	Profit	(Loss)	Accum.	A/C Equity	50% Margin
1	1/5/96	S	89 3/4	Sell 1				$89,750.00	$44,875.00
PP	1/12/96	L	89 1/2	PP2	2/8		$ 130.00	$89,880.00	$45,005.00
2	1/19/96	L	93 3/8	Buy 2					
PP	1/25/96	S	92 5/8	PP1		- 6/8	$ (740.00)	$89,010.00	$44,135.00
3	1/30/96	L	95	Buy 1					
PP	1/31/96	S	92	PP1		-3	$ (3,860.00)	$85,890.00	$41,015.00
4	2/5/96	L	95	Buy 1					
PP	2/15/96	S	96 3/8	PP1	1 3/8		$ (2,605.00)	$87,145.00	$42,270.00
5	2/21/96	L	97 7/8	Buy 1					
PP	3/8/96	S	100	PP1	2 1/8		$ (600.00)	$89,150.00	$44,275.00
6	3/13/96	S	98 3/4	Sell 2					
PP	4/1/96	L	90 1/8	PP1	8 5/8		$ 7,905.00	$97,655.00	$52,780.00
7	4/9/96	S	89 3/8	Sell 1					
PP	4/16/96	L	90 3/4	PP1		-1 3/8	$ 6,410.00	$96,160.00	$51,285.00
8	4/19/96	S	88 1/8	Sell 1					
PP	4/26/96	L	89 1/4	PP1		-1 1/8	$ 5,165.00	$94,915.00	$50,040.00
9	5/2/96	S	88 5/8	Sell 1					
PP	5/13/96	L	89 7/8	PP1		-1 2/8	$ 3,795.00	$93,545.00	$48,670.00
10	5/14/96	L	91	Buy 2					
PP	5/31/96	S	99 3/8	PP1	8 3/8		$12,050.00	$101,800.00	$56,925.00
11	6/4/96	L	101 3/8	Buy 1					
PP	6/18/96	S	102 1/2	PP1	1 1/8		$13,055.00	$102,805.00	$57,930.00
12	6/24/96	L	104 5/8	Buy 1					
13	7/5/96	S	101 7/8	Sell 2		-2 6/8	$10,185.00	$99,935.00	$55,060.00
PP	7/26/96	L	102 1/8	PP1		- 2/8	$ 9,815.00	$99,565.00	$54,690.00
14	7/30/96	L	102 1/4	Buy 2					
PP	8/9/96	S	100 1/2	PP2		-1 6/8	$ 7,945.00	$97,695.00	$52,820.00
15	8/9/96	S	97 1/8	Sell 3					
PP	8/20/96	L	91 1/2	PP1	5 5/8		$13,450.00	$103,200.00	$58,325.00
16	8/21/96	S	87 1/8	Sell 1					
PP	8/26/96	L	90 3/8	PP1		-3 1/4	$10,080.00	$99,830.00	$54,955.00
17	8/27/96	L	91 3/4	Buy 2					
PP	9/20/96	S	92 5/8	PP1	7/8		$10,835.00	$100,585.00	$55,710.00

1996

Philip Morris - Gann Swing Chartist®

Basic Swing Plan (Real Time)

Fibonacci Trader®

Trade #	Date	L/S	Price	Rule #	Profit	(Loss)	Accum.	A/C Equity	50% Margin
18	9/25/96	S	90 1/2	Sell 2					
PP	10/1/96	L	91	PP2		- 1/2	$ 10,215.00	$99,965.00	$55,090.00
19	10/16/96	L	94 7/8	Buy 2					
PP	10/18/96	S	93 3/4	PP2		-1 1/8	$ 8,970.00	$98,720.00	$53,845.00
20	11/6/96	L	97 3/8	Buy 1					
PP	11/29/96	S	103 1/4	PP1	5 7/8		$ 14,725.00	$104,475.00	$59,600.00
21	12/5/96	L	107 7/8	Buy 1					
PP	12/12/96	S	113 3/4	PP1	5 7/8		$ 20,480.00	$110,230.00	$65,355.00

197

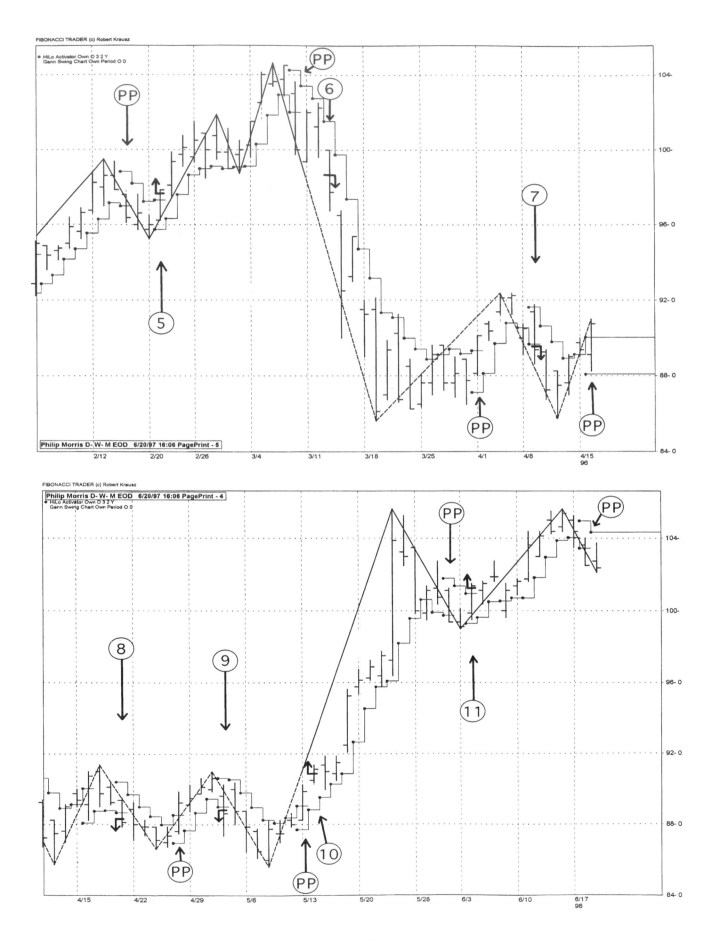

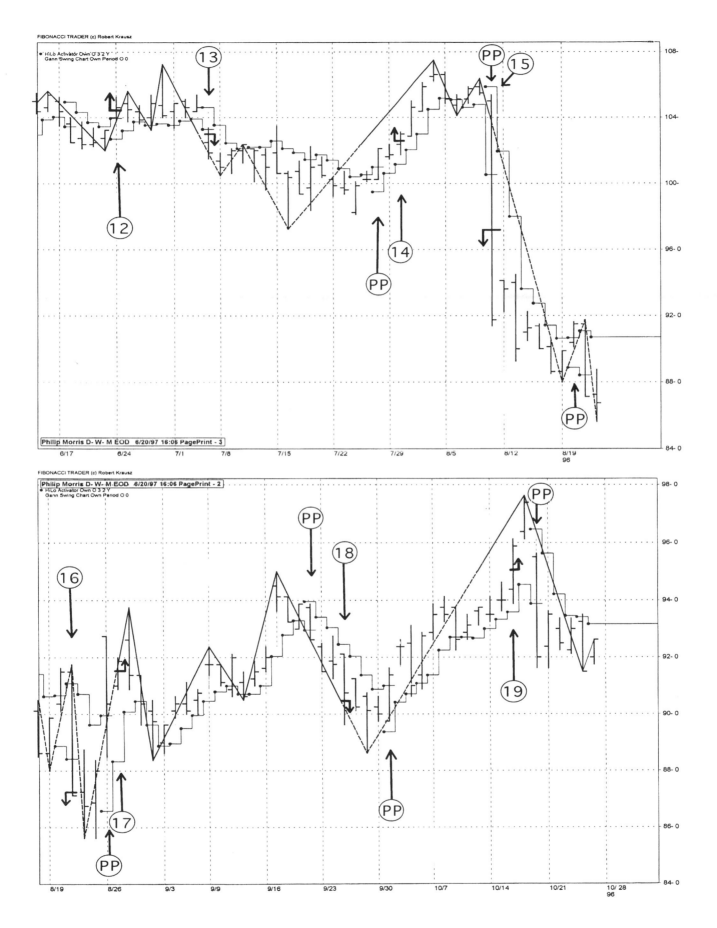

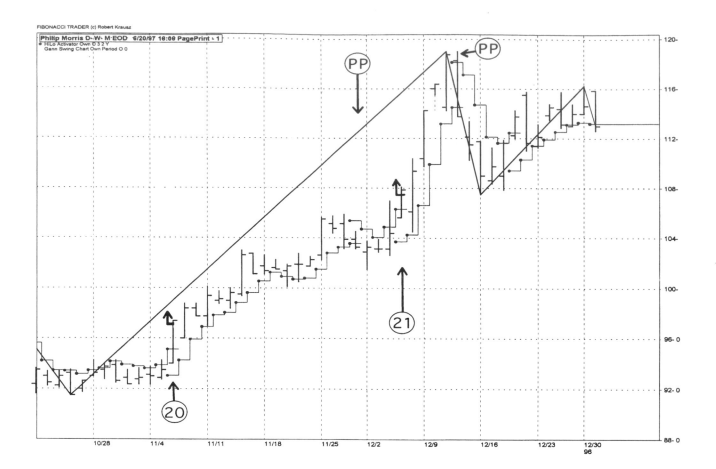

J.P. MORGAN - 1992-1996 (5 YRS.) EOD.
BASIC SWING PLAN - COMPOSITE
GANN SWING CHARTIST - FIBONACCI TRADER ®

With 100% Margin

Beginning Equity	$63,500.00	Ending Equity	$83,760.00
Total Net Profit	$32,500.00	Gross Loss	($61,250.00)
Gross Profit	$93,750.00	Total Commissions	$12,240.00
Total No. Trades	102	Percentage Profitable	52%
No. Winning Trades	53	No. Losing Trades	49

Largest Winning Trade	$6,125.00	Largest Losing Trade	($2,500.00)
Average Winning Trade	$1,700.07	Average Losing Trade	($1,250.00)
Max. Consecutive Winners	4	Max. Consecutive Losses	4
Average Average Drawdown (%)	8.06%	Average Drawdown ($)	($5,858.00)

Return on Account	6%
Profit/Drawdown Ratio	5.55

With 50% Margin

Beginning Equity	$31,750.00	Ending Equity	$52,010.00
Total Net Profit	$32,500.00	Gross Loss	($61,250.00)
Gross Profit	$93,750.00	Total Commissions	$12,240.00
Total No. Trades	102	Percentage Profitable	52%
No. Winning Trades	53	No. Losing Trades	10

Largest Winning Trade	$6,125.00	Largest Losing Trade	($2,500.00)
Average Winning Trade	$1,768.87	Average Losing Trade	($6,125.00)
Max. Consecutive Winners	4	Max. Consecutive Losses	4
Average Drawdown (%)	15.17%	Average Drawdown ($)	($5,858.00)

Average Return on Account	13%
Profit/Drawdown Ratio	5.55

Notes:
1) Each trade is equal to 1,000 shares.
2) Initial account is equal to what it would cost
   to trade 1,000 shares at a price/share at that time.
3) Commission is equal to 12 cents per round turn per share.
4) Plan handles less or more shares, percentages are the same.

J.P. MORGAN - 1992
BASIC SWING PLAN
GANN SWING CHARTIST - FIBONACCI TRADER®

With 100% Margin

Beginning Equity	$63,500.00	Ending Equity	$69,975.00
Total Net Profit	$8,875.00	Gross Loss	($9,375.00)
Gross Profit	$18,250.00	Total Commissions	$2,400.00
Total No. Trades	20	Percentage Profitable	50%
No. Winning Trades	10	No. Losing Trades	10

Largest Winning Trade	$4,375.00	Largest Losing Trade	($1,875.00)
Average Winning Trade	$1,825.00	Average Losing Trade	($937.50)
Ratio Average Win/Loss	1.95	Average Trade	$443.75
Max. Consecutive Winners	3	Max. Consecutive Losses	3
Largest Consecutive Drawdown (%)	6.50%	Largest Consecutive Drawdown	($4,815.00)

Return on Account	10%
Profit/Drawdown Ratio	1.84

With 50% Margin

Beginning Equity	$31,750.00	Ending Equity	$38,225.00
Total Net Profit	$8,875.00	Gross Loss	($9,375.00)
Gross Profit	$18,250.00	Total Commissions	$2,400.00
Total No. Trades	20	Percentage Profitable	50%
No. Winning Trades	10	No. Losing Trades	10

Largest Winning Trade	$4,375.00	Largest Losing Trade	($1,875.00)
Average Winning Trade	$1,825.00	Average Losing Trade	($937.50)
Ratio Average Win/Loss	1.95	Average Trade	$443.75
Max. Consecutive Winners	3	Max. Consecutive Losses	3
Largest Consecutive Drawdown (%)	11.39%	Largest Consecutive Drawdown	($4,815.00)

Return on Account	20%
Profit/Drawdown Ratio	1.84

Notes:
1) Each trade is equal to 1,000 shares.
2) Initial account is equal to what it would cost
   to trade 1,000 shares at a price/share at that time.
3) Commission is equal to 12 cents per round turn.
4) Plan handles less or more shares.

1992
J.P. Morgan - Gann Swing Chartist®
Basic Swing Plan (End of Day)

Fibonacci Trader®

Trade #	Date	L/S	Price	Rule #	Profit	(Loss)	Accum.	A/C Equity	50% Margin
1	12/20/91	L	63 1/2	Buy 1				$63,500.00	$31,750.00
PP	1/2/92	S	67 7/8	PP1	4 3/8		$ 4,255.00	$67,755.00	$36,005.00
2	1/7/92	L	69	Buy 1					
PP	1/9/92	S	67 1/2	PP1		-1 4/8	$ 2,635.00	$66,135.00	$34,385.00
3	1/13/92	S	66 1/2	Sell 2					
PP	2/4/92	L	62 1/8	PP1	4 3/8		$ 6,890.00	$70,390.00	$38,640.00
4	2/7/92	S	61 3/8	Sell 1					
PP	2/20/92	L	60 1/2	PP1	7/8		$ 7,645.00	$71,145.00	$39,395.00
5	2/25/92	L	60 7/8	Buy 2					
PP	2/28/92	S	60 1/8	PP1		- 6/8	$ 6,775.00	$70,275.00	$38,525.00
6	3/6/92	S	57 5/8	Sell 2					
PP	4/22/92	L	54 1/4	PP2	3 3/8		$10,030.00	$73,530.00	$41,780.00
7	4/22/92	L	55 5/8	Buy 1					
PP	5/13/92	S	56 1/4	PP1	5/8		$10,535.00	$74,035.00	$42,285.00
8	5/20/92	L	56 7/8	Buy 1					
PP	5/26/92	S	55	PP1		-1 7/8	$ 8,540.00	$72,040.00	$40,290.00
9	5/29/92	L	57 3/8	Buy 1					
PP	6/10/92	S	55 1/2	PP1		-1 7/8	$ 6,545.00	$70,045.00	$38,295.00
10	6/17/92	S	54	Sell 2					
PP	6/23/92	L	54 1/4	PP1		- 2/8	$ 6,175.00	$69,675.00	$37,925.00
11	7/2/92	L	57 3/4	Buy 1					
PP	7/15/92	S	60 1/4	PP1	2 4/8		$ 8,555.00	$72,055.00	$40,305.00
12	7/28/92	L	60 1/4	Buy 1					
13	8/19/92	S	59 3/8	Sell 2		- 7/8	$ 7,560.00	$71,060.00	$39,310.00
PP	8/27/92	L	59 3/4	PP1		- 3/8	$ 7,065.00	$70,565.00	$38,815.00
14	9/4/92	L	60 1/8	Buy 2					
PP	10/5/92	S	61	PP1	7/8		$ 7,820.00	$71,320.00	$39,570.00
15	10/15/92	L	61 7/8	Buy 1					
PP	10/22/92	S	61 7/8	PP1	0		$ 7,700.00	$71,200.00	$39,450.00
16	10/30/92	L	63	Buy 1					
PP	11/12/92	S	63 3/8	PP1	3/8		$ 7,955.00	$71,455.00	$39,705.00
17	11/13/92	S	63 1/4	Sell 2					
PP	11/25/92	L	62 3/8	PP1		- 7/8	$ 6,960.00	$70,460.00	$38,710.00

1992
J.P. Morgan - Gann Swing Chartist®
Basic Swing Plan (End of Day)

Fibonacci Trader®

18	12/1/92	S	61	Sell 1				$37,715.00
PP	12/7/92	L	61 7/8	PP1	- 7/8	$ 5,965.00	$69,465.00	$37,715.00
19	12/8/92	L	62 7/8	Buy 2				
PP	12/15/92	S	62 3/4	PP1	- 1/8	$ 5,720.00	$69,220.00	$37,470.00
20	12/18/92	L	64 1/4	Buy 1				
PP	1/4/93	S	65 1/8	PP1	7/8	$ 6,475.00	$69,975.00	$38,225.00

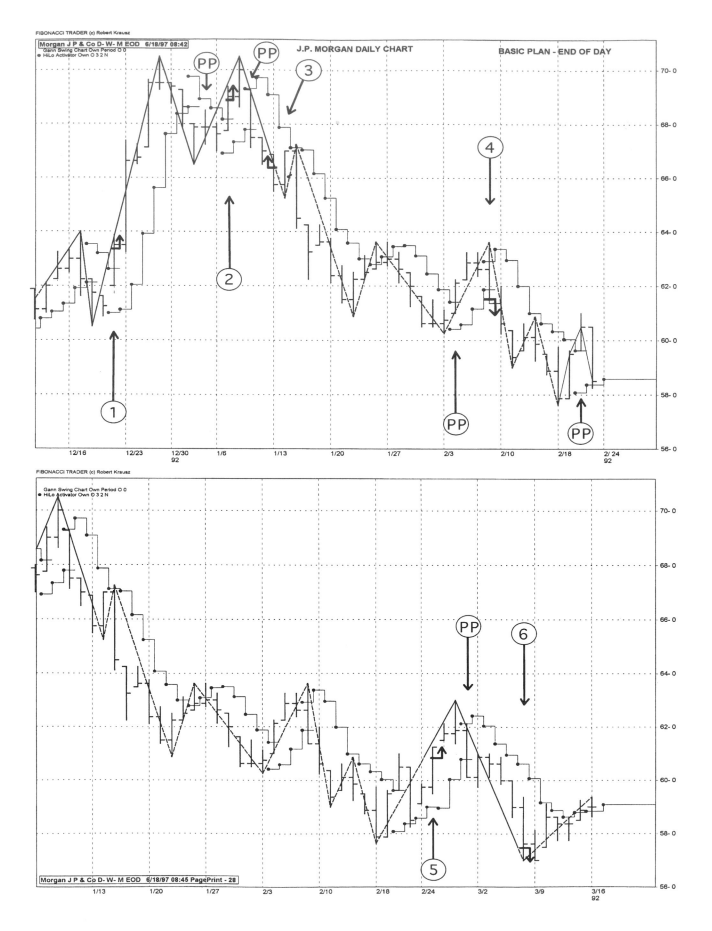

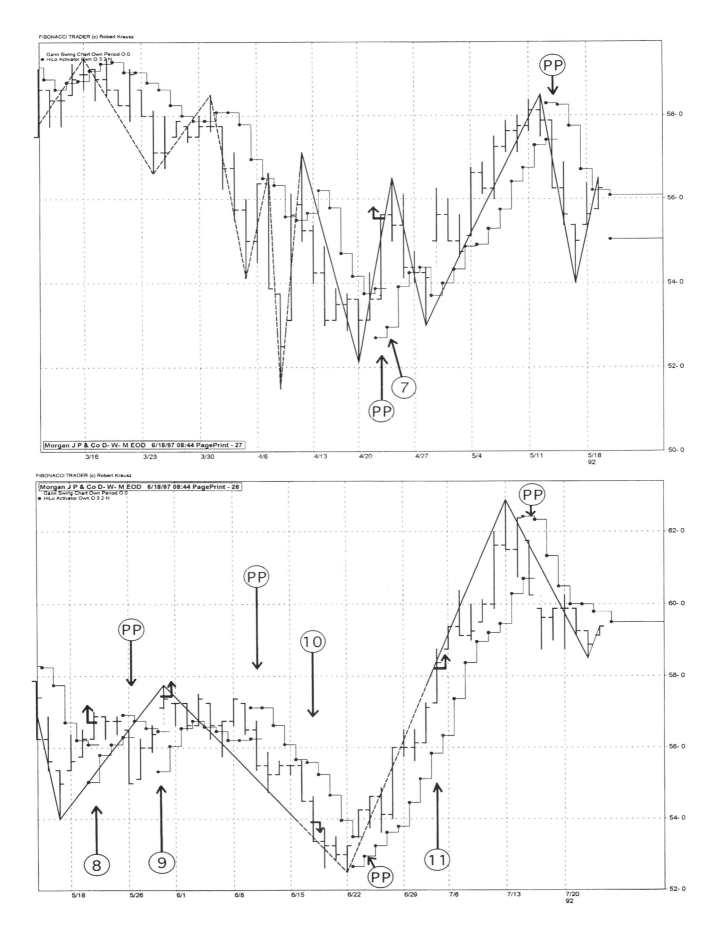

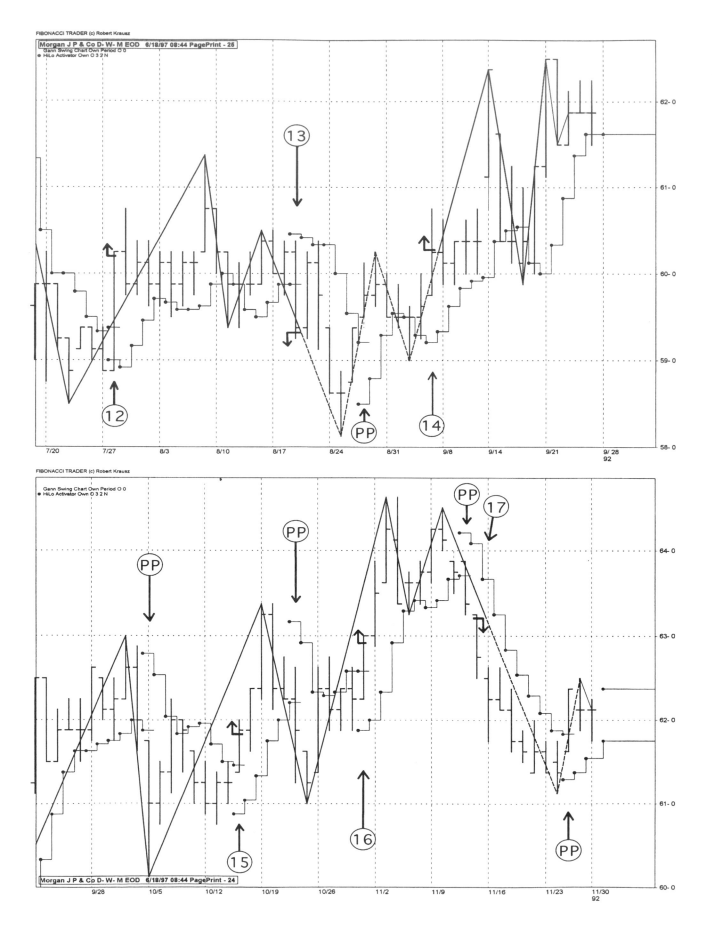

J.P. MORGAN - 1993
BASIC SWING PLAN
GANN SWING CHARTIST - FIBONACCI TRADER®

With 100% Margin

Beginning Equity	$63,375.00	Ending Equity	$66,855.00
Total Net Profit	$6,000.00	Gross Loss	($15,500.00)
Gross Profit	$21,500.00	Total Commissions	$2,520.00
Total No. Trades	21	Percentage Profitable	48%
No. Winning Trades	10	No. Losing Trades	11

Largest Winning Trade	$6,125.00	Largest Losing Trade	($2,250.00)
Average Winning Trade	$2,150.00	Average Losing Trade	($1,409.09)
Ratio Average Win/Loss	1.53	Average Trade	$285.71
Max. Consecutive Winners	3	Max. Consecutive Losses	4
Largest Consecutive Drawdown (%)	12.22%	Largest Consecutive Drawdown	($8,695.00)

Return on Account	5%
Profit/Drawdown Ratio	0.69

With 50% Margin

Beginning Equity	$31,687.50	Ending Equity	$35,167.50
Total Net Profit	$6,000.00	Gross Loss	($15,500.00)
Gross Profit	$21,500.00	Total Commissions	$2,520.00
Total No. Trades	21	Percentage Profitable	48%
No. Winning Trades	10	No. Losing Trades	11

Largest Winning Trade	$6,125.00	Largest Losing Trade	($2,250.00)
Average Winning Trade	$2,150.00	Average Losing Trade	($1,409.09)
Ratio Average Win/Loss	1.53	Average Trade	$285.71
Max. Consecutive Winners	3	Max. Consecutive Losses	4
Largest Consecutive Drawdown (%)	22.04%	Largest Consecutive Drawdown	($8,695.00)

Return on Account	11%
Profit/Drawdown Ratio	0.69

Notes:
1) Each trade is equal to 1,000 shares.
2) Initial account is equal to what it would cost
   to trade 1,000 shares at a price/share at that time.
3) Commission is equal to 12 cents per round turn.
4) Plan handles less or more shares.

1993
J.P. Morgan - Gann Swing Chartist®
Basic Swing Plan (End of Day)

Trade #	Date	L/S	Price	Rule #	Profit	(Loss)	Accum.	A/C Equity	50% Margin
1	1/14/93	S	63 3/8	Sell 2				$63,375.00	$31,687.50
2	2/4/93	L	61 1/4	Buy 2	2 1/8		$ 2,005.00	$65,380.00	$33,692.50
PP	2/12/93	S	62 3/8	PP1	1 1/8		$ 3,010.00	$66,385.00	$34,697.50
3	2/19/93	L	62 1/2	Buy 1					
PP	3/19/93	S	67 3/8	PP1	4 7/8		$ 7,765.00	$71,140.00	$39,452.50
4	4/2/93	S	67 1/8	Sell 2					
PP	4/8/93	L	68 3/4	PP1		-1 5/8	$ 6,020.00	$69,395.00	$37,707.50
5	4/12/93	L	70	Buy 2					
PP	4/20/93	S	71 1/2	PP1	1 4/8		$ 7,400.00	$70,775.00	$39,087.50
6	4/26/93	S	66 3/4	Sell 2					
PP	5/4/93	L	69	PP1		-2 2/8	$ 5,030.00	$68,405.00	$36,717.50
7	5/7/93	S	66 5/8	Sell 1					
PP	5/11/93	L	68 3/8	PP1		-1 6/8	$ 3,160.00	$66,535.00	$34,847.50
8	5/13/93	S	66 3/8	Sell 1					
PP	5/19/93	L	66 3/4	PP1		- 3/8	$ 2,665.00	$66,040.00	$34,352.50
9	5/26/93	L	68 1/8	Buy 2					
10	6/3/93	S	66 1/8	Sell 2		-2	$ 545.00	$63,920.00	$32,232.50
PP	6/11/93	L	65 3/8	PP1	6/8		$ 1,175.00	$64,550.00	$32,862.50
11	6/17/93	L	67 1/4	Buy 2					
PP	6/23/93	S	65 1/2	PP1		-1 6/8	$ (695.00)	$62,680.00	$30,992.50
12	6/28/93	L	67 3/8	Buy 1					
PP	7/14/93	S	70 1/8	PP1	2 6/8		$ 1,935.00	$65,310.00	$33,622.50
13	7/23/93	S	69 5/8	Sell 2					
PP	7/27/93	L	71	PP1		-1 3/8	$ 440.00	$63,815.00	$32,127.50
14	7/29/93	L	73	Buy 2					
PP	8/6/93	S	71 3/4	PP1		-1 2/8	$ (930.00)	$62,445.00	$30,757.50
15	8/11/93	L	72 3/4	Buy 1					
PP	8/19/93	S	73 1/4	PP1	4/8		$ (550.00)	$62,825.00	$31,137.50
16	8/24/93	L	74 3/8	Buy 1					
PP	9/14/93	S	75 7/8	PP1	1 4/8		$ 830.00	$64,205.00	$32,517.50
17	9/21/93	S	74 1/2	Sell 2					
PP	9/24/93	L	76	PP1		-1 4/8	$ (790.00)	$62,585.00	$30,897.50
18	10/7/93	S	77	Sell 1					

1993
J.P. Morgan - Gann Swing Chartist®
Basic Swing Plan (End of Day)

Fibonacci Trader®

PP	11/9/93	L	70 7/8	PP1	6 1/8		$ 5,215.00	$68,590.00	$36,902.50
19	11/19/93	S	69 1/4	Sell 1					
PP	11/26/93	L	69 7/8	PP1		- 5/8	$ 4,470.00	$67,845.00	$36,157.50
20	11/29/93	L	71	Buy 2	2/8				
PP	12/7/93	S	71 1/4	PP1			$ 4,600.00	$67,975.00	$36,287.50
21	12/16/93	L	71 7/8	Buy 1					
PP	12/27/93	S	70 7/8	PP1	-1		$ 3,480.00	$66,855.00	$35,167.50

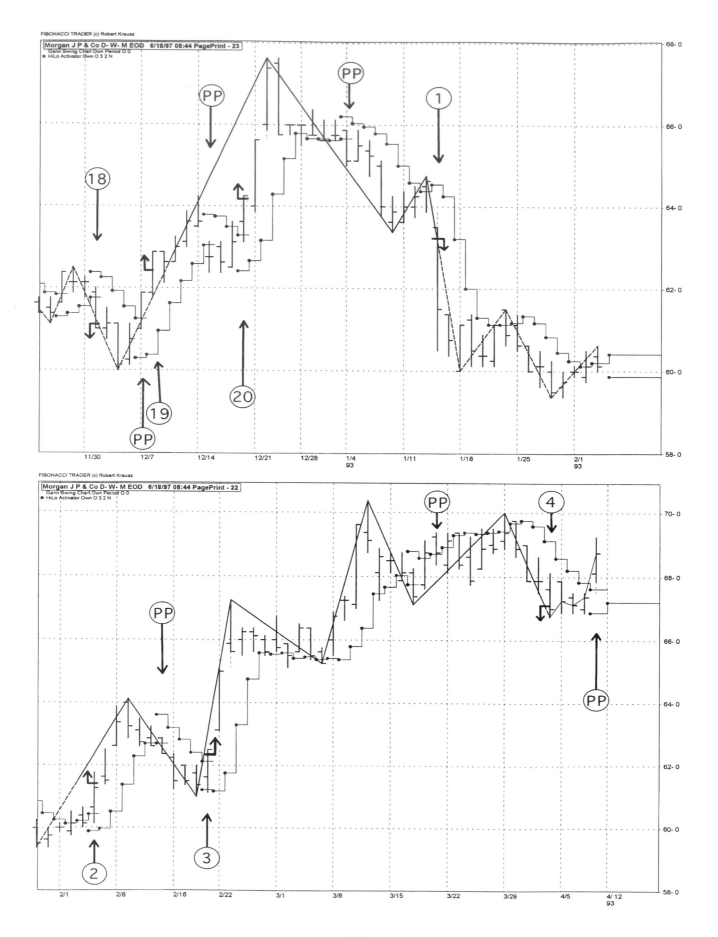

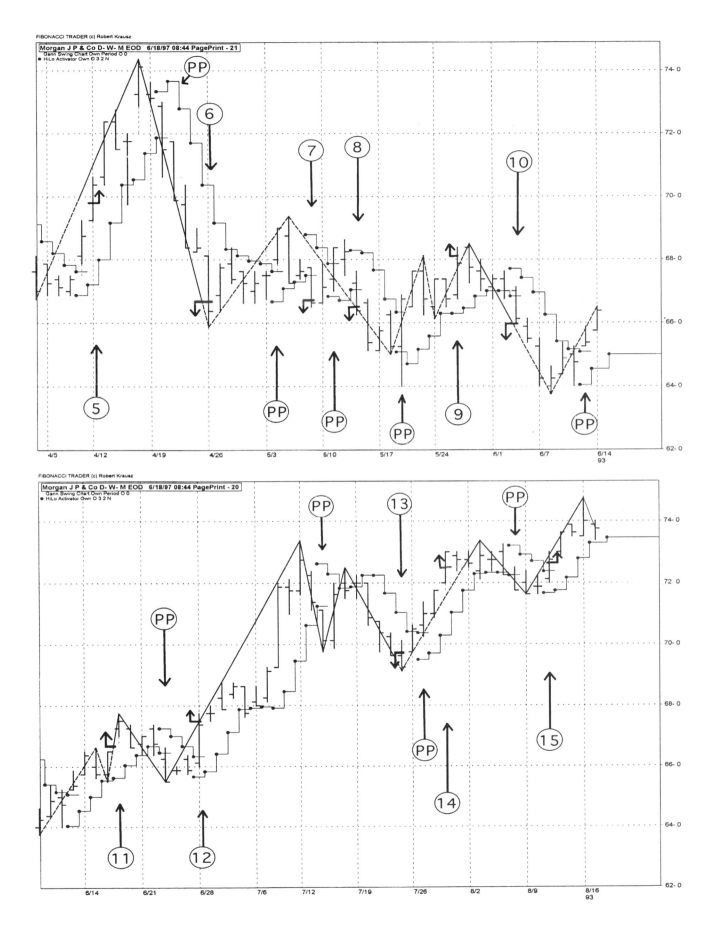

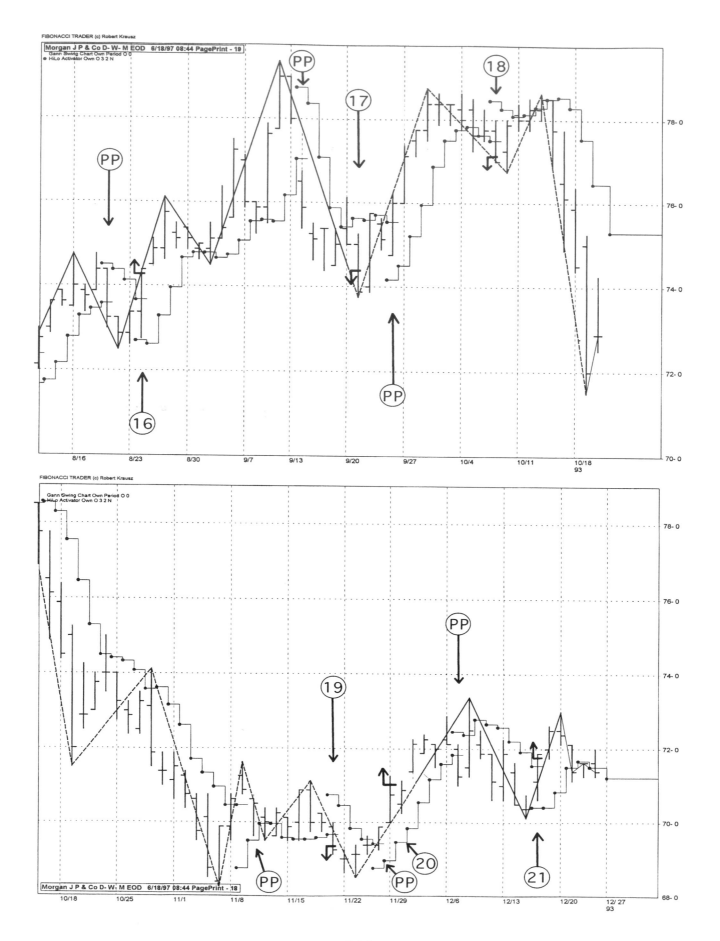

J.P. MORGAN - 1994
BASIC SWING PLAN
GANN SWING CHARTIST - FIBONACCI TRADER®

With 100% Margin

Beginning Equity	$69,750.00	Ending Equity	$78,095.00
Total Net Profit	$10,625.00	Gross Loss	($5,125.00)
Gross Profit	$15,750.00	Total Commissions	$2,280.00
Total No. Trades	19	Percentage Profitable	58%
No. Winning Trades	11	No. Losing Trades	8

Largest Winning Trade	$2,500.00	Largest Losing Trade	($1,750.00)
Average Winning Trade	$1,431.82	Average Losing Trade	($640.63)
Ratio Average Win/Loss	2.24	Average Trade	$559.21
Max. Consecutive Winners	4	Max. Consecutive Losses	3
Largest Consecutive Drawdown (%)	3.63%	Largest Consecutive Drawdown	($2,860.00)

Return on Account	12%
Profit/Drawdown Ratio	3.72

With 50% Margin

Beginning Equity	$34,875.00	Ending Equity	$43,220.00
Total Net Profit	$10,625.00	Gross Loss	($5,125.00)
Gross Profit	$15,750.00	Total Commissions	$2,280.00
Total No. Trades	19	Percentage Profitable	58%
No. Winning Trades	11	No. Losing Trades	8

Largest Winning Trade	$2,500.00	Largest Losing Trade	($1,750.00)
Average Winning Trade	$1,431.82	Average Losing Trade	($640.63)
Ratio Average Win/Loss	2.24	Average Trade	$559.21
Max. Consecutive Winners	4	Max. Consecutive Losses	3
Largest Consecutive Drawdown (%)	6.51%	Largest Consecutive Drawdown	($2,860.00)

Return on Account	24%
Profit/Drawdown Ratio	3.72

Notes:
1) Each trade is equal to 1,000 shares.
2) Initial account is equal to what it would cost
   to trade 1,000 shares at a price/share at that time.
3) Commission is equal to 12 cents per round turn.
4) Plan handles less or more shares.

1994
J.P. Morgan - Gann Swing Chartist®
Basic Swing Plan (End of Day)

Fibonacci Trader®

Trade #	Date	L/S	Price	Rule #	Profit	(Loss)	Accum.	A/C Equity	50% Margin
1	12/30/93	S	69 3/4	Sell 2				$69,750.00	$34,875.00
PP	1/11/94	L	69 5/8	PP1	1/8		$ 5.00	$69,755.00	$34,880.00
2	1/19/94	S	70	Sell 1					
PP	1/27/94	L	70 3/8	PP1		- 3/8	$ (490.00)	$69,260.00	$34,385.00
3	2/3/94	S	70 3/4	Sell 1					
PP	2/14/94	L	69 1/4	PP1	1 4/8		$ 890.00	$70,640.00	$35,765.00
4	2/17/94	S	68 1/8	Sell 1					
PP	3/11/94	L	65 7/8	PP1	2 2/8		$ 3,020.00	$72,770.00	$37,895.00
5	3/17/94	S	65	Sell 1					
PP	4/6/94	L	62 1/2	PP1	2 4/8		$ 5,400.00	$75,150.00	$40,275.00
6	4/13/94	S	62 3/4	Sell 1					
PP	5/5/94	L	62 3/8	PP1	3/8		$ 5,655.00	$75,405.00	$40,530.00
7	5/12/94	S	61 5/8	Sell 1					
PP	5/13/94	L	63 3/8	PP1		-1 6/8	$ 3,785.00	$73,535.00	$38,660.00
8	5/16/94	L	63 1/8	Buy 2					
PP	6/7/94	S	65 1/8	PP1	2		$ 5,665.00	$75,415.00	$40,540.00
9	6/16/94	S	64 7/8	Sell 2					
PP	7/7/94	L	62 3/8	PP1	2 4/8		$ 8,045.00	$77,795.00	$42,920.00
10	7/12/94	S	61 1/2	Sell 1					
PP	7/19/94	L	61 5/8	PP1		- 1/8	$ 7,800.00	$77,550.00	$42,675.00
11	7/29/94	L	62 3/8	Buy 2					
PP	8/9/94	S	62 3/8	PP1	0		$ 7,680.00	$77,430.00	$42,555.00
12	8/11/94	L	63 1/2	Buy 1					
PP	8/19/94	S	63 1/4	PP1		- 2/8	$ 7,310.00	$77,060.00	$42,185.00
13	8/29/94	L	65	Buy 1					
PP	9/7/94	S	64 7/8	PP1		- 1/8	$ 7,065.00	$76,815.00	$41,940.00
14	9/13/94	S	63 1/8	Sell 2					
PP	10/11/94	L	61	PP1	2 1/8		$ 9,070.00	$78,820.00	$43,945.00
15	10/11/94	L	61 1/8	Buy 2					
PP	10/20/94	S	60 3/8	PP1		- 6/8	$ 8,200.00	$77,950.00	$43,075.00
16	10/27/94	L	61	Buy 1					
PP	11/2/94	S	60 1/2	PP1		- 4/8	$ 7,580.00	$77,330.00	$42,455.00
17	11/8/94	L	61 3/8	Buy 1					

1994

J.P. Morgan - Gann Swing Chartist®

Basic Swing Plan (End of Day)

Fibonacci Trader®

18	11/14/94	S	60 1/8	Sell 2		-1 2/8	$ 6,210.00	$75,960.00	$41,085.00
PP	11/28/94	L	58 3/4	PP1	1 3/8		$ 7,465.00	$77,215.00	$42,340.00
19	12/8/94	S	58 1/8	Sell 1			$ 8,345.00	$78,095.00	
PP	1/4/95	L	57 1/8	PP1	1				$43,220.00

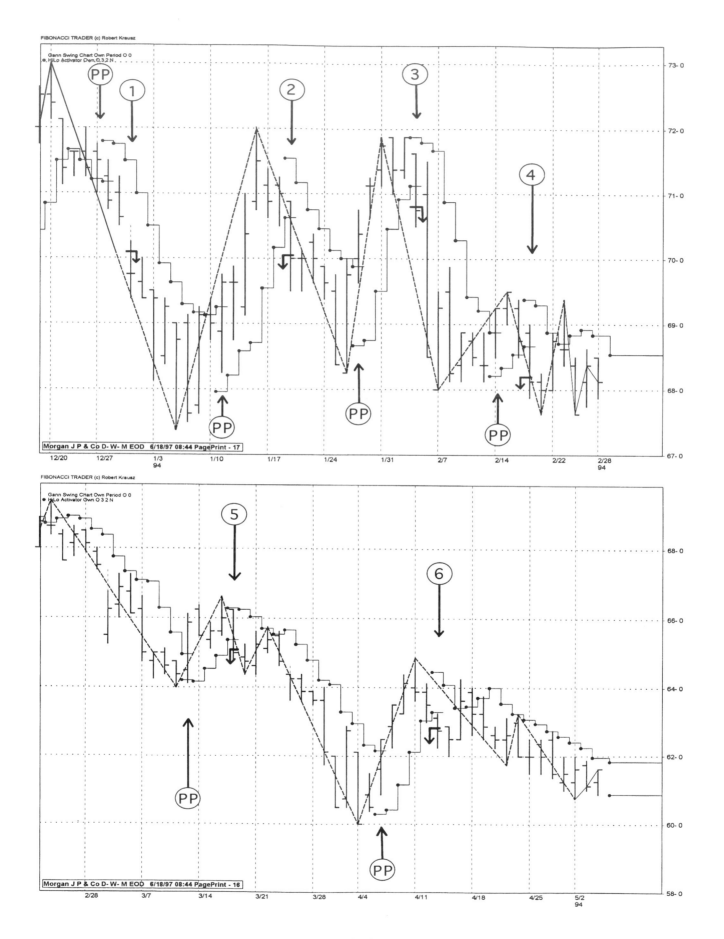

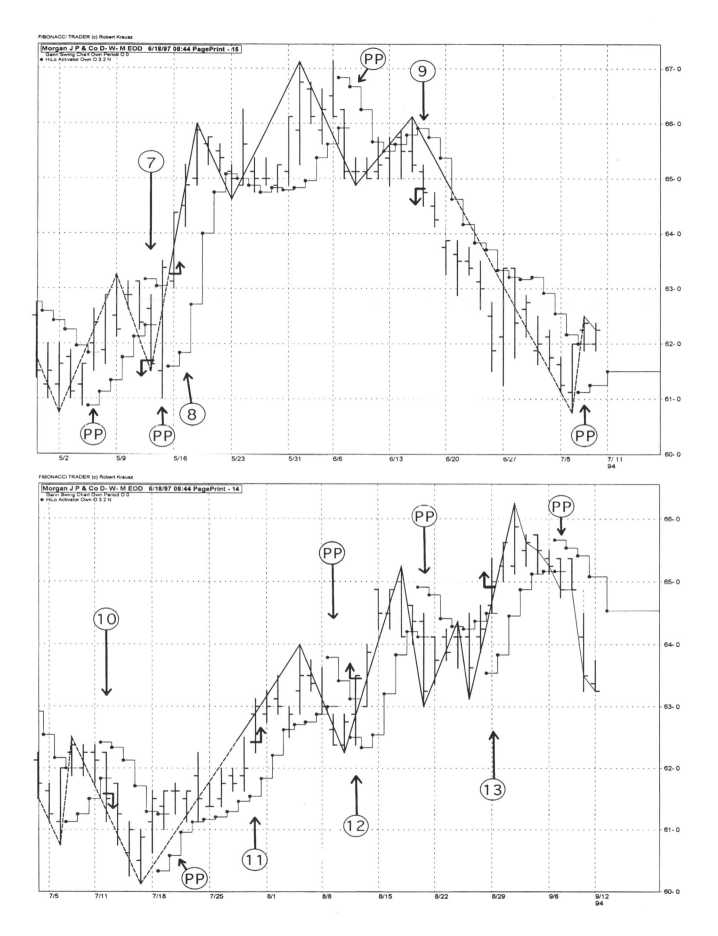

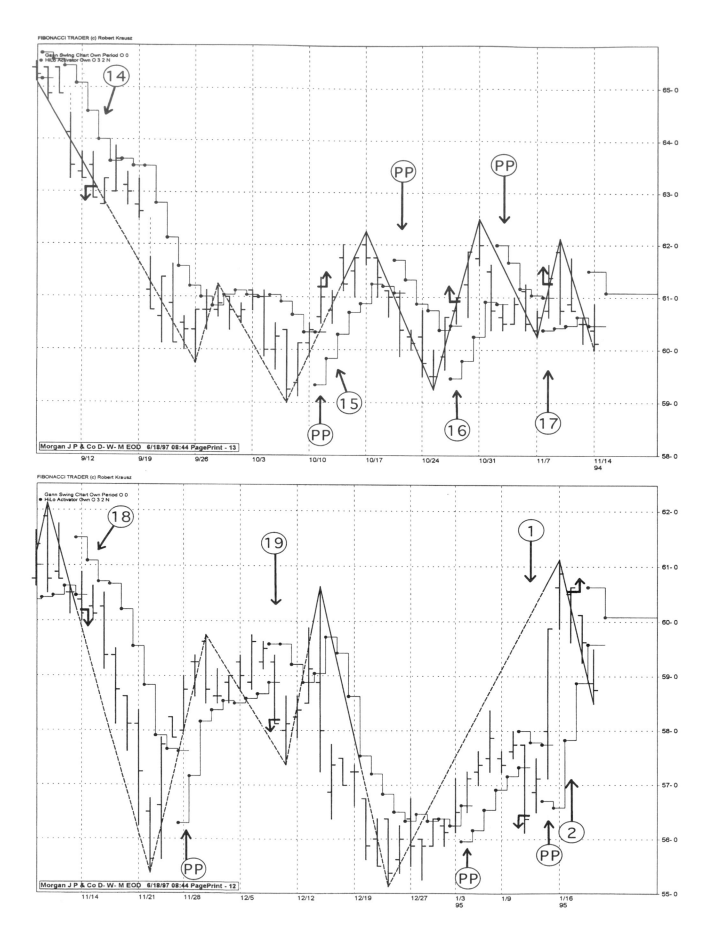

J.P. MORGAN - 1995
BASIC SWING PLAN
GANN SWING CHARTIST - FIBONACCI TRADER®

With 100% Margin

Beginning Equity	$56,375.00	Ending Equity	$60,225.00
Total Net Profit	$6,250.00	Gross Loss	($12,500.00)
Gross Profit	$18,750.00	Total Commissions	$2,400.00
Total No. Trades	20	Percentage Profitable	55%
No. Winning Trades	11	No. Losing Trades	9

Largest Winning Trade	$5,500.00	Largest Losing Trade	($1,875.00)
Average Winning Trade	$1,704.55	Average Losing Trade	($1,388.89)
Ratio Average Win/Loss	1.23	Average Trade	$312.50
Max. Consecutive Winners	4	Max. Consecutive Losses	2
Largest Consecutive Drawdown (%)	6.63%	Largest Consecutive Drawdown	($3,740.00)

Return on Account	7%
Profit/Drawdown Ratio	1.67

With 50% Margin

Beginning Equity	$28,187.50	Ending Equity	$32,037.50
Total Net Profit	$6,250.00	Gross Loss	($12,500.00)
Gross Profit	$18,750.00	Total Commissions	$2,400.00
Total No. Trades	20	Percentage Profitable	55%
No. Winning Trades	11	No. Losing Trades	9

Largest Winning Trade	$5,500.00	Largest Losing Trade	($1,875.00)
Average Winning Trade	$1,704.55	Average Losing Trade	($1,388.89)
Ratio Average Win/Loss	1.23	Average Trade	$312.50
Max. Consecutive Winners	4	Max. Consecutive Losses	2
Largest Consecutive Drawdown (%)	13.27%	Largest Consecutive Drawdown	($3,740.00)

Return on Account	14%
Profit/Drawdown Ratio	1.67

Notes:
1) Each trade is equal to 1,000 shares.
2) Initial account is equal to what it would cost
   to trade 1,000 shares at a price/share at that time.
3) Commission is equal to 12 cents per round turn.
4) Plan handles less or more shares.

1995
J.P. Morgan - Gann Swing Chartist®
Basic Swing Plan (End of Day)

Fibonacci Trader®

Trade #	Date	L/S	Price	Rule #	Profit	(Loss)	Accum.	A/C Equity	50% Margin
1	1/11/95	S	56 3/8	Sell 1				$56,375.00	$28,187.50
PP	1/13/95	L	58	PP2		-1 5/8	$ (1,745.00)	$54,630.00	$26,442.50
2	1/16/95	L	60 5/8	Buy 2					
PP	1/19/95	S	58 3/4	PP1		-1 7/8	$ (3,740.00)	$52,635.00	$24,447.50
3	1/23/95	L	60	Buy 1					
PP	2/9/95	S	62 7/8	PP1	2 7/8		$ (985.00)	$55,390.00	$27,202.50
4	2/17/95	S	62 5/8	Sell 2					
PP	2/23/95	L	63	PP1		- 3/8	$ (1,480.00)	$54,895.00	$26,707.50
5	2/24/95	L	63 3/4	Buy 2					
PP	3/7/95	S	64	PP1	2/8		$ (1,350.00)	$55,025.00	$26,837.50
6	3/13/95	S	61	Sell 2					
PP	3/24/95	L	60 1/4	PP1	6/8		$ (720.00)	$55,655.00	$27,467.50
7	4/10/95	S	61 3/4	Sell 1					
8	4/13/95	L	63 3/4	Buy 2		-2	$ (2,840.00)	$53,535.00	$25,347.50
PP	4/26/95	S	65 1/8	PP1	1 3/8		$ (1,585.00)	$54,790.00	$26,602.50
9	5/1/95	L	65 3/4	Buy 1					
PP	6/7/95	S	71 1/4	PP1	5 4/8		$ 3,795.00	$60,170.00	$31,982.50
10	6/14/95	L	71 3/4	Buy 1					
PP	6/23/95	S	71 1/2	PP1		- 2/8	$ 3,425.00	$59,800.00	$31,612.50
11	7/6/95	L	71 3/4	Buy 1					
PP	7/13/95	S	73 1/8	PP1	1 3/8		$ 4,680.00	$61,055.00	$32,867.50
12	7/19/95	S	69 5/8	Sell 2					
PP	7/24/95	L	71 1/2	PP2		-1 7/8	$ 2,685.00	$59,060.00	$30,872.50
13	8/15/95	S	71 5/8	Sell 1					
PP	8/18/95	L	72 5/8	PP1		-1	$ 1,565.00	$57,940.00	$29,752.50
14	8/22/95	S	71 1/2	Sell 1					
PP	8/25/95	L	71 7/8	PP1	3/8		$ 1,820.00	$58,195.00	$30,007.50
15	8/28/95	L	72 3/4	Buy 2					
PP	9/7/95	S	73 5/8	PP2	7/8		$ 2,575.00	$58,950.00	$30,762.50
16	9/12/95	L	74 3/4	Buy 1					
PP	9/21/95	S	76 5/8	PP1	1 7/8		$ 4,330.00	$60,705.00	$32,517.50
17	9/27/95	L	77 1/8	Buy 1					
PP	10/19/95	S	79 7/8	PP1	2 6/8		$ 6,960.00	$63,335.00	$35,147.50

J.P. Morgan - Gann Swing Chartist®
Basic Swing Plan (End of Day)

Fibonacci Trader®

18	10/25/95	S	76 5/8	Sell 2				$33,277.50
PP	10/27/95	L	78 3/8	PP1	-1 6/8	$ 5,090.00	$61,465.00	
19	11/13/95	S	76	Sell 1				
PP	11/16/95	L	77 3/4	PP1	-1 6/8	$ 3,220.00	$59,595.00	$31,407.50
20	11/29/95	L	79 1/8	Buy 2				
PP	12/11/95	S	79 7/8	PP1	6/8	$ 3,850.00	$60,225.00	$32,037.50

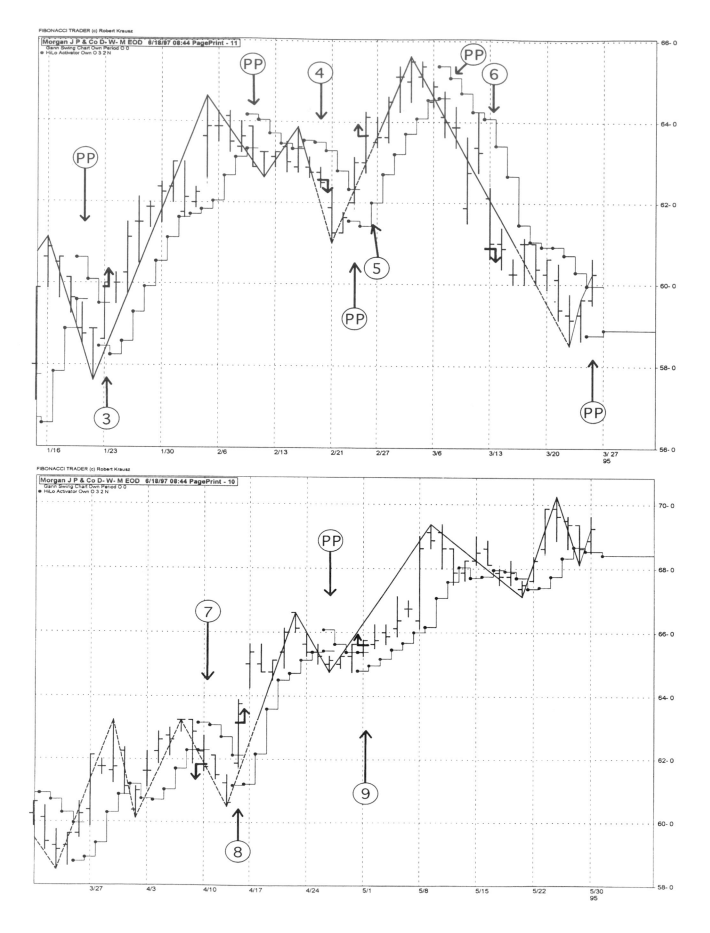

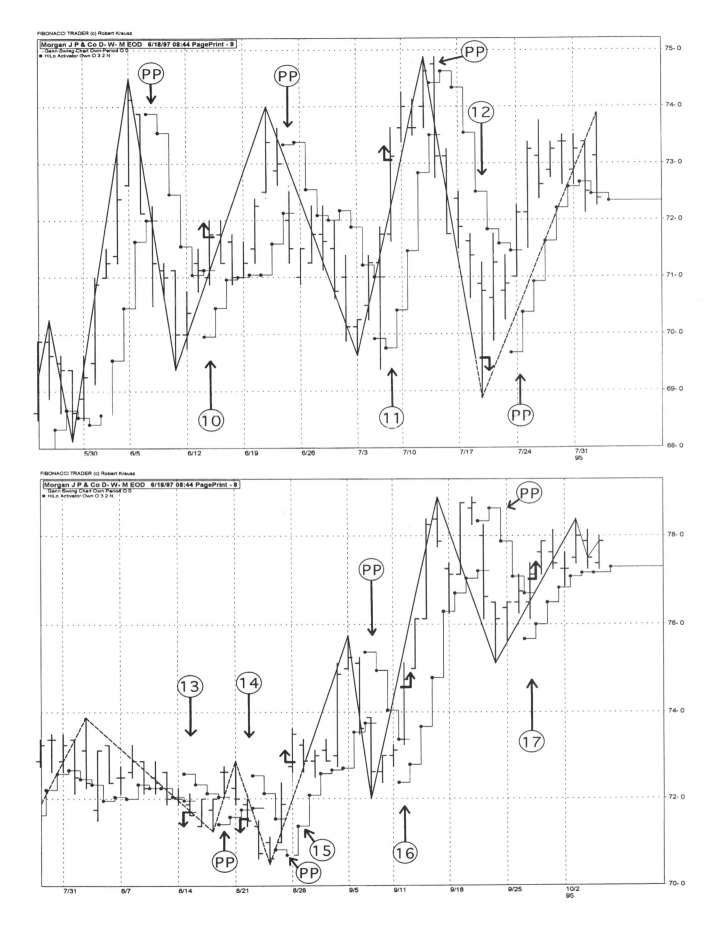

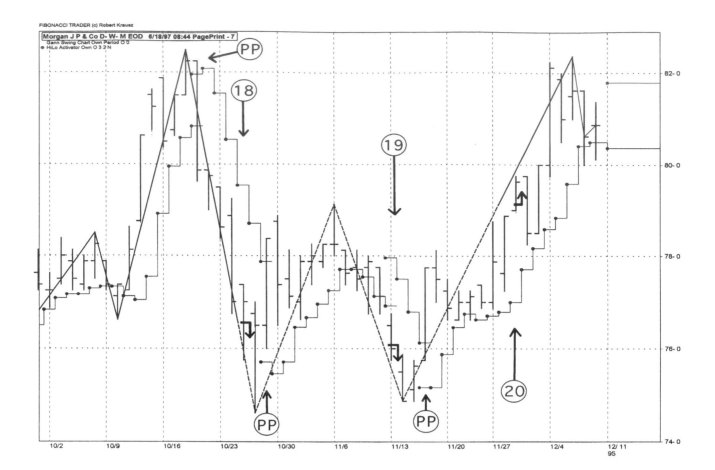

J.P. MORGAN - 1996
BASIC SWING PLAN
GANN SWING CHARTIST - FIBONACCI TRADER®

With 100% Margin

Beginning Equity	$81,125.00	Ending Equity	$79,235.00
Total Net Profit	$750.00	Gross Loss	($18,750.00)
Gross Profit	$19,500.00	Total Commissions	$2,640.00
Total No. Trades	22	Percentage Profitable	50%
No. Winning Trades	11	No. Losing Trades	11

Largest Winning Trade	$3,500.00	Largest Losing Trade	($2,500.00)
Average Winning Trade	$1,772.73	Average Losing Trade	($1,704.55)
Ratio Average Win/Loss	1.04	Average Trade	$34.09
Max. Consecutive Winners	4	Max. Consecutive Losses	3
Largest Consecutive Drawdown (%)	11.32%	Largest Consecutive Drawdown	($9,180.00)

Return on Account	-2%
Profit/Drawdown Ratio	0.08

With 50% Margin

Beginning Equity	$40,562.50	Ending Equity	$38,672.50
Total Net Profit	$750.00	Gross Loss	($18,750.00)
Gross Profit	$19,500.00	Total Commissions	$2,640.00
Total No. Trades	22	Percentage Profitable	50%
No. Winning Trades	11	No. Losing Trades	11

Largest Winning Trade	$3,500.00	Largest Losing Trade	($2,500.00)
Average Winning Trade	$1,772.73	Average Losing Trade	($1,704.55)
Ratio Average Win/Loss	1.04	Average Trade	$34.09
Max. Consecutive Winners	4	Max. Consecutive Losses	3
Largest Consecutive Drawdown (%)	22.63%	Largest Consecutive Drawdown	($9,180.00)

Return on Account	-5%
Profit/Drawdown Ratio	0.08

Notes:
1) Each trade is equal to 1,000 shares.
2) Initial account is equal to what it would cost
   to trade 1,000 shares at a price/share at that time.
3) Commission is equal to 12 cents per round turn.
4) Plan handles less or more shares.

1996
J.P. Morgan - Gann Swing Chartist®
Basic Swing Plan (End of Day)

Fibonacci Trader®

Trade #	Date	L/S	Price	Rule #	Profit	(Loss)	Accum.	A/C Equity	50% Margin
1	1/2/96	L	81 1/8	Buy 1				$81,125.00	$40,562.50
PP	1/4/96	S	79	PP1		-2 1/8	$ (2,245.00)	$78,880.00	$38,317.50
2	1/5/96	S	78 5/8	Sell 2					
PP	1/16/96	L	76 3/4	PP2	1 7/8		$ (490.00)	$80,635.00	$40,072.50
3	2/6/96	S	80	Sell 1					
PP	2/8/96	L	81 3/4	PP1		-1 6/8	$ (2,360.00)	$78,765.00	$38,202.50
4	2/12/96	L	81 3/4	Buy 2					
PP	2/16/96	S	81	PP1		- 6/8	$ (3,230.00)	$77,895.00	$37,332.50
5	2/20/96	S	79 1/2	Sell 2					
PP	2/23/96	L	82 1/2	PP1		-3	$ (6,350.00)	$74,775.00	$34,212.50
6	2/26/96	L	82 7/8	Buy 2					
PP	3/7/96	S	84	PP1	1 1/8		$ (5,345.00)	$75,780.00	$35,217.50
7	3/18/96	L	82 1/2	Buy 1					
PP	3/27/96	S	83 1/4	PP1	6/8		$ (4,715.00)	$76,410.00	$35,847.50
8	4/1/96	L	84 7/8	Buy 1					
PP	4/4/96	S	83 1/8	PP1		-1 6/8	$ (6,585.00)	$74,540.00	$33,977.50
9	4/8/96	S	82	Sell 2					
PP	4/15/96	L	80 3/8	PP2	1 5/8		$ (5,080.00)	$76,045.00	$35,482.50
10	5/2/96	S	82 7/8	Sell 1					
11	5/8/96	L	84 3/8	Buy 2		-1 4/8	$ (6,700.00)	$74,425.00	$33,862.50
PP	5/28/96	S	87 1/2	PP1	3 1/8		$ (3,695.00)	$77,430.00	$36,867.50
12	6/5/96	L	88 1/8	Buy 1					
13	6/10/96	S	85 5/8	Sell 2		-2 4/8	$ (6,315.00)	$74,810.00	$34,247.50
PP	6/25/96	L	85 3/4	PP1		- 1/8	$ (6,560.00)	$74,565.00	$34,002.50
14	7/3/96	L	86 5/8	Buy 2					
15	7/5/96	S	84 1/8	Sell 2		-2 4/8	$ (9,180.00)	$71,945.00	$31,382.50
PP	7/17/96	L	83 1/4	PP2	7/8		$ (8,425.00)	$72,700.00	$32,137.50
16	8/1/96	L	86 3/8	Buy 2					
PP	8/26/96	S	89 7/8	PP1	3 4/8		$ (5,045.00)	$76,080.00	$35,517.50
17	9/9/96	L	89	Buy 1					
PP	9/19/96	S	90	PP1	1		$ (4,165.00)	$76,960.00	$36,397.50
18	10/2/96	S	87 1/2	Sell 2					
PP	10/18/96	L	85	PP2	2 4/8		$ (1,785.00)	$79,340.00	$38,777.50

228

1996
J.P. Morgan - Gann Swing Chartist®
Basic Swing Plan (End of Day)

Fibonacci Trader®

19	11/12/96	S	86 7/8	Sell 1				$37,032.50
20	11/15/96	L	88 1/2	Buy 2	-1 5/8	$ (3,530.00)	$77,595.00	
PP	12/3/96	S	91 3/8	PP1	2 7/8	$ (775.00)	$80,350.00	$39,787.50
21	12/6/96	L	94 1/2	Buy 1				
PP	12/12/96	S	93 3/8	PP1	-1 1/8	$ (2,020.00)	$79,105.00	$38,542.50
22	12/17/96	L	97 3/8	Buy 1				
PP	12/31/96	S	97 5/8	PP1	2/8	$ (1,890.00)	$79,235.00	$38,672.50

229

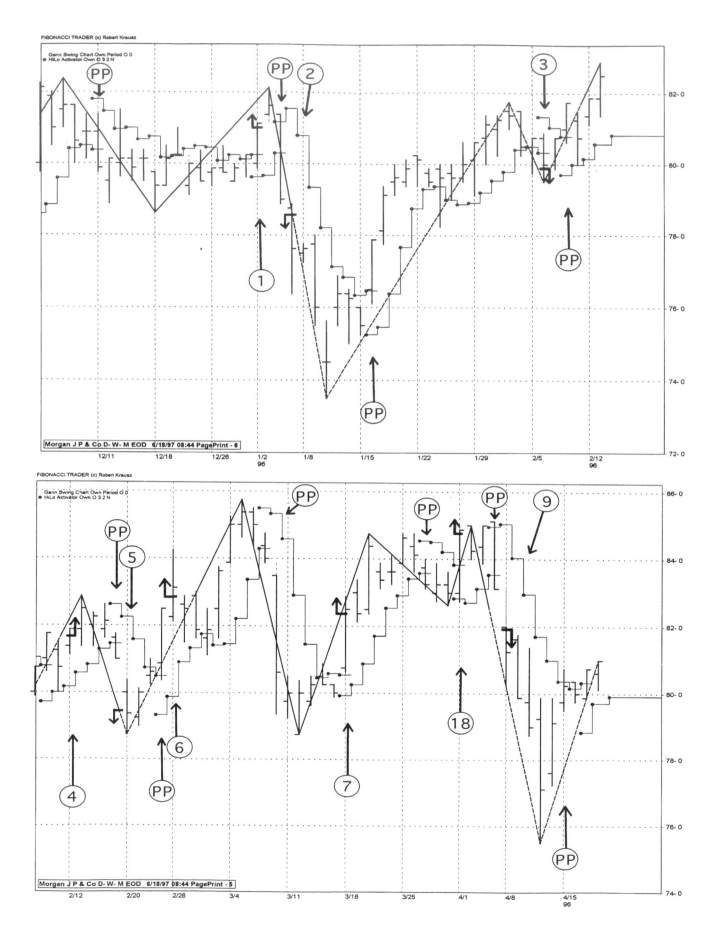

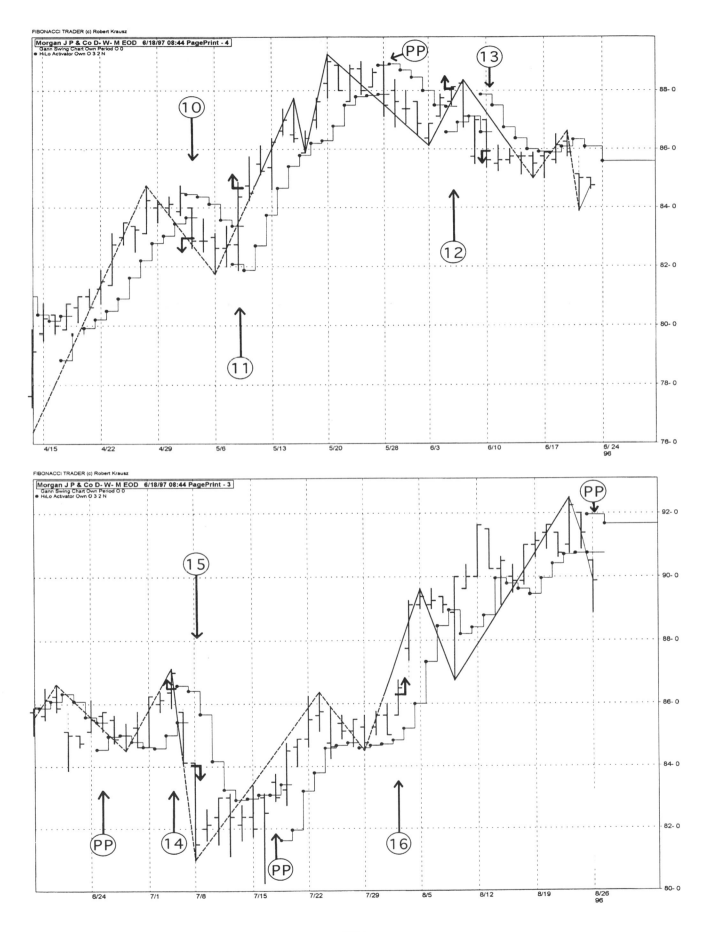

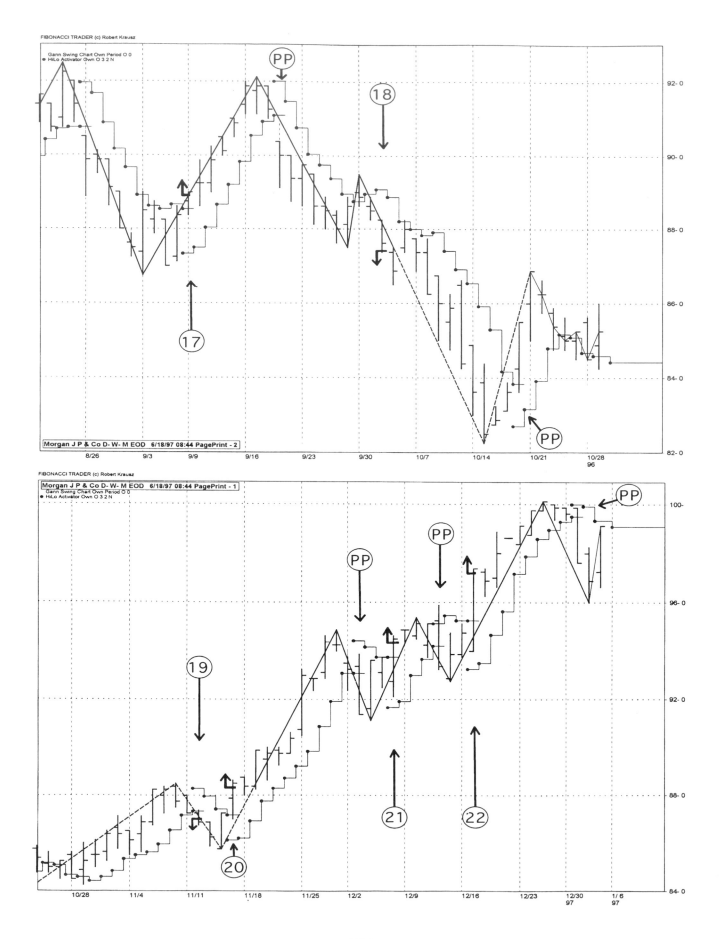

INTEL - 1992-1996 (5 YRS.) EOD.
BASIC SWING PLAN - COMPOSITE
GANN SWING CHARTIST - FIBONACCI TRADER ®

With 100% Margin

Beginning Equity	$11,250.00	Ending Equity	$67,990.00
Total Net Profit	$68,500.00	Gross Loss	($56,500.00)
Gross Profit	$125,000.00	Total Commissions	$11,760.00
Total No. Trades	98	Percentage Profitable	45%
No. Winning Trades	44	No. Losing Trades	54

Largest Winning Trade	$13,875.00	Largest Losing Trade	($3,250.00)
Average Winning Trade	$2,840.91	Average Losing Trade	($1,046.30)
Max. Consecutive Winners	3	Max. Consecutive Losses	4
Average Drawdown (%)	12.98%	Average Drawdown ($)	($4,620.00)

Average Return on Account	37%
Profit/Drawdown Ratio	14.83

With 50% Margin

Beginning Equity	$5,625.00	Ending Equity	$62,365.00
Total Net Profit	$68,500.00	Gross Loss	($56,500.00)
Gross Profit	$125,000.00	Total Commissions	$11,760.00
Total No. Trades	98	Percentage Profitable	45%
No. Winning Trades	44	No. Losing Trades	10

Largest Winning Trade	$13,875.00	Largest Losing Trade	($3,250.00)
Average Winning Trade	$2,840.91	Average Losing Trade	($5,650.00)
Max. Consecutive Winners	3	Max. Consecutive Losses	4
Average Drawdown (%)	21.82%	Average Drawdown ($)	($4,620.00)

Average Return on Account	74%
Profit/Drawdown Ratio	14.83

Notes:
1) Each trade is equal to 1,000 shares.
2) Initial account is equal to what it would cost
   to trade 1,000 shares at a price/share at that time.
3) Commission is equal to 12 cents per round turn per share.
4) Plan handles less or more shares, percentages are the same.

INTEL - 1992
BASIC SWING PLAN
GANN SWING CHARTIST - FIBONACCI TRADER®

With 100% Margin

Beginning Equity	$11,250.00	Ending Equity	$19,935.00
Total Net Profit	$10,125.00	Gross Loss	($2,750.00)
Gross Profit	$12,875.00	Total Commissions	$1,440.00
Total No. Trades	12	Percentage Profitable	33%
No. Winning Trades	4	No. Losing Trades	8

Largest Winning Trade	$5,625.00	Largest Losing Trade	($1,125.00)
Average Winning Trade	$3,218.75	Average Losing Trade	($343.75)
Ratio Average Win/Loss	9.36	Average Trade	$843.75
Max. Consecutive Winners	1	Max. Consecutive Losses	4
Largest Consecutive Drawdown (%)	9.90%	Largest Consecutive Drawdown	($1,585.00)

Return on Account	77%
Profit/Drawdown Ratio	6.39

With 50% Margin

Beginning Equity	$5,625.00	Ending Equity	$14,310.00
Total Net Profit	$10,125.00	Gross Loss	($2,750.00)
Gross Profit	$12,875.00	Total Commissions	$1,440.00
Total No. Trades	12	Percentage Profitable	33%
No. Winning Trades	4	No. Losing Trades	8

Largest Winning Trade	$5,625.00	Largest Losing Trade	($1,125.00)
Average Winning Trade	$3,218.75	Average Losing Trade	($343.75)
Ratio Average Win/Loss	9.36	Average Trade	$843.75
Max. Consecutive Winners	1	Max. Consecutive Losses	4
Largest Consecutive Drawdown (%)	15.26%	Largest Consecutive Drawdown	($1,585.00)

Return on Account	154%
Profit/Drawdown Ratio	6.39

Notes:
1) Each trade is equal to 1,000 shares.
2) Initial account is equal to what it would cost
   to trade 1,000 shares at a price/share at that time.
3) Commission is equal to 12 cents per round turn.
4) Plan handles less or more shares.

1992

Intel - Gann Swing Chartist®

Basic Swing Plan (End of Day)

Fibonacci Trader®

Trade #	Date	L/S	Price	Rule #	Profit	(Loss)	Accum.	A/C Equity	50% Margin
1	12/23/91	L	11 1/4	Buy 1				$11,250.00	$5,625.00
PP	2/18/92	S	16 1/8	PP1	4 7/8		$ 4,755.00	$16,005.00	$10,380.00
2	2/21/92	L	16 7/8	Buy 1					$9,135.00
3	3/5/92	S	15 3/4	Sell 2		-1 1/8	$ 3,510.00	$14,760.00	
PP	4/6/92	L	14 3/8	PP1	1 3/8		$ 4,765.00	$16,015.00	$10,390.00
4	4/10/92	S	12 3/4	Sell 1					
5	4/30/92	L	13 1/8	Buy 2		- 3/8	$ 4,270.00	$15,520.00	$9,895.00
PP	5/12/92	S	12 7/8	PP1		- 2/8	$ 3,900.00	$15,150.00	$9,525.00
6	5/14/92	S	12 1/8	Sell 2					
PP	5/22/92	L	12 1/4	PP1		- 1/8	$ 3,655.00	$14,905.00	$9,280.00
7	6/19/92	L	13	Buy 2					
PP	7/17/92	S	14	PP1	1		$ 4,535.00	$15,785.00	$10,160.00
8	7/20/92	S	14	Sell 2					
PP	7/23/92	L	14 1/2	PP1		- 4/8	$ 3,915.00	$15,165.00	$9,540.00
9	7/29/92	L	14 3/4	Buy 2					
PP	8/6/92	S	14 5/8	PP1		- 1/8	$ 3,670.00	$14,920.00	$9,295.00
10	9/3/92	L	15 1/4	Buy 2					
PP	10/1/92	S	15 7/8	PP1		5/8	$ 4,175.00	$15,425.00	$9,800.00
11	10/5/92	S	15 1/2	Sell 2					
12	10/19/92	L	16 3/8	Buy 1		- 7/8	$ 3,180.00	$14,430.00	$8,805.00
PP	12/30/92	S	22	PP1	5 5/8		$ 8,685.00	$19,935.00	$14,310.00

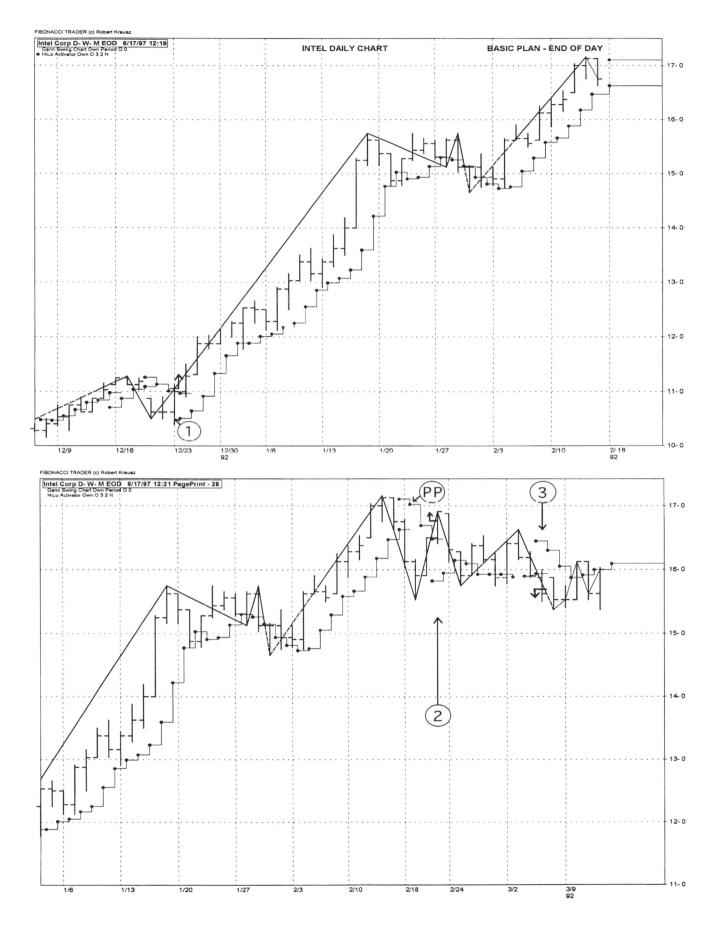

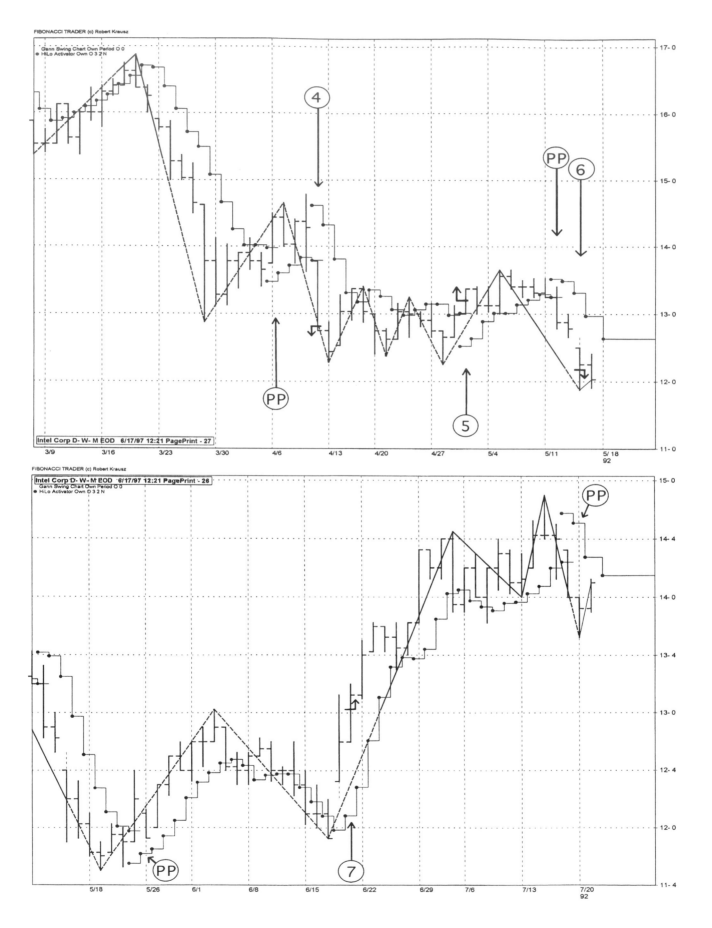

FIBONACCI TRADER (c) Robert Krausz

Gann Swing Chart Own Period O 0
● HiLo Activator Own O 3 2 N

Intel Corp D- W- M EOD 6/17/97 12:21 PagePrint - 27

FIBONACCI TRADER (c) Robert Krausz

Intel Corp D- W- M EOD 6/17/97 12:21 PagePrint - 26
Gann Swing Chart Own Period O 0
● HiLo Activator Own O 3 2 N

238

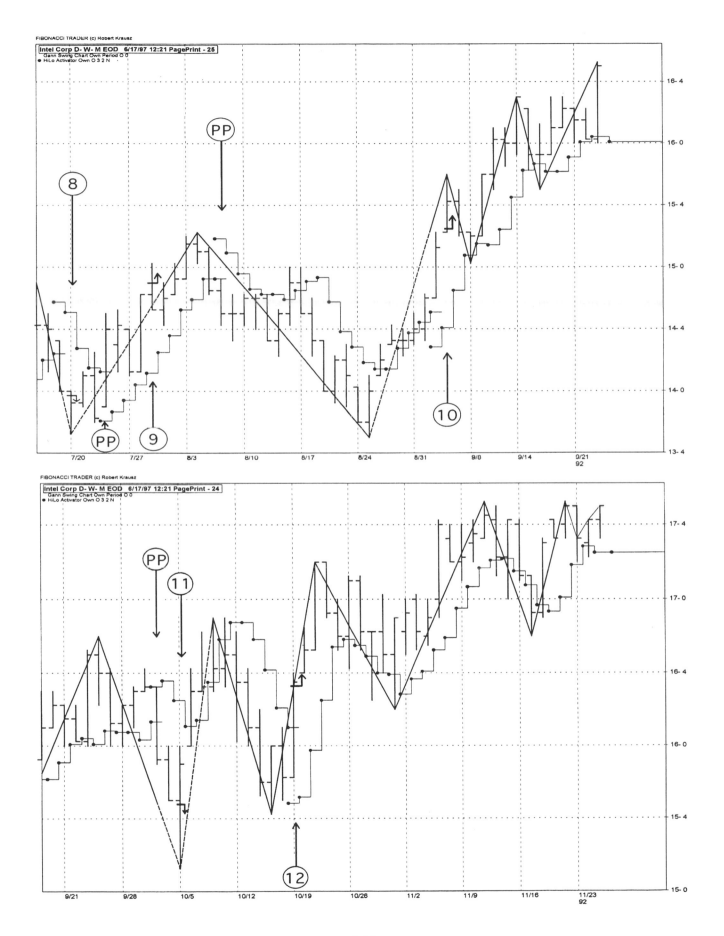

INTEL - 1993
BASIC SWING PLAN
GANN SWING CHARTIST - FIBONACCI TRADER®

With 100% Margin

Beginning Equity	$22,750.00	Ending Equity	$21,105.00
Total Net Profit	$875.00	Gross Loss	($12,000.00)
Gross Profit	$12,875.00	Total Commissions	$2,520.00
Total No. Trades	21	Percentage Profitable	38%
No. Winning Trades	8	No. Losing Trades	13

Largest Winning Trade	$4,500.00	Largest Losing Trade	($2,000.00)
Average Winning Trade	$1,609.38	Average Losing Trade	($923.08)
Ratio Average Win/Loss	1.74	Average Trade	$41.67
Max. Consecutive Winners	1	Max. Consecutive Losses	4
Largest Consecutive Drawdown (%)	25.91%	Largest Consecutive Drawdown	($7,030.00)

Return on Account	-7%
Profit/Drawdown Ratio	0.12

With 50% Margin

Beginning Equity	$11,375.00	Ending Equity	$9,730.00
Total Net Profit	$875.00	Gross Loss	($12,000.00)
Gross Profit	$12,875.00	Total Commissions	$2,520.00
Total No. Trades	21	Percentage Profitable	38%
No. Winning Trades	8	No. Losing Trades	13

Largest Winning Trade	$4,500.00	Largest Losing Trade	($2,000.00)
Average Winning Trade	$1,609.38	Average Losing Trade	($923.08)
Ratio Average Win/Loss	1.74	Average Trade	$41.67
Max. Consecutive Winners	1	Max. Consecutive Losses	4
Largest Consecutive Drawdown (%)	44.62%	Largest Consecutive Drawdown	($7,030.00)

Return on Account	-14%
Profit/Drawdown Ratio	0.12

Notes:
1) Each trade is equal to 1,000 shares.
2) Initial account is equal to what it would cost
   to trade 1,000 shares at a price/share at that time.
3) Commission is equal to 12 cents per round turn.
4) Plan handles less or more shares.

1993
Intel - Gann Swing Chartist®
Basic Swing Plan (End of Day)

Fibonacci Trader®

Trade #	Date	L/S	Price	Rule #	Profit	(Loss)	Accum.	A/C Equity	50% Margin
1	1/5/93	L	22 3/4	Buy 1				$22,750.00	$11,375.00
PP	1/28/93	S	27 1/4	PP1	4 4/8		$ 4,380.00	$27,130.00	$15,755.00
2	2/8/93	S	26 1/2	Sell 2					
PP	2/9/93	L	27 5/8	PP1		-1 1/8	$ 3,135.00	$25,885.00	$14,510.00
3	2/10/93	L	28	Buy 2					
PP	2/16/93	S	26 3/8	PP1		-1 5/8	$ 1,390.00	$24,140.00	$12,765.00
4	2/22/93	L	28 7/8	Buy 2					
PP	3/17/93	S	28 5/8	PP1		- 2/8	$ 1,020.00	$23,770.00	$12,395.00
5	3/19/93	S	28 3/4	Sell 2					
PP	4/7/93	L	28 1/2	PP1	2/8		$ 1,150.00	$23,900.00	$12,525.00
6	4/12/93	L	29 1/8	Buy 2					
PP	4/16/93	S	27 3/8	PP1		-1 6/8	$ (720.00)	$22,030.00	$10,655.00
7	4/19/93	S	24 3/4	Sell 2					
PP	4/29/93	L	23 7/8	PP1	7/8		$ 35.00	$22,785.00	$11,410.00
8	5/11/93	S	24 7/8	Sell 1					
PP	5/18/93	L	25 1/4	PP1		- 3/8	$ (460.00)	$22,290.00	$10,915.00
9	5/19/93	L	25 5/8	Buy 2					
PP	6/9/93	S	27 7/8	PP1	2 2/8		$ 1,670.00	$24,420.00	$13,045.00
10	6/9/93	S	28 1/2	Sell 2					
PP	6/14/93	L	29 1/8	PP1		- 5/8	$ 925.00	$23,675.00	$12,300.00
11	6/18/93	S	27 5/8	Sell 1					
PP	6/28/93	L	28	PP1		- 3/8	$ 430.00	$23,180.00	$11,805.00
12	7/1/93	S	27	Sell 1					
PP	7/8/93	L	27 3/8	PP1		- 3/8	$ (65.00)	$22,685.00	$11,310.00
13	7/15/93	S	26 1/4	Sell 1					
PP	7/26/93	L	26 3/8	PP1		- 1/8	$ (310.00)	$22,440.00	$11,065.00
14	8/6/93	L	28 1/2	Buy 2					
PP	9/7/93	S	31	PP1	2 4/8		$ 2,070.00	$24,820.00	$13,445.00
15	9/8/93	S	30 5/8	Sell 2					
PP	9/9/93	L	32 3/8	PP1		-1 6/8	$ 200.00	$22,950.00	$11,575.00
16	9/9/93	L	32 3/8	Buy 2					
PP	9/14/93	S	31 5/8	PP1		- 6/8	$ (670.00)	$22,080.00	$10,705.00
17	9/22/93	L	33 5/8	Buy 1					
PP	10/5/93	S	35	PP1	1 3/8		$ 585.00	$23,335.00	$11,960.00

1993

Intel – Gann Swing Chartist®

Basic Swing Plan (End of Day)

Fibonacci Trader®

18	11/3/93	S	30 7/8	Sell 2					
PP	11/10/93	L	31 3/4	PP1	- 7/8		$ (410.00)	$22,340.00	$10,965.00
19	11/15/93	S	30	Sell 1					
PP	11/24/93	L	30	PP1		0	$ (530.00)	$22,220.00	$10,845.00
20	12/1/93	L	30 7/8	Buy 2					
PP	12/6/93	S	28 7/8	PP1	-2		$ (2,650.00)	$20,100.00	$8,725.00
21	12/22/93	L	29 7/8	Buy 2					
PP	12/31/93	S	31	PP1		1 1/8	$ (1,645.00)	$21,105.00	$9,730.00

242

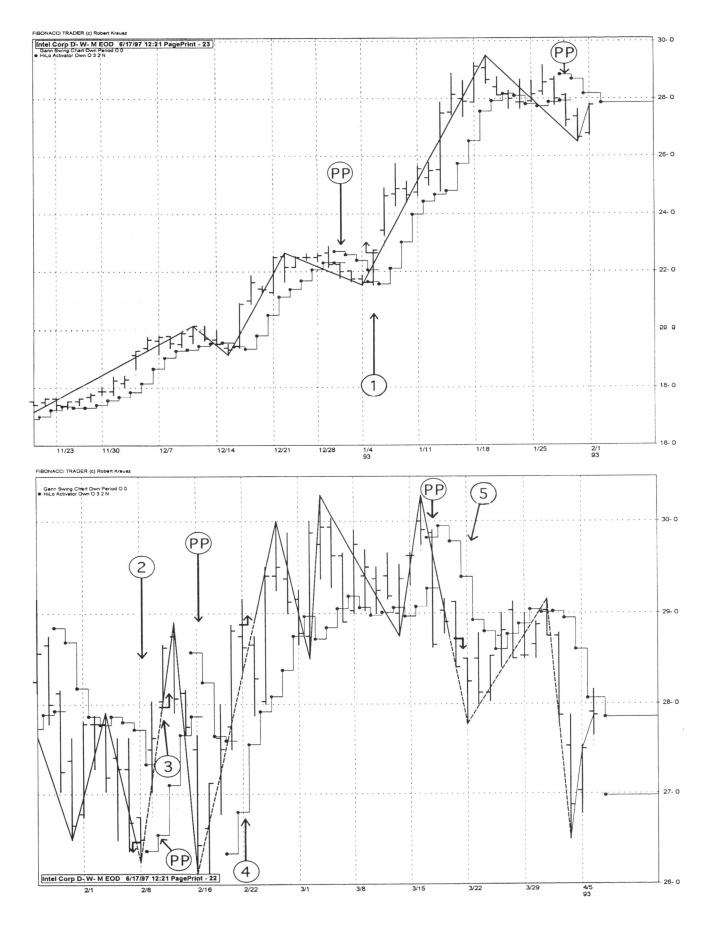

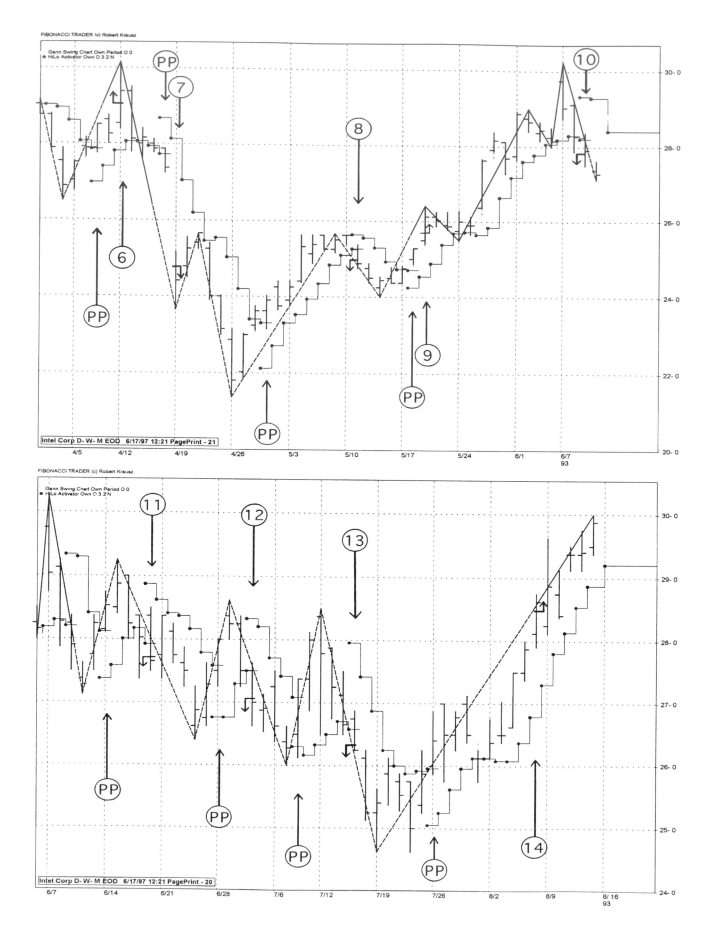

244

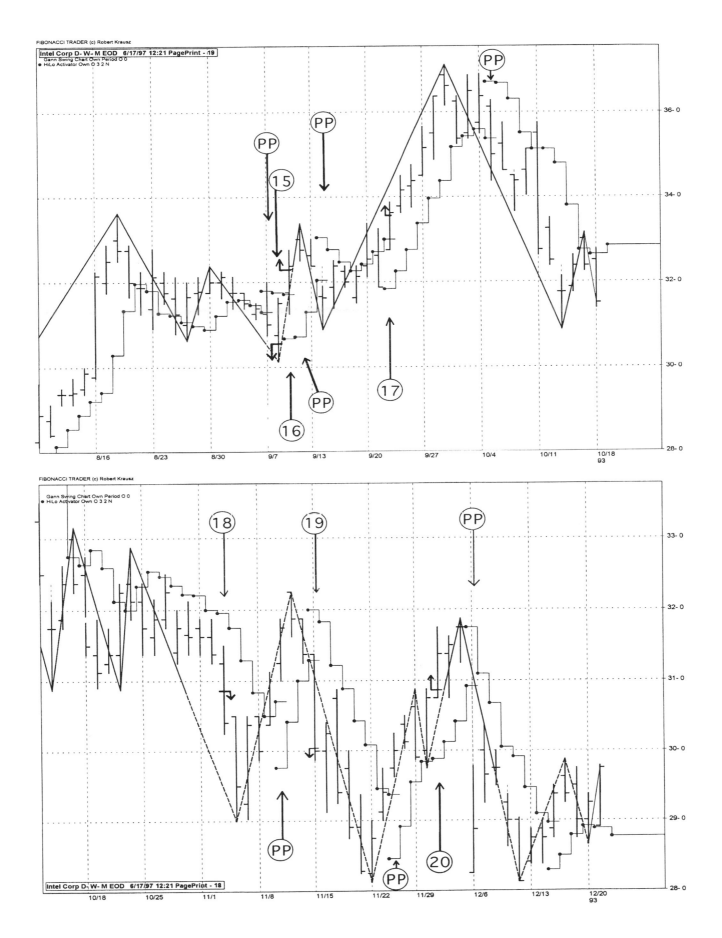

INTEL - 1994
BASIC SWING PLAN
GANN SWING CHARTIST - FIBONACCI TRADER®

With 100% Margin

Beginning Equity	$31,875.00	Ending Equity	$29,000.00
Total Net Profit	$125.00	Gross Loss	($11,000.00)
Gross Profit	$11,125.00	Total Commissions	$3,000.00
Total No. Trades	25	Percentage Profitable	44%
No. Winning Trades	11	No. Losing Trades	14

Largest Winning Trade	$2,500.00	Largest Losing Trade	($1,250.00)
Average Winning Trade	$1,011.36	Average Losing Trade	($785.71)
Ratio Average Win/Loss	1.29	Average Trade	$5.00
Max. Consecutive Winners	3	Max. Consecutive Losses	3
Largest Consecutive Drawdown (%)	12.91%	Largest Consecutive Drawdown	($4,260.00)

Return on Account	-9%
Profit/Drawdown Ratio	0.03

With 50% Margin

Beginning Equity	$15,937.50	Ending Equity	$13,062.50
Total Net Profit	$125.00	Gross Loss	($11,000.00)
Gross Profit	$11,125.00	Total Commissions	$3,000.00
Total No. Trades	25	Percentage Profitable	44%
No. Winning Trades	11	No. Losing Trades	14

Largest Winning Trade	$2,500.00	Largest Losing Trade	($1,250.00)
Average Winning Trade	$1,011.36	Average Losing Trade	($785.71)
Ratio Average Win/Loss	1.29	Average Trade	$5.00
Max. Consecutive Winners	3	Max. Consecutive Losses	3
Largest Consecutive Drawdown (%)	24.96%	Largest Consecutive Drawdown	($4,260.00)

Return on Account	-18%
Profit/Drawdown Ratio	0.03

Notes:
1) Each trade is equal to 1,000 shares.
2) Initial account is equal to what it would cost
   to trade 1,000 shares at a price/share at that time.
3) Commission is equal to 12 cents per round turn.
4) Plan handles less or more shares.

1994

Intel - Gann Swing Chartist®

Basic Swing Plan (End of Day)

Fibonacci Trader®

Trade #	Date	L/S	Price	Rule #	Profit	(Loss)	Accum.	A/C Equity	50% Margin
1	1/4/94	L	31 7/8	Buy 1				$31,875.00	$15,937.50
PP	1/17/94	S	33 1/8	PP1	1 2/8		$ 1,130.00	$33,005.00	$17,067.50
2	1/24/94	L	32 3/4	Buy 1					
PP	1/26/94	S	31 3/4	PP1		-1	$ 10.00	$31,885.00	$15,947.50
3	2/4/94	S	30 3/4	Sell 2					
PP	2/9/94	L	32	PP1		-1 2/8	$ (1,360.00)	$30,515.00	$14,577.50
4	2/15/94	L	32 1/4	Buy 2					
PP	3/1/94	S	33 3/8	PP1	1 1/8		$ (355.00)	$31,520.00	$15,582.50
5	3/4/94	L	34 3/4	Buy 1					
PP	3/10/94	S	34 3/4	PP1	0		$ (475.00)	$31,400.00	$15,462.50
6	3/15/94	L	35 5/8	Buy 1					
PP	3/24/94	S	35 1/8	PP1		- 4/8	$ (1,095.00)	$30,780.00	$14,842.50
7	4/5/94	L	34 3/8	Buy 1					
PP	4/12/94	S	34	PP2		- 3/8	$ (1,590.00)	$30,285.00	$14,347.50
8	4/13/94	S	32 5/8	Sell 2					
PP	4/22/94	L	30 1/8	PP1	2 4/8		$ 790.00	$32,665.00	$16,727.50
9	5/2/94	S	30 1/4	Sell 1					
PP	5/18/94	L	29 5/8	PP1	5/8		$ 1,295.00	$33,170.00	$17,232.50
10	5/31/94	L	30 7/8	Buy 2					
PP	6/6/94	S	30 7/8	PP1	0		$ 1,175.00	$33,050.00	$17,112.50
11	6/8/94	S	29 7/8	Sell 2					
PP	6/14/94	L	30 5/8	PP1		- 6/8	$ 305.00	$32,180.00	$16,242.50
12	6/20/94	S	29 3/8	Sell 1					
PP	7/8/94	L	28 1/2	PP1	7/8		$ 1,060.00	$32,935.00	$16,997.50
13	7/13/94	L	30 3/8	Buy 2					
PP	7/15/94	S	29 7/8	PP1		- 4/8	$ 440.00	$32,315.00	$16,377.50
14	7/20/94	S	28 1/4	Sell 2					
PP	7/22/94	L	29 1/4	PP2		-1	$ (680.00)	$31,195.00	$15,257.50
15	8/4/94	S	28 5/8	Sell 1					
PP	8/10/94	L	29 7/8	PP1		-1 2/8	$ (2,050.00)	$29,825.00	$13,887.50
16	8/11/94	L	30 1/8	Buy 2					
PP	9/1/94	S	32 1/8	PP1	2		$ (170.00)	$31,705.00	$15,767.50
17	9/7/94	L	33 1/8	Buy 1					

1994

Intel - Gann Swing Chartist®

Basic Swing Plan (End of Day)

Fibonacci Trader®

PP	9/12/94	S	32 1/4	PP1		- 7/8	$ (1,165.00)	$30,710.00	$14,772.50
18	9/15/94	L	33 1/2	Buy 1					
PP	9/21/94	S	32 5/8	PP1		- 7/8	$ (2,160.00)	$29,715.00	$13,777.50
19	9/23/94	S	31 7/8	Sell 2					
PP	10/10/94	L	30 1/4	PP1	1 5/8		$ (655.00)	$31,220.00	$15,282.50
20	10/13/94	S	29 3/8	Sell 1					
PP	10/19/94	L	30	PP1		- 5/8	$ (1,400.00)	$30,475.00	$14,537.50
21	10/25/94	S	29 1/2	Sell 1					
PP	10/27/94	L	30 1/4	PP1		- 6/8	$ (2,270.00)	$29,605.00	$13,667.50
22	10/28/94	L	30 1/2	Buy 2					
PP	11/4/94	S	30 1/8	PP1		- 3/8	$ (2,765.00)	$29,110.00	$13,172.50
23	11/14/94	L	31 1/8	Buy 1					
PP	11/30/94	S	31 7/8	PP2	6/8		$ (2,135.00)	$29,740.00	$13,802.50
24	12/6/94	L	32 1/4	Buy 1					
PP	12/8/94	S	31 3/8	PP1		- 7/8	$ (3,130.00)	$28,745.00	$12,807.50
25	12/12/94	S	30 5/8	Sell 2					
PP	12/20/94	L	30 1/4	PP2	3/8		$ (2,875.00)	$29,000.00	$13,062.50

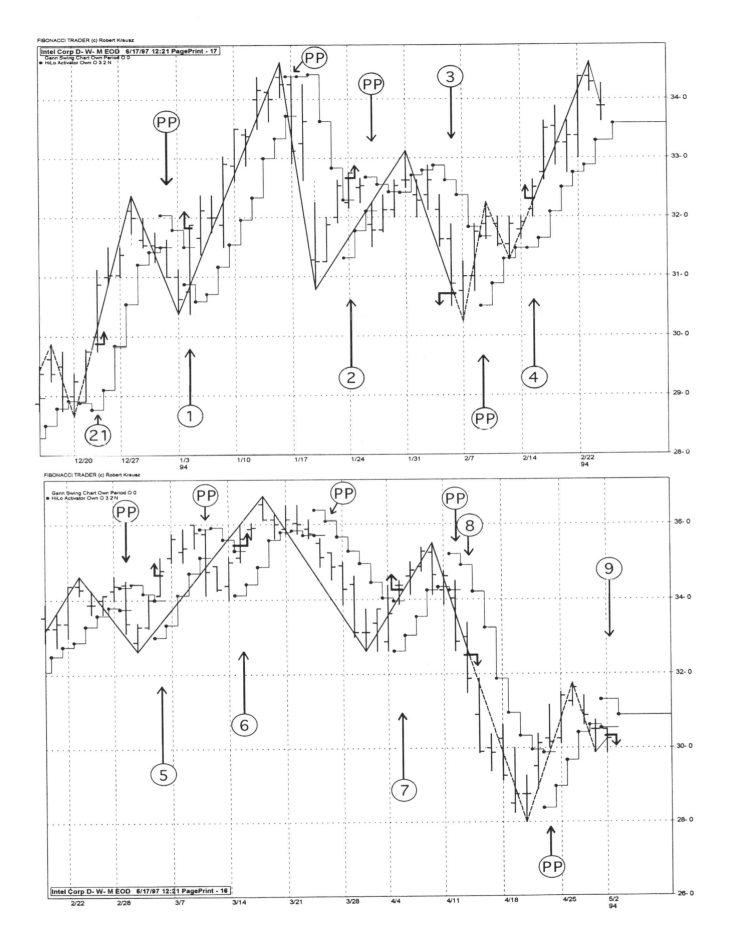

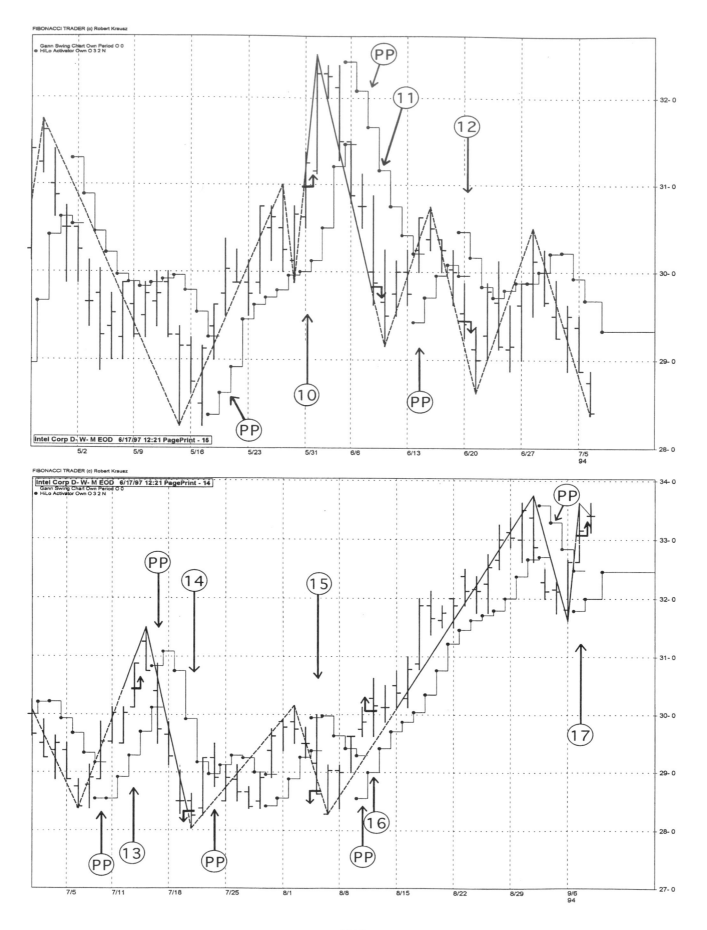

250

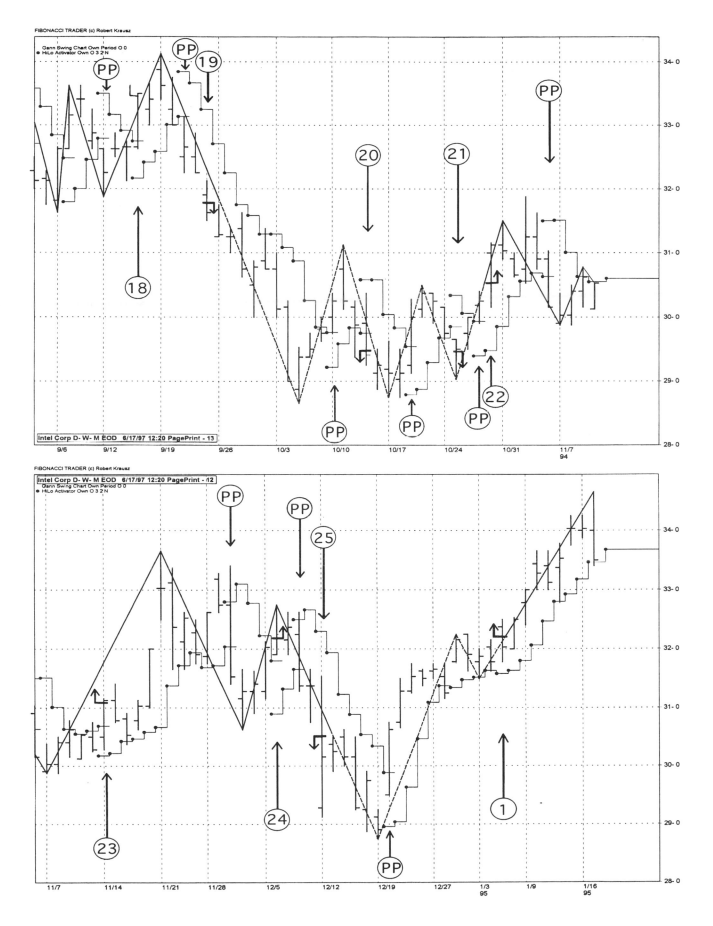

INTEL - 1995
BASIC SWING PLAN
GANN SWING CHARTIST - FIBONACCI TRADER®

With 100% Margin

Beginning Equity	$32,250.00	Ending Equity	$54,960.00
Total Net Profit	$24,750.00	Gross Loss	($10,625.00)
Gross Profit	$35,375.00	Total Commissions	$2,040.00
Total No. Trades	17	Percentage Profitable	53%
No. Winning Trades	9	No. Losing Trades	8

Largest Winning Trade	$12,750.00	Largest Losing Trade	($2,125.00)
Average Winning Trade	$3,930.56	Average Losing Trade	($1,328.13)
Ratio Average Win/Loss	2.96	Average Trade	$1,455.88
Max. Consecutive Winners	3	Max. Consecutive Losses	4
Largest Consecutive Drawdown (%)	9.43%	Largest Consecutive Drawdown	($4,980.00)

Return on Account	70%
Profit/Drawdown Ratio	4.97

With 50% Margin

Beginning Equity	$16,125.00	Ending Equity	$38,835.00
Total Net Profit	$24,750.00	Gross Loss	($10,625.00)
Gross Profit	$35,375.00	Total Commissions	$2,040.00
Total No. Trades	17	Percentage Profitable	53%
No. Winning Trades	9	No. Losing Trades	8

Largest Winning Trade	$12,750.00	Largest Losing Trade	($2,125.00)
Average Winning Trade	$3,930.56	Average Losing Trade	($1,328.13)
Ratio Average Win/Loss	2.96	Average Trade	$1,455.88
Max. Consecutive Winners	3	Max. Consecutive Losses	4
Largest Consecutive Drawdown (%)	13.58%	Largest Consecutive Drawdown	($4,980.00)

Return on Account	141%
Profit/Drawdown Ratio	4.97

Notes:
1) Each trade is equal to 1,000 shares.
2) Initial account is equal to what it would cost
   to trade 1,000 shares at a price/share at that time.
3) Commission is equal to 12 cents per round turn.
4) Plan handles less or more shares.

252

1995

Intel - Gann Swing Chartist®
Basic Swing Plan (End of Day)

Fibonacci Trader®

Trade #	Date	L/S	Price	Rule #	Profit	(Loss)	Accum.	A/C Equity	50% Margin
1	1/5/95	L	32 1/4	Buy 2				$32,250.00	$16,125.00
PP	1/31/95	S	34 5/8	PP1	2 3/8		$ 2,255.00	$34,505.00	$18,380.00
2	2/2/95	L	36 1/8	Buy 1					
PP	2/23/95	S	39	PP1	2 7/8		$ 5,010.00	$37,260.00	$21,135.00
3	2/24/95	S	39 1/8	Sell 2					
4	3/3/95	L	40 1/4	Buy 2		-1 1/8	$ 3,765.00	$36,015.00	$19,890.00
PP	3/17/95	S	40 3/8	PP1	1/8		$ 3,770.00	$36,020.00	$19,895.00
5	3/20/95	L	41 5/8	Buy 1					
PP	3/30/95	S	43 1/8	PP2	1 4/8		$ 5,150.00	$37,400.00	$21,275.00
6	4/3/95	L	44 1/4	Buy 1					
PP	5/30/95	S	57	PP2	12 6/8		$17,780.00	$50,030.00	$33,905.00
7	6/2/95	L	58 1/4	Buy 1					
PP	6/6/95	S	56 1/8	PP1		-2 1/8	$15,535.00	$47,785.00	$31,660.00
8	6/15/95	L	57 1/2	Buy 1					
PP	6/27/95	S	62 5/8	PP1	5 1/8		$20,540.00	$52,790.00	$36,665.00
9	7/6/95	L	65 1/2	Buy 1					
PP	7/19/95	S	65 1/4	PP2		- 2/8	$20,170.00	$52,420.00	$36,295.00
10	7/25/95	L	68 5/8	Buy 1					
PP	7/28/95	S	67 1/8	PP1		-1 4/8	$18,550.00	$50,800.00	$34,675.00
11	8/2/95	S	62 1/2	Sell 2					
PP	8/8/95	L	64 1/4	PP2		-1 6/8	$16,680.00	$48,930.00	$32,805.00
12	8/21/95	S	60 3/8	Sell 1					
PP	8/31/95	L	61 3/8	PP1		-1	$15,560.00	$47,810.00	$31,685.00
13	9/14/95	S	63 3/4	Sell 1					
PP	9/28/95	L	60 7/8	PP2	2 7/8		$18,315.00	$50,565.00	$34,440.00
14	10/4/95	S	58 3/4	Sell 1					
PP	10/5/95	L	60 7/8	PP1		-2 1/8	$16,070.00	$48,320.00	$32,195.00
15	10/6/95	L	62 3/4	Buy 2					
PP	11/7/95	S	68 7/8	PP2	6 1/8		$22,075.00	$54,325.00	$38,200.00
16	11/15/95	S	64 7/8	Sell 2					
PP	12/8/95	L	63 1/4	PP1	1 5/8		$23,580.00	$55,830.00	$39,705.00
17	12/14/95	S	60	Sell 1					
PP	12/20/95	L	60 3/4	PP2		- 6/8	$22,710.00	$54,960.00	$38,835.00

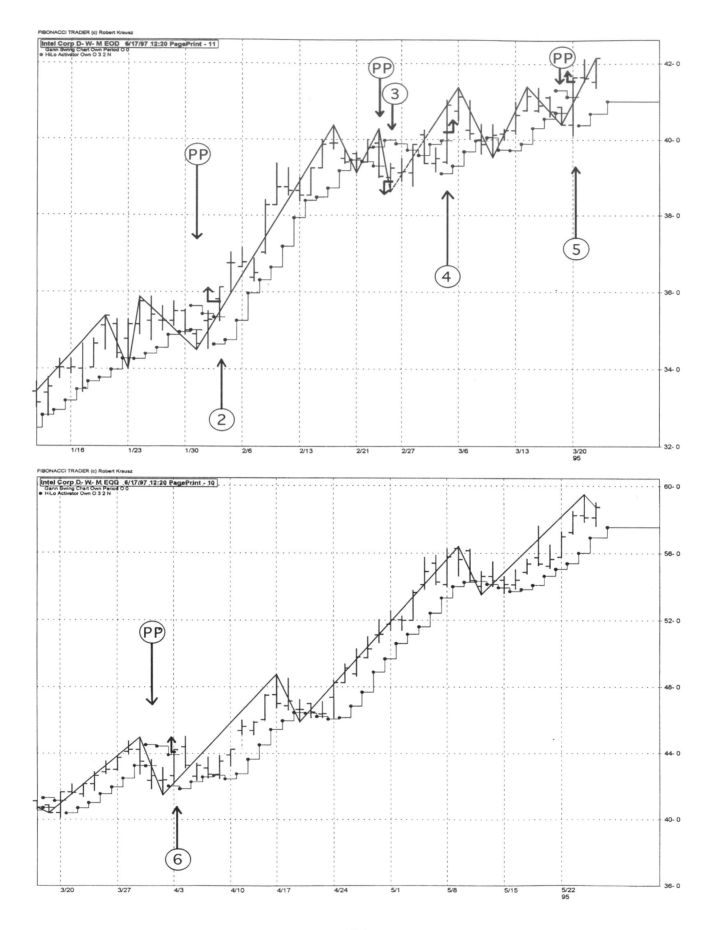

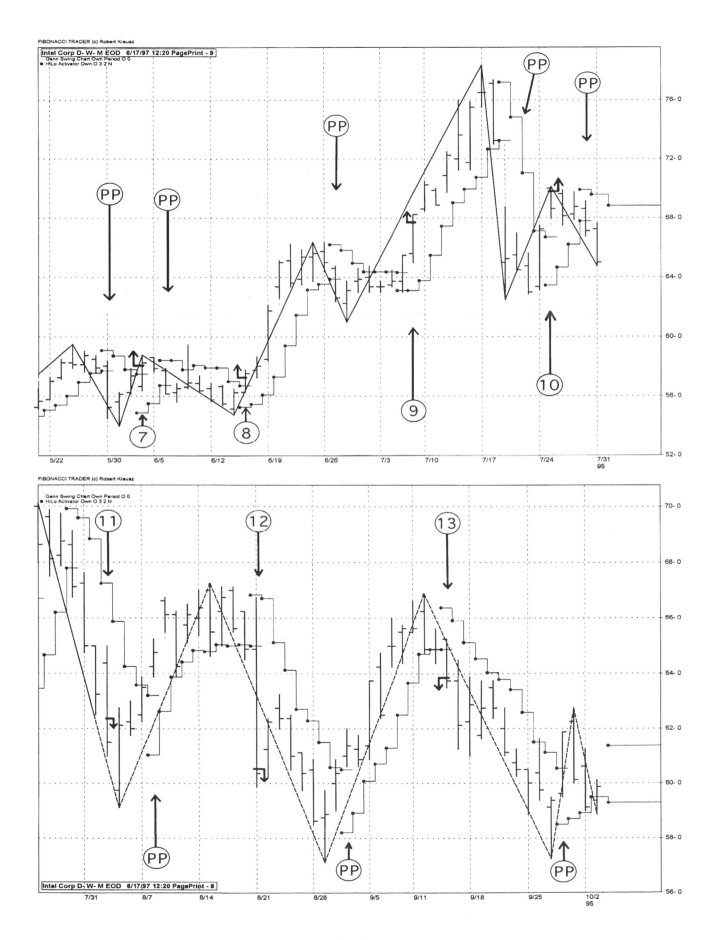

FIBONACCI TRADER (c) Robert Krausz

Intel Corp D- W- M EOD 6/17/97 12:20 PagePrint - 9
Gann Swing Chart Own Period O 0
● HiLo Activator Own O 3 2 N

FIBONACCI TRADER (c) Robert Krausz

Gann Swing Chart Own Period O 0
● HiLo Activator Own O 3 2 N

Intel Corp D- W- M EOD 6/17/97 12:20 PagePrint - 8

INTEL - 1996
BASIC SWING PLAN
GANN SWING CHARTIST - FIBONACCI TRADER®

With 100% Margin

Beginning Equity	$56,750.00	Ending Equity	$86,615.00
Total Net Profit	$32,625.00	Gross Loss	($20,125.00)
Gross Profit	$52,750.00	Total Commissions	$2,760.00
Total No. Trades	23	Percentage Profitable	52%
No. Winning Trades	12	No. Losing Trades	11

Largest Winning Trade	$13,250.00	Largest Losing Trade	($5,125.00)
Average Winning Trade	$4,395.83	Average Losing Trade	($1,829.55)
Ratio Average Win/Loss	2.40	Average Trade	$1,418.48
Max. Consecutive Winners	3	Max. Consecutive Losses	2
Largest Consecutive Drawdown (%)	6.76%	Largest Consecutive Drawdown	($5,245.00)

Return on Account	53%
Profit/Drawdown Ratio	6.22

With 50% Margin

Beginning Equity	$28,375.00	Ending Equity	$58,240.00
Total Net Profit	$32,625.00	Gross Loss	($20,125.00)
Gross Profit	$52,750.00	Total Commissions	$2,760.00
Total No. Trades	23	Percentage Profitable	52%
No. Winning Trades	12	No. Losing Trades	11

Largest Winning Trade	$13,250.00	Largest Losing Trade	($5,125.00)
Average Winning Trade	$4,395.83	Average Losing Trade	($1,829.55)
Ratio Average Win/Loss	2.40	Average Trade	$1,418.48
Max. Consecutive Winners	3	Max. Consecutive Losses	2
Largest Consecutive Drawdown (%)	10.66%	Largest Consecutive Drawdown	($5,245.00)

Return on Account	105%
Profit/Drawdown Ratio	6.22

Notes:
1) Each trade is equal to 1,000 shares.
2) Initial account is equal to what it would cost
   to trade 1,000 shares at a price/share at that time.
3) Commission is equal to 12 cents per round turn.
4) Plan handles less or more shares.

257

1996

Intel - Gann Swing Chartist®
Basic Swing Plan (End of Day)

Fibonacci Trader®

Trade #	Date	L/S	Price	Rule #	Profit	(Loss)	Accum.	A/C Equity	50% Margin
1	1/4/96	S	56 3/4	Sell 3				$56,750.00	$28,375.00
PP	1/23/96	L	52 3/4	PP1	4		$ 3,880.00	$60,630.00	$32,255.00
2	2/5/96	L	57 1/2	Buy 2					$31,760.00
PP	2/13/96	S	57 1/8	PP1		- 3/8	$ 3,385.00	$60,135.00	$31,760.00
3	2/21/96	L	59 1/4	Buy 1					
PP	2/29/96	S	58 7/8	PP1		- 3/8	$ 2,890.00	$59,640.00	$31,265.00
4	3/1/96	S	57 1/8	Sell 2					
PP	3/11/96	L	55 1/4	PP1	1 7/8		$ 4,645.00	$61,395.00	$33,020.00
5	3/20/96	S	55 1/2	Sell 1					
PP	3/27/96	L	56 1/2	PP2		-1	$ 3,525.00	$60,275.00	$31,900.00
6	4/8/96	L	60 1/4	Buy 2					
PP	4/12/96	S	59 5/8	PP1		- 5/8	$ 2,780.00	$59,530.00	$31,155.00
7	4/16/96	L	64	Buy 3					
PP	4/29/96	S	68 1/8	PP1	4 1/8		$ 6,785.00	$63,535.00	$35,160.00
8	5/13/96	L	71 3/4	Buy 1					
PP	5/17/96	S	71 1/8	PP1		- 5/8	$ 6,040.00	$62,790.00	$34,415.00
9	5/28/96	L	72 1/2	Buy 1					
PP	6/7/96	S	75 1/4	PP1	2 6/8		$ 8,670.00	$65,420.00	$37,045.00
10	6/12/96	L	76 3/4	Buy 1					
11	6/14/96	S	73 1/2	Sell 2		-3 2/8	$ 5,300.00	$62,050.00	$33,675.00
PP	6/24/96	L	73	PP2	4/8		$ 5,680.00	$62,430.00	$34,055.00
12	7/5/96	S	72 1/8	Sell 1					
PP	7/17/96	L	71	PP2	1 1/8		$ 6,685.00	$63,435.00	$35,060.00
13	7/23/96	S	69 1/2	Sell 1					
PP	7/25/96	L	71 7/8	PP2		-2 3/8	$ 4,190.00	$60,940.00	$32,565.00
14	8/1/96	L	75 7/8	Buy 2					
PP	8/20/96	S	79 1/2	PP1	3 5/8		$ 7,695.00	$64,445.00	$36,070.00
15	8/22/96	L	83	Buy 1					
16	8/30/96	S	80 1/8	Sell 2		-2 7/8	$ 4,700.00	$61,450.00	$33,075.00
17	9/4/96	L	82 1/4	Buy 2					
PP	9/30/96	S	95 1/2	PP1	13 2/8		$17,830.00	$74,580.00	$46,205.00
18	10/2/96	L	99	Buy 1					
PP	10/10/96	S	99 7/8	PP1	7/8		$18,585.00	$75,335.00	$46,960.00

1996
Intel - Gann Swing Chartist®
Basic Swing Plan (End of Day)

Fibonacci Trader®

	Date	L/S	Price	Signal					
19	10/11/96	L	105 3/8	Buy 1					
PP	10/21/96	S	107 3/4	PP1	2 3/8		$ 20,840.00	$77,590.00	$49,215.00
20	10/29/96	S	104 3/4	Sell 2					
PP	10/31/96	L	109 7/8	PP1		-5 1/8	$ 15,595.00	$72,345.00	$43,970.00
21	11/5/96	L	111 1/8	Buy 2					
PP	11/13/96	S	119 1/2	PP1	8 3/8		$ 23,850.00	$80,600.00	$52,225.00
22	11/19/96	L	120 3/4	Buy 1					
PP	12/16/96	S	130 5/8	PP2	9 7/8		$ 33,605.00	$90,355.00	$61,980.00
23	12/18/96	L	135 3/4	Buy 1					
PP	12/23/96	S	132 1/4	PP1		-3 4/8	$ 29,985.00	$86,735.00	$58,360.00

259

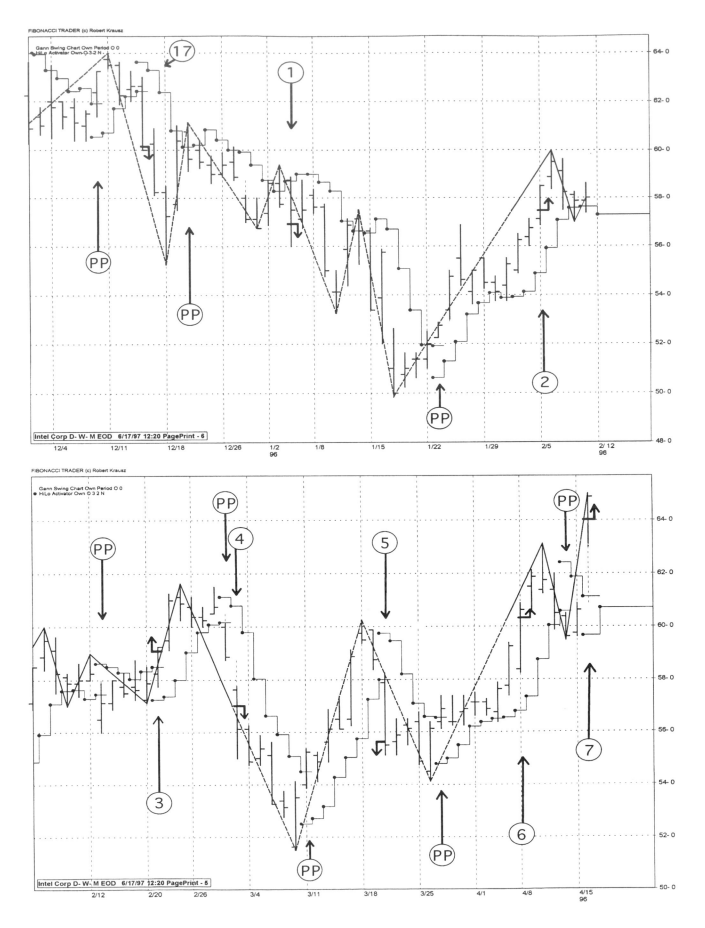

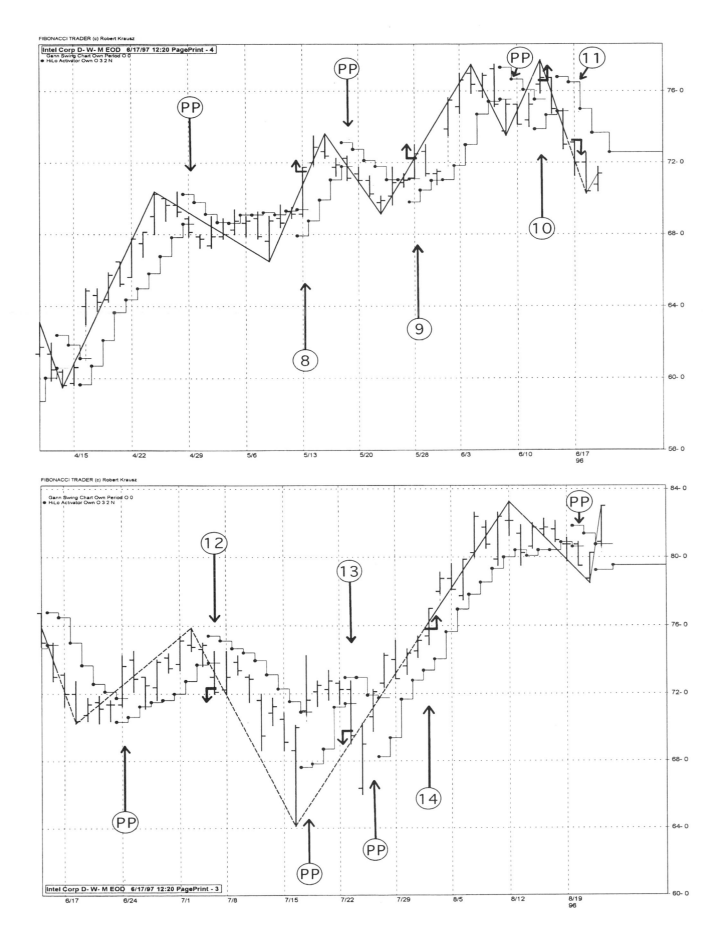

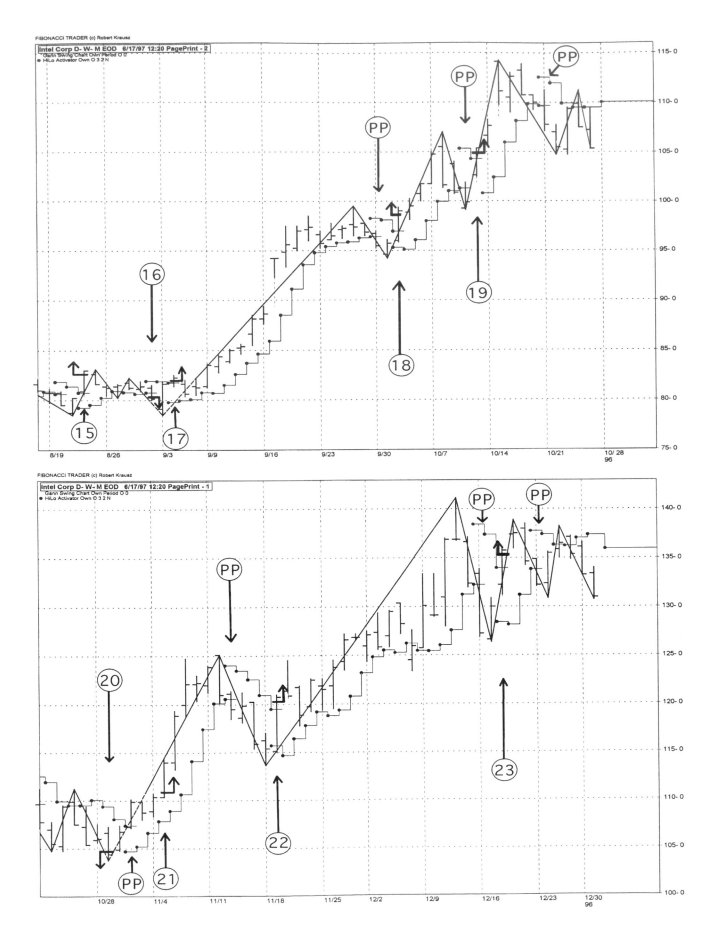

NEW GANN SWING CHARTIST©

PROFESSIONAL SWING PLAN

"REAL TIME"

FOR U.S. T-BONDS
1991 - 1996

> # Trading is 75% psychological,
> # the rest is simple.

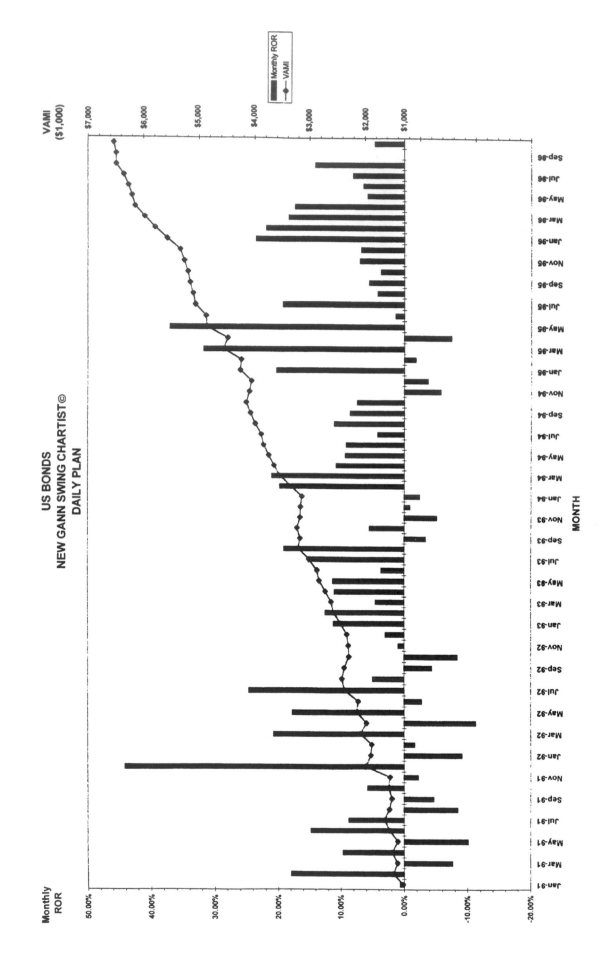

US BONDS
NEW GANN SWING CHARTIST©
DAILY PLAN

PROFESSIONAL SWING PLAN (REAL TIME)
GENERAL NOTES AND COMMENTS

This plan is very different to the Basic Plan. The emphasis is on trading in harmony with the daily rhythm of the markets.

Trading is all about following the direction and speed of a river. The markets, like the river, will always take the course of least resistance. This plan tries to do the same. Commissions are cheap compared to being on the wrong side of the market.

Accurate and consistent execution of this plan calls for vigilance and full focus. Also, you must be willing to not marry a position; change direction if the market demands it. That is why it is called a Professional Plan.

The major difference to the Basic Plan can be listed as followed:

1. This plan trades against the trend as well as with the trend.

2. Profit Protection rules are used so hard earned profits are not given back too easily.

3. We take profits at Target points on part of our total position (each new trade is 3 contracts, see Check List of Results).
   Note: these target points are market denominated and not some arbitrary money amount dreamt up by you or me.

4. You can add (Pyramid) to your position under specific conditions.

5. Re-entering the market if you got out (via the rules) too early is an integral part of the plan.

6. The HiLo Activator of the WEEKLY plotted into the Daily bars becomes a functional rule for this plan. This introduces you to the concept of Multiple Time Frames and how useful they can be for mechanical trading plans.

ALL THE RULES ARE ILLUSTRATED. THE MORE COMPLEX RULES ARE FULLY DETAILED. PLEASE UNDERSTAND THEM CLEARLY BEFORE YOU START CHECKING OUT THE 6-YEAR BACK TEST.

PROFESSIONAL GANN SWING PLAN

TREND TRADING

QUALIFIER TO BUY

1.   Gann Swing Chart should show a Solid Line.

ENTRY RULE (TO BUY)

1.   Go Long on the "Close" above HiLo Activator (by 2 ticks on the T-Bonds).

QUALIFIER TO SELL

1.   Gann Swing Chart should show a Dashed Line.

ENTRY RULE (TO SELL)

1.   Go Short on the "Close" below HiLo Activator (by 2 ticks on the T-Bonds).

CONTRA TREND TRADING

QUALIFIERS TO BUY

1.   Gann Swing Chart should be a Dashed Line.
2.   Close above the HiLo Activator.

ENTRY RULE (TO BUY)

1.   Go Long when prices pass the High of the bar that "closed" above the HiLo Activator. Does not have to be the very next bar.

QUALIFIERS TO SELL

1.   Gann Swing Chart should be a Solid Line.
2.   Close below the HiLo Activator.

ENTRY RULE (TO SELL)

1.   Go "Short" when prices pass the Low of the bar that "closed" below the HiLo Activator. Does not have to be the very next bar.

SEE ILLUSTRATED RULES

SPECIAL ENTRY RULE (LONG OR SHORT)

QUALIFIERS TO BUY

Price Penetrates <u>NEXT</u> period's HiLo Activator.

ENTRY RULE (TO BUY)

Go Long on the 3 tick penetration of the <u>NEXT</u> time period's HiLo Activator (the Weekly). Do not wait for the "close".

QUALIFIERS TO SELL

Price penetrates <u>NEXT</u> period's HiLo Activator.

ENTRY RULE (TO SELL))

Go Short with a 3 tick penetration of the <u>NEXT</u> time period's HiLo Activator (the Weekly). Do not wait for the "close".

Note: The Weekly HiLo Activator is plotted in Line formation (Step formation is not needed).

SPECIAL STOP AND REVERSE RULE

1.   If <u>LONG</u>, Stop and Reverse 2 ticks past nearest VALLEY.
2.   If <u>SHORT</u>, Stop and Reverse 2 ticks past nearest PEAK.

RE-ENTRY RULE

If Profit Protection point is hit (see Profit Protection Rule) <u>BUT</u> there is NO reverse signal, then you can **Re-Enter** when the previous Peak or Valley is passed by 2 ticks (T-Bonds).

Note: Waiting for a "close" past a previous Peak or Valley is optional; the results are based on <u>not</u> waiting for the "close".

SEE ILLUSTRATIONS

TARGETS
(USE WHICHEVER IS HIT FIRST)

1. Take profits on 1/3 of your positions on the "close" of first bar that causes the Slope of the swing to change. This applies →→→→→ even if it is a loss.
2. Take profits on 1/3 of your contracts at NEXT period's HiLo Activator (the Weekly).

Note: Continue to take profits and/or losses at each new target point.

PYRAMID RULES

1. Pyramid (add) 1/3 of your original position at a Trend Change point (ie: if Long and the Swing Chart changes to Solid Line = Uptrend).
2. Pyramid (add) 1/3 of your original position when a previous Peak or Valley is taken out (passed). No Illustration needed.

PROFIT PROTECTION RULES
(USE WHICHEVER IS HIT FIRST)

1. Any 38.2% retracement of previous swing.
2. Any 2 tick penetration of the Daily HiLo.

SEE ILLUSTRATIONS

SUGGESTIONS FOR A DAILY CHECKLIST

It is suggested that you study the rules and check out the results trade by trade before you design your own checklist. Yes, I know it is a lot of work and it would be easier if I provided one for you. But, I also know that if you do it for yourself, it will have much more meaning at a subconscious level.

Many of you are aware that I have worked with traders for 20 years helping with their psychological approach to trading. Over the years I have learned that trading and analysis are two different disciplines.

Relaxed trading needs confidence, not just at the conscious level (that is the easy part). But, as 75% of trading is a psychological affair that can only be mastered if your subconscious mind Is also satisfied that you have a valid trading methodology.

To be a competent analyst satisfying your mind at a conscious level is sufficient, but to be a truly competent trader it is your subconscious mind that must be totally satisfied. How can we attempt to do this?

The simplest route is to do as much <u>Back track</u> (back test) as you possibly can. This fulfills two jobs:

Firstly, you learn the rules; feel them in your very bones. It helps you to understand how they perform under fire, when things go against you. After a multi year back track, you will know that if you had 4 or 5 losses consecutively, and yet the plan survived. When it occurs in real trading (as surely it will) you will not be shocked, and you will be able to take the next trade. That is what trading is all about.

My attitude is on public record: without a back tested plan with fixed rules, you have nothing. That is, if you want to use a mechanical plan.

Secondly, and believe it or not, this is the more important of the two; through the process of repetition, repetition, repetition, the subconscious starts accepting the validity of the plan. The more repetition, checking those trades day by day, rule by rule, the greater the chance of total acceptance at a subconscious level. Of course, if your plan does not have positive mathematical expectations then all the back testing in the world will be of no use (continued on page 269).

ENTRY RULES WITH THE TREND
TREND TRADING

Trend Trading Rule: Long Entry (Buy)

UPTREND

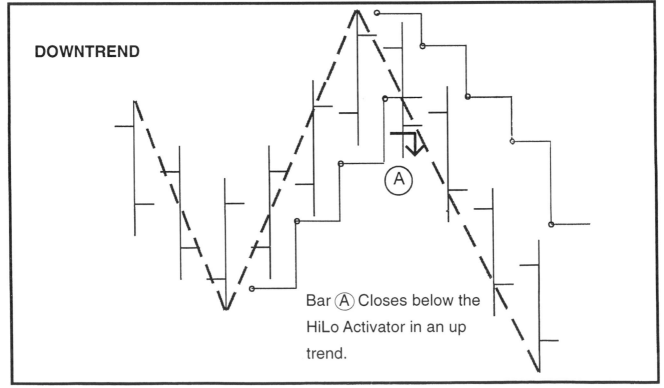

(A)

Bar (A) Closes above the HiLo Activator in an up trend.

Trend Trading Rule: Short Entry (Sell)

DOWNTREND

(A)

Bar (A) Closes below the HiLo Activator in an up trend.

ENTRY RULE AGAINST THE TREND
CONTRA TREND TRADING

Contra Trend Trading: Long Entry (Buy)

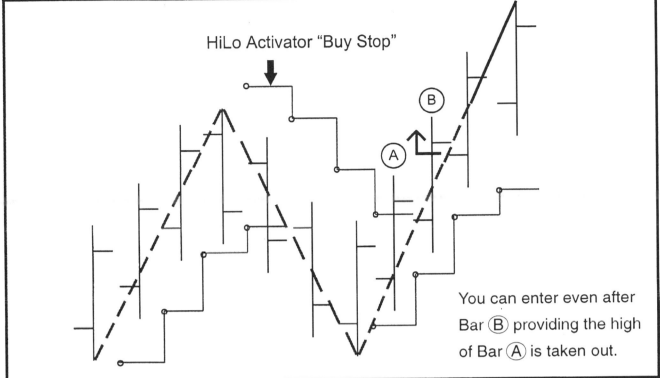

HiLo Activator "Buy Stop"

You can enter even after Bar (B) providing the high of Bar (A) is taken out.

Contra Trend Trading: Short Entry (Sell)

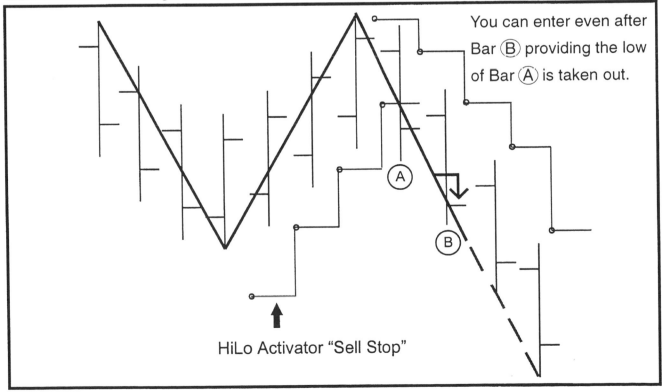

You can enter even after Bar (B) providing the low of Bar (A) is taken out.

HiLo Activator "Sell Stop"

SPECIAL ENTRY RULE

This rule introduces you to incorporating the NEXT time periods HiLo Activator. (The NEXT time period up from the Daily is the WEEKLY.) Therefore, it is the Weekly bars highs and lows that produce the Weekly HiLo Activator. (See Advanced Section for calculations.) The weekly in this case is plotted in line formation as shown (no steps).

1. Bar Ⓐ goes below the weekly HiLo Activator and closes below it by 3 ticks.

2. Bar Ⓑ , if prices go back above the weekly HiLo Activator by 3 ticks, this is the ACTION POINT.

STOP & REVERSE for the "Special Entry Rule"

It is important to understand this rule. If the "Special Entry Rule" fails, instead of just "stopping" out of a trade, the plan reverses in the opposite direction. (That is why it is called a "Professional Plan".)

If you buy on Bar Ⓑ (as shown) but the rally fails, this rule may help you get back with the trend on Bar Ⓒ , as the Downtrend resumes. The plan reverses to the "short" side 3 ticks below the previous valley. That is the ACTION POINT.

SPECIAL ENTRY RULE

Special Rule: Take Action 3 Ticks Past NEXT Period's HiLo Activator Line

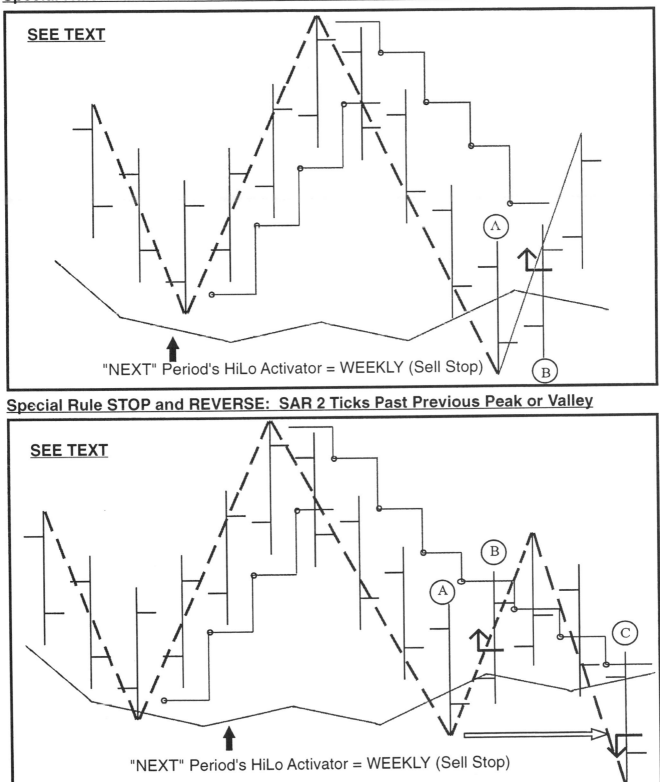

SEE TEXT

"NEXT" Period's HiLo Activator = WEEKLY (Sell Stop)

Special Rule STOP and REVERSE: SAR 2 Ticks Past Previous Peak or Valley

SEE TEXT

"NEXT" Period's HiLo Activator = WEEKLY (Sell Stop)

RE-ENTRY RULE WITH THE TREND

Re-Entry Rule

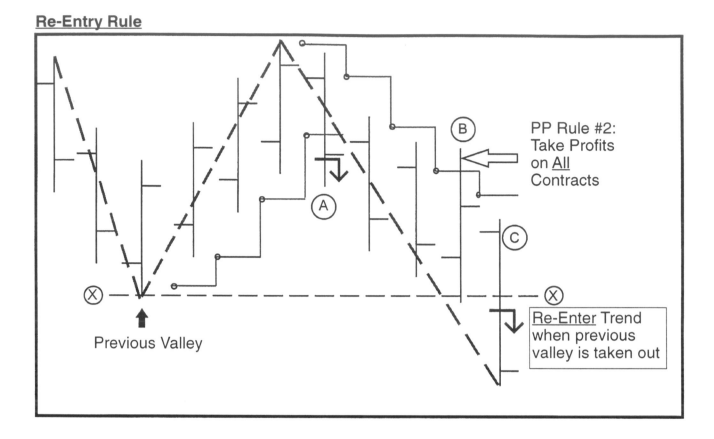

PP Rule #2:
Take Profits
on <u>All</u>
Contracts

A

B

C

<u>Re-Enter</u> Trend
when previous
valley is taken out

Previous Valley

RE-ENTRY RULE   **EXPLANATION**

As this plan is sensitive and hugs the price movements closely, we may exit a position but the trend continues in the original direction. This rule helps to re-enter in the market's direction. Ⓐ - Ⓑ - Ⓒ shows the sequence of events that trigger the Re-Entry Rule.

BAR A = Trend is down and the plan sells below the HiLo Activator.

BAR B = Price goes above the HiLo Activator "Buy Stop" by 2 ticks and we exit the trade as per Profit Protection Rule #2 (see that rule).

BAR C = Re-Entry Rule kicks in. Why?
    1. Trend is still Down.
    2. Prices take our (pass) the previous Valley at Ⓧ------------------------Ⓧ.

Not too complicated, was it?

Checklist (continued from page 263.)

Now, back to our checklist. What rule seems the most important to you? This should be number 1 on your list. Go through the rules and place them in your own order. This process gives you a chance to personalize the plan.

Let's say that "Direction of Trend" is your priority, then it could show:

1. IS THE TREND   UP ❏   DOWN ❏

The next focus for you may be:

2. DIRECTION OF SLOPE   UP ❏   DOWN ❏

These two points could lead you to the question:

3. USE   TREND ❏ OR   COUNTER TREND RULES ❏

(Obviously, if the Trend is up and the Slope is also up, then using Trend Trading Rules looking to buy would be more appropriate.)

Some other points your checklist may include are:
Price level of the previous Peak (Resistance). _ _ _ _ _ _
Price level of the previous Valley (Support). _ _ _ _ _ _ _
At what price is the Daily HiLo Activator? _ _ _ _ _ _ _ _
At what price is the Weekly HiLo Activator? _ _ _ _ _ _ _
Where are the Targets?   1) _ _ _ _ _ _2) _ _ _ _ _ _
Any Pyramid potentials - Where? _ _ _ _ _ _ _ _ _ _ _
At what price level are the Profit Protection Points? _ _ _ _

I am sure you get the idea. You may have to adjust this a few times before you feel comfortable with the results. Once you have a checklist that you are happy with it should be an automatic part of your daily analysis and action plan. A place for the date and the contract are obvious. Some of you may want to include potential "action points" and even your daily positions, plus results.

Using your final checklist, I suggest paper trading your plan until it has become automatic. It is imperative that you do your "thinking" before you trade. The trading should be part of a confident flow at one with the markets, following your rules mechanically. A personalized checklist will help you to achieve this.

TARGET RULES

TARGET RULE #1

The purpose of this rule is twofold:

1. To take some profit.

2. It reduces your risk exposure by 33 1/3%.

By trading multiple contracts, money management techniques are easier to implement. Follow the rule as shown. Use Rule 1 or 2, whichever is hit first. Keep on taking profits every time a rule is hit.

TARGET RULE #2

Once again we take profits on 1/3 of our position at a specified market driven spot; but **now** we use the NEXT periods HiLo Activator (THE WEEKLY). (Calculations are given in the Advanced Section.) If prices go below or touch the WEEKLY HiLo Activator = take profit on 1/3 of your short position.

<u>Note</u>: Long position is exactly opposite.

TARGET RULES

Use Whichever is hit first

Target #1: Take Profit on 1/3 of Position on Close of 1st Slope Change

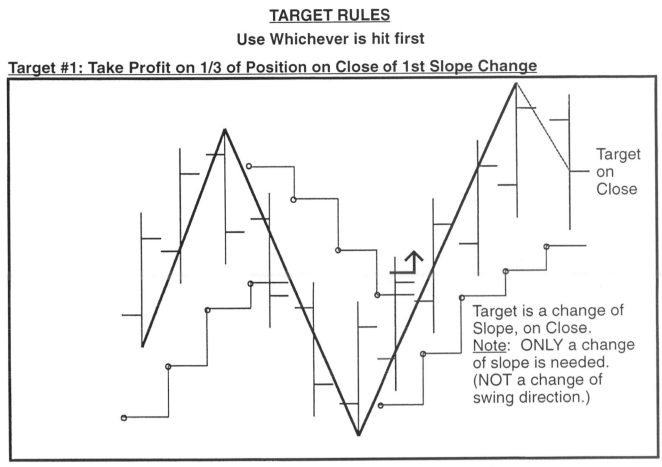

Target on Close

Target is a change of Slope, on Close.
Note: ONLY a change of slope is needed.
(NOT a change of swing direction.)

Target #2: Take Profit on 1/3 of Position at Next Period HiLo Indicator

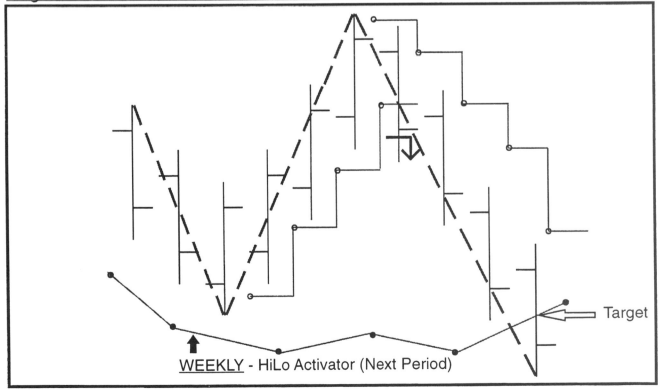

Target

WEEKLY - HiLo Activator (Next Period)

PYRAMID POINTS - RULE #1

ADD TO YOUR LONG POSITION (BUY)

You can "pyramid" 1/3 of your original entry position when prices pass the previous Peak (shown at (X)------------------------(X) **providing:**

1. The plan is already long.

2. The trend was DOWN (dashed line) and changes to UPTREND (solid line) as prices take out previous peak.

ADD TO YOUR SHORT POSITION (SELL)

You can "pyramid" 1/3 of your original entry position when prices fall below the previous Valley (shown at (X)------------------------(X) **providing:**

1. The plan is already short.

2. The trend was UP (solid line) and changes to DOWNTREND (dashed line) as prices take out previous valley.

278

PYRAMID POINTS - RULE #1

Pyramid Point: After Long Entry (Buy)

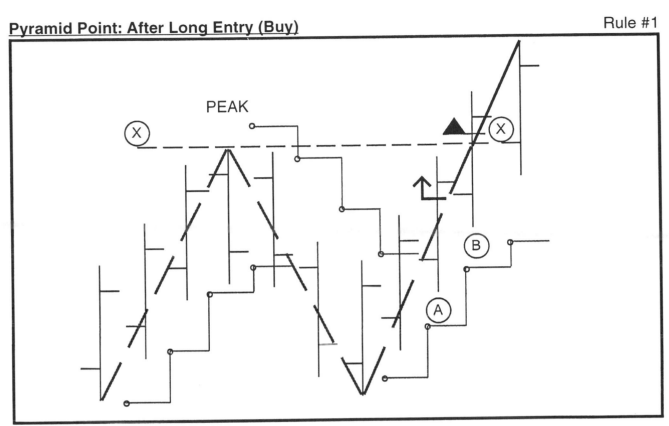

Pyramid Point: After Short Entry (Sell)

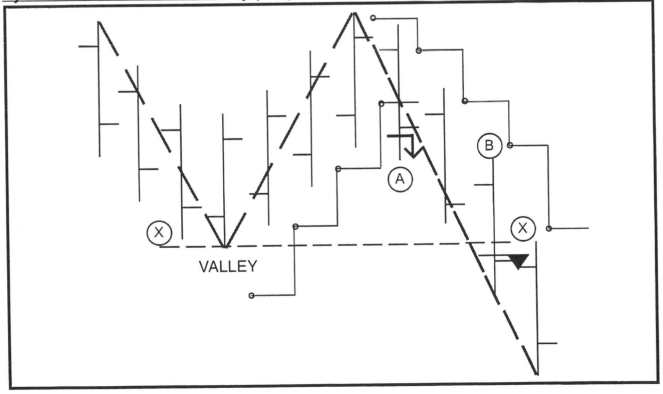

PROFIT PROTECTION RULES (PP RULES)

PROFIT PROTECTION (PP) RULE #1 (After Upswing)

Profits are not easy to come by. Hence these two rules. Both are market driven and not random numbers.

The market rises from a Valley Ⓐ to a Peak Ⓑ . If prices retrace 38.2% of that swing, the plan takes profit on <u>all</u> positions and waits for the next entry signal.

<u>Note</u>: Downswings are exactly opposite.

PROFIT PROTECTION (PP) RULE #2 (If Short)

After taking a "sell" signal (short) and prices rally to go above the HiLo Activator "Buy Stop" by 2 ticks, then take profits on all contracts.

Do not wait for the "close".

If "Long" (after a Buy Signal) exactly the opposite applies.

PROFIT PROTECTION RULES (PP RULES)

Profit Protection Rule #1: 38.2% Retracement of Prior Swing

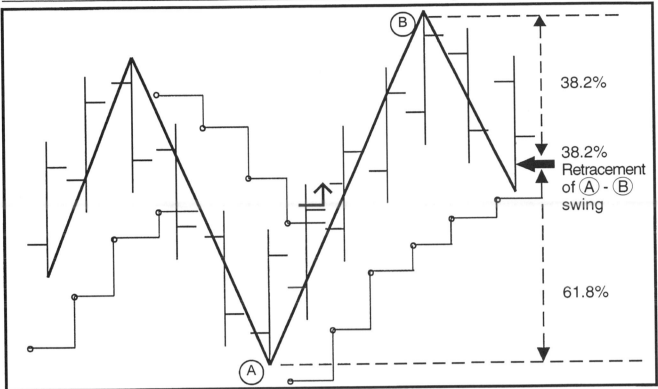

Profit Protection Rule #2: Penetration of Own Period HiLo Activator

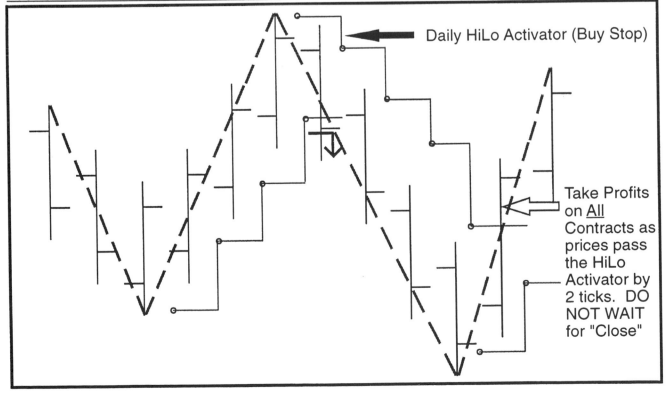

Beginning Equity	$30,000.00	Ending Equity	$52,500.00
Total Net Profit	$22,500.00		
Gross Profit	$65,281.25	Gross Loss	($42,781.25)
Total No. Trades	60	Percentage Profitable	47%
No. Winning Trades	28	No. Losing Trades	32

Largest Winning Trade	$9,406.25	Largest Losing Trade	($4,500.00)
Average Winning Trade	$2,331.47	Average Losing Trade	($1,336.91)
Ratio Average Win/Loss	1.74	Average Trade	$375.00
Max. Consecutive Winners	5	Max. Consecutive Losses	5
Largest Consecutive Drawdown (%)	16%	Largest Consecutive Drawdown	($6,343.75)

Return on Account	75%
Profit/Drawdown Ratio	3.55

NOTES:

1) Initial A/C Size = $30,000

2) Pyramids only 1/3 of original position

1991
US BONDS
NEW GANN SWING CHARTIST ©
DAILY PLAN

TRADE#	DATE	L/S	PRICE	CTR.	RULE #	PROFIT	(LOSS)	ACCUM.	MO. PROFIT/(LOSS)	A/C EQUITY
1	1/2/91	L	76.30	3	Contra 1					$30,000.00
T	1/3/91	S	77.30	1	T2	32		32		$31,000.00
2	1/4/91	S	77.26	5	Special Rule	56		88		$32,750.00
PP	1/9/91	L	76.18	3	PP1	120		208		$36,500.00
3	1/9/91	S	75.08	3	Re-entry Rule					
T	1/10/91	L	75.15	1	T1		(7)	201		$36,281.25
T	1/15/91	L	74.28	1	T1	19		220		$36,875.00
T	1/16/91	L	74.29	1	T1	11		231		$37,218.75
4	1/17/91	S	74.10	3	Re-entry Rule					
PP	1/17/91	L	75.26	3	PP1		(144)	87		$32,718.75
5	1/18/91	L	77.21	3	Contra 1					
6	1/18/91	S	77.14	6	Special Rule		(21)	66		$32,062.50
PP	1/23/91	L	77.01	3	PP1	39		105		$33,281.25
7	1/25/91	S	77.24	3	Re-entry Rule					
PP	1/25/91	L	76.23	3	PP2		(99)	6	6	$30,187.50
8	2/1/91	L	77.15	3	Re-entry Rule					
T	2/6/91	S	79.01	1	T1	50		56		$31,750.00
PP	2/8/91	S	78.13	2	PP2	60		116		$33,625.00
9	2/8/91	L	79.12	3	Re-entry Rule					
PP	2/11/91	S	79.02	3	PP1		(30)	86		$32,687.50
10	2/20/91	S	78.12	3	Trend 1					
T	2/22/91	L	78.02	1	T2	10		96		
T	2/25/91	L	78.07	1	T1	5		101		$33,156.25
11	3/4/91	L	75.30	1	T1	78		179	173	$35,593.75
PP	3/8/91	L	76.27	3	Contra 1		(33)	146		$34,562.50
12	3/8/91	S	76.16	3	PP1					
PP	3/11/91	L	75.26	3	Re-entry Rule		(24)	122		$33,812.50
13	3/14/91	L	76.02	3	PP1					
PP	3/15/91	L	77.01	3	Trend 1		(60)	62		$31,937.50
14	3/18/91	S	76.13	3	PP1					
PYR	3/19/91	S	75.24	3	Contra 1					
T	3/20/91	S	75.11	1	PYR 1					
PP	3/21/91	L	75.10	2	T1	28		90		$32,812.50
15	3/25/91	L	75.18	2	PP1		(1)	89		$32,781.25
PP	3/26/91	L	75.29	3	Contra 1					
16	3/27/91	S	75.15	3	PP2		(42)	47		$31,468.75
T	3/28/91	L	76.07	3	Re-entry Rule					
		S	76.24	1	T2	17		64		$32,000.00

283

1991
US BONDS
NEW GANN SWING CHARTIST ©
DAILY PLAN

TRADE#	DATE	L/S	PRICE	CTR.	RULE #	PROFIT	(LOSS)	ACCUM.	MO. PROFIT/(LOSS)	A/C EQUITY
17	4/1/91	S	76.21	5	Special Rule	28		92	(87)	$32,875.00
18	4/2/91	L	77.01	6	Re-entry Rule		(36)	56		$31,750.00
PYR	4/4/91	L	77.04	1	PYR 1					
T	4/8/91	S	77.24	2	T1	46		102		$33,187.50
PP	4/9/91	S	77.09	2	PP2	13		115		$33,593.75
19	4/10/91	S	77.06	3	Contra 1					
PP	4/12/91	L	77.01	3	PP1	15		130		$34,062.50
20	4/12/91	L	77.25	3	Trend 1					
T	4/16/91	S	78.04	1	T1	11		141		$34,406.25
PP	4/18/91	S	77.25	2	PP2	0		141		$34,406.25
21	4/19/91	S	77.13	3	Contra 1					
T	4/22/91	L	76.19	1	T2	26		167		$35,218.75
22	4/23/91	L	76.21	5	Special Rule	48		215		$36,718.75
PP	4/25/91	S	77.06	3	PP1	51		266		$38,312.50
23	4/29/91	L	77.26	3	Re-entry Rule					
PP	4/30/91	S	77.09	3	PP1		(45)	221		$36,906.25
24	4/30/91	L	77.30	3	Re-entry Rule					
PP	5/3/91	S	77.21	3	PP1		(27)	194	102	$36,062.50
25	5/6/91	S	77.12	3	Contra 1					
PP	5/7/91	L	77.20	3	PP1		(24)	170		$35,312.50
26	5/10/91	S	76.30	3	Re-entry Rule					
T	5/10/91	L	76.18	1	T2	12		182		$35,687.50
PYR	5/10/91	S	76.15	1	PYR 1					
T	5/13/91	L	76.27	1	T1	3		185		$35,781.25
T	5/15/91	L	76.05	1	T1	25		210		$36,562.50
T	5/16/91	L	76.10	1	T1	20		230		$37,187.50
27	5/17/91	S	75.26	3	Re-entry Rule					
PP	5/17/91	L	76.26	3	PP2		(96)	134		$34,187.50
28	5/21/91	L	77.07	3	Contra 1					
PP	5/23/91	S	76.21	3	PP1		(54)	80		$32,500.00
29	5/30/91	L	77.11	3	Trend 1					
T	5/30/91	S	77.12	1	T2	1		81		$32,531.25
30	5/31/91	S	77.09	5	Special Rule		(4)	77	(117)	$32,406.25
PYR	6/4/91	S	76.12	1	PYR 1					
T	6/10/91	L	75.01	2	T1	144		221		$36,906.25
PP	6/14/91	L	75.03	2	PP2	111		332		$40,375.00
31	6/17/91	L	75.10	3	Contra 1					
PP	6/18/91	S	74.23	3	PP2		(57)	275		$38,593.75

1991
US BONDS
NEW GANN SWING CHARTIST ©
DAILY PLAN

TRADE#	DATE	L/S	PRICE	CTR.	RULE #	PROFIT	(LOSS)	ACCUM.	MO. PROFIT/(LOSS)	A/C EQUITY
32	6/20/91	L	75.15	3	Re-entry Rule					
PP	6/21/91	S	74.24	3	PP1		(69)	206		$36,437.50
33	6/28/91	L	75.13	3	Trend 1					
T	6/28/91	S	75.21	1	T2	8		214		$36,687.50
T	7/1/91	S	75.21	1	T1	8		222		$36,937.50
T	7/2/91	S	75.21	1	T1	8		230	153	$37,187.50
34	7/8/91	S	74.25	3	Contra 1					
T	7/10/91	L	74.30	1	T1		(5)	225		$37,031.25
PP	7/11/91	L	75.08	2	PP2		(30)	195		$36,093.75
35	7/11/91	L	75.16	3	Trend 1					
T	7/15/91	S	75.31	1	T1	15		210		$36,562.50
T	7/16/91	S	75.28	1	T1	12		222		$36,937.50
PP	7/17/91	S	75.17	1	PP1	1		223		$36,968.75
36	7/18/91	S	75.12	3	Contra 1					
PP	7/19/91	L	75.21	3	PP1		(27)	196		$36,125.00
37	7/24/91	L	76.07	3	Trend 1					
T	7/29/91	S	76.17	1	T1	10		206		$36,437.50
PP	8/8/91	S	78.07	2	PP2	128		334	104	$40,437.50
38	8/13/91	L	79.03	3	Re-entry Rule					
PP	8/16/91	S	79.10	3	PP1	21		355		$41,093.75
39	8/19/91	L	80.09	3	Re-entry Rule					
PP	8/19/91	S	79.13	3	PP1		(84)	271		$38,468.75
40	8/26/91	S	79.06	3	Contra 1					
T	8/27/91	L	79.15	1	T1		(9)	262		$38,187.50
PP	8/28/91	L	79.22	2	PP1		(32)	230		$37,187.50
41	8/28/91	L	80.10	3	Trend 1					
PP	8/30/91	S	80.08	3	PP1		(6)	224	(110)	$37,000.00
42	9/9/91	L	81.04	3	Re-entry Rule					
PP	9/11/91	S	80.20	3	PP2		(48)	176		$35,500.00
43	9/12/91	L	81.09	3	Re-entry Rule					
PP	9/13/91	S	81.07	3	PP1		(6)	170		$35,312.50
44	9/20/91	L	82.11	3	Re-entry Rule					
T	9/23/91	S	82.07	1	T1		(4)	166		$35,187.50
T	9/25/91	S	81.29	1	T1		(14)	152		$34,750.00
T	10/2/91	S	82.27	1	T1	16		168	(56)	$35,250.00
45	10/4/91	L	83.12	3	Re-entry Rule			168		$35,250.00
T	10/8/91	S	83.03	1	T1		(9)	159		$34,968.75
PP	10/9/91	S	83.01	2	PP1		(22)	137		$34,281.25

1991
US BONDS
NEW GANN SWING CHARTIST ©
DAILY PLAN

TRADE#	DATE	L/S	PRICE	CTR.	RULE #	PROFIT	(LOSS)	ACCUM.	MO. PROFIT/(LOSS)	A/C EQUITY
46	10/9/91	S	82.15	3	Trend 1					
T	10/9/91	L	81.27	1	T2	20		157		$34,906.25
47	10/9/91	L	81.30	5	Special Rule	34		191		$35,968.75
48	10/10/91	S	81.24	6	Special Rule		(18)	173		$35,406.25
49	10/11/91	L	81.30	6	Special Rule		(18)	155		$34,843.75
PP	10/17/91	S	82.15	3	PP1	51		206		$36,437.50
50	10/17/91	S	81.21	3	Special Rule					
51	10/18/91	L	81.27	6	Special Rule		(18)	188		$35,875.00
52	10/18/91	S	81.04	6	Special Rule		(69)	119		$33,718.75
T	10/23/91	L	80.25	1	T1	11		130		$34,062.50
53	10/24/91	L	81.10	5	Special Rule		(12)	118		$33,687.50
PP	10/28/91	S	81.00	3	PP1		(30)	88		$32,750.00
54	10/28/91	L	81.02	3	Special Rule					
T	10/31/91	S	82.25	1	T1	55		143		$34,468.75
PP	11/1/91	S	82.15	2	PP2	90		233	65	$37,281.25
55	11/8/91	L	83.05	3	Trend 1					
T	11/11/91	S	83.13	1	T1	8		241		$37,531.25
PP	11/13/91	S	83.01	2	PP1		(8)	233		$37,281.25
56	11/20/91	S	83.01	3	Contra 1					
PP	11/21/91	L	83.01	3	PP1	0				
57	11/21/91	S	82.15	3	Re-entry Rule					
PP	11/26/91	L	82.19	3	PP2		(12)	221		$36,906.25
58	11/27/91	S	81.31	3	Re-entry Rule					
59	11/27/91	L	82.04	6	Special Rule		(15)	206	(27)	$36,437.50
PYR	12/4/91	L	84.06	1	PYR 2					
T	12/9/91	S	84.19	2	T1	158		364		$41,375.00
T	12/10/91	S	84.16	1	T1	76		440		$43,750.00
PP	12/11/91	S	84.07	1	PP2	67		507		$45,843.75
60	12/19/91	L	85.09	3	Re-entry Rule					
PP	1/2/92	S	87.16	3	PP2	213		720	514	$52,500.00

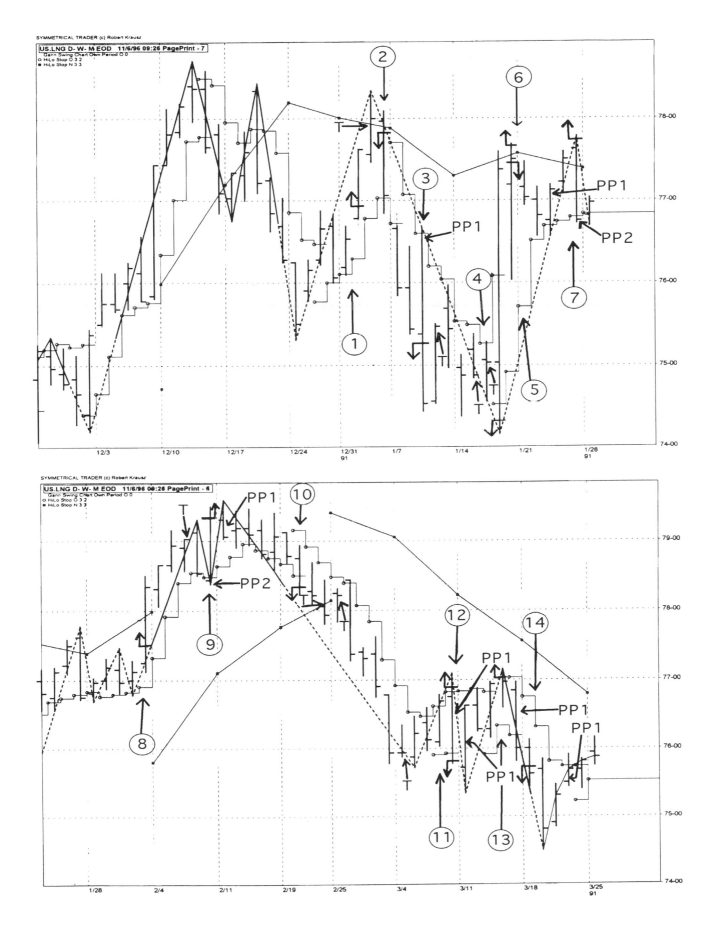

SYMMETRICAL TRADER (c) Robert Krausz

US.LNG D- W- M EOD 11/6/96 09:26 PagePrint - 7
Gann Swing Chart Own Period O 0
O HiLo Stop O 3 2
■ HiLo Stop N 3 3

SYMMETRICAL TRADER (c) Robert Krausz

US.LNG D- W- M EOD 11/6/96 09:26 PagePrint - 6
Gann Swing Chart Own Period O 0
O HiLo Stop O 3 2
■ HiLo Stop N 3 3

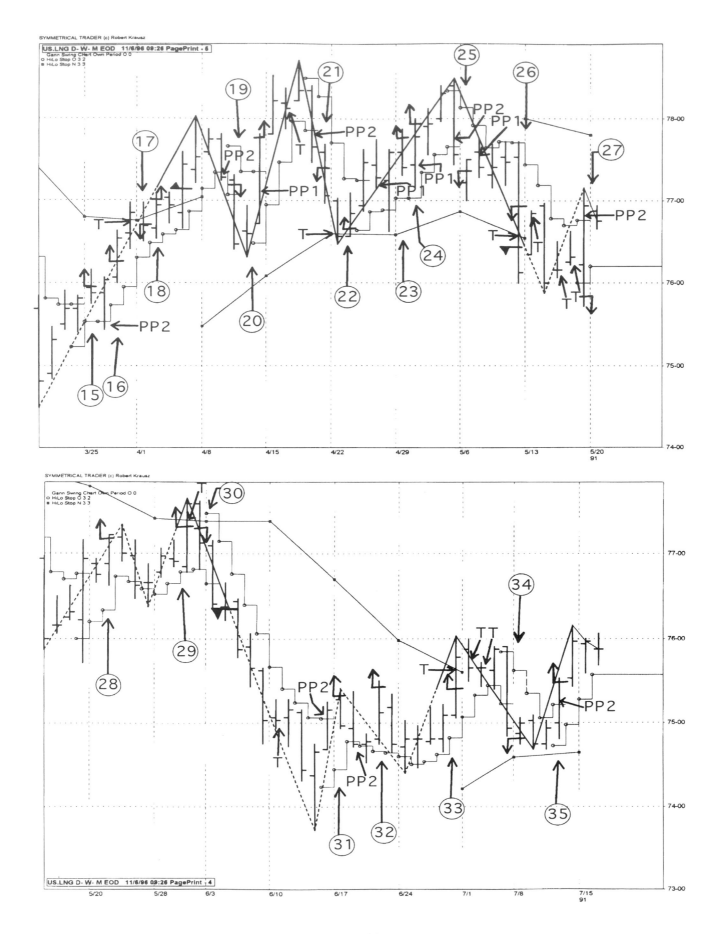

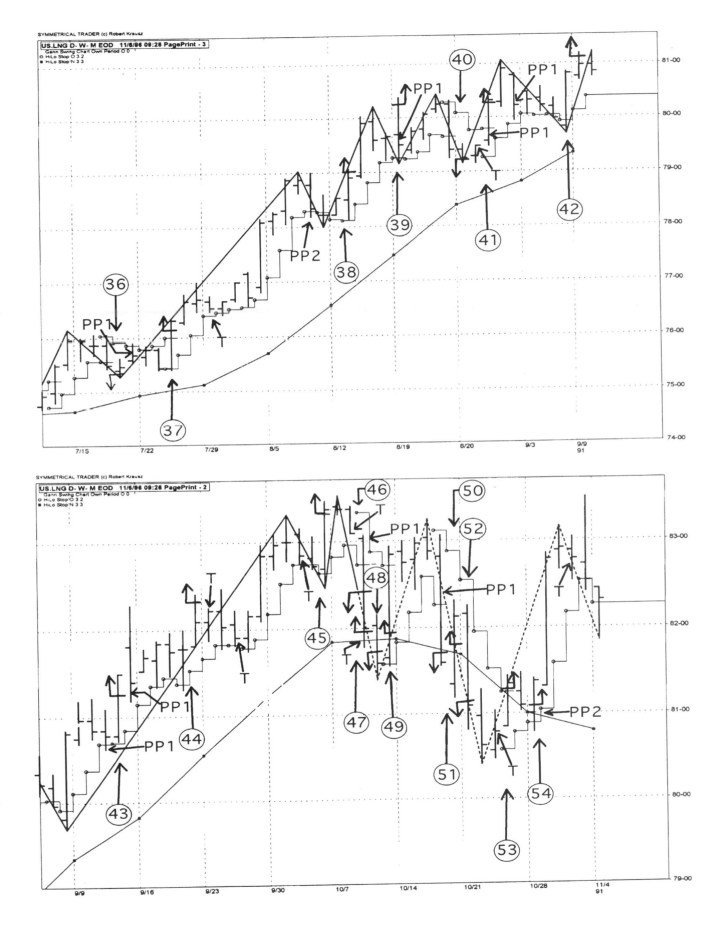

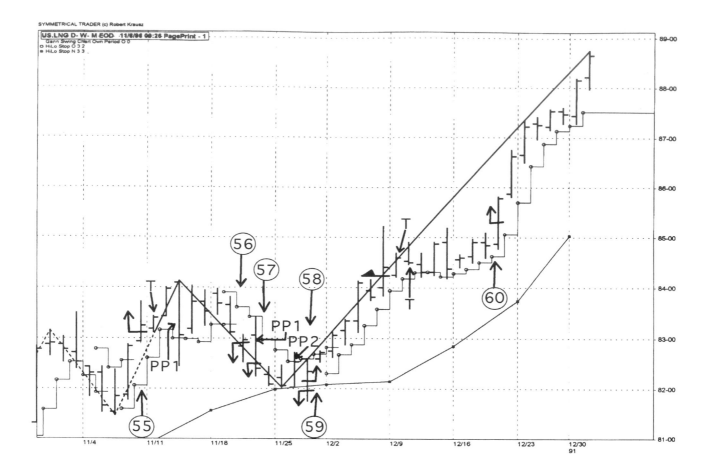

1992
NEW GANN SWING CHARTIST ©
DAILY PLAN

Beginning Equity	$30,000.00	Ending Equity	$39,125.00
Total Net Profit	$9,125.00		
Gross Profit	$47,531.25	Gross Loss	($38,406.25)
Total No. Trades	57	Percentage Profitable	39%
No. Winning Trades	22	No. Losing Trades	35

Largest Winning Trade	$4,312.50	Largest Losing Trade	($3,000.00)
Average Winning Trade	$2,160.51	Average Losing Trade	($1,097.32)
Ratio Average Win/Loss	1.97	Average Trade	$160.09
Max. Consecutive Winners	3	Max. Consecutive Losses	8
Largest Consecutive Drawdown (%)	15%	Largest Consecutive Drawdown	($5,031.25)

Return on Account	30%
Profit/Drawdown Ratio	1.81

NOTES:
1) Initial A/C Size = $30,000
2) Pyramids only 1/3 of original position

1992
US BONDS
NEW GANN SWING CHARTIST ©
DAILY PLAN

TRADE#	DATE	L/S	PRICE	CTR.	RULE #	PROFIT	(LOSS)	ACCUM.	MO. PROFIT/(LOSS)	A/C EQUITY
1	1/7/92	L	88.29	3	Re-entry Rule					$30,000.00
PP	1/8/92	S	88.27	3	PP1		(6.00)	(6)		$29,812.50
2	1/13/92	S	87.23	3	Contra 1					
PYR	1/14/92	S	87.10	1	PYR 1					
T	1/14/92	L	87.03	2	T2	40		34		$31,062.50
3	1/14/92	L	87.06	5	Special Rule	8		42		$31,312.50
4	1/16/92	S	86.17	6	Special Rule		(63.00)	(21)		$29,343.75
PP	1/20/92	L	86.29	3	PP2		(36.00)	(57)		$28,218.75
5	1/23/92	S	85.22	3	Re-entry Rule					
T	1/27/92	L	85.16	1	T1	6		(51)		$28,406.25
PP	1/28/92	L	86.01	2	PP1		(22.00)	(73)		$27,718.75
6	1/29/92	L	86.12	3	Contra 1					
PP	1/29/92	S	86.03	3	PP1		(27.00)	(100)		$26,875.00
7	1/29/92	S	85.06	3	Re-entry Rule					
T	1/31/92	L	84.30	1	T1	8		(92)		$27,125.00
PP	2/4/92	L	85.04	2	PP2	4		(88)	(88)	$27,250.00
8	2/13/92	S	84.06	3	Re-entry Rule					
PP	2/20/92	L	84.01	3	PP1	15		(73)		$27,718.75
9	2/27/92	L	84.25	3	Contra 1					
T	2/28/92	S	84.29	1	T2	4		(69)		$27,843.75
PP	3/2/92	S	84.12	2	PP1		(34.00)	(103)	(15)	$26,781.25
10	3/2/92	S	84.06	3	Trend 1					
T	3/5/92	L	83.17	1	T1	21		(82)		$27,437.50
T	3/6/92	S	82.26	1	T2	44		(38)		$28,812.50
11	3/6/92	L	82.29	4	Special Rule	41		3		$32,718.75
PP	3/11/92	S	83.25	3	PP1	84		87		$33,843.75
12	3/11/92	S	83.13	3	Trend 1					
T	3/12/92	L	82.21	1	T2	36		123		$35,968.75
13	3/13/92	L	82.23	5	Special Rule	68		191		$35,406.25
14	3/13/92	S	82.11	6	Special Rule		(18.00)	173		$35,500.00
T	3/16/92	L	82.08	1	T1	3		176		$34,312.50
PP	3/17/92	L	82.30	2	PP1		(38.00)	138		$32,343.75
15	3/25/92	L	83.28	3	Contra 1					
PP	3/26/92	S	83.07	3	PP1		(63.00)	75	178	$31,968.75
16	4/1/92	L	84.08	3	Re-entry Rule					
17	4/2/92	S	84.04	6	Special Rule		(12.00)	63		$30,468.75
18	4/3/92	L	84.20	6	Special Rule		(48.00)	15		$30,531.25
T	4/6/92	S	84.22	1	T1	2		17		$30,593.75
T	4/7/92	S	84.22	1	T1	2		19		
19	4/8/92	S	84.06	4	Trend 1		(14.00)	5		$30,156.25

1992
US BONDS
NEW GANN SWING CHARTIST ©
DAILY PLAN

TRADE#	DATE	L/S	PRICE	CTR.	RULE #	PROFIT	(LOSS)	ACCUM.	MO. PROFIT/(LOSS)	A/C EQUITY
PP	4/9/92	L	84.16	3	PP1		(30.00)	(25)		$29,218.75
20	4/9/92	L	85.06	3	Trend 1					$26,875.00
PP	4/10/92	S	84.13	3	PP1		(75.00)	(100)		
21	4/20/92	S	84.08	3	Contra 1					$27,250.00
T	4/20/92	L	83.28	1	T2	12		(88)		
PYR	4/23/92	S	83.00	1	PYR 1					$28,312.50
T	4/24/92	L	83.06	1	T1	34		(54)		$28,687.50
PP	4/29/92	L	83.14	2	PP2	12		(42)	(117)	
22	4/29/92	L	83.28	3	Contra 1					$29,187.50
T	5/6/92	S	84.12	1	T2	16		(26)		
PYR	5/8/92	L	85.11	1	PYR 1					
T	5/12/92	S	85.12	1	T1	48		22		$30,687.50
PP	5/14/92	S	85.06	2	PP2	37		59		$31,843.75
23	5/15/92	L	85.31	3	Re-entry Rule					
T	5/15/92	S	85.30	1	T1		(1.00)	58		$31,812.50
PP	5/18/92	S	85.22	2	PP2		(18.00)	40		$31,250.00
24	5/21/92	S	85.13	3	Contra 1					
PP	5/22/92	L	85.27	3	PP3		(42.00)	(2)		$29,937.50
25	5/22/92	S	85.07	3	Re-entry Rule					
T	5/26/92	L	84.18	1	T2	21		19		$30,593.75
26	5/27/92	L	84.21	5	Special Rule	36		55		$31,718.75
PP	5/27/92	S	85.11	3	PP1	66		121	163	$33,781.25
27	6/1/92	S	84.25	3	Special Rule					
28	6/1/92	L	84.31	6	Special Rule		(18.00)	103		$33,218.75
PP	6/2/92	L	85.14	3	PP1	45		148		$34,625.00
29	6/9/92	S	85.00	3	Contra 1					
PP	6/11/92	S	85.11	3	PP1		(33.00)	115		$33,593.75
30	6/25/92	L	86.25	3	Trend 1					
PP	6/30/92	L	86.17	3	PP2		(24.00)	91	(30)	$32,843.75
31	7/1/92	S	87.04	3	Re-entry Rule					
T	7/7/92	S	88.22	1	T1	50		141		$34,406.25
T	7/8/92	S	88.21	1	T1	49		190		$35,937.50
PP	7/10/92	S	88.11	1	PP2	39		229		$37,156.25
32	7/14/92	S	87.29	3	Contra 1					
PP	7/15/92	L	88.15	3	PP1		(54.00)	175		$35,468.75
33	7/15/92	L	88.19	3	Trend 1					
PP	7/16/92	S	88.16	3	PP1		(9.00)	166		$35,187.50
34	7/22/92	L	89.03	3	Re-entry Rule					
T	7/30/92	S	90.30	1	T1	59		225		$37,031.25
T	7/31/92	S	90.29	1	T1	58		283		$38,843.75

293

1992
US BONDS
NEW GANN SWING CHARTIST ©
DAILY PLAN

TRADE#	DATE	L/S	PRICE	CTR.	RULE #	PROFIT	(LOSS)	ACCUM.	MO. PROFIT/(LOSS)	A/C EQUITY
T	8/6/92	S	91.06	1	T1	67		350	259	$40,937.50
35	8/7/92	L	92.04	3	Re-entry Rule					
PP	8/13/92	S	92.07	3	PP1	9		359		$41,218.75
36	8/17/92	S	91.16	3	Contra 1					
PP	8/18/92	L	92.04	3	PP1		(60.00)	299		$39,343.75
37	8/24/92	S	91.09	3	Re-entry Rule					
T	8/24/92	L	91.04	1	T2	5		304		$39,500.00
38	8/27/92	L	91.06	5	Special Rule	6		310		$39,687.50
T	8/31/92	S	91.07	1	T1	1		311		$39,718.75
T	9/3/92	S	92.02	1	T1	28		339		$40,593.75
PYR	9/4/92	L	93.09	1	PYR 1					
T	9/9/92	S	93.13	1	T1	71		410		$42,812.50
PP	9/10/92	S	93.14	1	PP2	5		415	65	$42,968.75
39	9/11/92	L	94.09	3	Re-entry Rule					
PP	9/11/92	S	93.09	3	PP2		(96.00)	319		$39,968.75
40	9/12/92	L	94.12	3	Re-entry Rule					
PP	9/12/92	S	93.27	3	PP1		(51.00)	268		$38,375.00
41	9/15/92	S	93.00	3	Trend 1					
T	9/17/92	L	92.21	1	T1	11		279		$38,718.75
T	9/18/92	L	93.00	1	T1	0				
42	9/22/92	L	92.00	1	T2	32		311		$39,718.75
T	9/25/92	L	92.04	3	Special Rule					
T	9/29/92	S	92.24	1	T1	20		331		$40,343.75
T	9/30/92	S	92.18	1	T1	14		345		$40,781.25
PP	10/1/92	S	92.14	1	PP2	10		355	(60)	$41,093.75
43	10/1/92	L	93.03	3	Re-entry Rule					
PP	10/2/92	S	92.17	3	PP1		(54.00)	301		$39,406.25
44	10/3/92	L	93.21	3	Re-entry Rule					
PP	10/3/92	S	93.07	3	PP1		(42.00)	259		$38,093.75
45	10/6/92	S	92.05	3	Trend 1					
T	10/7/92	L	91.19	1	T2	18		277		$38,656.25
46	10/8/92	L	91.19	5	Special Rule	36		313		$39,781.25
47	10/9/92	S	90.30	6	Special Rule		(33.00)	280		$38,750.00
T	10/12/92	L	90.29	1	T1	1		281		$38,781.25
PP	10/14/92	L	91.13	2	PP2		(30.00)	251		$37,843.75
48	10/19/92	S	90.09	3	Re-entry Rule					
PP	10/22/92	L	90.11	3	PP2		(6.00)	245	(110)	$37,656.25
49	11/6/92	S	89.09	3	Re-entry Rule					
PP	11/10/92	L	89.16	3	PP1		(21.00)	224		$37,000.00
50	11/11/92	L	89.31	3	Contra 1					

1992
US BONDS
NEW GANN SWING CHARTIST ©
DAILY PLAN

TRADE#	DATE	L/S	PRICE	CTR.	RULE #	PROFIT	(LOSS)	ACCUM.	MO. PROFIT/(LOSS)	A/C EQUITY
PYR	11/12/92	L	90.23	1	PYR 1					
T	11/13/92	S	90.27	2	T2	56		280		$38,750.00
51	11/16/92	S	90.24	2	T1	26		306		$39,562.50
T	11/17/92	L	90.29	1	T1		(5.00)	301		$39,406.25
52	11/18/92	L	91.05	5	Special Rule		(26.00)	275		$38,593.75
53	11/19/92	S	90.28	6	Special Rule		(27.00)	248		$37,750.00
T	11/25/92	L	91.03	1	T1		(7.00)	241		$37,531.25
PYR	11/27/92	S	90.14	1	PYR 2					
T	12/1/92	L	90.18	1	T1	10		251		$37,843.75
PP	12/2/92	L	90.23	1	PP2	5		256	11	$38,000.00
54	12/4/92	L	91.16	3	Special Rule					
T	12/11/92	S	92.16	1	T1	32		288		$39,000.00
T	12/12/92	S	92.08	1	T1	24		312		$39,750.00
PP	12/13/92	S	92.03	1	PP2	19		331		$40,343.75
55	12/17/92	L	92.26	3	Re-entry Rule					
T	12/18/92	S	92.21	1	T1		(5.00)	326		$40,187.50
T	12/23/92	S	93.19	1	T1	25		351		$40,968.75
T	12/24/92	S	93.16	1	T1	22		373		$41,656.25
56	12/29/92	S	92.29	3	Contra 1					
PP	12/29/92	L	93.10	3	PP1		(39.00)	334		$40,437.50
57	12/31/92	S	92.26	3	Re-entry Rule					
PP	1/4/93	L	93.08	3	PP1		(42.00)	292	36	$39,125.00

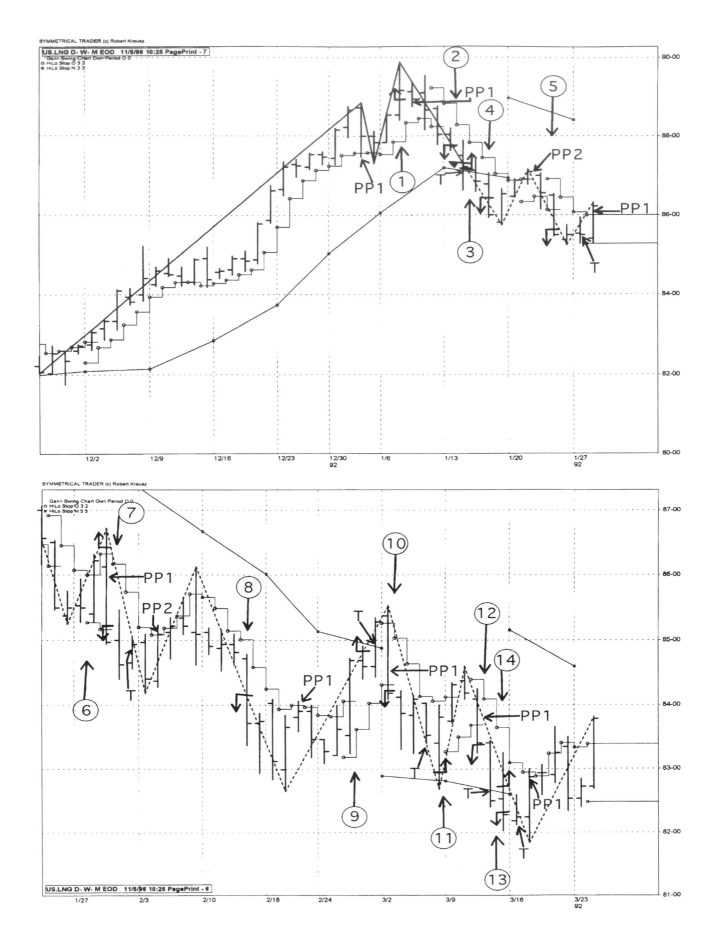

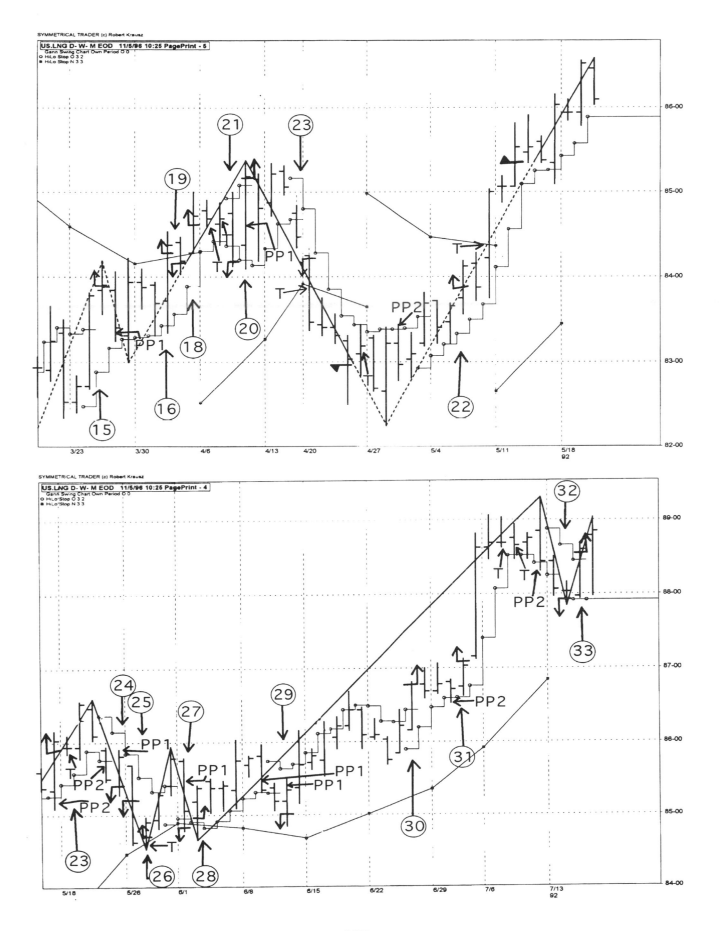

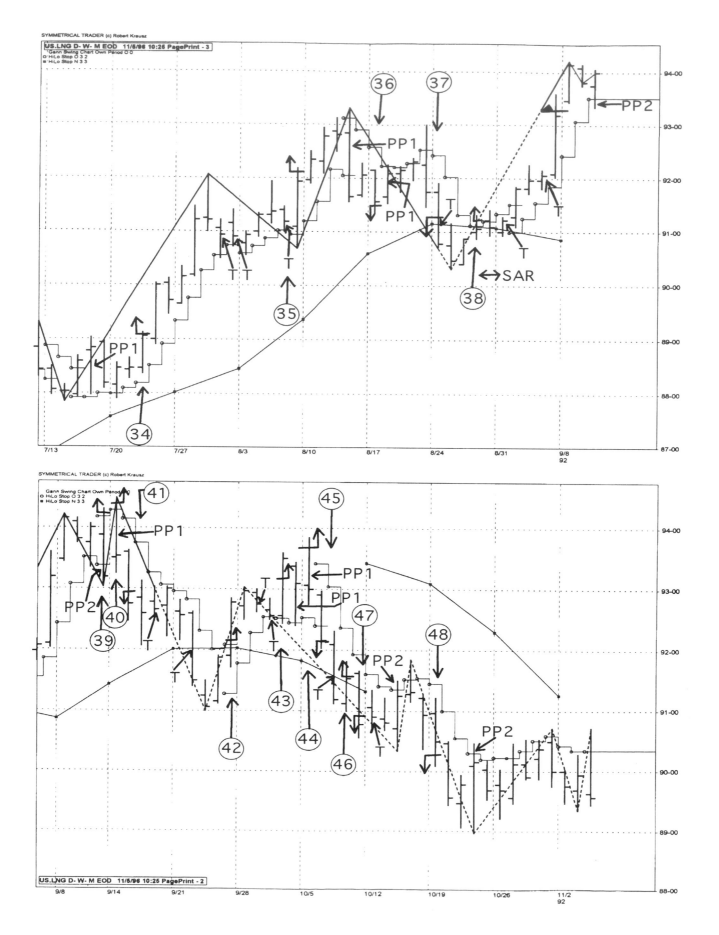

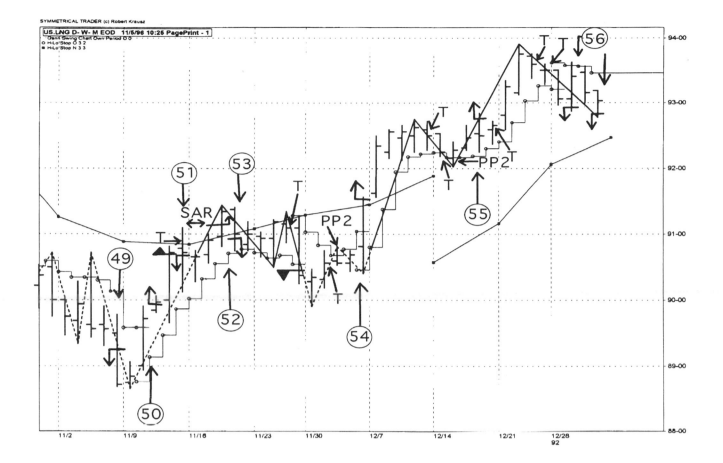

US.LNG D- W- M EOD   11/5/96 10:25 PagePrint - 1
Gann Swing Chart Own Period 0 0
O HiLo'Stop O 3 2
■ HiLo'Stop N 3 3

Beginning Equity	$30,000.00	Ending Equity	$65,843.75
Total Net Profit	$35,843.75		
Gross Profit	$70,031.25	Gross Loss	($34,187.50)
Total No. Trades	45	Percentage Profitable	56%
No. Winning Trades	25	No. Losing Trades	20

Largest Winning Trade	$11,312.50	Largest Losing Trade	($3,656.25)
Average Winning Trade	$2,801.25	Average Losing Trade	($1,709.38)
Ratio Average Win/Loss	1.64	Average Trade	$796.53
Max. Consecutive Winners	4	Max. Consecutive Losses	3
Largest Consecutive Drawdown (%)	10%	Largest Consecutive Drawdown	($5,312.50)

Return on Account	119%
Profit/Drawdown Ratio	6.75

NOTES:
1) Initial A/C Size = $30,000
2) Pyramids only 1/3 of original position

1993
US BONDS
NEW GANN SWING CHARTIST ©
DAILY PLAN

TRADE#	DATE	L/S	PRICE	CTR.	RULE #	PROFIT	(LOSS)	ACCUM.	MO. PROFIT/(LOSS)	A/C EQUITY
1	1/4/93	L	93.29	3	Trend 1					$30,000.00
T	1/5/93	S	93.29	1	T1		(5)	(5)		$29,843.75
T	1/6/93	S	93.24	1	T1		(24)	(29)		$29,093.75
PP	1/7/93	S	93.05	1	PP2					
2	1/8/93	S	92.11	3	Contra 1					
PYR	1/8/93	S	92.01	1	PYR 1					
T	1/11/93	L	92.08	1	T1	3		(26)		$29,187.50
T	1/13/93	L	92.16	1	T1		(5)	(31)		$29,031.25
PP	1/14/93	L	92.23	1	PP1		(12)	(43)		$28,656.25
3	1/15/93	L	93.05	3	Contra 1					
T	1/15/93	S	93.27	1	T2	22		(21)		$29,343.75
T	1/18/93	S	93.25	1	T1	20		(1)		$29,968.75
PYR	1/19/93	L	93.28	1	PYR 1					
PP	1/21/93	S	93.24	2	PP2	15		14		$30,437.50
4	1/22/93	L	94.21	3	Re-entry Rule					
T	1/27/93	S	95.05	1	T1	16		30		$30,937.50
T	2/2/93	S	95.10	1	T1	21		51		$31,593.75
T	2/8/93	S	96.13	1	T1	56		107	107	$33,343.75
5	2/16/93	L	96.27	3	Re-entry Rule					
T	2/17/93	S	96.22	1	T1		(5)	102		$33,187.50
T	2/25/93	S	98.24	1	T1	61		163		$35,093.75
T	2/26/93	S	99.08	1	T1	77		240	133	$37,500.00
6	3/3/93	L	100.13	3	Re-entry Rule					
PP	3/5/93	S	101.01	3	PP	60		300		$39,375.00
7	3/8/93	L	102.13	3	Re-entry Rule					
PP	3/9/93	S	101.07	3	PP1		(114)	186		$35,812.50
8	3/12/93	S	100.14	3	Contra 1					
PYR	3/12/93	S	99.01	1	PYR 1					
T	3/15/93	L	98.18	2	T2	120		306		$39,562.50
T	3/16/93	L	99.10	1	T1	36		342		$40,687.50
T	3/17/93	L	99.12	1	T1	34		376		$41,750.00
9	3/19/93	L	100.11	3	Contra 1					
T	3/22/93	S	100.03	1	T1		(8)	368		$41,500.00
T	3/24/93	S	100.07	1	T1		(4)	364		$41,375.00
PP	3/25/93	S	99.30	1	PP2		(13)	351		$40,968.75
10	3/26/93	S	98.24	3	Trend 1					
T	3/29/93	L	98.21	1	T2	3		354		$41,062.50
PP	3/30/93	L	99.22	2	PP2		(60)	294	54	$39,187.50
11	4/2/93	S	98.08	3	Special Rule					
T	4/3/93	L	98.05	1	T1	3		297		$39,281.25

1993
US BONDS
NEW GANN SWING CHARTIST ©
DAILY PLAN

TRADE#	DATE	L/S	PRICE	CTR.	RULE #	PROFIT	(LOSS)	ACCUM.	MO. PROFIT/(LOSS)	A/C EQUITY
PP	4/6/93	L	98.30	2	PP1		(44)	253		$37,906.25
12	4/7/93	L	99.05	3	Contra 1					
T	4/8/93	S	100.14	1	T2	43		296		$39,250.00
T	4/14/93	S	101.29	1	T1	89		385		$42,031.25
PP	4/19/93	S	101.17	1	PP2	77		462		$44,437.50
13	4/27/93	S	100.25	3	Contra 1					
T	4/27/93	L	100.04	1	T2	21		483		$45,093.75
14	4/29/93	L	100.12	5	Special Rule	26		509		$45,906.25
15	4/30/93	S	100.12	6	Special Rule					
PYR	4/30/93	S	99.27	1	PYR 2				138	$43,500.00
PP	5/3/93	L	100.27	4	PP1		(77)	432		
16	5/3/93	L	101.01	3	Trend 1					
T	5/5/93	S	102.02	1	T2	33		465		$44,531.25
17	5/5/93	S	102.00	5	Special Rule	62		527		$46,468.75
T	5/10/93	L	101.27	1	T1	5		532		$46,625.00
PYR	5/13/93	S	99.29	1	PYR 1					
T	5/17/93	L	99.30	2	T1	132		664		$50,750.00
PP	5/20/93	L	100.04	1	PP2		(6)	658		$50,562.50
18	5/27/93	L	100.27	3	Contra 1					
PP	5/28/93	S	100.04	3	PP1		(69)	589	157	$48,406.25
19	6/1/93	L	101.04	3	Special Rule		(15)	574		$47,937.50
20	6/4/93	S	100.31	6	Special Rule		(18)	556		$47,375.00
T	6/7/93	L	101.17	1	T1		(58)	498		$45,562.50
21	6/9/93	L	101.28	5	Special Rule					
T	6/10/93	S	101.24	1	T1		(4)	494		$45,437.50
T	6/16/93	S	102.19	1	T1	23		517		$46,156.25
T	6/22/93	S	103.10	1	T1	46		563		$47,593.75
22	6/24/93	L	103.21	3	Re-entry Rule					
T	6/30/93	S	104.25	1	T1	36		599	56	$48,718.75
PP	7/7/93	S	104.12	2	PP2	46		645		$50,156.25
23	7/13/93	L	105.22	3	Re-entry Rule					
T	7/19/93	S	106.26	1	T1	36		681		$51,281.25
PP	7/20/93	S	106.06	2	PP1	32		713		$52,281.25
24	7/22/93	S	105.21	3	Contra 1					
T	7/23/93	L	104.19	1	T2	34		747		$53,343.75
25	7/26/93	L	104.21	5	Special Rule	64		811		$55,343.75
PP	7/28/93	S	104.13	3	PP2		(24)	787		$54,593.75
26	7/28/93	L	105.06	3	Special Rule					
T	8/2/93	S	106.08	1	T1	34		821		$55,656.25
T	8/4/93	S	106.09	1	T1	35		856		$56,750.00

1993
US BONDS
NEW GANN SWING CHARTIST ©
DAILY PLAN

TRADE#	DATE	L/S	PRICE	CTR.	RULE #	PROFIT	(LOSS)	ACCUM.	MO. PROFIT/(LOSS)	A/C EQUITY
T	8/5/93	S	106.06	1	T1	32		888	243	$57,750.00
27	8/9/93	L	106.29	3	Re-entry Rule		(9)	879		$57,468.75
PP	8/13/93	S	106.26	3	PP1					
28	8/20/93	L	107.26	3	Re-entry Rule					
T	9/1/93	S	110.12	1	T1	82		961		$60,031.25
T	9/8/93	S	112.21	1	T1	155		1116		$64,875.00
PP	9/9/93	S	111.23	1	PP2	125		1241	353	$68,781.25
29	9/10/93	S	111.04	3	Contra 1					
PP	9/11/93	L	111.25	3	PP1		(63)	1178		$66,812.50
30	9/15/93	S	110.26	3	Re-entry Rule					
PP	9/16/93	L	111.06	3	PP1		(36)	1142		$65,687.50
31	9/21/93	S	109.29	3	Special Rule					
32	9/22/93	L	110.07	6	Special Rule		(30)	1112		$64,750.00
PP	9/29/93	S	111.09	3	PP1	102		1214		$67,937.50
33	9/30/93	S	111.04	3	Contra 1					
PP	10/5/93	L	111.20	3	PP1		(48)	1166	(75)	$66,437.50
34	10/8/93	L	112.15	3	Re-entry Rule					
PP	10/13/93	S	112.16	3	PP2	3		1169		$66,531.25
35	10/14/93	L	113.14	3	Re-entry Rule					
PP	10/18/93	S	113.17	3	PP1	9		1178		$66,812.50
36	10/21/93	S	112.10	3	Trend 1					
T	10/22/93	L	111.11	1	T2	31		1209		$67,781.25
T	10/26/93	L	111.00	1	T1	42		1251		$69,093.75
PP	10/29/93	L	111.10	1	PP2	32		1283	117	$70,093.75
37	11/1/93	S	109.24	3	Re-entry Rule					
T	11/3/93	L	108.15	1	T1	41		1324		$71,375.00
T	11/8/93	L	108.09	1	T1	47		1371		$72,843.75
PP	11/11/93	S	107.30	3	Re-entry Rule					
38	11/12/93	L	109.05	3	PP2		(117)	1254		$69,187.50
PP	11/15/93	L	109.10	3	Contra 1					
39	11/17/93	S	108.31	3	PP1		(33)	1221		$68,156.25
PP	11/18/93	S	108.11	3	Trend 1					
40	11/19/93	S	107.08	1	PYR 2	21		1242		$68,812.50
PYR	11/23/93	L	107.29	4	PP2					
PP	11/29/93	L	108.12	3	Contra 1					
41	11/30/93	S	107.19	3	PP1		(75)	1167		$66,468.75
PP	12/6/93	L	109.06	3	Re-entry Rule				(116)	$66,843.75
42	12/8/93	S	109.18	3	T1	12		1179		
T	12/10/93	S	109.04	3	Special Rule		(4)	1175		$66,718.75
43	12/20/93	L	108.10	3	PP2	78		1253		$69,156.25

1993
US BONDS
NEW GANN SWING CHARTIST ©
DAILY PLAN

TRADE#	DATE	L/S	PRICE	CTR.	RULE #	PROFIT	(LOSS)	ACCUM.	MO. PROFIT/(LOSS)	A/C EQUITY
44	12/21/93	S	107.17	3	Re-entry Rule					
PP	12/22/93	L	108.19	3	PP2		(102)	1151		$65,968.75
45	12/22/93	L	109.08	3	Re-entry Rule					
T	12/23/93	S	109.16	1	T2	8		1159		$66,218.75
PP	12/28/93	S	109.02	2	PP2		(12)	1147	(20)	$65,843.75

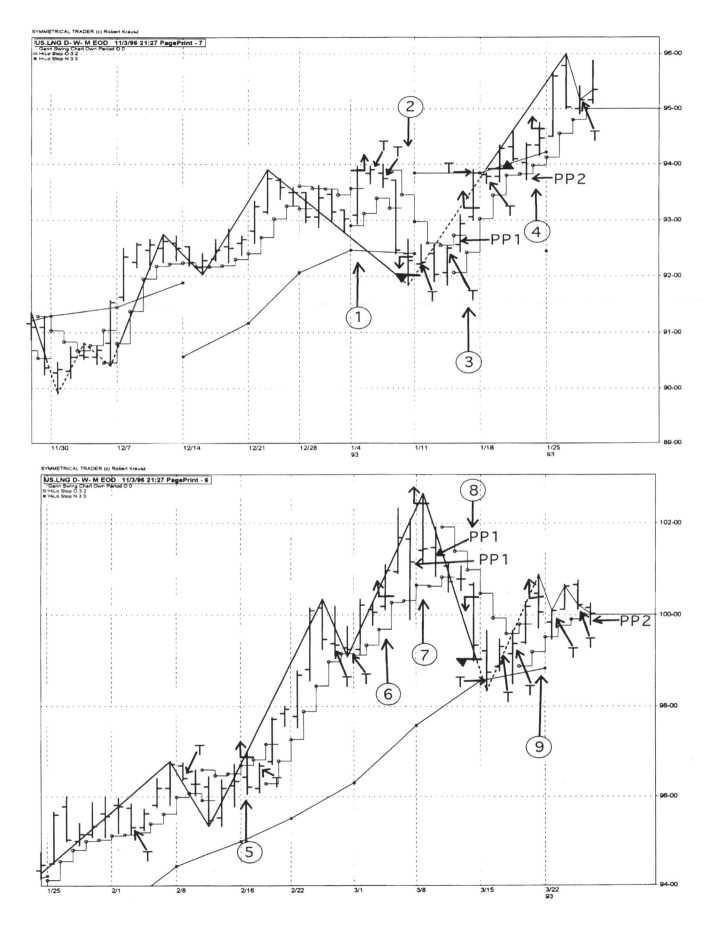

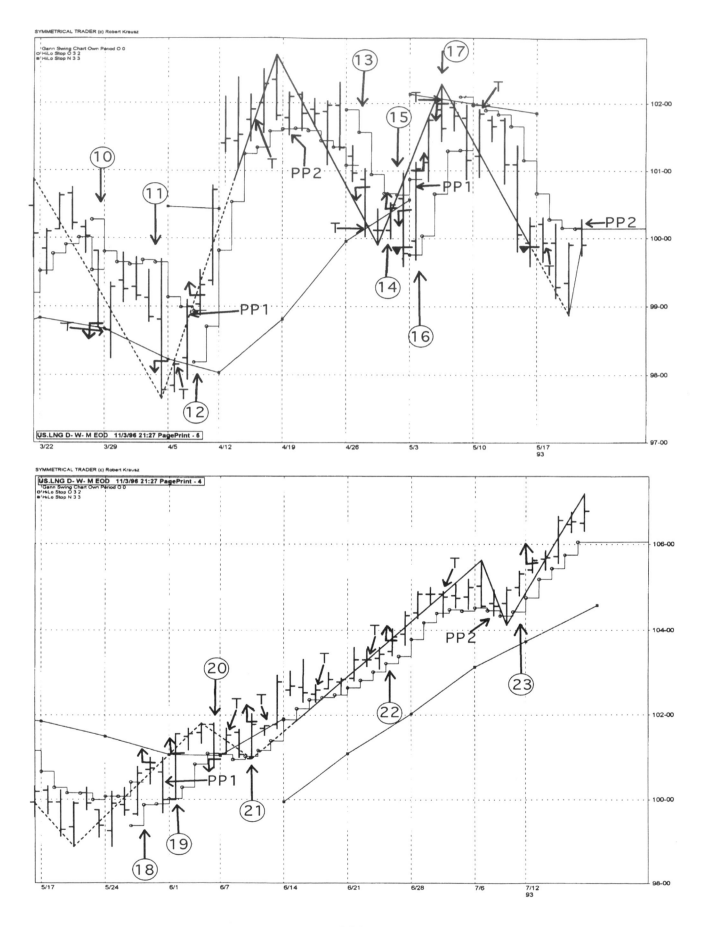

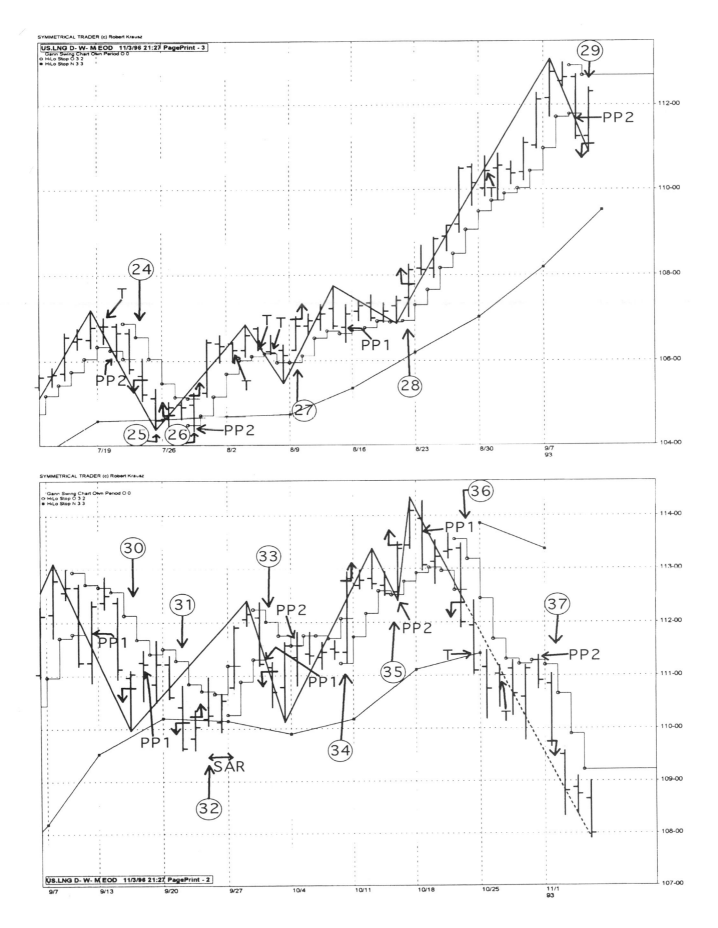

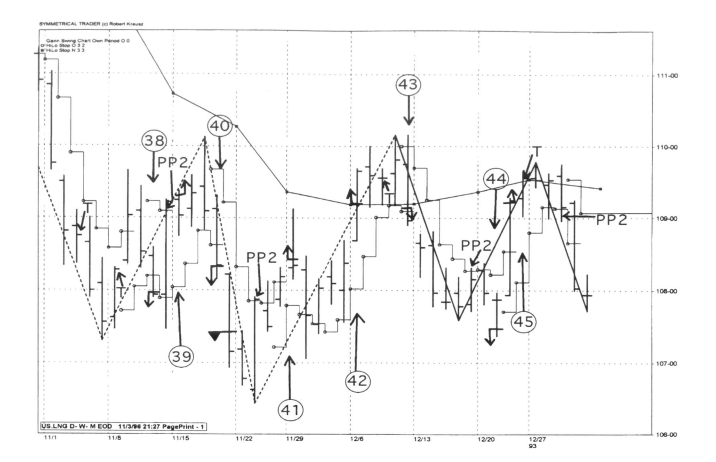

1994
NEW GANN SWING CHARTIST ©
DAILY PLAN

Beginning Equity	$30,000.00	Ending Equity	$68,687.50
Total Net Profit	$38,687.50		
Gross Profit	$63,625.00	Gross Loss	($24,937.50)
Total No. Trades	51	Percentage Profitable	51%
No. Winning Trades	26	No. Losing Trades	25

Largest Winning Trade	$11,312.50	Largest Losing Trade	($2,250.00)
Average Winning Trade	$2,447.12	Average Losing Trade	($997.50)
Ratio Average Win/Loss	2.45	Average Trade	$758.58
Max. Consecutive Winners	6	Max. Consecutive Losses	5
Largest Consecutive Drawdown (%)	15%	Largest Consecutive Drawdown	($5,687.50)

Return on Account	129%
Profit/Drawdown Ratio	6.80

NOTES:

1) Initial A/C Size = $30,000

2) Pyramids only 1/3 of original position

1994
US BONDS
NEW GANN SWING CHARTIST ©
DAILY PLAN

TRADE#	DATE	L/S	PRICE	CTR.	RULE #	PROFIT	(LOSS)	ACCUM.	MO. PROFIT/(LOSS)	A/C EQUITY
1	12/31/93	S	107.30	3	Contra 1					$30,000.00
PYR	1/3/94	S	107.19	1	PYR 1		(12)	(12)		$29,625.00
PP	1/5/94	L	107.31	4	PP2		(3)	(15)		$29,531.25
2	1/10/94	L	109.23	3	Contra 1					
PYR	1/10/94	L	109.26	1	PYR 1					
T	1/11/94	S	109.27	2	T1	8		(7)		$29,781.25
PP	1/13/94	S	109.14	2	PP2		(21)	(28)		$29,125.00
3	1/14/94	S	109.09	3	Contra 1					
T	1/17/94	L	108.23	1	T2	18		(10)		$29,687.50
4	1/18/94	L	109.13	5	Trend 1					
T	1/24/94	S	109.19	1	T1	6		(4)		$29,875.00
PP	1/25/94	S	109.06	2	PP2		(14)	(18)		$29,437.50
5	1/26/94	S	108.28	3	Contra 1					
PP	1/26/94	L	109.12	3	PP1		(48)	(66)		$27,937.50
6	1/27/94	L	110.07	4	Trend 1/PYR2					
T	1/28/94	S	110.21	2	T1	28		(38)		$28,812.50
T	1/31/94	S	110.19	1	T1	12		(26)		$29,187.50
PP	2/1/94	S	110.09	1	PP1	2		(24)	(24)	$29,250.00
7	2/2/94	S	109.16	3	Contra 1			(24)		$29,250.00
PP	2/4/94	L	109.30	3	PP1		(42)	(66)		$27,937.50
8	2/4/94	S	108.31	3	Re-entry Rule					
T	2/8/94	L	107.23	1	T1	40		(26)		$29,187.50
PP	2/10/94	L	108.13	2	PP2	36		10		$30,312.50
9	2/17/94	S	107.13	3	Re-entry Rule					
T	2/22/94	L	106.17	1	T1	28		38		$31,187.50
T	2/25/94	L	105.04	1	T1	73		111		$33,468.75
T	2/28/94	L	105.27	1	T1	50		161	185	$35,031.25
10	3/1/94	S	104.25	3	Re-entry Rule					
T	3/3/94	L	103.28	1	T1	29		190		$35,937.50
PP	3/7/94	L	104.13	2	PP1	24		214		$36,687.50
11	3/10/96	S	103.08	3	Re-entry Rule					
T	3/14/94	S	103.05	1	T1	3		217		$36,781.25
PP	3/15/94	L	103.24	2	PP2		(32)	185		$35,781.25
12	3/17/94	L	104.16	3	Contra 1					
PP	3/18/94	L	103.24	3	PP1		(72)	113		$33,531.25
13	3/18/94	S	103.06	3	Trend 1					
PP	3/22/94	S	103.12	3	PP1		(18)	95		$32,968.75
14	3/23/94	L	104.02	3	Contra 1					
PP	3/24/94	S	103.14	3	PP1		(60)	35		$31,093.75
15	3/24/94	S	102.12	3	Trend 1					

1994
US BONDS
NEW GANN SWING CHARTIST ©
DAILY PLAN

TRADE#	DATE	L/S	PRICE	CTR.	RULE #	PROFIT	(LOSS)	ACCUM.	MO. PROFIT/(LOSS)	A/C EQUITY
PYR	3/25/94	S	102.08	1	PYR 2					
T	4/5/94	L	99.10	2	T1	196		231		$37,218.75
PP	4/6/94	L	99.23	2	PP2	166		397	236	$42,406.25
16	4/12/94	L	100.03	3	Contra 1					
PP	4/14/94	S	99.14	3	PP1		(63)	334		$40,437.50
17	4/14/94	S	99.04	3	Trend 1					
PYR	4/19/94	S	97.15	1	PYR 2					
PP	4/20/94	L	98.20	4	PP1	41		375		$41,718.75
18	4/22/94	L	100.17	3	Contra 1					
PYR	4/25/94	L	100.22	1	PYR 1					
19	4/28/94	S	100.22	7	Special Rule	15		390		$42,187.50
T	5/3/94	L	98.23	1	T1	63		453		$44,156.25
PP	5/5/94	L	99.09	2	PP2	90		543	146	$46,968.75
20	5/6/94	S	98.02	3	Re-entry Rule					
PYR	5/6/94	S	97.08	1	PYR 1					
PP	5/11/94	L	97.19	4	PP2	34		577		$48,031.25
21	5/17/94	L	98.16	3	Contra 1					
T	5/17/94	S	99.18	1	T2	34		611		$49,093.75
22	5/20/94	S	99.09	5	Special Rule	50		661		$50,656.25
T	5/24/94	L	98.20	1	T1	21		682		$51,312.50
PP	5/25/94	L	98.26	2	PP1	30		712		$52,250.00
23	5/31/94	S	97.21	3	Re-entry Rule					
T	6/1/94	L	97.04	1	T2	17		729		$52,781.25
PP	6/1/94	L	98.14	3	PP1		(46)	683	140	$51,343.75
24	6/3/94	L	99.09	3	Contra 1					
PYR	6/4/94	L	100.15	1	PYR 1					
T	6/7/94	S	100.13	2	T	72		755		$53,593.75
PP	6/8/94	S	100.00	2	PP2	8		763		$53,843.75
25	6/16/94	S	98.26	3	Contra 1					
T	6/17/94	L	98.07	1	T1	19		782		$54,437.50
26	6/22/94	L	98.11	5	Special Rule	30		812		$55,375.00
PP	6/24/94	S	98.20	3	PP3	27		839		$56,218.75
27	6/24/94	S	98.09	3	Special Rule					
PYR	6/27/94	L	97.16	1	PYR 1					
PP	6/27/94	L	98.03	4	PP1		(1)	838		$56,187.50
28	6/30/94	S	97.05	3	Re-entry Rule					
T	7/5/94	L	97.01	1	T1	4		842		$56,312.50
PP	7/7/94	L	97.09	2	PP2		(8)	834	151	$56,062.50
29	7/8/94	S	96.11	3	Re-entry Rule					
T	7/12/94	L	96.07	1	T1	4		838		$56,187.50

311

1994
US BONDS
NEW GANN SWING CHARTIST ©
DAILY PLAN

TRADE#	DATE	L/S	PRICE	CTR.	RULE #	PROFIT	(LOSS)	ACCUM.	MO. PROFIT/(LOSS)	A/C EQUITY
PYR	3/25/94	S	102.08	1	PYR 2					
T	4/5/94	L	99.10	2	T1	196		231		$37,218.75
PP	4/6/94	L	99.23	2	PP2	166		397	236	$42,406.25
16	4/12/94	L	100.03	3	Contra 1					
PP	4/14/94	S	99.14	3	PP1		(63)	334		$40,437.50
17	4/14/94	S	99.04	3	Trend 1					
PYR	4/19/94	S	97.15	1	PYR 2					
PP	4/20/94	L	98.20	4	PP1	41		375		$41,718.75
18	4/22/94	L	100.17	3	Contra 1					
PYR	4/25/94	L	100.22	1	PYR 1					
19	4/28/94	S	100.22	7	Special Rule	15		390		$42,187.50
T	5/3/94	L	98.23	1	T1	63		453		$44,156.25
PP	5/5/94	L	99.09	2	PP2	90		543	146	$46,968.75
20	5/6/94	S	98.02	3	Re-entry Rule					
PYR	5/6/94	S	97.08	1	PYR 1					
PP	5/11/94	L	97.19	4	PP2	34		577		$48,031.25
21	5/17/94	L	98.16	3	Contra 1					
T	5/17/94	S	99.18	1	T2	34		611		$49,093.75
22	5/20/94	S	99.09	5	Special Rule	50		661		$50,656.25
T	5/24/94	L	98.20	1	T1	21		682		$51,312.50
PP	5/25/94	L	98.26	2	PP1	30		712		$52,250.00
23	5/31/94	S	97.21	3	Re-entry Rule					
T	6/1/94	L	97.04	1	T2	17		729		$52,781.25
PP	6/1/94	L	98.14	3	PP1		(46)	683	140	$51,343.75
24	6/3/94	L	99.09	3	Contra 1					
PYR	6/4/94	L	100.15	1	PYR 1					
T	6/7/94	S	100.13	2	T	72		755		$53,593.75
PP	6/8/94	S	100.00	2	PP2	8		763		$53,843.75
25	6/16/94	S	98.26	3	Contra 1					
T	6/17/94	L	98.07	1	T1	19		782		$54,437.50
26	6/22/94	L	98.11	5	Special Rule	30		812		$55,375.00
PP	6/24/94	S	98.20	3	PP3	27		839		$56,218.75
27	6/24/94	L	98.09	3	Special Rule					
PYR	6/27/94	S	97.16	1	PYR 1					
PP	6/27/94	L	98.03	4	PP1		(1)	838		$56,187.50
28	6/30/94	S	97.05	3	Re-entry Rule					
T	7/5/94	L	97.01	1	T1	4		842		$56,312.50
PP	7/7/94	L	97.09	2	PP2		(8)	834	151	$56,062.50
29	7/8/94	S	96.11	3	Re-entry Rule					
T	7/12/94	L	96.07	1	T1	4		838		$56,187.50

1994
US BONDS
NEW GANN SWING CHARTIST ©
DAILY PLAN

TRADE#	DATE	L/S	PRICE	CTR.	RULE #	PROFIT	(LOSS)	ACCUM.	MO. PROFIT/(LOSS)	A/C EQUITY
PP		L	96.16	2	PP2		(10)	828		$55,875.00
30	7/13/94	L	98.10	3	Contra 1					$56,031.25
T	7/15/94	S	98.15	1	T1	5		833		$55,156.25
PP	7/18/94	S	97.28	2	PP2		(28)	805		
31	7/20/94	L	98.18	3	Trend 1					$55,875.00
T	7/29/94	S	99.09	1	T2	23		828		$57,312.50
T	7/29/94	S	100.00	1	T1	46		874		$58,406.25
PP	8/1/94	S	99.21	1	PP2	35		909	75	
32	8/3/94	S	98.12	3	Contra 1					
PP	8/5/94	L	98.18	3	PP2		(18)	891		$57,843.75
33	8/11/94	S	97.20	3	Special Rule					
PYR	8/11/94	S	97.10	1	PYR 1					$57,250.00
34	8/11/94	L	97.23	7	Special Rule		(19)	872		$60,437.50
PP	8/12/94	S	98.25	3	PP1	102		974		
35	8/18/94	S	98.04	3	Trend 1					$60,906.25
T	8/18/94	L	97.21	1	T2	15		989		
36	8/19/94	L	97.23	5	Special Rule	26		1015		$62,406.25
T	8/23/94	S	98.13	1	T1	22		1037		$63,656.25
T	8/29/94	S	98.31	1	T1	40		1077		$64,875.00
PP	9/1/94	S	98.30	1	PP1	39		1116	207	
37	9/2/94	S	98.12	3	Contra 1					
T	9/6/94	L	97.23	1	T2	21		1137		$65,531.25
T	9/6/94	L	97.19	1	T2	25		1162		$66,312.50
T	9/7/94	L	97.20	1	T1	24		1186		$67,062.50
38	9/8/94	S	97.12	3	Trend 1					
T	9/9/94	L	95.31	1	T1	45		1231		$68,468.75
PP	9/12/94	L	96.17	2	PP2	54		1285		$70,156.25
39	9/14/94	S	95.19	3	Re-entry Rule					
T	9/16/94	L	95.28	1	T1		(9)	1276		$69,875.00
T	9/19/94	L	95.19	1	T1					
PP	9/22/94	L	95.22	1	PP2		(3)	1273		$69,781.25
40	9/28/94	S	94.24	3	Re-entry Rule					
T	9/29/94	L	95.04	1	T1		(12)	1261		$69,406.25
T	9/30/94	L	93.29	1	T1	25		1286		$70,187.50
PP	10/6/94	L	94.16	1	PP2	8		1294	178	$70,437.50
41	10/7/94	L	94.23	3	Contra 1					
T	10/11/94	S	94.24	1	T1	1		1295		$70,468.75
T	10/12/94	S	95.20	1	T2	29		1324		$71,375.00
T	10/13/94	S	95.20	1	T2	29		1353		$72,281.25
42	10/14/94	S	94.27	3	Trend 1					

1994
US BONDS
NEW GANN SWING CHARTIST ©
DAILY PLAN

TRADE#	DATE	L/S	PRICE	CTR.	RULE #	PROFIT	(LOSS)	ACCUM.	MO. PROFIT/(LOSS)	A/C EQUITY
T	10/26/94	L	93.14	1	T1	45		1398		$73,687.50
T	10/27/94	L	93.18	1	T1	41		1439		$74,968.75
PP	10/28/94	L	94.04	1	PP2	23		1462	168	$75,687.50
43	11/1/94	S	93.15	3	Trend 1					
PP	11/4/94	L	93.19	3	PP2		(12)	1450		$75,312.50
44	11/4/94	S	92.25	3	Re-entry Rule					
T	11/8/94	L	92.30	1	T1		(5)	1445		$75,156.25
PP	11/9/94	L	93.04	2	PP2		(22)	1423		$74,468.75
45	11/10/94	L	93.21	3	Contra 1					
PP	11/10/94	S	93.09	3	PP1		(36)	1387		$73,343.75
46	11/11/94	S	92.08	3	Trend 1					
PP	11/14/94	L	92.31	3	PP1		(69)	1318		$71,187.50
47	11/15/94	L	92.26	3	Trend 1					
PP	11/16/94	S	93.16	3	PP1		(30)	1288		$70,250.00
48	11/23/94	L	94.04	3	Trend 1					
T	11/23/94	S	94.15	1	T2	11		1299		$70,593.75
T	11/28/94	S	94.23	1	T1	19		1318		$71,187.50
PP	11/29/94	S	94.09	1	PP2	5		1323	(139)	$71,343.75
49	12/2/94	L	95.20	3	Trend 1					
PP	12/7/94	S	95.13	3	PP1		(21)	1302		$70,687.50
50	12/14/94	L	96.19	3	Re-entry Rule					
T	12/15/94	S	96.04	1	T1		(15)	1287		$70,218.75
T	12/20/94	S	96.09	1	T1		(10)	1277		$69,906.25
PP	12/22/94	S	96.04	1	PP2		(15)	1262		$69,437.50
51	12/27/94	L	96.26	3	Re-entry Rule					
PP	12/28/94	S	96.18	3	PP1		(24)	1238	(85)	$68,687.50

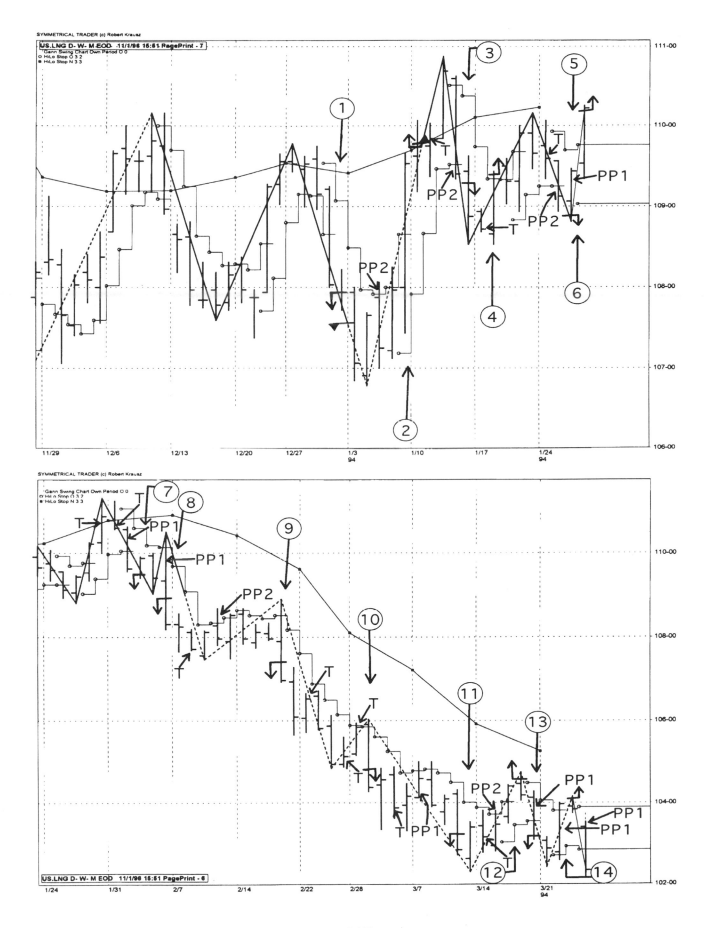

315

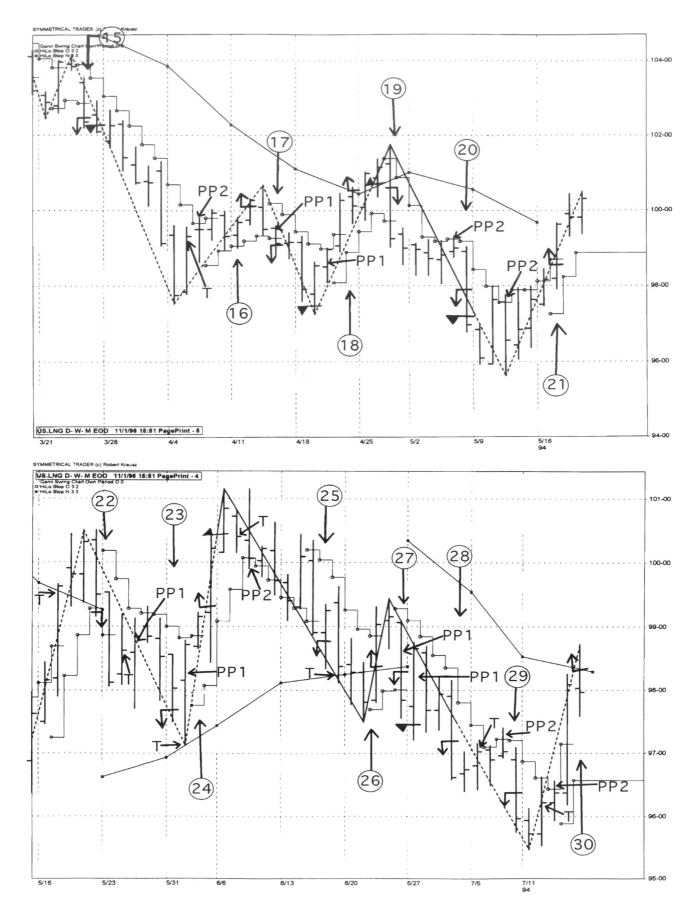

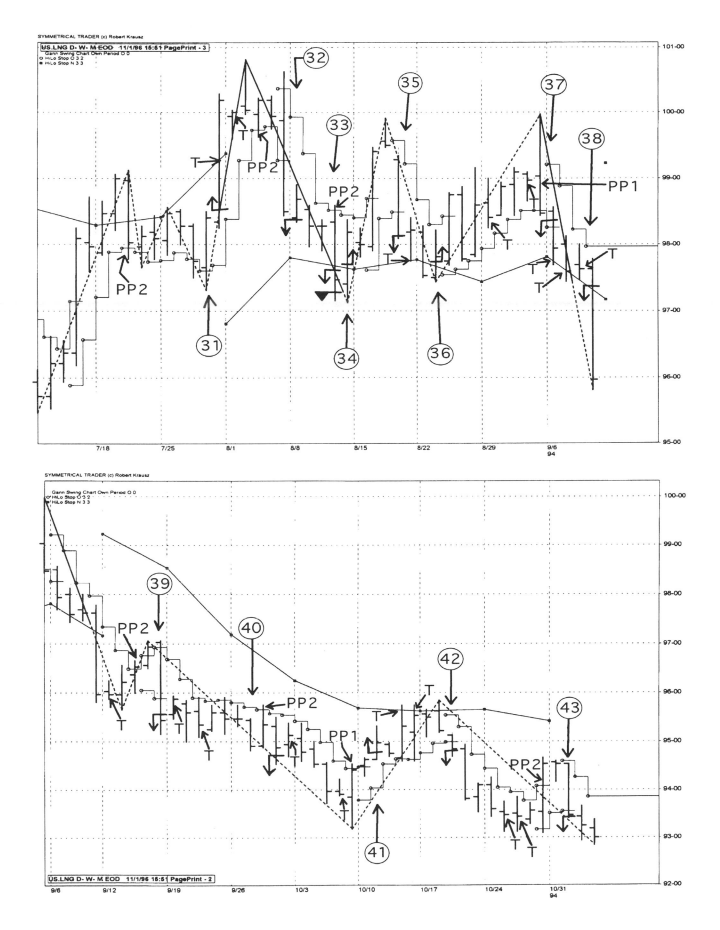

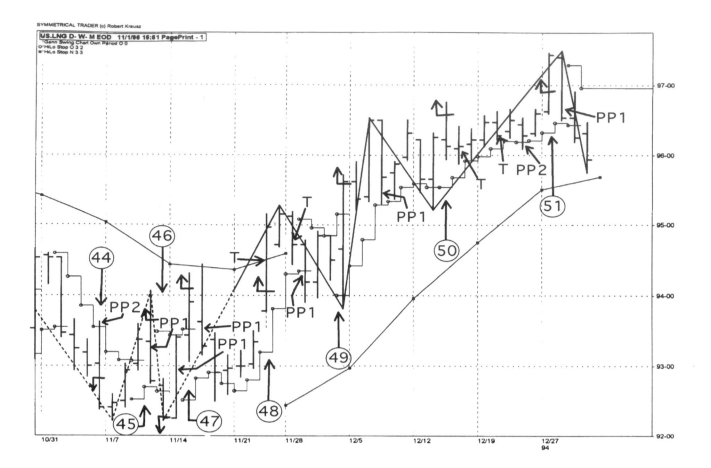

Beginning Equity	$30,000.00	Ending Equity	$93,312.50
Total Net Profit	$63,312.50		
Gross Profit	$87,500.00	Gross Loss	($24,187.50)
Total No. Trades	43	Percentage Profitable	56%
No. Winning Trades	24	No. Losing Trades	19

Largest Winning Trade	$11,593.75	Largest Losing Trade	($2,437.50)
Average Winning Trade	$3,645.83	Average Losing Trade	($1,273.03)
Ratio Average Win/Loss	2.86	Average Trade	$1,472.38
Max. Consecutive Winners	5	Max. Consecutive Losses	4
Largest Consecutive Drawdown (%)	9.00%	Largest Consecutive Drawdown	($5,156.25)

Return on Account	211%
Profit/Drawdown Ratio	12.28

<u>NOTES:</u>
1) Initial A/C Size = $30,000
2) Pyramids only 1/3 of original position

1995
US BONDS
NEW GANN SWING CHARTIST ©
DAILY PLAN

TRADE#	DATE	L/S	PRICE	CTR.	RULE #	PROFIT	(LOSS)	ACCUM.	MO. PROFIT/(LOSS)	A/C EQUITY
1	12/30/94	S	96.04	3	Contra 1					$30,000.00
T	1/3/95	L	95.21	1	T2	15		15		$30,468.75
PP	1/4/95	S	96.16	2	PP1		(24)	(9)		$29,718.75
2	1/4/95	L	96.13	3	Trend 1					
T	1/5/95	S	95.23	1	T1		(22)	(31)		$29,031.25
3	1/6/95	S	95.19	5	Special Rule		(52)	(83)		$27,406.25
4	1/6/95	L	95.25	6	Special Rule		(18)	(101)		$26,843.75
T	1/12/95	S	95.29	1	T1	4		(97)		$26,968.75
T	1/17/95	S	97.02	1	T1	41		(56)		$28,250.00
T	1/19/95	S	96.24	1	T1	31		(25)		$29,218.75
5	1/23/95	S	95.29	3	Contra 1					
T	1/24/95	L	95.28	1	T1	1		(24)		$29,250.00
T	1/25/95	L	95.20	2	T2	9		(15)		$29,531.25
6	1/25/95	L	95.23	5	Special Rule					
PYR	1/27/95	L	97.11	1	PYR 2					
PP	2/2/95	S	97.20	4	PP2	192		177	177	$35,531.25
7	2/3/95	L	98.22	3	Re-entry Rule					
T	2/6/95	S	99.06	1	T1	16		193		$36,031.25
T	2/7/95	S	99.03	1	T1	13		206		$36,437.50
PP	2/8/95	S	98.28	1	PP2	6		212		$36,625.00
8	2/10/95	S	98.17	3	Contra 1					
T	2/11/95	L	98.12	1	T1	5		217		$36,781.25
PP	2/14/95	L	98.23	2	PP1		(12)	205		$36,406.25
9	2/14/95	L	99.02	3	Trend 1					
PP	2/16/95	S	99.06	3	PP1	12		217		$36,781.25
10	2/23/95	L	100.03	3	Re-entry Rule					
PP	2/23/95	S	99.27	3	PP1		(24)	193		$36,031.25
11	2/28/95	L	100.19	3	Re-entry Rule					
PP	3/2/95	S	100.06	3	PP1		(39)	154	(23)	$34,812.50
12	3/6/95	S	99.03	3	Contra 1					
PYR	3/6/95	S	98.29	1	PYR 1					
T	3/6/95	L	98.22	2	T2	26		180		$35,625.00
13	3/8/95	L	98.26	5	Special Rule	12		192		$36,000.00
PYR	3/14/95	L	101.02	1	PYR 1					
T	3/15/95	S	101.29	2	T1	198		390		$42,187.50
T	3/17/95	S	101.22	1	T1	92		482		$45,062.50
T	3/20/95	S	101.11	1	T1	81		563		$47,593.75
14	3/22/95	S	100.23	3	Contra 1					

320

1995
US BONDS
NEW GANN SWING CHARTIST ©
DAILY PLAN

TRADE#	DATE	L/S	PRICE	CTR.	RULE #	PROFIT	(LOSS)	ACCUM.	MO. PROFIT/(LOSS)	A/C EQUITY
T	3/23/95	L	100.18	1	T1	5		568		$47,750.00
PP	3/24/95	L	101.09	2	PP 2		(36)	532		$46,625.00
15	3/24/95	L	101.21	3	Trend 1				360	
PP	3/28/95	S	101.15	3	PP1		(18)	514		$46,062.50
16	4/7/95	L	102.12	3	Re-entry Rule					
PP	4/7/95	S	101.25	3	PP1		(57)	457		$44,281.25
17	4/17/95	L	102.27	3	Re-entry Rule					
PP	4/17/95	S	102.09	3	PP1		(54)	403	(111)	$42,593.75
18	5/3/95	L	103.03	3	Re-entry Rule					
T	5/8/95	S	106.07	1	T1	100		503		$45,718.75
T	5/11/95	S	106.19	1	T1	112		615		$49,218.75
T	5/12/95	S	106.17	1	T1	110		725		$52,656.25
19	5/17/95	L	108.08	3	Re-entry Rule					
PP	5/18/95	S	107.14	3	PP1		(78)	647		$50,218.75
20	5/24/95	L	108.19	3	Re-entry Rule					
T	5/26/95	S	109.13	1	T1	26		673		$51,031.25
T	6/5/95	S	112.11	1	T1	120		793		$54,781.25
T	6/6/95	S	112.13	1	T1	122		915	512	$58,593.75
21	6/9/95	S	111.17	3	Contra 1	33		948		$59,625.00
PP	6/13/95	L	111.06	3	PP1		(17)	931		$59,093.75
22	6/13/95	L	111.31	3	Trend 1					
T	6/15/95	S	111.12	1	T1					
PP	6/16/95	S	111.06	2	PP1		(50)	881		$57,531.25
23	6/20/95	L	112.11	3	Trend 1					
T	6/23/95	S	112.27	1	T1	16		897		$58,031.25
PP	6/26/95	S	112.08	2	PP2		(6)	891		$57,843.75
24	6/29/95	S	111.29	3	Contra 1					
T	6/30/95	L	111.08	1	T1	21		912		$58,500.00
T	7/1/95	L	111.09	1	T1	20		932		$59,125.00
25	7/5/95	L	111.20	4	Trend 1	9		941	26	$59,406.25
T	7/10/95	L	113.06	1	T1	50		991		$60,968.75
PP	7/11/95	S	112.18	2	PP1	60		1051		$62,843.75
26	7/18/95	S	111.00	3	Contra 1					
PYR	7/18/95	S	110.18	1	PYR 1					
T	7/24/95	L	108.20	2	T1	152		1203	370	$67,593.75
PP	7/25/95	L	109.03	2	PP2	108		1311		$70,968.75
27	8/10/95	S	107.27	3	Trend 1					
PYR	8/11/95	S	107.10	1	PYR 2			1311		$70,968.75

1995
US BONDS
NEW GANN SWING CHARTIST ©
DAILY PLAN

TRADE#	DATE	L/S	PRICE	CTR.	RULE #	PROFIT	(LOSS)	ACCUM.	MO. PROFIT/(LOSS)	A/C EQUITY
PP	8/15/95	L	107.22	4	PP1	3		1314		$71,062.50
28	8/21/95	L	108.07	3	Contra 1					
T	8/22/95	S	107.29	1	T1		(10)	1304		$70,750.00
29	8/23/95	S	107.20	5	Trend 1		(38)	1266		$69,562.50
PP	8/24/95	L	108.14	3	PP2		(78)	1188		$67,125.00
30	8/25/95	L	108.28	3	Contra 1					
PYR	8/25/95	L	109.08	1	PYR 1					
T	8/29/95	S	110.03	1	T1	39		1227		$68,343.75
T	9/6/95	S	111.28	1	T1	96		1323		$71,343.75
T	9/7/95	S	111.16	1	T1	84		1407	96	$73,968.75
31	9/12/95	L	112.05	3	Re-entry Rule					
T	9/15/95	S	112.23	1	T1	18		1425		$74,531.25
PP	9/18/95	S	112.09	2	PP1	8		1433		$74,781.25
32	9/20/95	L	113.00	3	Trend 1					
PP	9/21/95	S	112.09	3	PP1		(69)	1364		$72,625.00
33	9/22/95	S	111.03	3	Trend 1					
34	9/23/95	L	110.31	6	Special Rule	12		1376		$73,000.00
T	9/26/95	S	111.04	1	T1	5		1381		$73,156.25
35	9/27/95	S	110.24	5	Special Rule		(14)	1367		$72,718.75
36	9/27/95	L	110.28	6	Special Rule		(12)	1355		$72,343.75
PYR	10/4/95	L	113.04	1	PYR 1					
PP	10/6/95	S	112.28	4	PP2	184		1539	132	$78,093.75
37	10/12/95	L	114.08	3	Re-entry Rule					
T	10/16/95	S	115.09	1	T1	33		1572		$79,125.00
T	10/18/95	S	115.07	1	T1	31		1603		$80,093.75
PP	10/20/95	S	114.23	1	PP2	15		1618		$80,562.50
38	10/27/95	S	114.11	3	Trend 1					
T	10/27/95	L	113.23	1	T2	20		1638		$81,187.50
PP	10/27/95	L	114.14	2	PP1		(6)	1632	93	$81,000.00
39	11/1/95	L	115.28	3	Trend 1					
T	11/6/95	S	115.30	1	T1	2		1634		$81,062.50
PP	11/7/95	S	115.20	2	PP2		(16)	1618		$80,562.50
40	11/8/95	L	116.13	3	Trend 1					
PP	11/9/95	S	116.03	3	PP1		(30)	1588		$79,625.00
41	11/24/95	L	116.02	3	Trend 1					
T	11/28/95	S	116.09	1	T1	7		1595		$79,843.75
PYR	11/29/95	L	116.22	1	PYR 2					
T	12/5/95	S	118.28	1	T1	90		1685		$82,656.25

1995
US BONDS
NEW GANN SWING CHARTIST ©
DAILY PLAN

TRADE#	DATE	L/S	PRICE	CTR.	RULE #	PROFIT	(LOSS)	ACCUM.	MO. PROFIT/(LOSS)	A/C EQUITY
PP	12/7/95	S	118.13	2	PP2	130		1815	183	$86,718.75
42	12/18/95	S	117.08	3	Special Rule		(12)			
43	12/19/95	L	117.12	6	Special Rule			1803		$86,343.75
PYR	12/29/95	L	119.27	1	PYR 2					
T	1/2/96	S	119.26	2	T1	156		1959		$91,218.75
PP	1/4/96	S	119.11	2	PP2	47		2006	191	$92,687.50

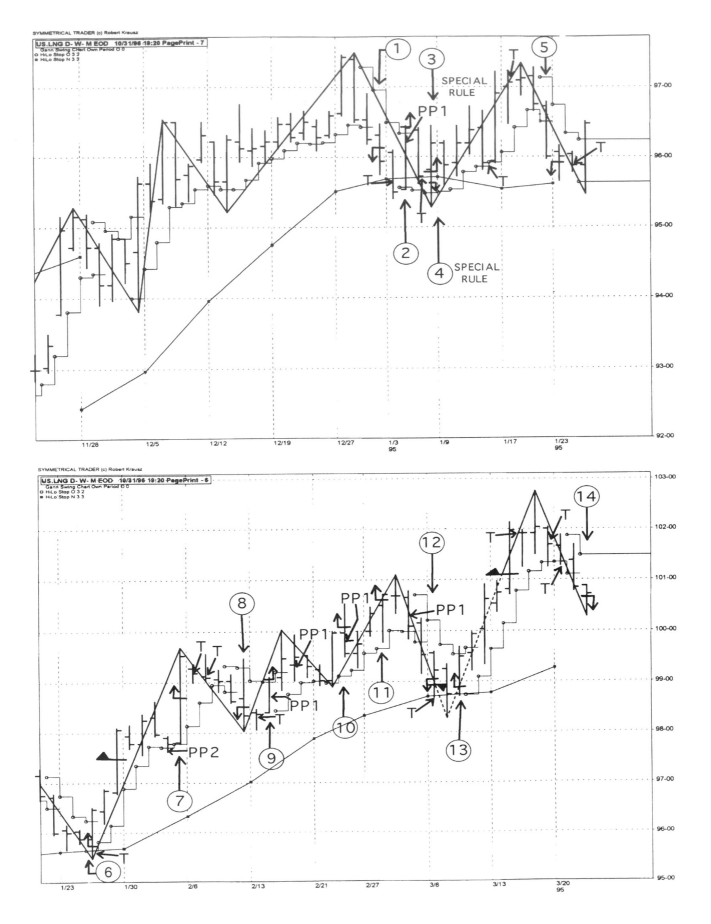

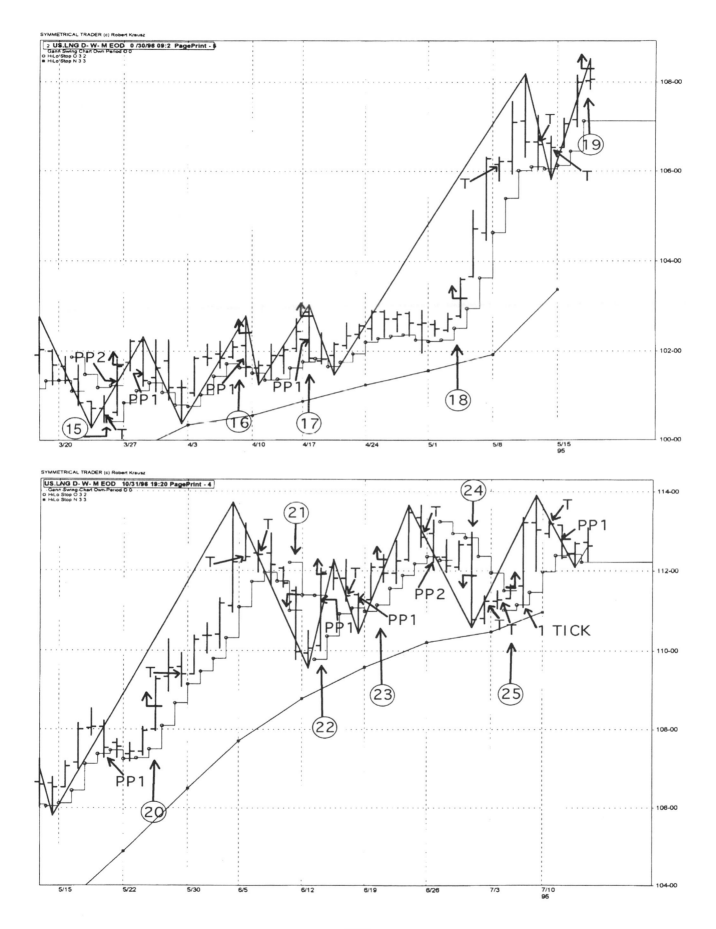

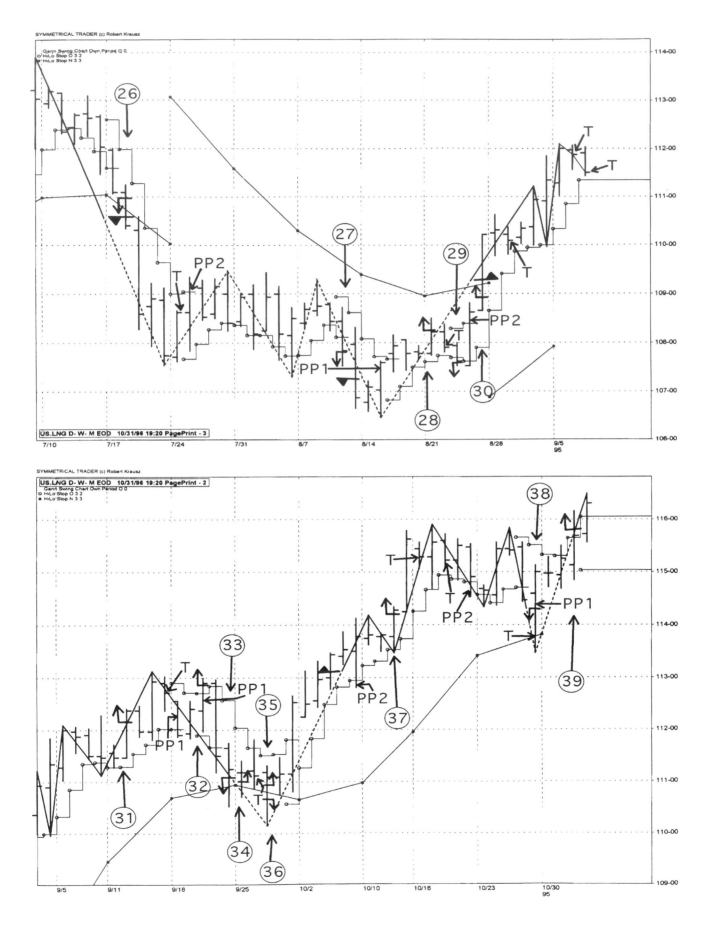

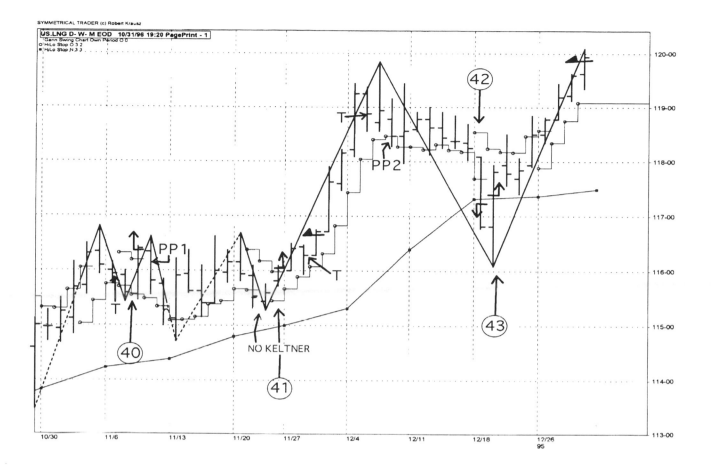

327

Beginning Equity	$30,000.00	**Ending Equity**	$93,968.75
Total Net Profit	$63,968.75		
Gross Profit	$87,000.00	**Gross Loss**	($23,031.25)
Total No. Trades	41	**Percentage Profitable**	56%
No. Winning Trades	23	**No. Losing Trades**	18

Largest Winning Trade	$10,937.50	**Largest Losing Trade**	($3,656.25)
Average Winning Trade	$3,782.61	**Average Losing Trade**	($1,279.51)
Ratio Average Win/Loss	2.96	**Average Trade**	$1,560.21
Max. Consecutive Winners	4	**Max. Consecutive Losses**	3
Largest Consecutive Drawdown (%)	6.92%	**Largest Consecutive Drawdown**	($3,968.75)

Return on Account	213%
Profit/Drawdown Ratio	16.12

NOTES:
1) Initial A/C Size = $30,000
2) Pyramids only 1/3 of original position

1996
US BONDS
NEW GANN SWING CHARTIST ©
DAILY PLAN

TRADE#	DATE	L/S	PRICE	CTR.	RULE #	PROFIT	(LOSS)	ACCUM.	MO. PROFIT/(LOSS)	A/C EQUITY
1	1/5/96	S	119.01	3	Contra 1					$30,000.00
T	1/8/96	L	118.26	1	T1	7		7		$30,218.75
T	1/10/96	L	117.19	1	T2	46		53		$31,656.25
2	1/16/96	L	117.25	4	Special Rule	40		93		$32,906.25
T	1/18/96	S	120.02	1	T	53		146		$34,562.50
PP	1/22/96	S	119.01	2	PP 2	34		180		$35,625.00
3	1/23/96	S	118.29	3	Contra 1					
T	1/24/96	L	119.12	1	T1		(15)	165		$35,156.25
PP	1/24/96	L	119.13	2	PP 2		(32)	133		$34,156.25
4	1/25/96	S	118.09	3	Re-entry Rule					
PP	1/26/96	L	118.01	3	PP 1	24		157	157	$34,906.25
5	2/12/96	L	119.02	3	Trend 1					
T	2/13/96	S	119.14	1	T2	12		169		$35,281.25
T	2/14/96	S	118.22	1	T1		(12)	157		$34,906.25
PP	2/15/96	S	118.20	1	PP1		(14)	143		$34,468.75
6	2/16/96	S	117.17	3	Contra 1					
PYR	2/16/96	S	117.12	1	PYR 1					
T	2/22/96	L	115.00	2	T1	162		305		$39,531.25
PP	2/23/96	L	115.16	2	PP 2	125		430		$43,437.50
7	2/23/96	S	113.29	3	Re-entry Rule					
T	2/27/96	L	113.26	1	T1	3		433		$43,531.25
PP	3/1/96	L	114.05	2	PP2		(16)	417	260	$43,031.25
8	3/4/96	L	114.20	3	Contra 1					
PP	3/6/96	S	114.01	3	PP1		(57)	360		$41,250.00
9	3/6/96	S	113.24	3	Trend 1					
PYR	3/8/96	S	112.10	1	PYR 2					
T	3/12/96	L	110.26	2	T1	188		548		$47,125.00
PP	3/19/96	L	110.16	2	PP2	162		710		$52,187.50
10	3/21/96	L	111.02	3	Contra 1					
T	3/22/96	S	110.25	1	T1		(9)	701		$51,906.25
T	3/26/96	S	111.20	1	T1	18		719		$52,468.75
PP	3/27/96	S	110.25	1	PP1		(9)	710		$52,187.50
11	3/27/96	S	110.08	3	Trend 1					
T	3/29/96	L	110.13	1	T1		(6)	704		$52,000.00
PP	4/1/96	L	110.19	2	PP2		(22)	682	265	$51,312.50
12	4/2/96	L	110.28	3	Contra 1					
13	4/4/96	S	110.17	6	Trend 1		(33)	649		$50,281.25
PYR	4/5/96	S	109.08	1	PYR 2					

1996
US BONDS
NEW GANN SWING CHARTIST ©
DAILY PLAN

TRADE#	DATE	L/S	PRICE	CTR.	RULE #	PROFIT	(LOSS)	ACCUM.	MO. PROFIT/(LOSS)	A/C EQUITY
T	4/9/96	L	108.12	2	T1	138		787		$54,593.75
PP	4/12/96	L	108.16	2	PP2	89		876		$57,375.00
14	4/15/96	L	109.02	3	Contra 1					
T	4/17/96	S	108.25	1	T1		(9)	867		$57,093.75
15	4/18/96	S	108.12	3	Trend 1		(44)	823		$55,718.75
PP	4/19/96	L	108.21	1	PP1		(27)	796		$54,875.00
16	4/24/96	S	108.22	3	Trend 1					
T	4/25/96	L	108.29	1	T1		(7)	789		$54,656.25
PP	4/26/96	L	109.10	2	PP2		(40)	749		$53,406.25
17	4/30/96	S	108.05	3	Re-entry Rule					
PYR	5/2/96	S	106.20	1	PYR 1					
T	5/6/96	L	106.03	2	T	132		881		$57,531.25
PP	5/8/96	L	106.18	2	PP2	53		934	252	$59,187.50
18	5/9/96	L	106.31	3	Contra 1					
T	5/13/96	S	107.26	1	T	40		974		$60,437.50
PP	5/16/96	S	107.27	2	PP2	56		1030		$62,187.50
19	5/20/96	L	108.26	3	Re-entry Rule					
T	5/21/96	S	108.16	1	T1		(10)	1020		$61,875.00
PP	5/22/96	S	108.10	2	PP2		(32)	988		$60,875.00
20	5/22/96	L	109.04	3	Re-entry Rule					
21	5/23/96	S	108.19	6	Special Rule		(51)	937		$59,281.25
PYR	5/29/96	S	108.04	1	PYR 1					
T	5/30/96	L	107.08	2	T2	86		1023		$61,968.75
T	6/4/96	L	107.01	1	T1	50		1073		$63,531.25
PP	6/5/96	L	107.17	1	PP2	35		1108	174	$64,625.00
22	6/6/96	L	107.25	3	Contra 1					
PP	6/7/96	S	107.28	3	PP1	9		1117		$64,906.25
23	6/7/96	S	106.17	3	Trend 1					
PP	6/14/96	L	106.06	3	PP2	33		1150		$65,937.50
24	6/17/96	L	106.21	3	Contra 1					
PP	6/19/96	S	106.11	3	PP1		(30)	1120		$65,000.00
25	6/25/96	L	107.04	3	Trend 1					
T	6/27/96	S	107.20	1	T2	16		1136		$65,500.00
T	7/1/96	S	109.02	1	T1	62		1198		$67,437.50
T	7/2/96	S	108.18	1	T1	46		1244	136	$68,875.00
26	7/5/96	S	108.10	3	Special Rule					
T	7/5/96	L	106.00	1	T1	74		1318		$71,187.50
PYR	7/5/96	S	105.29	1	PYR 1					

1996
US BONDS
NEW GANN SWING CHARTIST ©
DAILY PLAN

TRADE#	DATE	L/S	PRICE	CTR.	RULE #	PROFIT	(LOSS)	ACCUM.	MO. PROFIT/(LOSS)	A/C EQUITY
T	7/9/96	L	106.14	1	T1	60		1378		$73,062.50
PP	7/10/96	L	106.22	2	PP2	27		1405		$73,906.25
27	7/11/96	L	107.04	3	Contra 1					
T	7/15/96	S	107.10	1	T1	6		1411		$74,093.75
PP	7/16/96	S	107.03	2	PP1		(2)	1409		$74,031.25
28	7/18/96	L	108.10	3	Re-entry Rule					
T	7/18/96	S	108.28	1	T2	18		1427		$74,593.75
T	7/19/96	S	108.18	1	T1	8		1435		$74,843.75
T	7/22/96	S	108.02	1	T1		(8)	1427		$74,593.75
29	7/19/96	S	108.25	3	Special Rule					
PP	7/23/96	L	108.15	3	PP1	30		1457		$75,531.25
30	7/24/96	S	107.22	3	Trend 1					
T	7/25/96	L	107.30	1	T1		(8)	1449		$75,281.25
T	7/26/96	L	108.02	1	T1		(12)	1437		$74,906.25
PP	7/30/96	L	108.01	1	PP1		(11)	1426	182	$74,562.50
31	8/1/96	L	108.27	3	Contra 1					
PYR	8/1/96	L	109.09	1	PYR 1					
T	8/1/96	S	109.19	2	T2	48		1474		$76,062.50
T	8/5/96	S	111.08	1	T1	77		1551		$78,468.75
T	8/6/96	S	111.03	1	T1	72		1623		$80,718.75
32	8/9/96	L	111.23	3	Re-entry Rule					
PP	8/13/96	S	111.12	3	PP1		(33)	1590		$79,687.50
33	8/13/96	S	110.13	3	Trend 1					
T	8/16/96	L	110.25	1	T1		(12)	1578		$79,312.50
PYR	8/23/96	S	109.31	1	PYR 2					
T	8/23/96	L	109.24	1	T2	21		1599		$79,968.75
T	8/27/96	L	108.14	1	T1	61		1660		$81,875.00
T	9/4/96	L	106.31	1	T1	110		1770	344	$85,312.50
34	9/6/96	S	106.00	3	Re-entry Rule					
PP	9/9/96	L	107.07	3	PP2		(117)	1653		$81,656.25
35	9/12/96	L	107.14	3	Trend 1					
T	9/13/96	S	108.19	1	T2	37		1690		$82,812.50
T	9/16/96	S	108.26	1	T1	44		1734		$84,187.50
T	9/17/96	S	108.04	1	T1	22		1756		$84,875.00
36	9/24/96	L	108.20	3	Trend 1					
PYR	9/25/96	L	109.01	1	PYR 2					
PP	9/30/96	S	109.05	4	PP1	55		1811	41	$86,593.75
37	10/2/96	L	110.12	3	Re-entry Rule					

1996
US BONDS
NEW GANN SWING CHARTIST ©
DAILY PLAN

TRADE#	DATE	L/S	PRICE	CTR.	RULE #	PROFIT	(LOSS)	ACCUM.	MO. PROFIT/(LOSS)	A/C EQUITY
T	10/7/96	S	111.05	1	T1	25		1836		$87,375.00
T	10/8/96	S	111.03	1	T1	23		1859		$88,093.75
PP	10/9/96	S	110.26	1	PP2	14		1873		$88,531.25
38	10/10/96	S	110.14	3	Contra 1					
T	10/11/96	L	110.19	1	T1		(5)	1868		$88,375.00
PP	10/15/96	L	110.27	2	PP2		(26)	1842		$87,562.50
39	10/17/96	L	111.04	3	Trend 1					
T	10/21/96	S	111.02	1	T1		(2)	1840		$87,500.00
PP	10/22/96	S	110.28	2	PP1		(16)	1824		$87,000.00
40	10/23/96	S	110.17	3	Contra 1					
T	10/24/96	L	110.19	1	T1		(2)	1822		$86,937.50
PP	10/25/96	L	110.21	2	PP1		(8)	1814		$86,687.50
41	10/29/96	L	111.01	3	Trend 1					
PYR	10/29/96	L	111.24	1	PYR 2					
T	10/31/96	S	113.00	2	T1	126		1940	129	$90,625.00
T	11/4/96	S	112.31	1	T1	62		2002		$92,562.50
PP	11/7/96	S	113.05	1	PP2	45		2047		$93,968.75
42	11/7/96	L	114.05	3	Re-entry Rule					

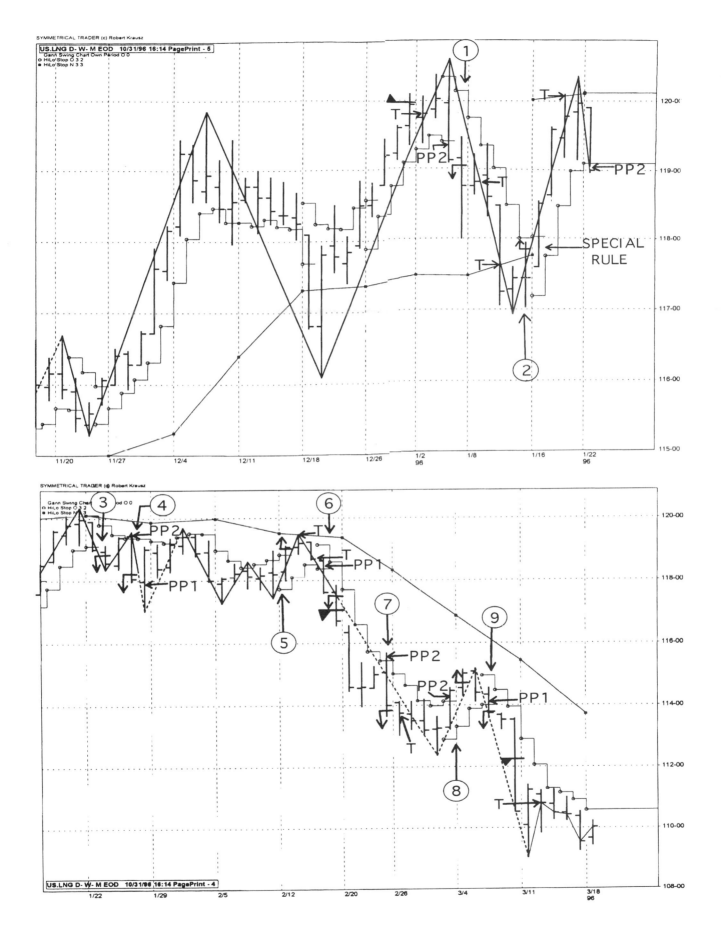

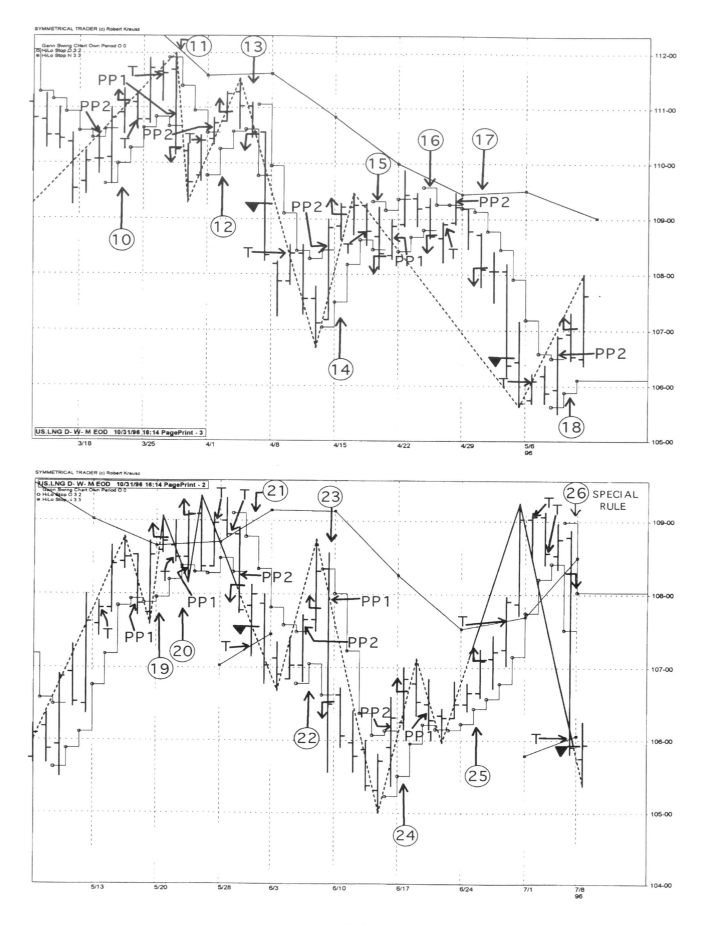

334

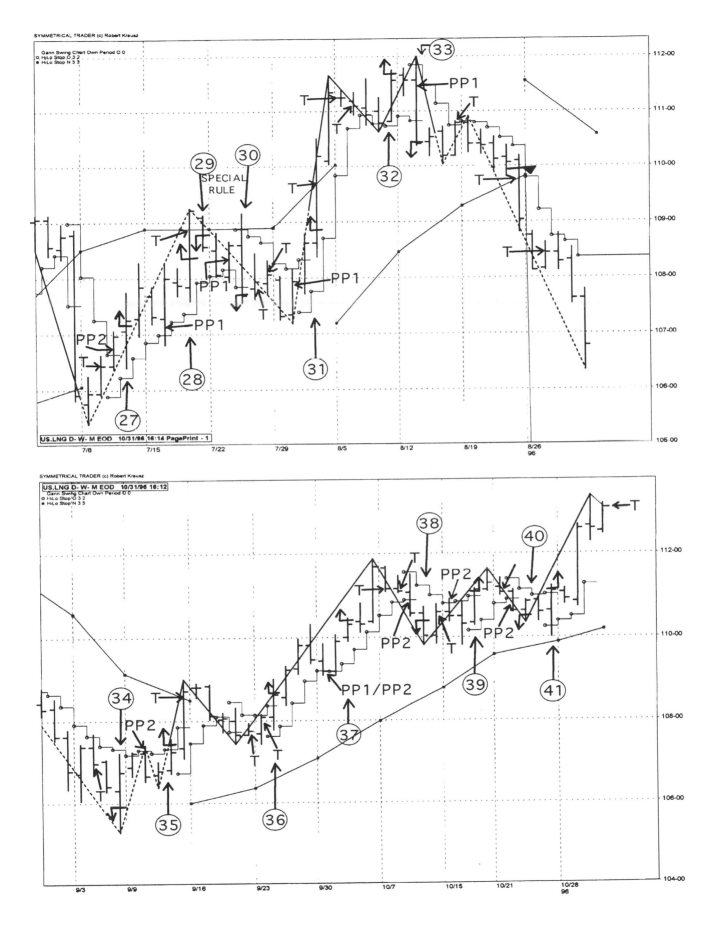

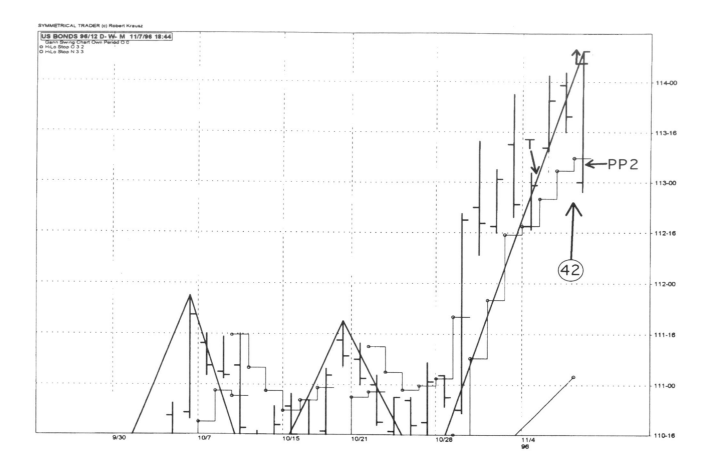

NEW GANN SWING CHARTIST©

BASIC SWING PLAN

FOR U.S. T-BONDS

"END OF DAY"

Rules are the same as the Basic Real Time Plan
But → Move the HiLo Activator 1 day forward

1992 - 1996

US T-BONDS: 1992
BASIC SWING PLAN
GANN SWING CHARTIST - FIBONACCI TRADER ®

Beginning Equity	$30,000.00	Ending Equity	$41,906.25
Total Net Profit	$11,906.25		
Gross Profit	$26,718.75	Gross Loss	($14,812.50)
Total No. Trades	24	Percentage Profitable	42%
No. Winning Trades	10	No. Losing Trades	14

Largest Winning Trade	$10,031.25	Largest Losing Trade	($2,718.75)
Average Winning Trade	$2,671.88	Average Losing Trade	($1,058.04)
Ratio Average Win/Loss	2.53	Average Trade	$496.09
Max. Consecutive Winners	3	Max. Consecutive Losses	4
Largest Consecutive Drawdown (%)	19.88%	Largest Consecutive Drawdown	($6,093.75)

Return on Account	40%
Profit/Drawdown Ratio	1.95

NOTES:
1) Initial A/C Size = $30,000

1992
US T- Bonds: Gann Swing Chartist®
Basic Swing Plan (End of Day)

Fibonacci Trader®

Trade#	Date	L/S	Price	Ctr.	Rule #	Profit	(Loss)	Accum.	A/C Equity
1	1/14/92	S	86.15	3	Sell 2				$30,000.00
PP	1/21/92	L	86.08	3	PP1	21		21	$30,656.25
2	1/23/92	S	84.21	3	Sell 1				
PP	1/28/92	L	85.07	3	PP2		(54)	(33)	$28,968.75
3	1/29/92	S	84.04	3	Sell 1				
PP	2/5/92	L	84.09	3	PP2		(15)	(48)	$28,500.00
4	2/13/92	S	83.05	3	Sell 3				
PP	2/26/92	L	83.07	3	PP2		(6)	(54)	$28,312.50
5	3/3/92	S	83.01	3	Sell 1				
PP	3/9/92	L	83.05	3	PP2		(12)	(66)	$27,937.50
6	3/11/92	S	82.18	3	Sell 1				
PP	3/18/92	L	82.05	3	PP2	39		(27)	$29,156.25
7	4/1/92	L	83.11	3	Buy 2				
PP	4/8/92	S	83.11	3	PP1	0		(27)	$29,156.25
8	4/9/92	L	84.11	3	Buy 1				
PP	4/16/92	S	83.20	3	PP1		(69)	(96)	$27,000.00
9	4/20/92	S	83.09	3	Sell 2				
PP	5/1/92	L	82.21	3	PP2	60		(36)	$28,875.00
10	5/12/92	L	84.16	3	Buy 2				
PP	5/21/92	S	84.21	3	PP1	15		(21)	$29,343.75
11	5/29/92	L	84.30	3	Buy 1				
PP	6/1/92	S	84.01	3	PP2		(87)	(108)	$26,625.00
12	6/5/92	L	85.03	3	Buy 3				
PP	6/10/92	S	84.13	3	PP2		(66)	(174)	$24,562.50
13	6/12/92	L	84.27	3	Buy 1				
PP	6/23/92	S	85.02	3	PP1	21		(153)	$25,218.75
14	6/25/92	L	85.30	3	Buy 1				
PP	7/10/92	S	87.19	3	PP1	159		6	$30,187.50
15	7/16/92	L	88.00	3	Buy 1				
PP	8/13/92	S	91.11	3	PP2	321		168	$35,250.00
16	8/19/92	L	91.10	3	Buy 1				
PP	8/21/92	S	90.28	3	PP2		(42)	126	$33,937.50
17	8/25/92	S	89.27	3	Sell 2				

1992
US T- Bonds: Gann Swing Chartist®
Basic Swing Plan (End of Day)

Fibonacci Trader®

Trade#	Date	L/S	Price	Ctr.	Rule #	Profit	(Loss)	Accum.	A/C Equity
PP	9/1/92	L	90.13	3	PP2		(54)	72	$32,250.00
18	9/4/92	L	92.15	3	Buy 2				
PP	9/11/92	S	92.11	3	PP1		(12)	60	$31,875.00
19	9/25/92	L	91.30	3	Buy 1				
PP	10/6/92	S	91.22	3	PP2		(24)	36	$31,125.00
20	10/9/92	S	90.05	3	Sell 2				
PP	10/22/92	L	89.18	3	PP2	57		93	$32,906.25
21	11/2/92	S	88.30	3	Sell 1				
PP	11/10/92	L	88.25	3	PP2	15		108	$33,375.00
22	11/12/92	L	89.25	3	Buy 2				
23	11/27/92	S	89.21	6	Sell 2		(12)	96	$33,000.00
PP	12/3/92	L	89.28	3	PP2		(21)	75	$32,343.75
24	12/4/92	L	90.22	6	Buy 1				
PP	12/28/92	S	92.07	3	PP1	147		222	$36,937.50

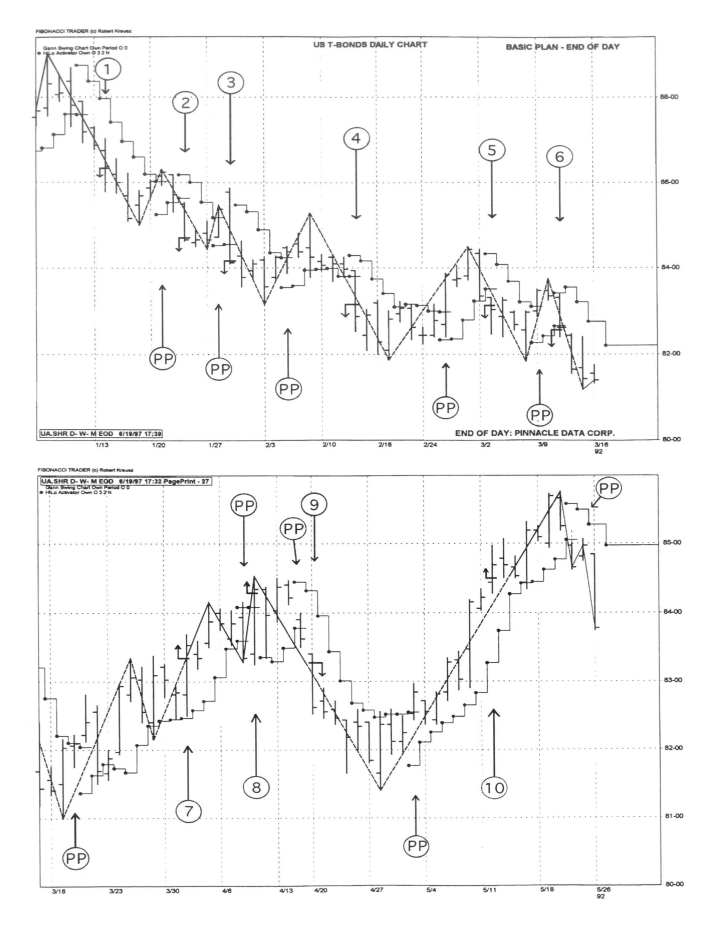

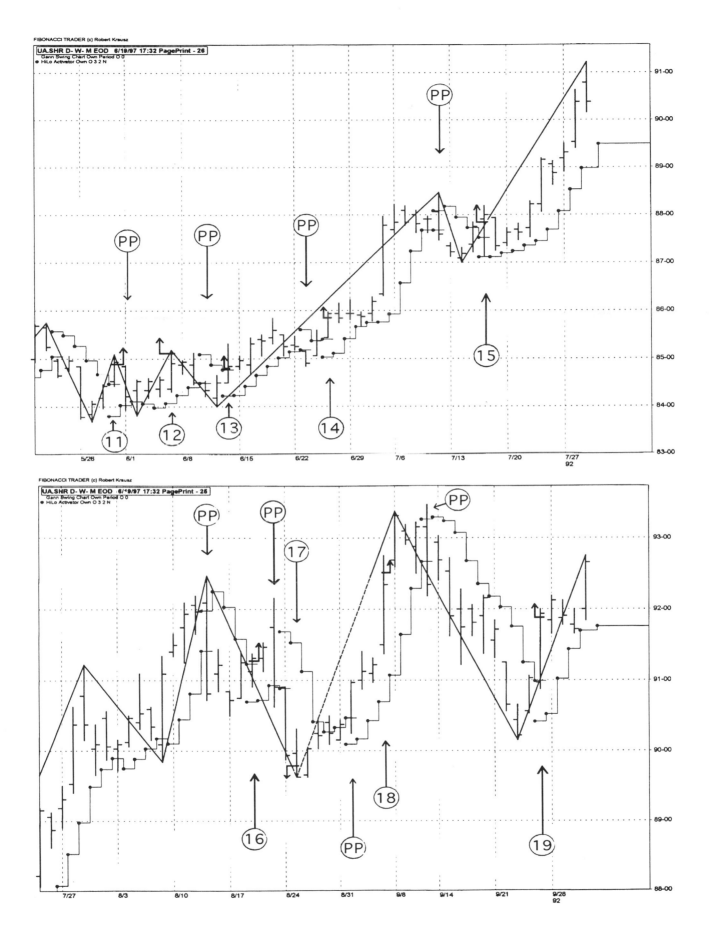

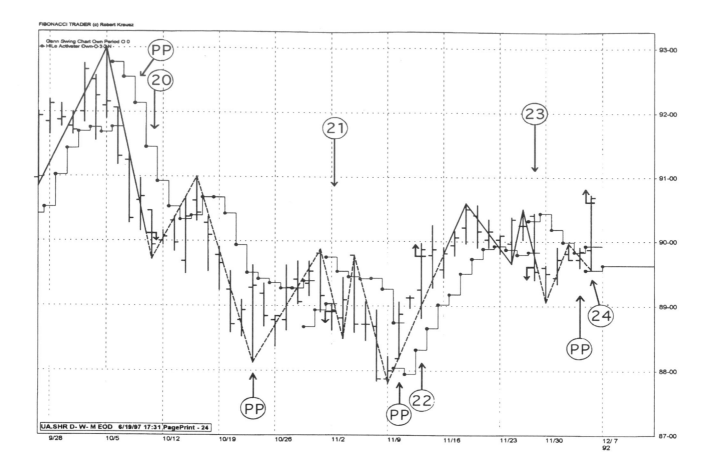

US T-BONDS: 1993
BASIC SWING PLAN
GANN SWING CHARTIST - FIBONACCI TRADER ®

Beginning Equity	$30,000.00	Ending Equity	$55,500.00
Total Net Profit	$25,500.00	Average Ticks/Mo.	
Gross Profit	$45,468.75	Gross Loss	($19,968.75)
Total No. Trades	21	Percentage Profitable	38%
No. Winning Trades	8	No. Losing Trades	13

Largest Winning Trade	$10,968.75	Largest Losing Trade	($4,218.75)
Average Winning Trade	$5,683.59	Average Losing Trade	($1,536.06)
Ratio Average Win/Loss	3.70	Average Trade	$1,214.29
Max. Consecutive Winners	2	Max. Consecutive Losses	3
Largest Consecutive Drawdown (%)	11.88%	Largest Consecutive Drawdown	($4,500.00)

Return on Account	85%
Profit/Drawdown Ratio	5.67

Notes:
1) Initial account size: $30,000

1993
US T- Bonds: Gann Swing Chartist®
Basic Swing Plan (End of Day)

Fibonacci Trader®

Trade#	Date	L/S	Price	Ctr.	Rule #	Profit	(Loss)	Accum.	A/C Equity
1	1/4/93	L	93.02	3	Buy 1				$30,000.00
PP	1/7/93	S	92.09	3	PP2		(75)	(75)	$27,656.25
2	1/8/93	S	91.14	3	Sell 2				
PP	1/14/93	L	91.27	3	PP2		(39)	(114)	$26,437.50
3	1/19/93	L	93.01	3	Buy 2				
PP	2/10/93	S	94.20	3	PP1	153		39	$31,218.75
4	2/18/93	L	96.28	3	Buy 1				
PP	3/5/93	S	99.14	3	PP2	246		285	$38,906.25
5	3/15/93	S	98.08	3	Sell 2				
PP	3/18/93	L	99.06	3	PP2		(90)	195	$36,093.75
6	3/26/93	S	97.29	3	Sell 1				
PP	4/7/93	L	98.06	3	PP2		(27)	168	$35,250.00
7	4/12/93	L	100.20	3	Buy 2				
PP	4/23/93	S	100.16	3	Sell 1		(12)	156	$34,875.00
8	5/3/93	L	100.06	3	Buy 1				
PP	5/7/93	S	100.10	3	PP2	12		168	$35,250.00
9	5/13/93	S	99.02	3	Sell 2				
PP	5/20/93	L	99.11	3	PP2		(27)	141	$34,406.25
10	6/11/93	L	101.14	3	Buy 2				
PP	7/21/93	S	105.03	3	PP2	351		492	$45,375.00
11	7/29/93	L	105.19	3	Buy 1				
PP	8/6/93	S	105.00	3	PP2		(57)	492	$45,375.00
12	8/9/93	L	105.31	3	Buy 3				
PP	8/13/93	S	105.27	3	PP2		(12)	480	$45,000.00
13	8/20/93	L	106.29	3	Buy 3				
PP	9/9/93	S	110.13	3	PP1	336		816	$55,500.00
14	9/21/93	S	109.04	3	Sell 2				
PP	9/23/93	L	110.01	3	PP2		(87)	729	$52,781.25
15	9/27/93	L	110.26	3	Buy 2				
PP	9/30/93	S	110.14	3	PP2		(36)	693	$51,656.25
16	10/8/93	L	111.31	3	Buy 1				
PP	10/19/93	S	112.01	3	PP2	6		699	$51,843.75
17	10/21/93	S	111.18	6	Sell 2				

1993

US T- Bonds: Gann Swing Chartist®

Basic Swing Plan (End of Day)

Fibonacci Trader®

Trade#	Date	L/S	Price	Ctr.	Rule #	Profit	(Loss)	Accum.	A/C Equity
PP	11/9/93	L	108.06	3	PP1	324		1023	$61,968.75
18	11/11/93	S	107.03	3	Sell 1				
PP	11/16/93	L	108.16	3	PP1		(135)	888	$57,750.00
19	11/18/93	S	107.16	3	Sell 1				
PP	11/24/93	L	107.07	3	PP1	27		915	$58,593.75
20	11/30/93	S	106.26	3	Sell 1				
PP	12/3/93	L	107.17	3	PP1		(69)	846	$56,437.50
21	12/22/93	L	108.13	3	Buy 1				
PP	12/30/93	S	107.29	3	PP2		(48)	798	$54,937.50

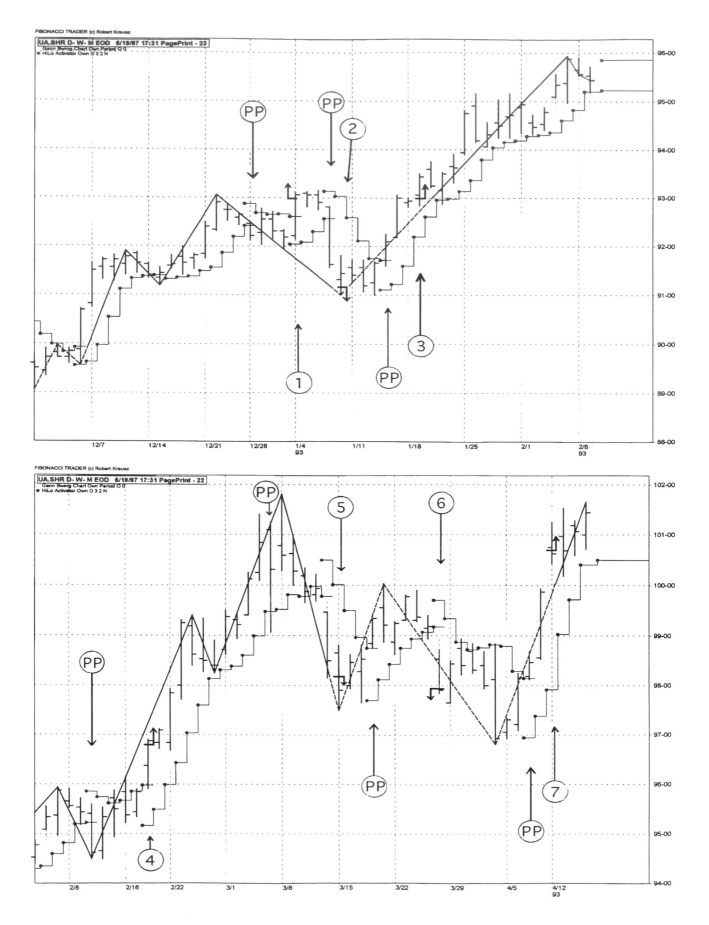

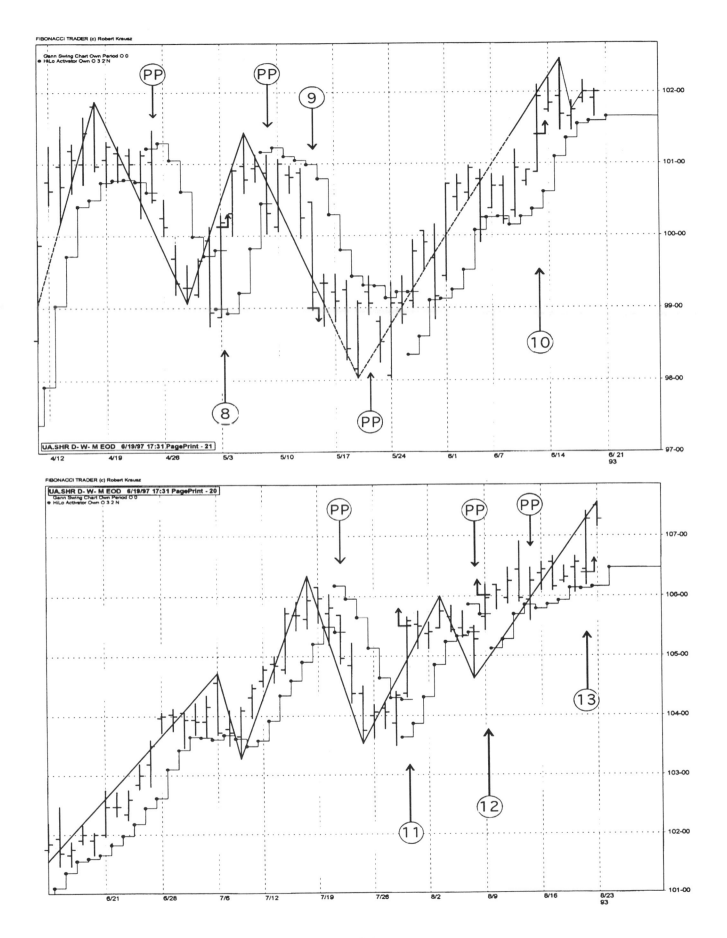

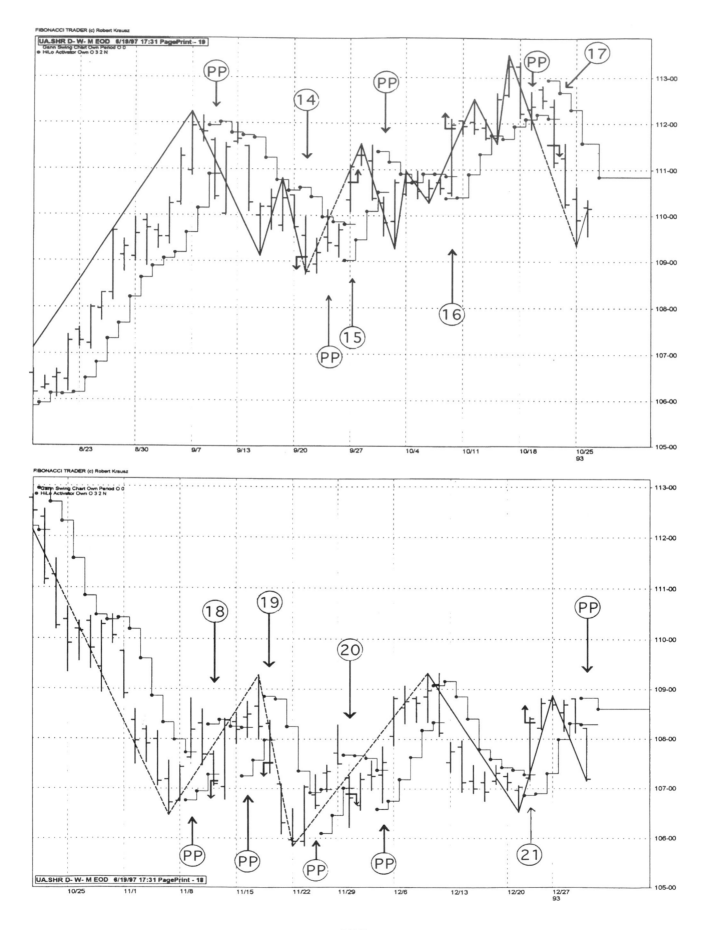

US T-BONDS: 1994
BASIC SWING PLAN
GANN SWING CHARTIST - FIBONACCI TRADER ®

Beginning Equity	$30,000.00	Ending Equity	$29,625.00
Total Net Profit	($375.00)	Average Ticks/Mo.	
Gross Profit	$31,031.25	Gross Loss	($31,406.25)
Total No. Trades	26	Percentage Profitable	27%
No. Winning Trades	7	No. Losing Trades	17

Largest Winning Trade	$ 13,218.75	Largest Losing Trade	($3,843.75)
Average Winning Trade	$4,433.04	Average Losing Trade	($1,847.43)
Ratio Average Win/Loss	2.40	Average Trade	($14.42)
Max. Consecutive Winners	3	Max. Consecutive Losses	6
Largest Consecutive Drawdown (%)	27.51%	Largest Consecutive Drawdown	($12,093.75)

Return on Account	-1%
Profit/Drawdown Ratio	-0.03

Notes:
1) Initial account size: $30,000

1994
US T- Bonds: Gann Swing Chartist®
Basic Swing Plan (End of Day)

Fibonacci Trader®

Trade#	Date	L/S	Price	Ctr.	Rule #	Profit	(Loss)	Accum.	A/C Equity
1	1/3/94	S	106.17	3	Sell 2				$30,000.00
PP	1/6/94	L	107.04	3	PP2		(57)	(57)	$28,218.75
2	1/10/94	L	108.29	3	Buy 2				$27,187.50
PP	1/13/94	S	108.18	3	PP1		(33)	(90)	$27,187.50
3	1/18/94	L	108.17	3	Buy 1				$26,625.00
PP	1/25/94	S	108.11	3	PP2		(18)	(108)	$26,625.00
4	1/27/94	L	109.12	3	Buy 1				$25,687.50
PP	2/1/94	S	109.02	3	PP2		(30)	(138)	$25,687.50
5	2/4/94	S	107.31	3	Sell 2				$38,906.25
PP	3/16/94	L	103.18	3	PP1	423		285	$38,906.25
6	3/18/94	S	102.11	3	Sell 1				$36,750.00
PP	3/22/94	L	103.02	3	PP2		(69)	216	$36,750.00
7	3/24/94	S	101.16	3	Sell 1				$43,968.75
PP	4/7/94	L	99.03	3	PP1	231		447	$43,968.75
8	4/14/94	S	98.09	3	Sell 1				$43,687.50
PP	4/20/94	L	98.12	3	PP2		(9)	438	$43,687.50
9	4/25/94	L	99.27	3	Buy 2				$41,250.00
PP	4/28/94	S	99.01	3	PP2		(78)	360	$41,250.00
10	5/6/94	S	96.20	3	Sell 2				$39,562.50
PP	5/16/94	L	97.06	3	PP2		(54)	306	$39,562.50
11	5/23/94	S	97.09	3	Sell 1				$37,500.00
PP	6/2/94	L	97.31	3	PP2		(66)	240	$37,500.00
12	6/6/94	L	99.21	3	Buy 2				$35,156.25
PP	6/10/94	S	98.28	3	PP1		(75)	165	$35,156.25
13	6/22/94	L	98.06	3	Buy 1				$31,875.00
PP	6/24/94	S	97.03	3	PP2		(105)	60	$31,875.00
14	6/27/94	S	96.21	3	Sell 2				$33,281.25
PP	7/14/94	L	96.06	3	PP2	45		105	$33,281.25
15	7/29/94	L	97.23	3	Buy 2				$35,812.50
PP	8/5/94	S	98.18	3	PP2	81		186	$35,812.50
16	8/11/94	S	96.15	3	Sell 2				$32,062.50
PP	8/16/94	L	97.23	3	PP2		(120)	66	$32,062.50
17	8/18/94	S	97.09	3	Sell 1				

352

1994
US T- Bonds: Gann Swing Chartist®
Basic Swing Plan (End of Day)

Trade#	Date	L/S	Price	Ctr.	Rule #	Profit	(Loss)	Accum.	A/C Equity
PP	8/24/94	L	97.19	3	PP2		(30)	36	$31,125.00
18	9/9/94	S	96.21	3	Sell 2			90	$32,812.50
PP	9/14/94	L	96.03	3	PP1	54			
19	9/16/94	S	94.25	3	Sell 3			186	$35,812.50
PP	10/10/94	L	93.25	3	PP1	96			
20	10/19/94	S	94.00	3	Sell 1			249	$37,781.25
PP	10/28/94	L	93.11	3	PP2	63			
21	11/2/94	S	92.13	3	Sell 1			237	$37,406.25
PP	11/9/94	L	92.17	3	PP1		(12)		
22	11/11/94	S	91.13	3	Sell 1			114	$33,562.50
PP	11/15/94	L	92.22	3	PP2		(123)		
23	11/15/94	L	93.02	3	Buy 2			15	$30,468.75
PP	11/17/94	S	92.01	3	PP2		(99)		
24	11/23/94	L	93.12	3	Buy 2			12	$30,375.00
PP	11/29/94	S	93.11	3	PP1		(3)		
25	12/2/94	L	94.25	3	Buy 1			(9)	$29,718.75
PP	12/13/94	S	94.18	3	PP2		(21)		
26	12/14/94	L	95.21	3	Buy 3			(12)	$29,625.00
PP	12/29/94	S	95.20	3	PP2		(3)		

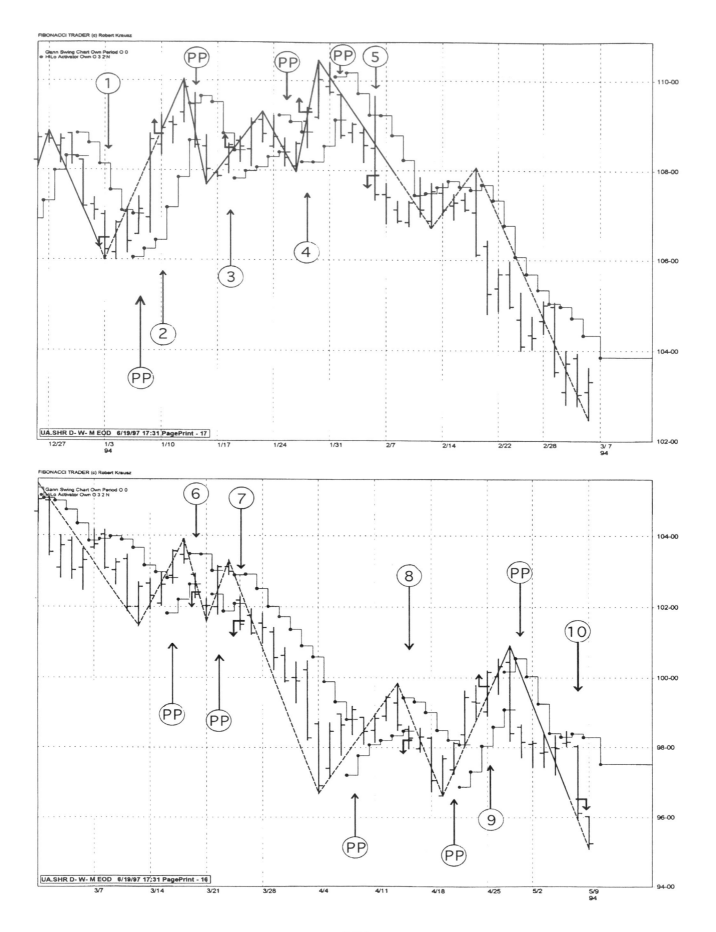

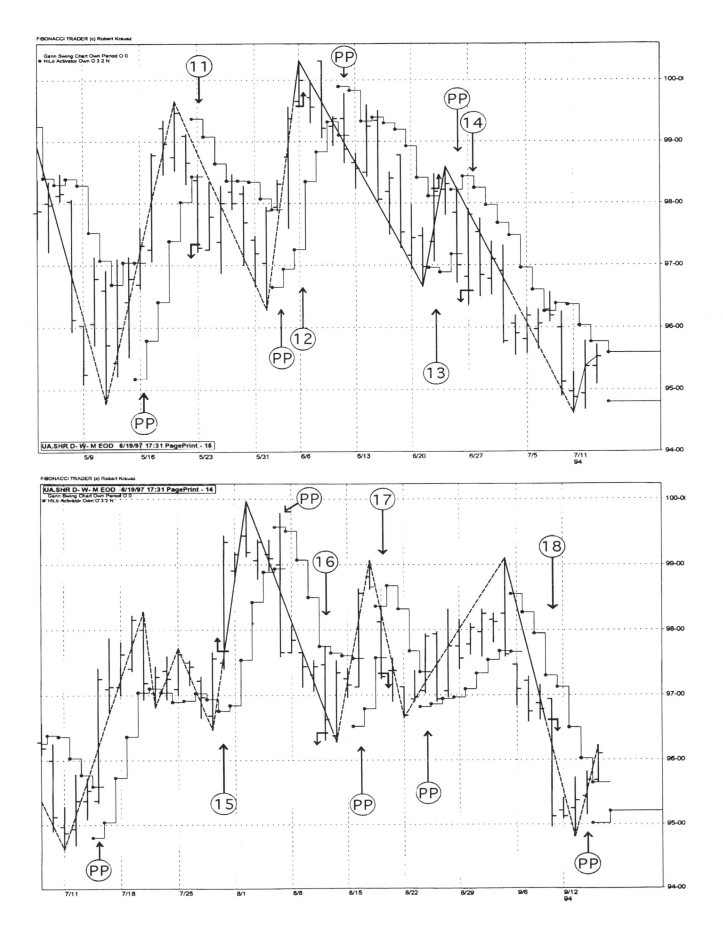

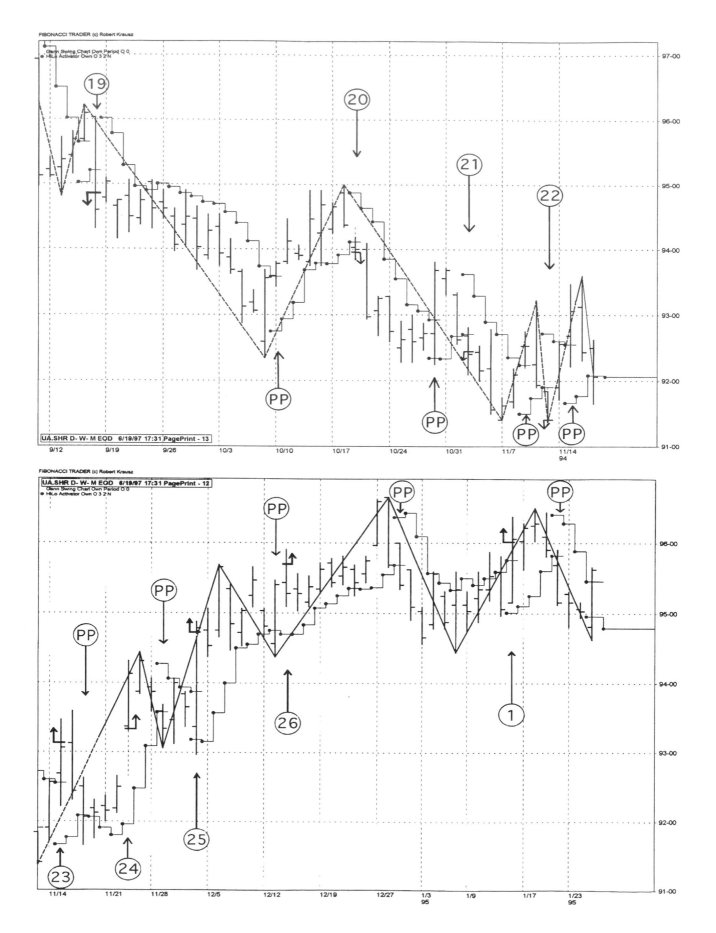

Beginning Equity	$30,000.00	Ending Equity	$49,500.00
Total Net Profit	$19,500.00	Average Ticks/Mo.	
Gross Profit	$53,437.50	Gross Loss	($33,937.50)
Total No. Trades	27	Percentage Profitable	52%
No. Winning Trades	14	No. Losing Trades	13

Largest Winning Trade	$ 22,781.25	Largest Losing Trade	($3,937.50)
Average Winning Trade	$3,816.96	Average Losing Trade	($2,610.58)
Ratio Average Win/Loss	1.46	Average Trade	$722.22
Max. Consecutive Winners	5	Max. Consecutive Losses	5
Largest Consecutive Drawdown (%)	26.07%	Largest Consecutive Drawdown	($9,187.50)

Return on Account	65%
Profit/Drawdown Ratio	2.12

Notes:
1) Initial account size: $30,000

US T- Bonds: Gann Swing Chartist®
Basic Swing Plan (End of Day)

Fibonacci Trader®

Trade#	Date	L/S	Price	Ctr.	Rule #	Profit	(Loss)	Accum.	A/C Equity
1	1/13/95	L	96.02	3	Buy 1				$30,000.00
PP	1/20/95	S	95.22	3	PP2		(36)	(36)	$28,875.00
2	1/25/95	L	95.20	3	Buy 1				
PP	2/9/95	S	97.25	3	PP1	111		75	$32,343.75
3	2/15/95	L	98.20	3	Buy 1				
PP	3/3/95	S	99.05	3	PP2	51		126	$33,937.50
4	3/6/95	S	98.01	3	Sell 2				
PP	3/8/95	L	98.24	3	PP2		(69)	57	$31,781.25
5	3/14/95	L	100.08	3	Buy 2				
PP	3/21/95	S	100.04	3	PP2		(12)	45	$31,406.25
6	3/24/95	L	100.26	3	Buy 1				
PP	3/29/95	S	100.11	3	PP2		(45)	0	$30,000.00
7	4/5/95	L	101.00	3	Buy 1				
PP	4/7/95	S	100.27	3	PP2		(15)	(15)	$29,531.25
8	4/13/95	L	101.19	3	Buy 1				
PP	4/19/95	S	100.30	3	PP2		(63)	(78)	$27,562.50
9	5/3/95	L	102.24	3	Buy 3				
PP	6/8/95	S	110.29	3	PP1	783		705	$52,031.25
10	6/13/95	L	111.04	3	Buy 1				
PP	6/27/95	S	111.09	3	PP1	15		720	$52,500.00
11	7/6/95	L	112.12	3	Buy 1				
PP	7/12/95	S	111.14	3	PP2		(90)	720	$52,500.00
12	7/18/95	S	109.24	3	Sell 2				
PP	7/25/95	L	108.10	3	PP1	138		858	$56,812.50
13	8/1/95	S	107.11	3	Sell 1				
PP	8/8/95	L	108.02	3	PP2		(93)	858	$56,812.50
14	8/11/95	S	106.15	3	Sell 3				
PP	8/16/95	L	106.30	3	PP2		(45)	813	$55,406.25
15	8/23/95	S	106.25	3	Sell 1				
PP	8/24/95	L	107.15	3	PP2		(66)	747	$53,343.75
16	8/24/95	L	107.25	6	Buy 1				
PP	9/8/95	S	110.12	3	PP2	249		996	$61,125.00
17	9/12/95	L	111.08	3	Buy 3				

1995
US T- Bonds: Gann Swing Chartist®
Basic Swing Plan (End of Day)

Fibonacci Trader®

Trade#	Date	L/S	Price	Ctr.	Rule #	Profit	(Loss)	Accum.	A/C Equity
PP	9/18/95	S	111.05	3	PP2		(9)	987	$60,843.75
18	9/20/95	L	112.02	3	Buy 1				
PP	9/21/95	S	111.00	3	PP2		(102)	885	$57,656.25
19	9/22/95	S	110.09	3	Sell 2				
PP	9/29/95	L	110.22	3	PP2		(39)	846	$56,437.50
20	10/3/95	L	112.08	3	Buy 2				
PP	10/20/95	S	113.31	3	PP2	165		1011	$61,593.75
21	10/24/95	L	114.19	3	Buy 1				
PP	10/26/95	S	113.24	3	PP2		(75)	936	$59,250.00
22	10/27/95	S	113.12	3	Sell 2				
PP	10/31/95	L	114.17	3	PP2		(111)	825	$55,781.25
23	11/1/95	L	114.31	3	Buy 1				
PP	11/7/95	S	114.24	3	PP1		(21)	804	$55,125.00
24	11/8/95	L	115.18	3	Buy 1				
PP	11/10/95	S	114.14	6	Sell 2		(108)	696	$51,750.00
PP	11/14/95	L	115.11	3	PP2		(87)	609	$49,031.25
26	11/29/95	L	115.24	3	Buy 2				
PP	12/8/95	S	117.06	3	PP2	138		747	$53,343.75
27	12/22/95	L	117.21	3	Buy 1				
PP	1/4/96	S	118.09	3	PP1	60		807	$55,218.75

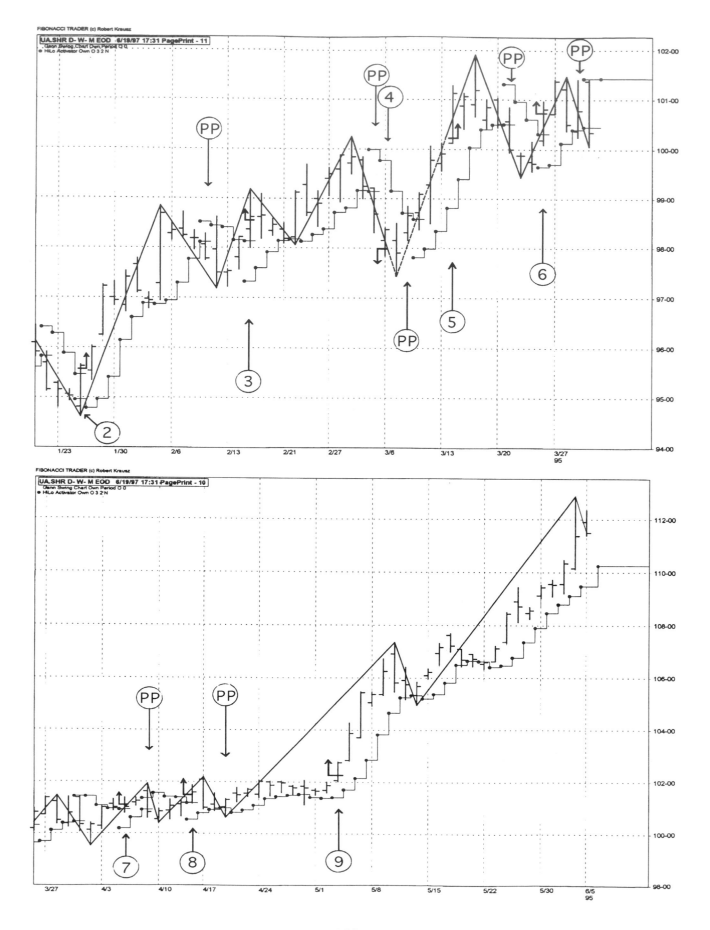

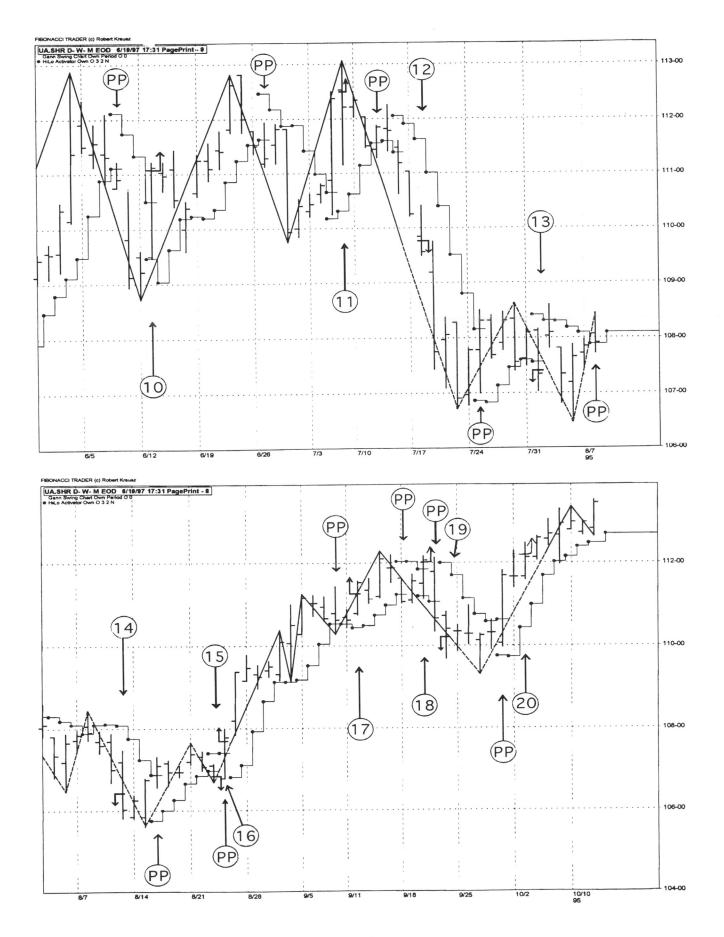

361

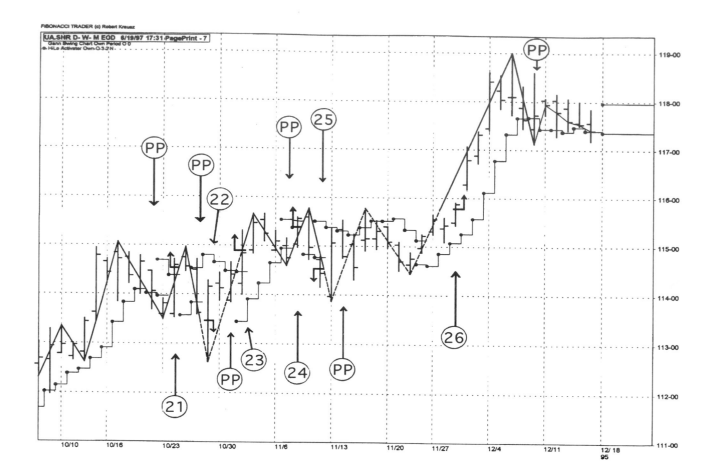

US T-BONDS: 1996
BASIC SWING PLAN
GANN SWING CHARTIST - FIBONACCI TRADER ®

Beginning Equity	$30,000.00	Ending Equity	$74,343.75
Total Net Profit	$44,343.75	Average Ticks/Mo.	
Gross Profit	$66,656.25	Gross Loss	($22,312.50)
Total No. Trades	26	Percentage Profitable	62%
No. Winning Trades	16	No. Losing Trades	10

Largest Winning Trade	$9,843.75	Largest Losing Trade	($3,750.00)
Average Winning Trade	$4,166.02	Average Losing Trade	($2,231.25)
Ratio Average Win/Loss	1.87	Average Trade	$1,705.53
Max. Consecutive Winners	4	Max. Consecutive Losses	2
Largest Consecutive Drawdown (%)	16.07%	Largest Consecutive Drawdown	($5,062.50)

Return on Account	148%
Profit/Drawdown Ratio	8.76

Notes:
1) Initial account size: $30,000

1996
US T- Bonds
Gann Swing Chartist® Basic Swing Plan (End of Day)

Fibonacci Trader®

Trade#	Date	L/S	Price	Ctr.	Rule #	Profit	(Loss)	Accum.	A/C Equity
1	1/16/96	L	117.21	3	Buy 1				$30,000.00
PP	1/23/96	S	117.26	3	PP2	15		15	$30,468.75
2	1/25/96	S	117.26	3	Sell 2				
PP	1/30/96	L	118.15	3	PP2		(63)	(48)	$28,500.00
3	1/31/96	L	118.22	3	Buy 2				
PP	2/2/96	S	117.27	3	PP2		(81)	(129)	$25,968.75
4	2/12/96	L	118.07	3	Buy 1				
PP	2/15/96	S	117.19	3	PP2		(63)	(192)	$24,000.00
5	2/16/96	S	116.19	3	Sell 2				
PP	3/1/96	L	113.05	3	PP2	330		138	$34,312.50
6	3/1/96	L	113.20	6	Buy 1				
PP	3/6/96	S	112.31	3	PP2		(63)	75	$32,343.75
7	3/8/96	S	111.17	3	Sell 2				
PP	3/20/96	L	109.31	3	PP1	150		225	$37,031.25
8	3/27/96	S	109.13	3	Sell 1				
PP	4/2/96	L	110.06	3	PP1		(75)	150	$34,687.50
9	4/4/96	S	109.22	3	Sell 1				
PP	4/12/96	L	108.00	3	PP2	162		312	$39,750.00
10	4/18/96	S	107.17	3	Sell 1				
PP	4/22/96	L	108.10	3	PP1		(75)	237	$37,406.25
11	4/24/96	S	107.27	3	Sell 1				
PP	5/8/96	L	106.01	3	PP1	174		411	$42,843.75
12	5/23/96	L	108.08	3	Buy 2				
PP	5/29/96	S	107.19	3	PP2		(63)	348	$40,875.00
13	5/29/96	S	107.10	3	Sell 2				
PP	6/5/96	L	106.26	3	PP1	48		396	$42,375.00
14	6/7/96	S	105.21	3	Sell 1				
PP	6/14/96	L	105.21	3	PP2	0		396	$42,375.00
15	6/25/96	L	106.09	3	Buy 2				
PP	7/5/96	S	106.23	3	PP2	42		438	$43,687.50
16	7/5/96	S	105.02	3	Sell 2				
PP	7/10/96	L	106.02	3	PP2		(96)	342	$40,687.50
17	7/24/96	S	106.27	3	Sell 1				

1996
US T- Bonds
Gann Swing Chartist® Basic Swing Plan (End of Day)

Fibonacci Trader®

Trade#	Date	L/S	Price	Ctr.	Rule #	Profit	(Loss)	Accum.	A/C Equity
PP	7/30/96	L	107.09	3	PP2		(42)	300	$39,375.00
18	8/1/96	L	108.13	3	Buy 2				
PP	8/8/96	S	109.30	3	PP2	147		447	$43,968.75
19	8/9/96	L	110.23	3	Buy 1				
PP	8/13/96	S	110.02	3	PP2		(63)	384	$42,000.00
20	8/13/96	S	109.25	3	Sell 2				
PP	9/12/96	L	106.14	3	PP2	321		705	$52,031.25
21	9/12/96	L	106.15	3	Buy 2				
PP	9/18/96	S	106.31	3	PP2	51		756	$53,625.00
22	9/24/96	L	107.25	3	Buy 1				
PP	10/9/96	S	109.23	3	PP1	186		942	$59,437.50
23	10/17/96	L	110.09	3	Buy 1				
PP	10/22/96	S	109.31	3	PP2		(30)	912	$58,500.00
24	10/29/96	L	111.24	3	Buy 1				
PP	12/4/96	S	114.28	3	PP2	300		1212	$67,875.00
25	12/5/96	S	113.20	3	Sell 2				
PP	12/19/96	L	112.22	3	PP1	90		1302	$70,687.50
26	12/31/96	S	112.05	3	Sell 1				
PP	1/14/97	L	110.30	3	PP1	117		1419	$74,343.75

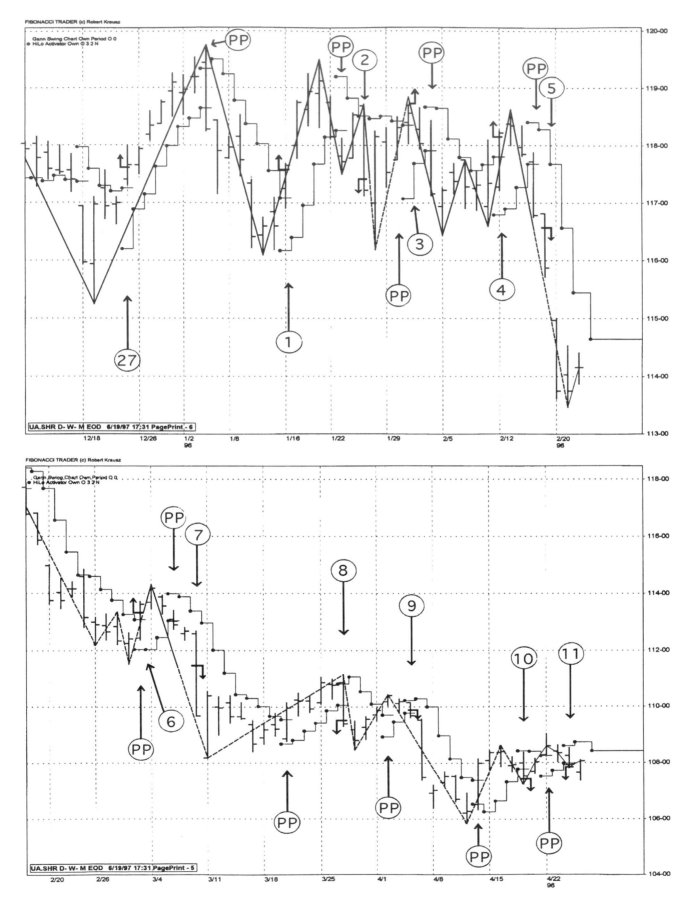

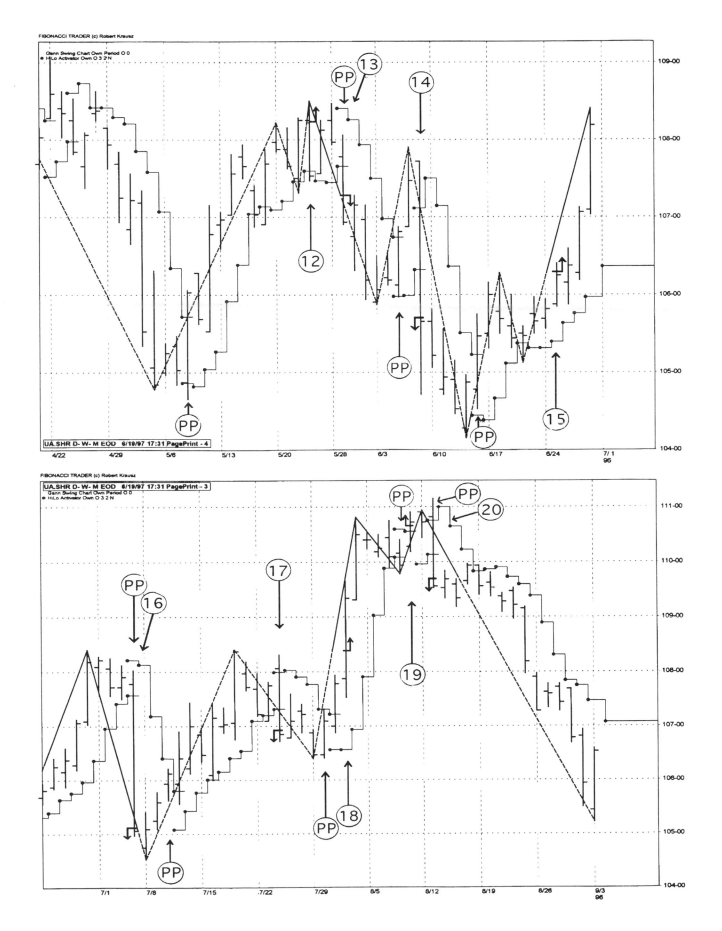

367

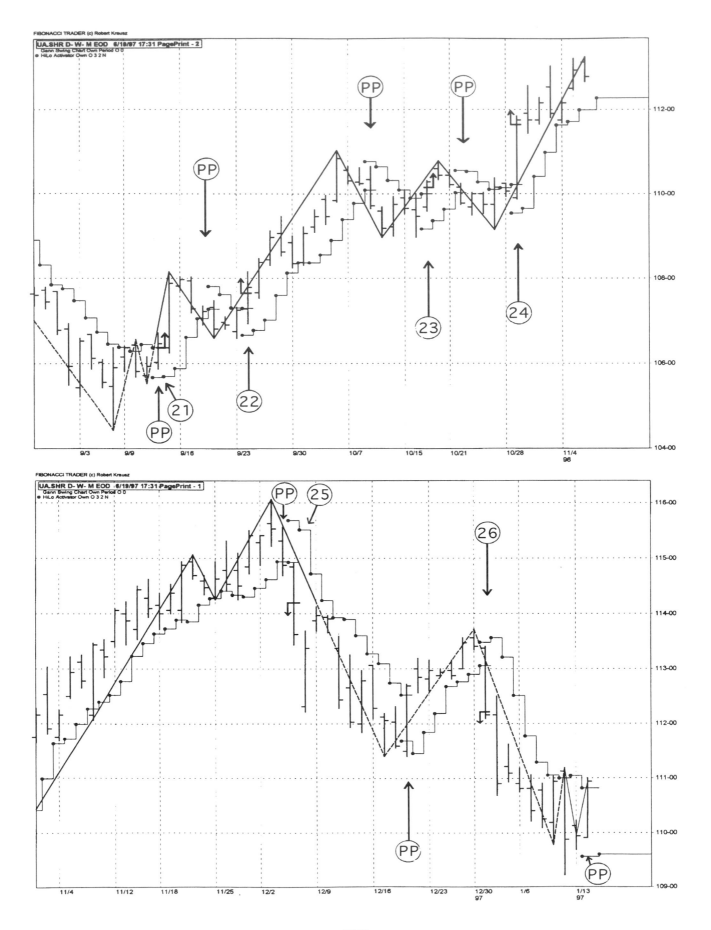

Beginning Equity	$30,000.00	Ending Equity	$68,968.75
Total Net Profit	$38,968.75		
Gross Profit	$52,875.00	Gross Loss	($13,906.25)
Total No. Trades	31	Percentage Profitable	58%
No. Winning Trades	18	No. Losing Trades	13

Largest Winning Trade	$7,000.00	Largest Losing Trade	($2,531.25)
Average Winning Trade	$2,937.50	Average Losing Trade	($1,069.71)
Ratio Average Win/Loss	2.75	Average Trade	$1,257.06
Max Consecutive Winners	3	Max Consecutive Losses	2
Largest Consecutive Drawdown (%)	9.82%	Largest Consecutive Drawdown	($4,156.25)

Return on Account (Before Comm.)	130%
Profit/Drawdown Ratio	9.38

NOTES:

1) Initial A/C Size = $30,000

2) Pyramids only 1/3 of original position.

3) **If you deduct $75 per trade for slippage and commission, the Ending Equity = $61,993.75.**

4) **This showed over 106% return on capital.**

5) This plan trades Trend and Countertrend.

1997
US BONDS
NEW GANN SWING CHARTIST ©
DAILY PLAN

TRADE#	DATE	L/S	PRICE	CTR.	RULE #	PROFIT	(LOSS)	ACCUM.	MO. PROFIT/(LOSS)	A/C EQUITY
1	12/31/96	S	112-05	3	Trend 1					$30,000.00
T	1/2/97	L	111-20	1	T2	17		17		$30,531.25
PYR	1/2/97	S	111-13	1	PYR 2	18		35		$31,093.75
PP	1/14/97	L	110-27	3	PP2	84		119		$33,718.75
2	1/24/97	S	109-25	3	Trend 1					
PP	1/28/97	L	110-08	3	PP1		(45)	74	74	$32,312.50
3	2/3/97	L	111-07	3	Contra 1					
PYR	2/3/97	L	111-11	1	PYR 1	2		76		$32,375.00
4	2/6/97	S	111-13	7	Special Rule	18		94		$32,937.50
5	2/7/97	L	112-06	6	Special Rule SAR		(75)	19		
T	2/10/97	S	112-00	1	T1		(6)	13		$30,406.25
PP	2/19/97	S	113-01	2	PP2	54		67		$32,093.75
6	2/21/97	S	112-15	3	Contra 1					
T	2/25/97	L	112-04	1	T1	11		78		$32,437.50
PP	3/7/97	L	110-10	2	PP2	132		210	136	$36,562.50
7	3/13/97	S	109-14	3	Trend 2					
T	3/14/97	L	108-27	1	T1	19		229		$37,156.25
PP	3/24/97	L	108-30	2	PP2	32		261		$38,156.25
8	3/25/97	L	109-12	3	Contra 1					
PP	3/25/97	S	109-04	3	PP1		(24)	237		$37,406.25
9	3/26/97	S	108-12	3	Trend 1					
PYR	3/27/97	S	108-06	1	PYR 1	36		273		$38,531.25
T	4/2/97	L	107-06	1	T1	38		311		$39,718.75
PP	4/15/97	L	107-02	2	PP2	84		395	185	$42,343.75
10	4/17/97	L	107-15	3	Trend 2					
T	4/18/97	S	107-23	1	T2	8		403		$42,593.75
11	4/23/97	S	107-18	3	Special Rule	6		409		
PP	4/28/97	L	107-02	3	PP1	48		457		$44,281.25
12	4/29/97	L	108-15	3	Trend 1					
T	5/5/97	S	109-21	1	T1	38		495		$45,468.75
PP	5/7/97	S	109-04	2	PP2	78		573	178	$47,906.25
13	5/9/97	L	109-27	3	Trend 1					
PP	5/13/97	S	109-19	3	PP1		(24)	549		$47,156.25

TRADE#	DATE	L/S	PRICE	CTR.	RULE #	PROFIT	(LOSS)	ACCUM.	MO. PROFIT/(LOSS)	A/C EQUITY
14	5/22/97	S	108-21	3	Contra 1					$47,125.00
T	5/27/97	L	108-22	1	T2		(1)	548		$46,937.50
PYR	5/27/97	S	108-18	1	PYR 1		(6)	542		$46,750.00
15	5/28/97	L	108-24	6	Special Rule		(6)	536	(37)	$48,000.00
T	6/5/97	S	110-00	1	T1	40		576		
PYR	6/6/97	L	110-12	1	PYR 1	51		627		$52,968.75
PP	6/24/97	S	111-31	3	PP2	108		735		
16	6/26/97	S	111-16	3	Contra 1					$52,843.75
T	6/27/97	L	111-20	1	T1		(4)	731		$52,781.25
PP	7/1/97	L	111-17	2	PP1		(2)	729	193	
17	7/2/97	L	112-02	3	Trend 1					$54,093.75
PYR	7/3/97	L	112-26	1	PYR 2	42		771		$55,656.25
T	7/8/97	S	113-20	1	T1	50		821		$59,781.25
PP	7/18/97	S	114-04	3	PP2	132		953		
18	7/22/97	L	114-28	3	Trend 1					$59,843.75
T	7/24/97	S	114-30	1	T1	2		955		$61,531.25
PP	8/1/97	S	115-23	3	PP1	54		1009	280	
19	8/1/97	S	114-14	3	Trend 2					$61,593.75
T	8/6/97	L	114-12	1	T1	2		1011		$61,281.25
PP	8/7/97	L	114-19	2	PP2		(10)	1001		
20	8/7/97	S	113-30	3	Re-entry 2					$61,906.25
T	8/8/97	L	113-10	1	T2	20		1021		$63,781.25
PP	8/13/97	L	113-00	2	PP2	60		1081		
21	8/18/97	L	113-14	3	Contra 1					$63,875.00
T	8/20/97	S	113-17	1	T1	3		1084		$63,250.00
PP	8/21/97	S	113-04	2	PP2		(20)	1064		
22	8/21/97	S	112-27	3	Trend 1					
T	8/25/97	L	112-02	1	T1	25		1089		$64,031.25
PP	8/27/97	L	112-17	2	PP2	20		1109	100	$64,656.25
23	9/5/97	S	112-17	3	Trend 1					
T	9/8/97	L	112-27	1	T1		(10)	1099		$64,343.75
PP	9/12/97	L	112-19	3	PP1		(4)	1095		$64,218.75
24	9/15/97	L	113-12	3	Contra 1					

1997
US BONDS
NEW GANN SWING CHARTIST ©
DAILY PLAN

TRADE#	DATE	L/S	PRICE	CTR.	RULE #	PROFIT	(LOSS)	ACCUM.	MO. PROFIT/(LOSS)	A/C EQUITY
T	9/19/97	S	115-21	1	T1	73		1168		$66,500.00
PP	9/25/97	S	115-11	2	PP2	126		1294		$70,437.50
25	9/30/97	S	115-08	3	Contra 1					
PP	10/1/97	L	115-27	3	PP1		(57)	1237	128	$68,656.25
26	10/1/97	L	116-11	3	Trend 1					
PP	10/3/97	S	117-07	3	PP1	84		1321		$71,281.25
27	10/9/97	S	115-10	3	Contra 1					
T	10/9/97	L	114-25	1	T2	17		1338		$71,812.50
PP	10/14/97	L	115-29	2	PP2		(38)	1300		$70,625.00
28	10/24/97	L	116-31	3	Contra 1					
PYR	10/28/97	L	118-20	1	PYR 1		(47)	1253		$69,156.25
PP	10/28/97	S	117-05	4	PP1	18		1271	34	$69,718.75
29	11/19/97	L	119-11	3	Trend 1					
PP	11/21/97	S	118-21	3	PP2		(66)	1205	(66)	$67,656.25
30	12/11/97	L	119-13	3	Trend 1					
T	12/16/97	S	120-04	1	T1	23		1228		$68,375.00
PP	12/17/97	S	119-17	2	PP2	8		1236		$68,625.00
31	12/18/97	L	120-15	3	Re-entry 2					
T	12/24/97	S	120-24	1	T1	9		1245		$68,906.25
PP	12/29/97	S	120-16	2	PP2	2		1247	42	$68,968.75

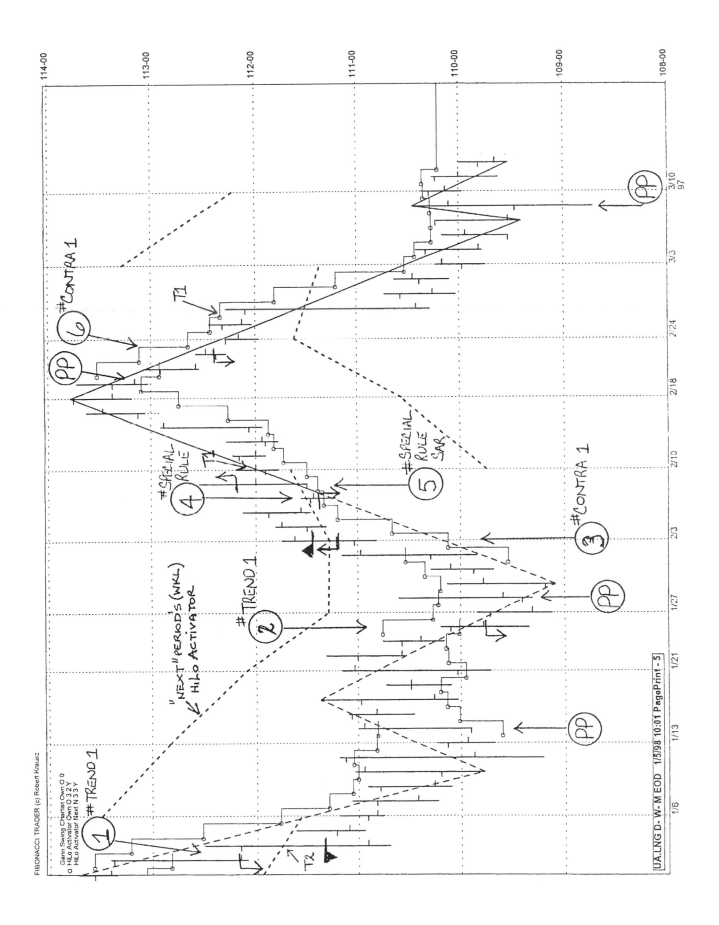

FIBONACCI TRADER (c) Robert Krausz

Gann Swing Chartist Own O 0
o HiLo Activator Own O 32 Y
HiLo Activator Next N 33 Y

UA.LNG D - W - M EOD 1/5/98 10:01 PagePrint - 5

373

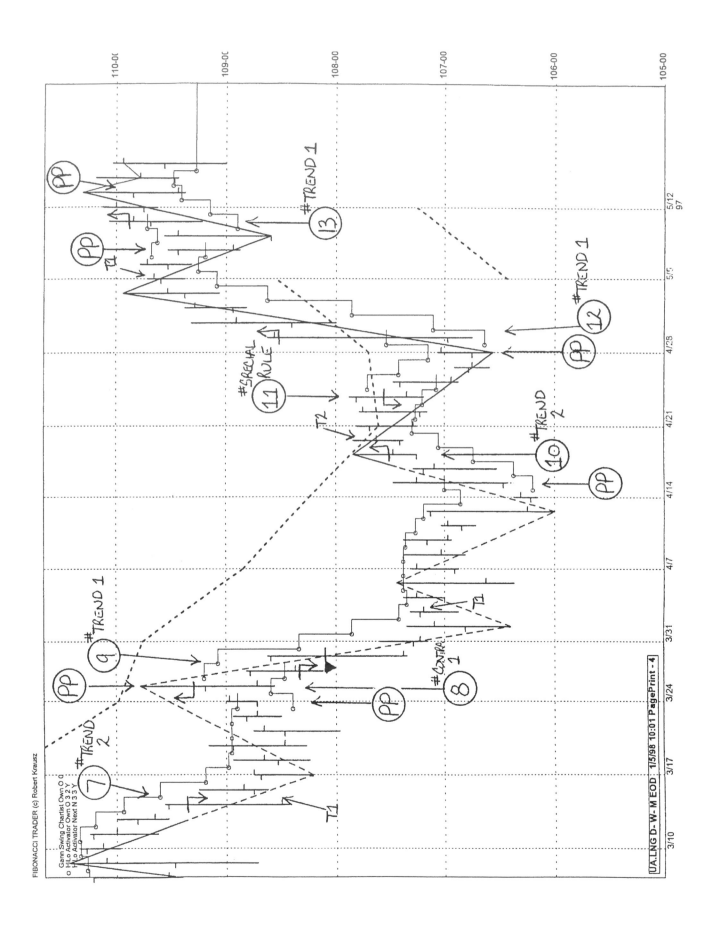

FIBONACCI TRADER (c) Robert Krausz

Gann Swing Chartist Own O q
o HiLo Activator Own O 3 2 Y
HiLo Activator Next N 3 3 Y

UA.LNG D- W- M EOD : 1/5/98 10:01 PagePrint - 4

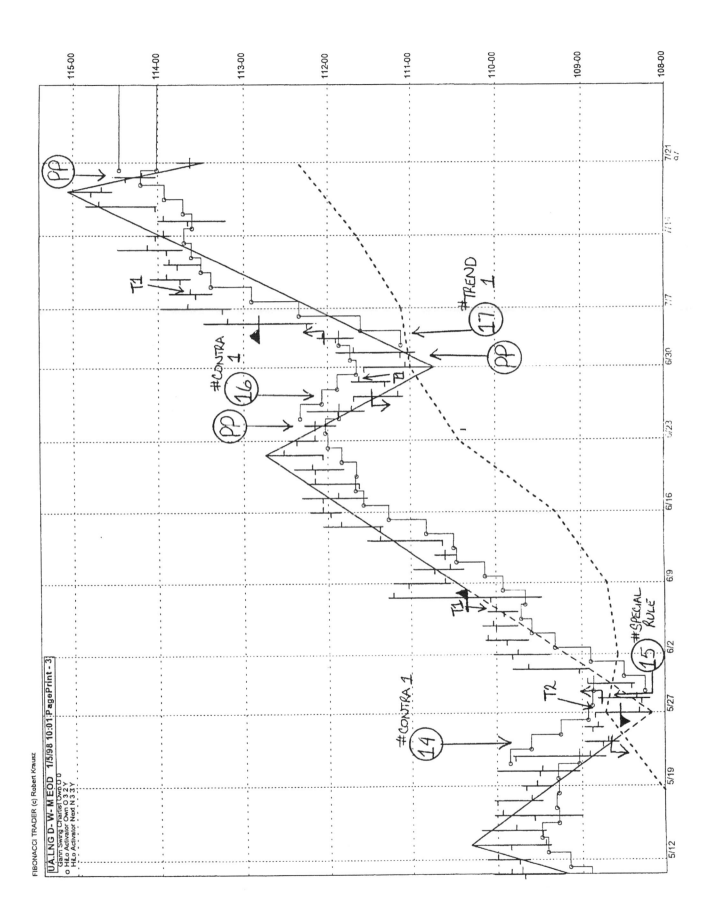

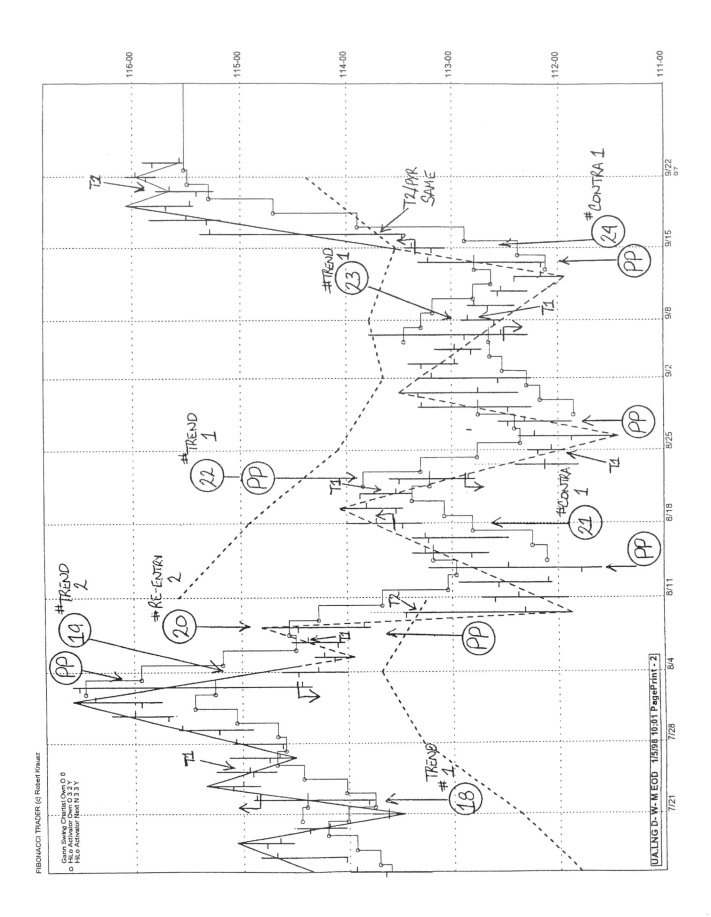

FIBONACCI TRADER (c) Robert Krausz

Gann Swing Chartist Own O 0
o HiLo Activator Own O 3 2 Y
   HiLo Activator Next N 3 3 Y

UA.LNG D- W- M EOD 1/5/98 10:01 PagePrint - 2

376

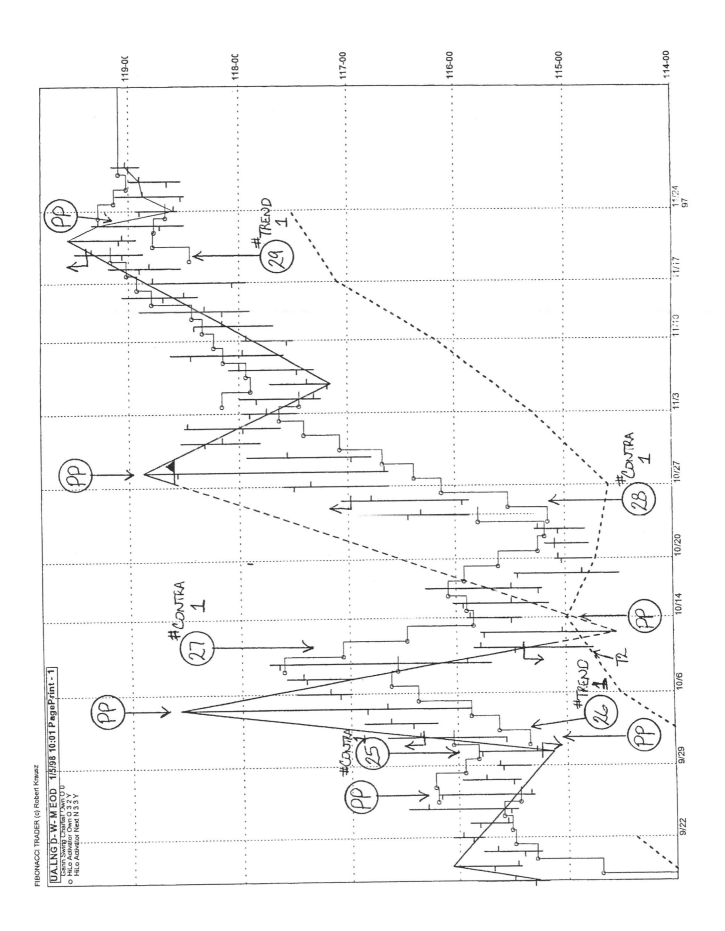

FIBONACCI TRADER (c) Robert Krausz

UA.LNG D- W- M EOD 1/5/98 10:01 PagePrint - 1
Gann Swing Charts / Own O O
o HiLo Activator Own O 3 2 Y
HiLo Activator Next N 3 3 Y

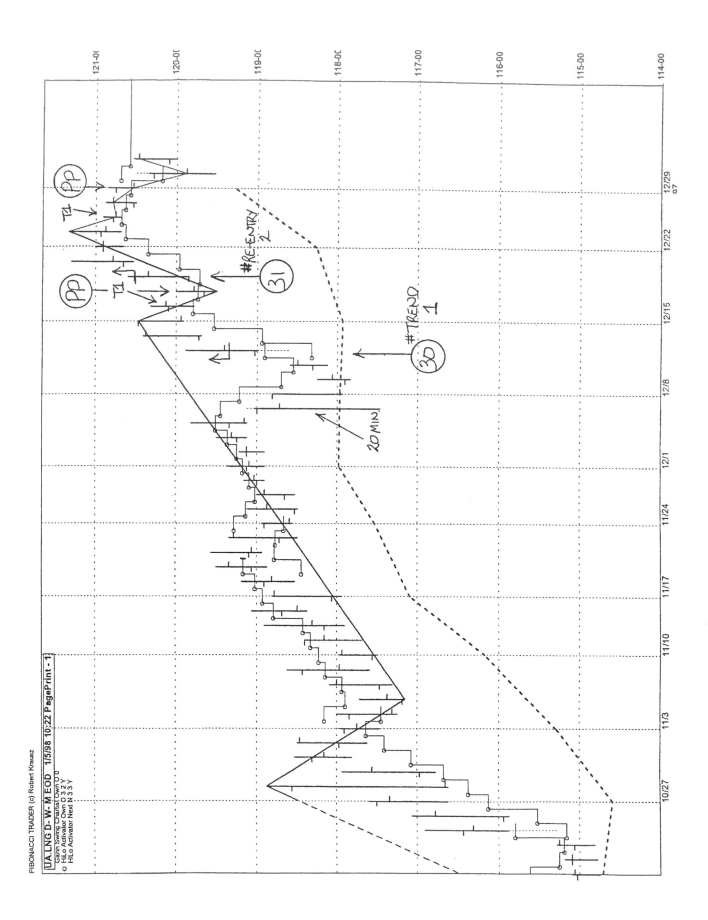

FIBONACCI TRADER (c) Robert Krausz

UA.LNG D-W-M EOD   1/5/98 10:22 PagePrint - 1
Gann Swing Chartist Down O U
o   HiLo Activator Own O 3 2 Y
    HiLo Activator Next N 3 3 Y

NEW GANN SWING CHARTIST©

ADVANCED CONCEPTS

> Trade only active markets.
> Keep out of slow, dead ones.
> W. D. Gann

LAWS OF MULTIPLE TIME FRAMES©

1. EVERY TIME FRAME HAS ITS OWN STRUCTURE.

2. THE HIGHER TIME FRAMES OVERRULE THE LOWER TIME FRAMES.

3. PRICES IN THE LOWER TIME FRAME STRUCTURE TEND TO RESPECT THE ENERGY POINTS OF THE HIGHER TIME FRAME STRUCTURE.

4. THE ENERGY POINTS OF SUPPORT/RESISTANCE CREATED BY THE HIGHER TIME FRAME'S VIBRATION (PRICES) CAN BE VALIDATED BY THE ACTION OF THE LOWER TIME PERIODS.

5. THE TREND CREATED BY THE NEXT TIME PERIOD ENABLES US TO DEFINE THE TRADABLE TREND.

6. WHAT APPEARS TO BE CHAOS IN ONE TIME PERIOD CAN BE ORDER IN ANOTHER TIME PERIOD.

MULTIPLE TIME FRAMES

A SIMPLE EXPLANATION

Any time period that you are interested in for trading or analysis has its own trend as well as its own Support and Resistance levels. Once you know what the direction of the trend is and where the Support and Resistance points are, you have an important part of what you need.

Actually, trading is a much simpler process than most people imagine. Complications arise due to the mindset that "more is better", "Ah, if I had just one more confirmation", or "I need one more crossing of that exponential moving average, then it will give me the 5 indicators confirming the signal." Of course, by then, the move is over!

The reality is that the structure of each time period is different. I am convinced that Gann was right and the markets are geometric in nature. Because each time period has its own structure, we are able to define the trend and the Support/Resistance levels for that specific period.

The 60-minute trend may be different to the Daily trend, yet it is part of that Daily trend, it has to be because without the 60-minute trend, the Daily trend could not exist. In other words, each time period is a self contained universe, yet it is very much a part of larger structure, both in price and in time. If this sounds like "Fractals" made famous by the Mandelbrot set, you are correct.

The Sierspinski gasket is an excellent representation of how a 5-minute bar chart is an integral part of the 15-minute, 30-minute, 60-minute, Daily, Weekly, and Monthly charts. The Sierspinski mathematical model shows a complicated concept at a simple level.

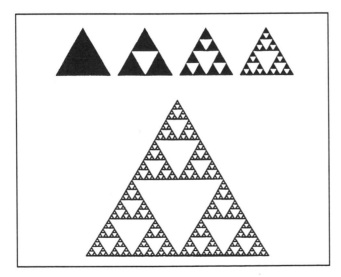

The Sierspinski gasket is used to show a simple triangle, representing the Monthly bar, produced by breaking it up into successively smaller units, ending up with, say, the 5-minute bars.

381

For trading purposes, we are interested only in three time frames.

OWN - NEXT - HIGH

Example:

If you are trading or analyzing the Daily bars, then that is defined as **OWN** period. The **NEXT** time period is the Weekly bar. The **HIGH** time period is the Monthly bar.

Going down the scale for intraday trading using the 30-minute bars, then your multiple time frame setup could look like this:

30-Minute Bars	=	OWN period
Daily Bars	=	NEXT period
Weekly Bars	=	HIGH period

For practical purposes, I will focus only on two time frames: OWN and NEXT. You will soon see why.

The definition of trend, as well as Support/Resistance, is kept the same irrespective of what time period we are looking at. Keeping the definition for all time periods the same enables us to define action points of the Daily bars (OWN Period) within the confines of the Weekly bars (NEXT Time Period).

In other words, we can use the Weekly (NEXT Period) trend and Support/Resistance points to guide us when and where to take action via the Daily bars (OWN Period). Why? Because the Weekly vibrations overrule the Daily. Please bear with me; the Advanced Charts will show the concept clearly.

What you are going to find is that the Weekly trend may be UP, but the Daily trend may be DOWN. It is these divergences between the two time periods that sometimes provide trading opportunities, because the Weekly trend can be more powerful than the Daily trend. And the Weekly Support/Resistance areas are stronger than the Daily Support/Resistance areas.

Naturally, the Daily trend will change before the Weekly, as it is the shorter time period. Of course, the 45-minute trend on an intraday chart will change faster than the Daily, for the same reason. Furthermore, Support (or Resistance) based on the Daily bars will be tested and possibly fail before the Support (or Resistance) based on the Weekly bars.

The first point to realize is that, like the Sierspinski gasket, a simple Weekly bar is produced by smaller units, in this case the 5 Daily bars.

ADVANCED CHART #1

Each Week; 1-4 is composed of five Daily bars. By drawing a "box" around the 5 days that make up the trading week, you can see not only the Weekly bar but also the price activity that took place during that week, on a Daily basis.

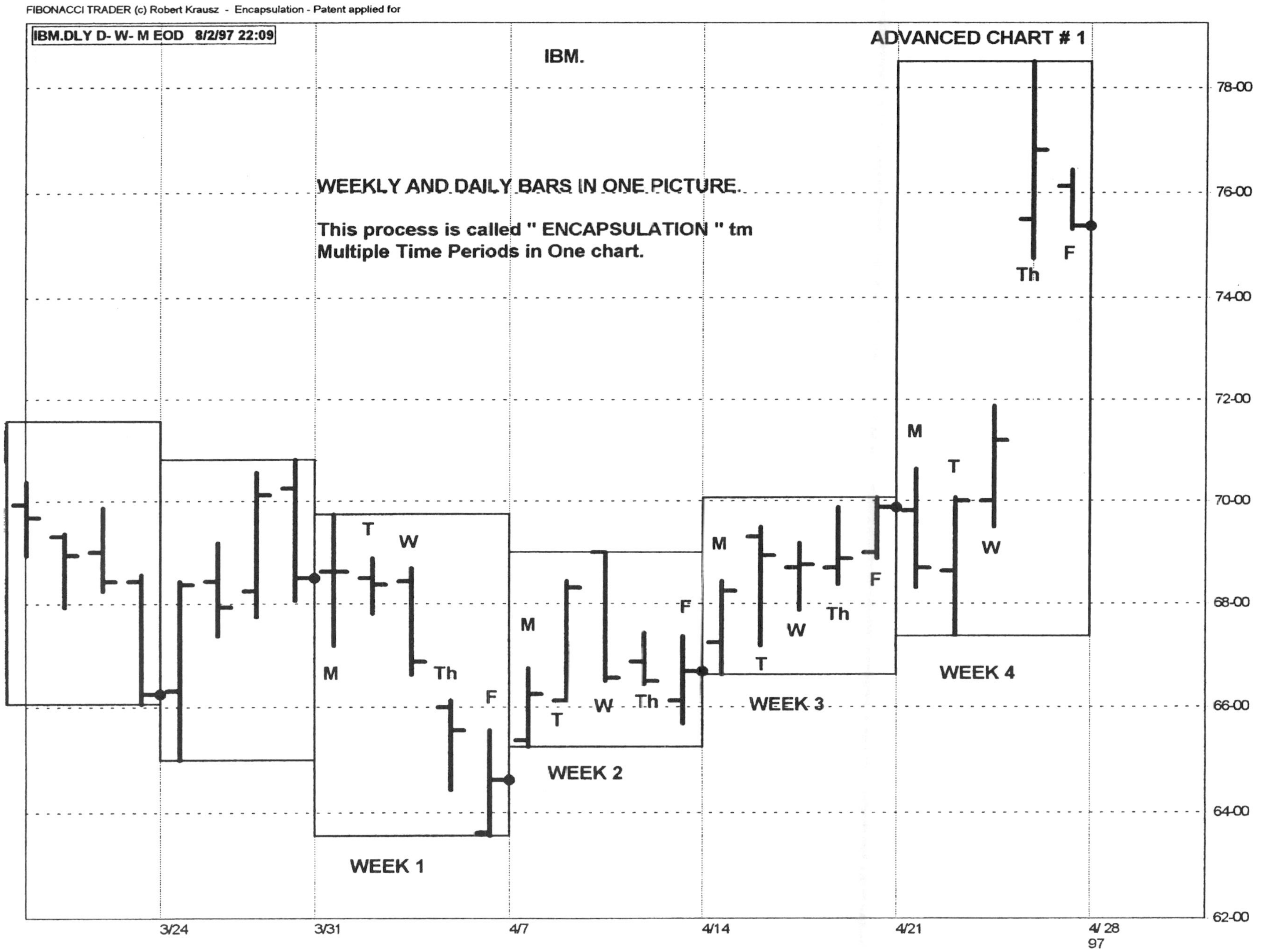

FIBONACCI TRADER (c) Robert Krausz - Encapsulation - Patent applied for

IBM.DLY D- W- M EOD 8/2/97 22:09

ADVANCED CHART # 1

IBM.

WEEKLY AND DAILY BARS IN ONE PICTURE.

This process is called " ENCAPSULATION " tm
Multiple Time Periods in One chart.

WEEK 4

WEEK 3

WEEK 2

WEEK 1

4/ 28
97

4/21

4/14

4/7

3/31

3/24

78-00

76-00

74-00

72-00

70-00

68-00

66-00

64-00

62-00

383

In this way, you capture the price vibrations for two time periods in one picture. This process is called ENCAPSULATION (in fact, I have applied for a patent for this). As we progress, the importance of this will become clear, as soon as we plot the Gann Swings for the Daily bars and the Gann Swing for the Weekly bars into one **Composite Swing Chart***.

ADVANCED CHART #2

This is the same IBM chart as Chart #1 <u>but</u> with the Daily Gann Swings plotted on the Daily bars. Please remember, Solid Line = Uptrend - Dashed Line = Downtrend. Note: During Week 3 on Thursday, the trend changed to UP. (Dashed Line changed to Solid Line when prices took out the previous Peak = week 2, Wednesday.)

One week later the prices gapped up nicely. Did someone know something?

ADVANCED CHART #3

In this chart I have removed the "Encapsulation" and shown another six weeks of Daily bars so you can get a feel of how the Daily swing picture develops. You can see that this potential trend reversal was again set up by Rising Valleys. (Which were the Low daily bars of Weeks 1, 2, 3 and 4.) More on this later.

ADVANCED CHART #4

This is an important chart. Please be sure you understand it. The "boxes" that surround the daily bars, in fact represent the WEEKLY bars. See Week 1, 2, 3 and 4, written from the bottom of the move upwards.

The Gann Swings displayed on this chart are the WEEKLY Swings derived from the WEEKLY bars.

ALL DEFINITIONS REMAIN THE SAME FOR THE WEEKLY BARS AS FOR THE DAILY BARS.

This includes Change of Swing direction. Please go back and check <u>all</u> of the definitions given in "Swing Trading Basics and Terminology". Because the definitions for both time periods are the same, we can apply the same logic to both.

When analyzing the Weekly swing you are interested in two things for starters. Direction of Slope and Trend. We define the Slope as <u>immediate direction of the swing</u>. From the Weekly Valley ② up to the Weekly Peak ③ the Weekly swing was in UPSLOPE mode.

From the Weekly Peak ③ down to Weekly Valley ④ the Weekly swing was in a DOWNSLOPE mode. As the slope defines the immediate direction of the market that is the direction we should be looking to trade in, via the Daily bars.

What does this mean? Simply put, if the Weekly Slope is UP we can look to buy, if and when the Daily bars give a buy signal. Don't worry, examples coming up. Conversely, if

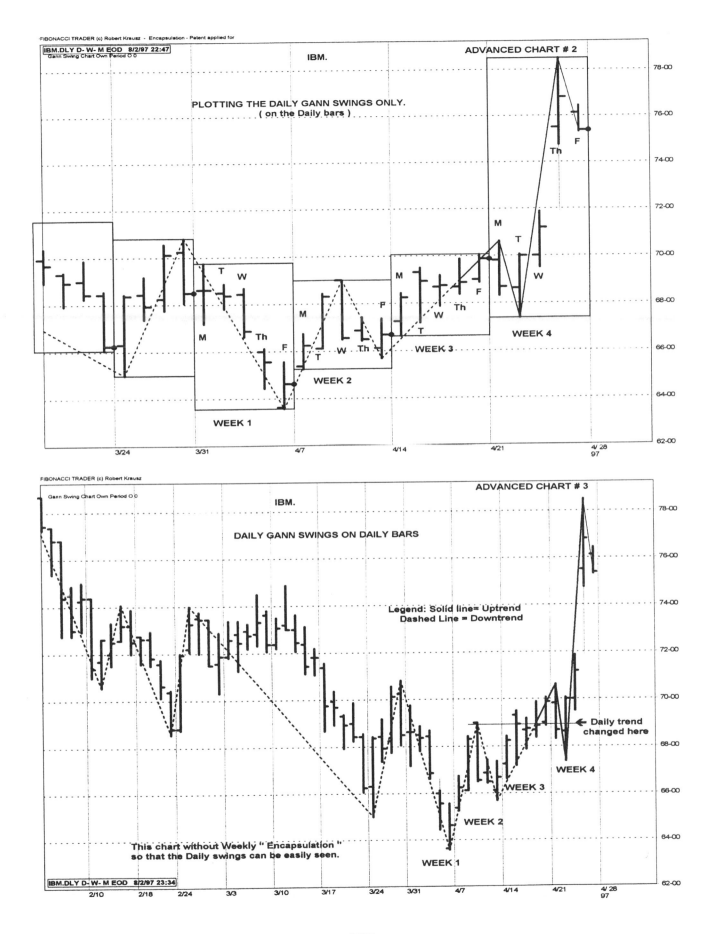

FIBONACCI TRADER (c) Robert Krausz - Encapsulation - Patent applied for

IBM.DLY D- W- M EOD 8/2/97 22:47
Gann Swing Chart Own Period O 0

IBM.

ADVANCED CHART # 2

PLOTTING THE DAILY GANN SWINGS ONLY.
(on the Daily bars)

Th
F
M
T
W
M
T
W
F
M
W
Th
F
T
W
Th
M
T
W
Th
F
T

WEEK 4

WEEK 3

WEEK 2

WEEK 1

3/24   3/31   4/7   4/14   4/21   4/ 28
97

78-00
76-00
74-00
72-00
70-00
68-00
66-00
64-00
62-00

FIBONACCI TRADER (c) Robert Krausz

Gann Swing Chart Own Period O 0

IBM.

ADVANCED CHART # 3

DAILY GANN SWINGS ON DAILY BARS

Legend: Solid line= Uptrend
Dashed Line = Downtrend

← Daily trend
changed here

WEEK 4

WEEK 3

WEEK 2

This chart without Weekly " Encapsulation "
so that the Daily swings can be easily seen.

WEEK 1

IBM.DLY D- W- M EOD 8/2/97 23:34

2/10   2/18   2/24   3/3   3/10   3/17   3/24   3/31   4/7   4/14   4/21   4/ 28
97

78-00
76-00
74-00
72-00
70-00
68-00
66-00
64-00
62-00

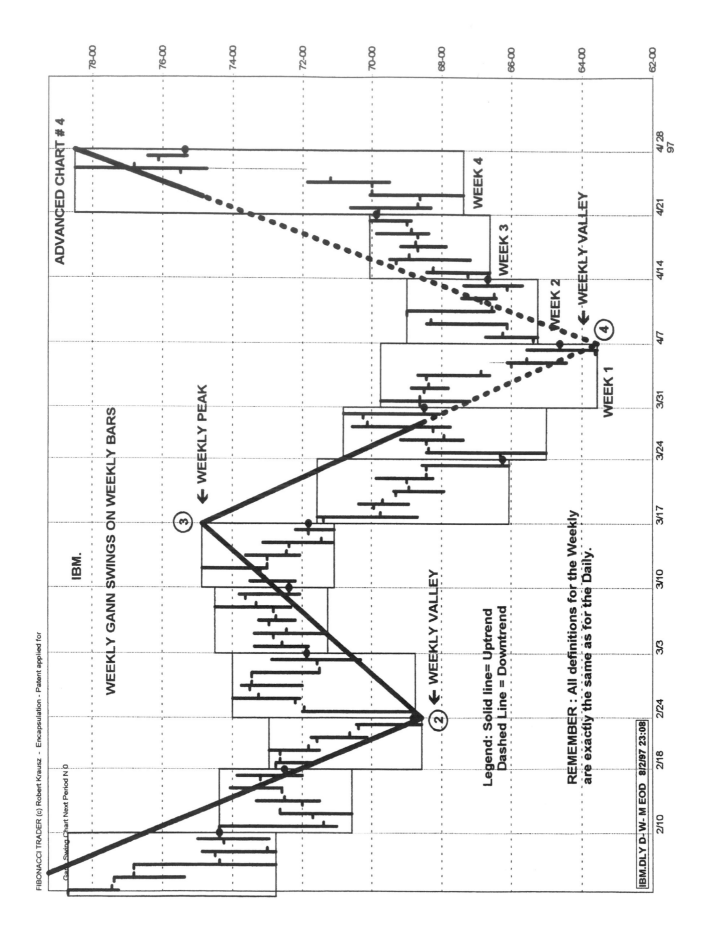

FIBONACCI TRADER (c) Robert Krausz - Encapsulation - Patent applied for

Gann Swing Chart Next Period N 0

IBM.

WEEKLY GANN SWINGS ON WEEKLY BARS

ADVANCED CHART # 4

← WEEKLY PEAK

③

← WEEKLY VALLEY

WEEK 4

WEEK 3

WEEK 2

← WEEKLY VALLEY

④

WEEK 1

Legend: Solid line= Uptrend
Dashed Line = Downtrend

REMEMBER : All definitions for the Weekly
are exactly the same as for the Daily.

IBM.DLY D-W- M EOD   8/2/97 23:08

② ← WEEKLY VALLEY

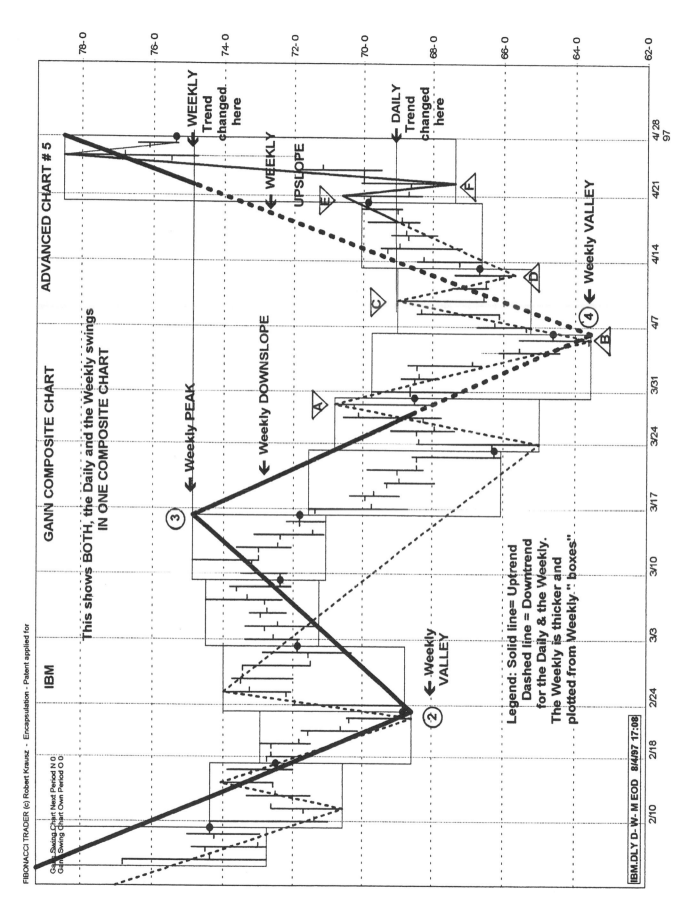

FIBONACCI TRADER (c) Robert Krausz - Encapsulation - Patent applied for

IBM   GANN COMPOSITE CHART   ADVANCED CHART # 5

This shows BOTH, the Daily and the Weekly swings
IN ONE COMPOSITE CHART

Gann Swing Chart Next Period N 0
Gann Swing Chart Own Period O 0

Legend: Solid line= Uptrend
Dashed line = Downtrend
for the Daily & the Weekly.
The Weekly is thicker and
plotted from Weekly "boxes"

IBM.DLY D-W- M EOD 8/4/97 17:08

← Weekly DOWNSLOPE

← Weekly PEAK

← Weekly VALLEY

← WEEKLY Trend changed here

← WEEKLY UPSLOPE

← DAILY Trend changed here

← Weekly VALLEY

387

the Weekly Slope is DOWN we can look to sell when the Daily bars give a sell signal.

So, during the Weekly Downslope from ③ to ④ you could be looking for an opportunity to sell the Daily in the direction of the Weekly Slope. These charts show IBM and I will also use some other contracts to demonstrate these ideas, so you can see they are not exclusive to US T-Bonds. The small "blob" on the right hand side of each weekly "box" (Encapsulation) is the closing price of the week.

ADVANCED CHART #5 GANN SWING COMPOSITE CHART

This charts shows BOTH the Daily and the Weekly swings in <u>one chart.</u> Swings ② ③ ④ are the Weekly, as in Chart 4. The Daily swings are labelled A - B - C - D - E - F. You can also see when the Daily trend changed as prices took out the Daily Peak "C" and when the Weekly trend changed as prices passed the Weekly Peak ③. The Daily trend changed to UP before the Weekly.

It is the Rising Valley Ⓓ that forced the Daily trend to change. Also note that the Rising Valley's Ⓓ and Ⓕ pushed the Weekly to eventually change trend as it took out the Weekly Peak ③.

This is what W. D. Gann had to say about higher bottoms (Rising Valleys) some 50 years ago:
"After commodities make a bottom and start in advance, if they continue to make higher bottoms and higher tops the trend is up."

In the same paragraph, he added:

"After it makes a third higher Bottom on a swing and goes through to a new high level or crosses the last top resistance level, it is indication of much higher prices."

The market is telling you, if you get Rising Daily Valleys then the opportunity exists for the Daily trend to change. This may give rise to a trend change on the Weekly. Although the Weekly trend did not change to UP until the 75.00 area, you did not have to wait to buy only after that point, because not only did you have Rising Daily Valleys but also the Weekly changed to an UPSLOPE long before this trend change occurred.

In reality the mechanical plans covered are stand alone plans. The concepts discussed here serve three purposes.
1. A better understanding of swing trading.
2. The realization that the lower time frames are an integral part of the higher time frames (fractals). The next step is to harness this knowledge by acting in the direction of the higher time periods trend and/or slope.
3. Eventually, for you to set up your own trading plan, either stand alone or incorporating your own tools.

Now let's go back to Advanced Chart #5. This is where the grasp of "Swing Trading

Basics" defined at the start of the book becomes important.

You can see that the Weekly swing from Peak ③ to Valley ④ was in an Uptrend by our definition but, it was in Downslope mode. Only at approximately 68.25 did the Weekly change to a Downtrend and Downslope mode.

But, the important point to realize is that the Daily was in a Downtrend mode all the time. In fact, from Daily Peak Ⓐ down to Daily Valley Ⓑ, the Weekly and the Daily were in tandem. Both Downtrend and Downslope.

To wait for this set up is too late if you are trading the Daily bars. Therefore, from a practical point of view, it is the Weekly Slope (ie: the immediate direction of the Weekly swing) that is crucial if you are analyzing or trading the Daily bars.

ADVANCED CHART #6
Once again this is a Composite chart. This time working with a recent daily Wheat chart that shows the Weekly and the Daily swings in one picture.

The Weekly swing from Peak ① to Valley ② is clearly in DOWNSLOPE mode for eleven weeks. (Even though the Weekly trend was up.) By the time the Weekly trend changed to a Downtrend, the move was nearly over.

The lesson is: IF you are using two time frames (ie: the Daily and the Weekly) pay attention to the Slope of the Weekly. You will find most of your winners will come when you trade the Daily bars in the Direction of the Weekly Slope.

Let's have a closer look at this 150 cent down move in the Wheat. At the simplest level there was a potential short sale when the Daily changed to a Downtrend as Daily Valley "B" was taken out at X ----- X.
Listen up!

There were 4 pieces of important information given to us by the market. Yes, 4.
1) Dropping Daily Peaks. Daily Peak "C" was lower than "A".
2) The Daily was in a Downslope from "C" to "E".
3) The Daily trend changed to Down at X ----- X.
4) The Weekly slope was Down (Downslope).

Where could your stop be? The only two logical market driven places can be Daily Peak "C" or Daily Peak "A". Why? Because these are nearest true resistance points, if you are swing trading.

So, which one to use? "A" or "C"? Obviously, the nearest. ie: "C" would be easier to hit. But, there are other points that should be taken into consideration before you decide. Firstly, if you are using multiple contracts, you could use both. That is one of the reasons I

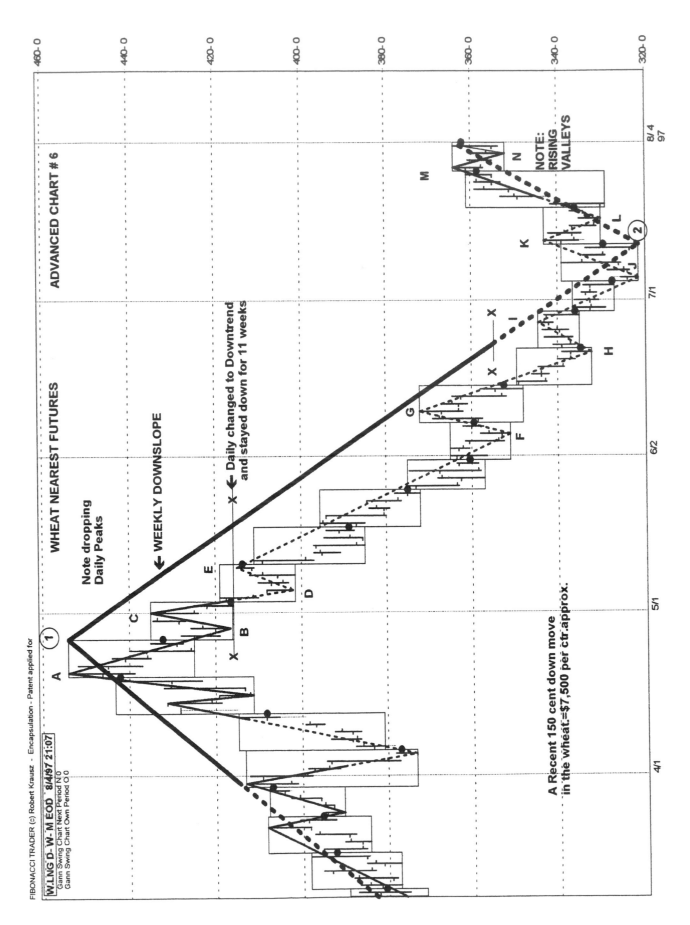

FIBONACCI TRADER (c) Robert Krausz - Encapsulation - Patent applied for

W.LNG D- W- M EOD 8/4/97 21:07
Gann Swing Chart Next Period N:0
Gann Swing Chart Own Period O:0

WHEAT NEAREST FUTURES   ADVANCED CHART # 6

Note dropping
Daily Peaks

← WEEKLY DOWNSLOPE

X ← Daily changed to Downtrend
and stayed down for 11 weeks

NOTE:
RISING
VALLEYS

A Recent 150 cent down move
in the wheat.=$7,500 per ctr.approx.

390

recommend trading multiple contracts. Example: if trading say, a 3 lot (or 30) then you have the luxury of taking what I call split decisions. Your stop can be on 1/3 of your position at "C" and 2/3 at "A" or the other way around. It depends on your plan.

The Second point is, what percentage of your capital does a loss at point "A" or "C" represent? What percentage of your trading capital, as far as margin is concerned, does this 3 lot in the Wheat represent? Have you backtested this entry and exit concept? Where is your trailing stop? Could you use the HiLo Activator on the Wheat also?

Hard questions have to be asked to become a competent professional trader. That's why some 90% fail. It's the hardest way to make an easy living. From Daily Peak Ⓔ down to Ⓕ is a dream trade, but note the following:
The Weekly Slope is Down.
The Daily Slope is Down.
The Daily is in Downtrend.

Does that say anything to you?

Let's look a litter closer at how this down move is trying to reverse even as I write this today (8/5/97). The Daily trend changed to Up, when for the first time after 11 weeks of Downtrend, a previous Daily Peak "K" was surpassed. As soon as Valley "L" formed, you knew it was higher than Daily Valley "J", which was the low of the entire move. You got it - Rising Valleys.

This potential bottoming process in Chart 6 was crystal clear. If it was that simple all the time swing trading would be easy. But, you would be surprised how often it happens if you watch a variety of contracts in the Futures Markets and heavily traded shares in the Stock Market. There are three patterns to keep an eagle eye on.

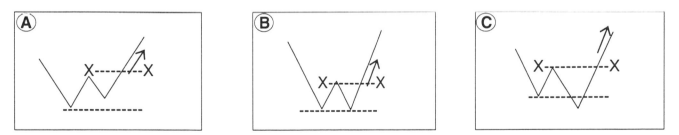

Of course there are more, but these three are worth checking out. Needless to say, the potential for a reversal becomes stronger when the previous Peak is taken out; that's when you go on full alert. Just think for a moment how encouraging it is, when this pattern sets up and one of the Buy Rules from the mechanical plans click in.

I promised to give you the calculation for the NEXT time periods HiLo Activator. Surprise! It is the same as for the Daily HiLo Activator, but we use the Weekly Highs and Lows. Take the latest three weeks high added together and divide the sum by 3. Now, plot it in Line formation (not in step formation). This is your Weekly (Next) buy stop. Do the same for the

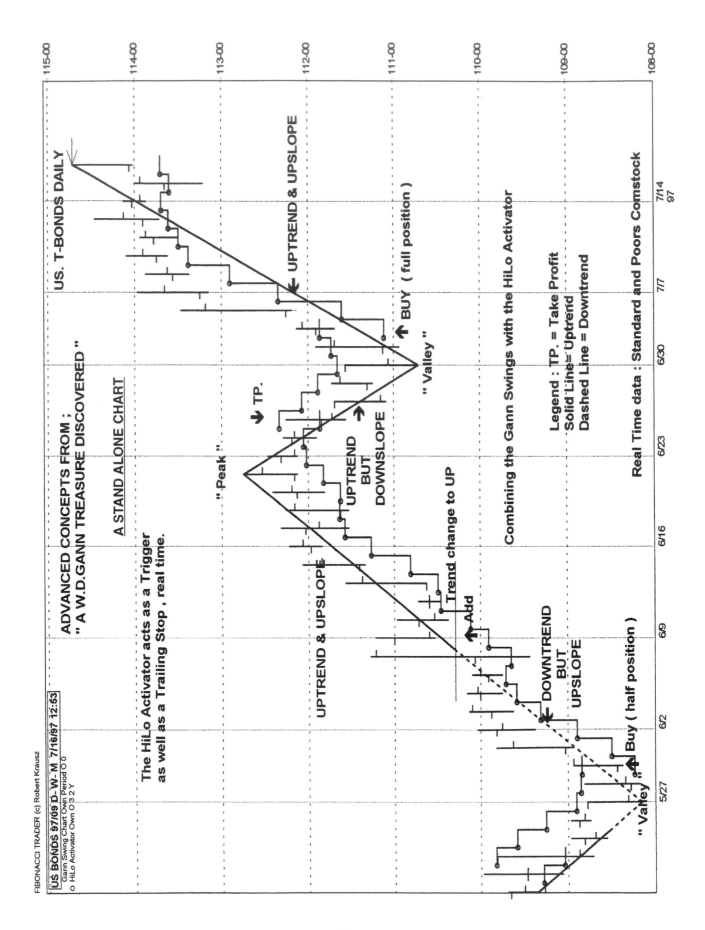

Weekly Lows and that is your Weekly (Next) sell stop. (I like simple concepts if possible.)

ADVANCED CHART #7 (next page)

Let's zoom in on the Wheat Chart #6. Where and how could we have taken action? You can see that I have numbered the Weekly "boxes" (Encapsulation™). Each "box" represents one week's trading. Not only do you have the Weekly and Daily Gann Swings but also the Daily and Weekly HiLo Activator.

Just because Advanced concepts are being looked at, it does not mean you can't use various rules to enter or exit the market from the mechanical plans. During Week 1, Wednesday prices closed below the Daily HiLo Activator and the Daily was in an Uptrend. This was a "sell" via the Professional Plan, Contra Trend Rule (check it out please). The Buy stop came up showing your trailing stop. This potential sell signal is indicated by a down arrow above Wednesday's bar.

As you work your way through these few trades you will realize that new ideas can pop up at any time, so be awake. After entry during Week 1, prices went down and made a low at Ⓑ during Week 2. If you are trading multiple contracts you may decide to take some "preset" profit on 1/3 of your contracts. How do you know what your "preset profit" should be?

If you do a few years backtest on the Wheat, taking the same entry signal (Contra Trend / close below sell stop rule in the Professional Plan), see how far prices move in your favor on the average, calculate the minimum. If they move in your favor, then check if it is worth it (ie: commissions, risk, etc.). Let us say that this comes out at 6¢, which is $300 per contract. If the statistics confirm it then that becomes your "preset" profit point for say 1/3 of your total contracts. That should pay for the trade. Treat your trading as a business. In this case, the short entry was at 435 3/4 and the low of that first down move at Ⓑ was 416 1/4 = over 19¢ move per contract ($950). Wednesday of Week 2 closed above the Daily HiLo Activator buy stop; if you followed the rules of the Professional Plan you would have been out of the trade totally at say, 432 1/4. (On Wheat intraday, I suggest you allow 3¢ for the Profit Protection Rule 2. Yes, I know the plan states a 2 tick penetration past the HiLo buy stop intraday → BUT that is for T-Bonds.) A profit of only 3¢ per contract. But, if you had a "preset" then one contract would yield 6¢. Clear?

The rhythm for most commodities is similar, but the vibration for each contract is different. So, you can use the same rules but the nuances will be different, as shown above. So, do not expect the S&P 500 to use exactly the same number of ticks for every entry and exit rule as the T-Bonds.

How do you know how many ticks to allow for the rules if you are trading Pork Bellies? Good question. Once you have worked your way through a few years of backtests shown here, you will have a really good idea how the rules work, whichever plan you choose.

Apply the same plan to the contract of your choice. You will quickly see what adjustments

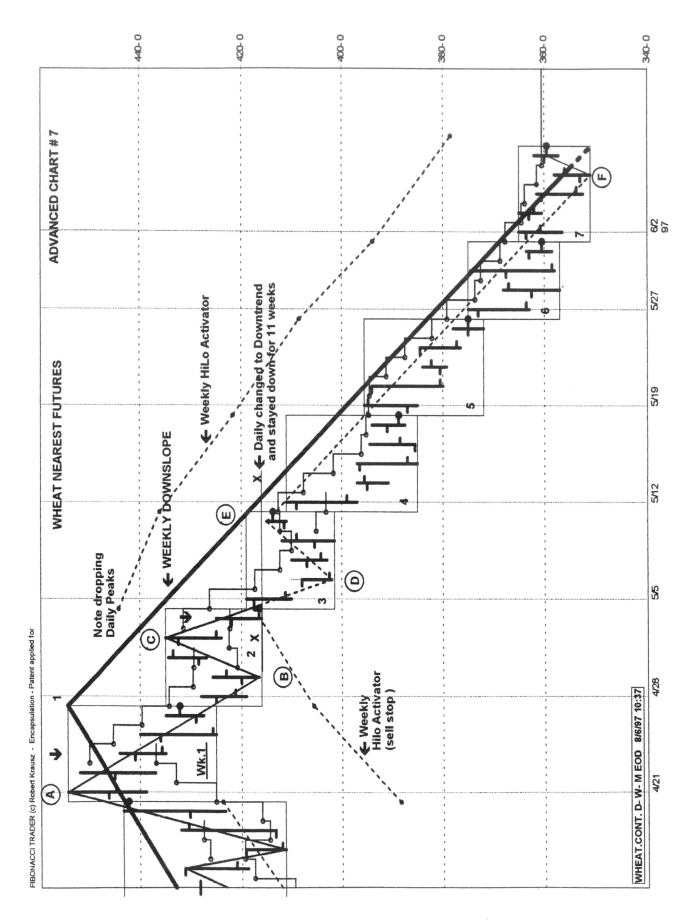

FIBONACCI TRADER (c) Robert Krausz - Encapsulation - Patent applied for

ADVANCED CHART # 7

WHEAT NEAREST FUTURES

Note dropping
Daily Peaks

← WEEKLY DOWNSLOPE

← Weekly HiLo Activator

X ← Daily changed to Downtrend
and stayed down for 11 weeks

Weekly
Hilo Activator
(sell stop)

Wk.1

WHEAT.CONT. D- W- M EOD 8/6/97 10:37

must be made to satisfy the vibration of your choice of commodities or shares. That is exactly what I do. The second step is to backtest that contract or stock to see how your "tick adjustment" worked. Please believe me, there is a direct correlation between how good your statistics are and how well you do in the markets.

There is no "holy grail". I do not have it nor does anyone else. What is important is to satisfy your subconscious mind and the only way to do that is to "personalize" and back test as much as possible. Even if you follow the plans exactly as presented in this book, you will have to really understand the rules and do plenty of backtrack of your own. Take nothing for granted.

Sure, I could give the tick value to use rule by rule for every commodity and stock as well as currency known to man, but this would defeat everything I have learned about what makes traders successful, and what separates them from the rest.

So, what's next? Still on Chart 7 on Friday of Week 2, again the Contra Trend Rule from the Professional Plan kicks in. But, we are getting a little help from our friends. Closing that day on the Weekly HiLo Activator and the Slope of the Weekly is certainly down. I am comfortable with that trade.

On Monday of Week 3 the Daily trend changed. On Tuesday a Valley formed at ⓓ. (Your "preset" profit point on 1/3 of your contracts was hit.) On Friday of that week prices closed above the HiLo Activator. But the close over the Buy stop was not by the 3¢ previously mentioned, therefore you can stay short. (The Weekly Slope is still down and so is the Daily trend.)

Even if you decided to jump ship on that Friday night's close, the rules would have put you back short on the next trading day. Which was Monday of Week 4. (Trend trading rule was hit below the HiLo Activator™ sell stop.) You had 4 weeks with nothing to do, just smile and say "thank you". Some $2000 move per contract. Who says that due to computers trends do not develop?

ADVANCED CHART #8 INTRADAY COMPOSITE CHART
This chart will be used to illustrate some important ideas (besides showing intraday possibilities for short term swing trading).

As this is an intraday chart, the multiple time frame set up for the 50-minute bars is:
    OWN   =   50-Minutes (The time period traded)
    NEXT   =   Daily
    HIGH   =   Weekly

Once again, for actual trading we are focusing only on two time periods, ie: the 50-minute and the Daily. Why the 50-minute and not the 60-minute bars? Good question.

I tend to divide the daily trading hours by a number from the Fibonacci series; 3, 5, 8, 13,

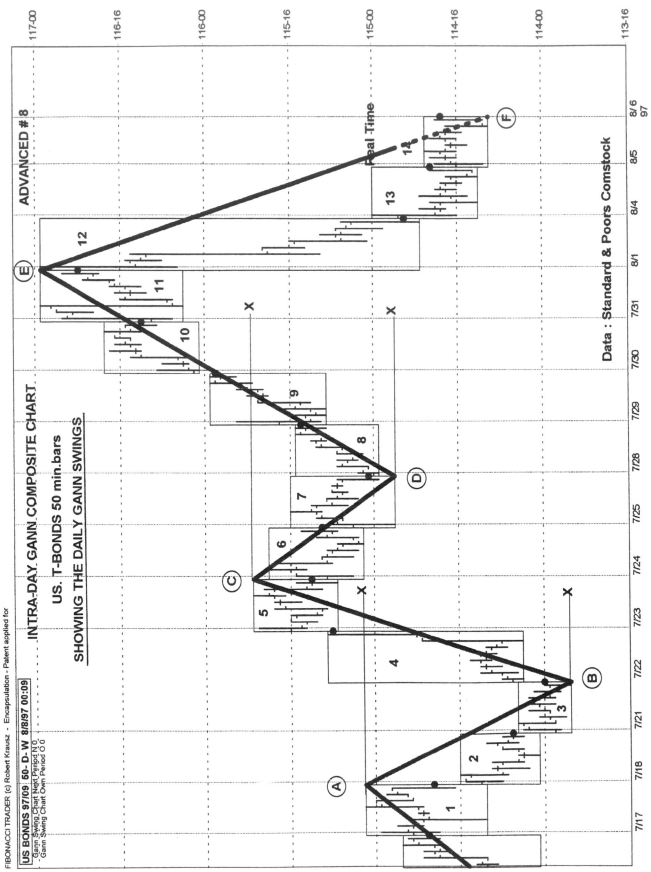

FIBONACCI TRADER (c) Robert Krausz - Encapsulation - Patent applied for

INTRA-DAY GANN COMPOSITE CHART

ADVANCED # 8

US. T-BONDS 50 min.bars

SHOWING THE DAILY GANN SWINGS

US BONDS 97/09 : 50- D- W 8/8/97 00:09

Gann Swing Chart Next Period N 0
Gann Swing Chart Own Period O 0

Data : Standard & Poors Comstock

Real Time

etc. The day bonds trade for 400 minutes; if you divide that by 8 you get the 50-minute bars. It also puts you 10 minutes ahead of the traders who follow the 60-minute bars. This 50-minute intraday chart is different from the previous charts. What do you see?
1. The 50-minute bars.
2. The Daily "box" encapsulating the 50-minute bars. (Each day is numbered.)
3. The DAILY SWINGS on the 50-minute bars. (Labelled Ⓐ - Ⓑ - Ⓒ - Ⓓ - Ⓔ - Ⓕ)
(Yes, I know it looks like Elliott Waves - don't even think about it.)

The concept here is to use the power of the Daily Swings to trade the 50-minute bars. That is to say we harness the energy of the Next (Daily) time period to trade Own (50-minute) period. In practice you can use the Slope, Trend, and Support/Resistance definitions of Daily to guide the trade direction of the 50-minute bar. Examining the implications of the Next period's properties can give you superior information.

SLOPE
Trade Entry via the 50-minute bars in the direction of the Daily Slope can improve the odds of a successful trade. During the Daily Upslope Ⓓ to Ⓔ, a "Long" position is more likely to "hit the spot". The same thought applies to selling during the Daily Downslope Ⓔ to Ⓕ.

TREND
During swings Ⓐ - Ⓑ - Ⓒ - Ⓓ and almost to Ⓕ the Daily was in an Uptrend mode. Taking note of the fact that IF the Daily Slope agreed with the Daily trend direction, then it would be helpful to the Longs. For this, see Ⓑ to Ⓒ and Ⓓ to Ⓔ. A useful confirmation.

SUPPORT AND RESISTANCE
Using the Support/Resistance points of the NEXT TIME PERIOD (in this case, the Daily) provides a mega-leap in swing trading concepts. Let's see what you think after you have back tracked some Daily and Intraday charts.

There are three important concepts at work:
1) Freedom to Fluctuate.
2) Failure of Support/Resistance.
3) Success of Support/Resistance.

Please remember that we are dealing with the Daily (Next) swings but trading the 50-minute bars.

"Freedom to fluctuate". What does this mean?
During the Daily swing Ⓐ - Ⓑ - Ⓒ a Daily Peak was established at Ⓐ and a Daily Valley at Ⓑ. Please follow carefully. The market told us that the Daily Support was at Ⓑ and the Daily Resistance at Ⓐ. Therefore you have an exact market defined price level of current Support and Resistance on a Daily basis. So long as prices stay between these two points, they are "Free to Fluctuate", setting up clearly defined trading opportunities within these two fixed points.

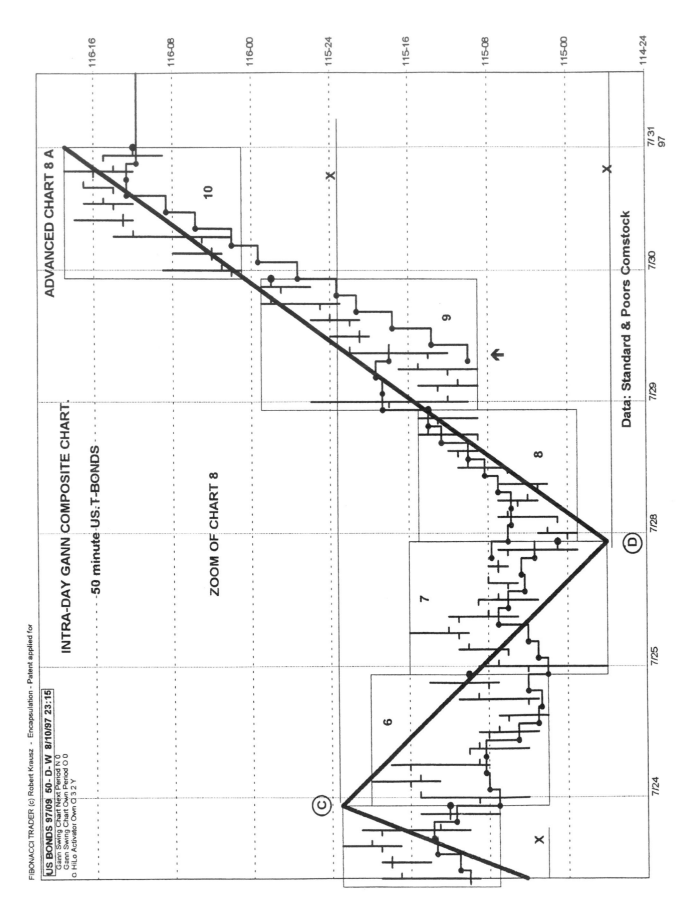

FIBONACCI TRADER (c) Robert Krausz - Encapsulation - Patent applied for

US BONDS 97/09 50- D- W 8/10/97 23:15
Gann Swing Chart Next Period N 0
Gann Swing Chart Own Period O 0
o HiLo Activator Own O 3 2 Y

INTRA-DAY GANN COMPOSITE CHART.

-50 minute-US:T-BONDS

ZOOM OF CHART 8

ADVANCED CHART 8 A

Data: Standard & Poors Comstock

What makes this concept different from other types of swing trading is that we use the 50-minutes' price activity within the Daily confines of Support/Resistance. In other words, we trade the 50-minute bars using the Daily energy points.

Look at swing C down to (D). The moment (D) was formed your Daily Support and Resistance levels were defined. So far so good. If prices proceeded upwards and surpassed Daily Peak (C), as shown by (C)---------(X), then the potential existed for higher prices. Why? Because the Daily Peak that represents Resistance failed and prices went higher.

Now, after (D) formed and if prices had gone down instead of up, then the support of the Daily Valley (D) could have failed. Furthermore, as (D) was the previous Valley, as per our definition, the Daily trend would have turned down. You can see this occurred on Day 12 as prices eventually crossed and closed below horizontal line (D)--------(X).

Well, having said that, how could you utilize this concept to trade the 50-minute bars? Any time during Upslope (D) - (E) you could have looked to buy via the 50-minute if you got a buy signal. Let's look at a few choices. You could take any retracements with a clearly defined stop loss at (D). You could have bought as soon as Upslope (D) - (E) started. You could have used one of your own favorite entry signals, as the Daily slope and the Daily trend were up. You could have bought the breakout above Peak (C) on the first 50-minute bar's close above the horizontal line (C)---------(X). You could easily think of taking a long position if the 50-minute bar closes above the HiLo Activator buy stop of the 50-minute, because that is the time frame we are working with.

This is shown on <u>ADVANCED CHART 8A</u> (which is a zoom of Chart #8). During Day 9 the fourth 50-minute bar of that day closed above the HiLo Activator buy stop. Marked with an arrow. Remember, the Daily trend was Up, the Slope was also Up. Of course Daily Valley (D) was above Daily Valley (B) = Rising Valleys. And we have not yet started to look at the 50-minute swings and how they show potential combinations with the Daily Gann Swings.

ADVANCED CHART #9
Chart 9 does exactly that; it combines the Daily and 50-minute Gann Swings with the HiLo Activator of the 50-minute. As you saw in Chart 8A, potential action was indicated on Day 9. Yes, the arrow is still there. But, now look at the 50-minute swings (H) - (I) - (J). During Day 9, the first 50-minute bar of the day surpassed the previous 50-minute Peak (I) around 115-16. The 50-minute had been in a Downtrend. 2 ticks past that previous Peak (I) the 50-minute turned positive, into an Uptrend. Three bars later, the same day, the HiLo Activator buy stop was hit.

Let's recap. A) The 50-minute changed to an Uptrend. B) The 50-minute was in Upslope mode. C) The Daily was in Upslope mode and in an Uptrend. D) The 50-minute's buy stop was hit. Now that's potential.

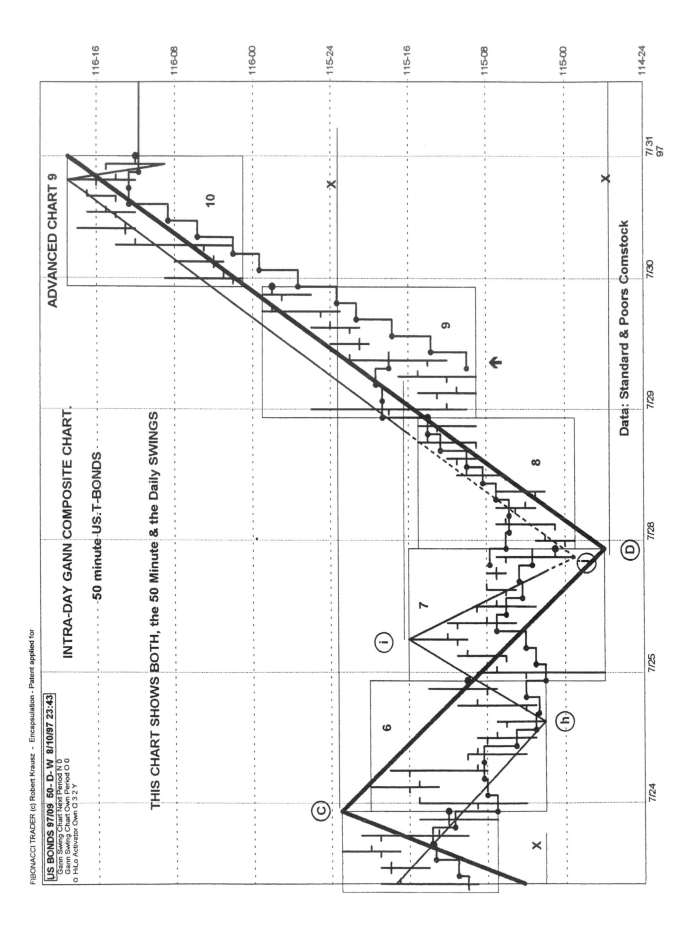

FIBONACCI TRADER (c) Robert Krausz - Encapsulation - Patent applied for

US BONDS 97/09 50- D- W 8/10/97 23:43
Gann Swing Chart Next Period N 0
Gann Swing Chart Own Period N 0
o HiLo Activator Own O 3 2 Y

ADVANCED CHART 9

INTRA-DAY GANN COMPOSITE CHART.

—50 minute US:T-BONDS

THIS CHART SHOWS BOTH, the 50 Minute & the Daily SWINGS

Data: Standard & Poors Comstock

NEW GANN SWING CHARTIST©

SWING DIRECTION
&
"NEUTRAL" SLOPE

> If you have no plan, you'll
> become part of someone else's.
> Robert Krausz

SWING DIRECTION & NEUTRAL SLOPE

These 7 charts will explain the following:

A) How the Swing changes direction.

B) How the Trend changes direction.

C) How the Swing becomes Neutral.

SWING DIRECTION CHART #1

Kicks off the action working our way through bar by bar. The Low of Bar 1 shows the end of a Downswing. As you can see, the Daily Trend is Up but the Slope is Down (the swing line is Solid = Uptrend).

On Bar 2 the Slope changes to up, BUT because we need TWO CONSECUTIVE Higher highs ONLY the Slope is changing and not the Swing. This line is drawn thinner than the Swing line. In the Fibonacci Trader® program it is plotted as a thin white line. Also note that because it is not yet a proper swing in the opposite direction, this thin white line is plotted to Bar 2's close (and not to the bar's high, if that only happens on a proper swing in the opposite direction). When this occurs, I call it "Neutral". You will soon see the reason why.

Please look at **Chart #2**. This shows the next day, Bar 3. On this day the prices once again go down. At this point the previous Daily Downslope is reestablished and something else happens. Correct. The previous Valley is taken out and the Trend changes to Down.

Yet, on Bar 4, again the Downtrend stalls, signified by a thin upslope plotted to the close of Bar 4. You can see this on **Chart #3**. Once again the swing is Neutral. As you have only one higher high but we need two consecutively for the slope to change.

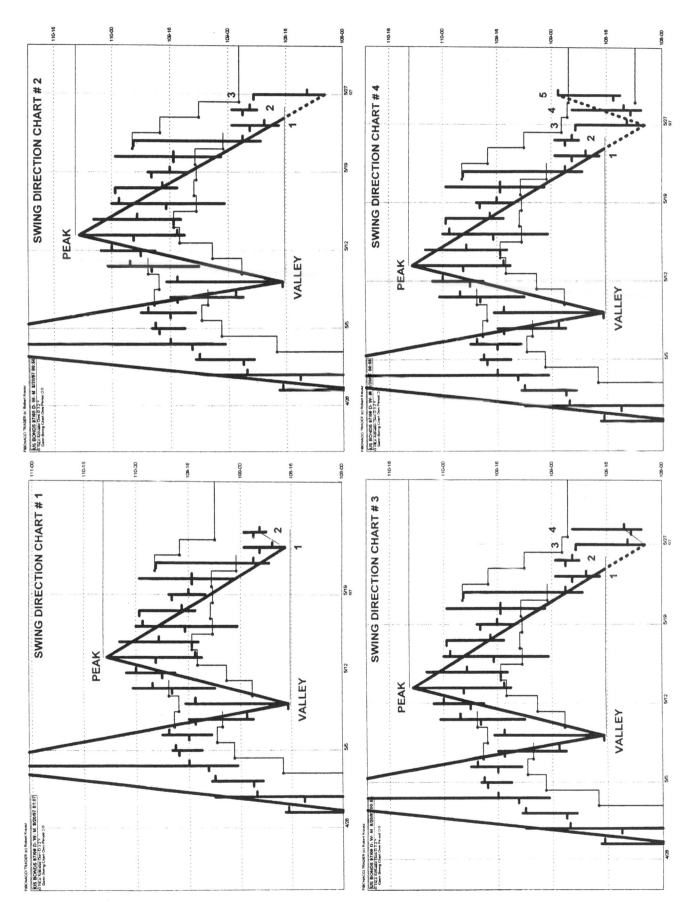

403

Chart #4 shows what happens when this occurs. Bar 5 gives us two consecutive higher highs and the Upslope is defined. Note: the Trend is still Down. Also, the Dashed line now goes to the high of Bar 5. Of course, you had a close above the HiLo Activator buy stop (Automatic).

Chart #5 shows you the prices heading higher but, by Swing charting definition, the Trend is still down and will stay down until the previous Peak is surpassed. Classic Downtrend but Upslope.

Chart #6 shows the Bar 9 making a Swing high, but not yet taking out the previous Peak around 116-08. On Bar 10 we get a Neutral slope plotted to Bar 10's close. Please note how the HiLo Activator followed the entire upmove. So, Bar 10's Neutral slope shows a stalling of the upward march of the market. Not surprising, as prices are so close to the previous Peak (Resistance).

Chart #7. Bingo. Bar 11 smashed above the Previous Peak and the trend changes to Up. Will you look at that close? But, please remember when the slope turned up, you had a clearly defined Upslope on Bar 5.

I could have shown you hundreds of Multiple Time Frame applications. The purpose of this Advanced section was to introduce you to the concept and the real potential of Gann Swing trading using 2 time periods. If it started your creative juices flowing, then the effort was well worth it.

I wish you peace and super trading,

Robert Krausz

Robert Krausz, MH.BCHE.

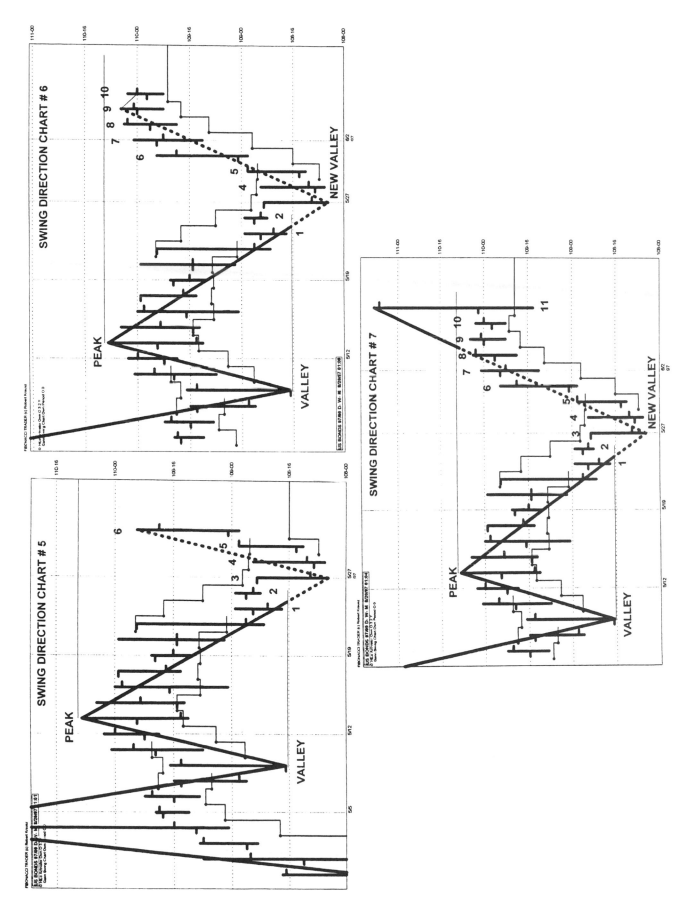

405

The Ten Trading Commandments©

i

Thou shalt not trade without a trading plan.

ii

Thou shalt backtest thy trading plan until it is inside thy very bones.

iii

Thou shalt follow thy backtested rules even if it hurts thine eyes and pocket.

iv

Thou shalt not listen to thy brother, nor thy wife, nor thy broker, only will thou listen to thyself.

v

Thou shalt ignore all rumors, even though they be from the highest in the land.

vi

The stairway to heaven is the trend, thou goest against it at thine own peril.

vii

The path to profit is strewn with fear and greed, conquer them and thou shalt be victorious.

viii

Thou shalt not risk thy bag of gold on one throw of the Dice.

ix

Thou shalt never trade unless thy stop is secured.

x

Miracles do happen, but nothing beats thine own preparation.

UPDATE & EXPLANATION

TO

"A W.D. GANN TREASURE DISCOVERED"

Many thanks for your comments and questions. Hopefully, this Update will cover most of them. To those of you who wrote to say thanks and are using the ideas profitably, I say 'well done - keep up the good work'. This applies especially to those who took advantage of the $25.00 offer to try the Fibonacci Trader™ program for 30 days to check out the rules in the book and to look at other commodities and shares of your choice.

Here are some answers:

1. The book (and I) only use the data for <u>T-Bonds</u> for the Day Session <u>only</u>.

2. If you currently update the "back adjusted" data for the Bonds, you may not get <u>exactly</u> the same price points as in the book. Of course, for Stocks and Shares it will be the same unless there has been a split in the stock, since publication.

3. **HiLo ACTIVATOR - WEEKLY ("NEXT" TIME PERIOD)**
   If you are using the Professional Plan (page 263) then the HiLo Activator of the WEEKLY comes into play via the rules for that plan. Most of you realized by looking at the charts for this plan that <u>we need to recalculate</u> the Weekly HiLo Activator IF a New High or New Low is made <u>during the week</u>. IE: Recalculate and replot if you get a new High or Low during the week. Of course, the Fibonacci Trader™ program does this automatically in Real Time, as this trading plan uses "real time" data.

4. **PEAKS & VALLEYS**
   Lots of questions about this...
   A) When using the "Re-Entry Rule", the plan uses "Minor Peaks/Valleys". It does NOT wait for the Gann Swing Peaks or Valleys.
   B) Can one use these "Minor Peaks/Valleys" for earlier entry at other times? The answer is "MAYBE" (but, this is not part of the plan.) I suggest that you check it VERY carefully on the contract of your choice. See charts below. Under Section 6, which shows these "Minor Peaks/Valleys".

5. Why doesn't the Swing always go to the Lowest Low or the Highest High? Especially the setup of Chart #7A (page 21 in the book) was questioned. Point #6 PLUS the attached charts should answer your questions.

6. CHART #7A (page 21 in the book)
    At point "D: (Bar 1) we have a Swing High (1 tick higher than the previous bar). Bar 2 makes a new high, but it also makes a Low that takes out the previous Valley point "C", thus changing to a Down Trend. Now, if the program would plot a line to this bar's high, then it would have to plot a line straight down the bar, to the Low. Of course, you would not see it. Therefore, if prices take out a previous Valley or Peak, this is the only way to handle it in a usable manner. This does not alter the results.

    CHART #7B
    This shows bars 2, 3, 4 continuing downwards and the down trend continues until Bar 5, this causes a minor upswing showed by a thin line ("white" in the Fibonacci Trader™ program). This forms a "Minor" Valley point at "E", which is the low of Bar 4. So far so good.

    CHART #7C
    Bar 6 gives a second consecutive higher high (by 1 tick) and then we have 5 days of Lower Lows (7, 8, 9, 10, 11) and the downtrend continues, until Bar 12 when we get a "minor" upswing. (Note the minor swing is plotted to the "close" of the bar and not the high or the low. This is shown in Chart #7D, and Bar 13 is still "neutral". A "Minor" Valley has formed.

    CHART #7E
    Bar 14 takes out the low of 11 and the downtrend continues (13 & 14 are two consecutive lower lows that are needed). Could you have sold again when the "minor" Valley was taken out? Maybe, but check it out. The trend is "down" and HiLo Sell Stop is above the prices.

NEW RULE

20 MIN RULE. Use only on Major government "number" days. Take action ONLY AFTER the High or the Low of the first 20 minute bar is taken out. I use this rule without fail. Please see the last page of 1997 Professional Plan Charts herewith. It was used during the week of 12/1/97. Of course, you need real time data for this rule as well as for the Professional Plan.

These answers should be of some help. Keep the questions coming (no more than 3 at a time please).

Wishing you good trading,

Robert Krausz

Robert Krausz, MH BCHE

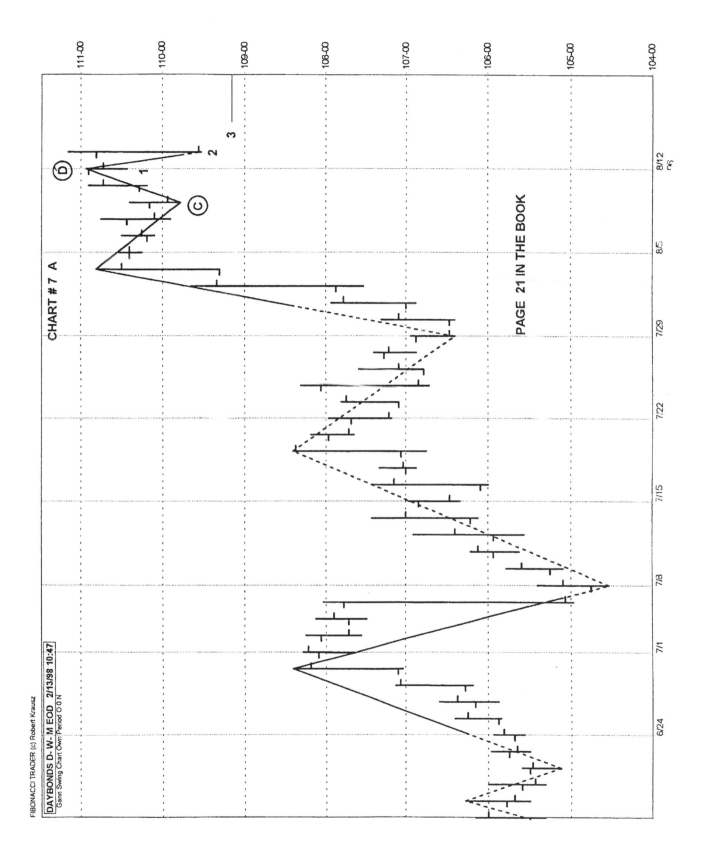

CHART # 7 A

PAGE 21 IN THE BOOK

DAYBONDS D- W- M EOD 2/13/98 10:47
Gann Swing Chart Own Period 0 0 N

409

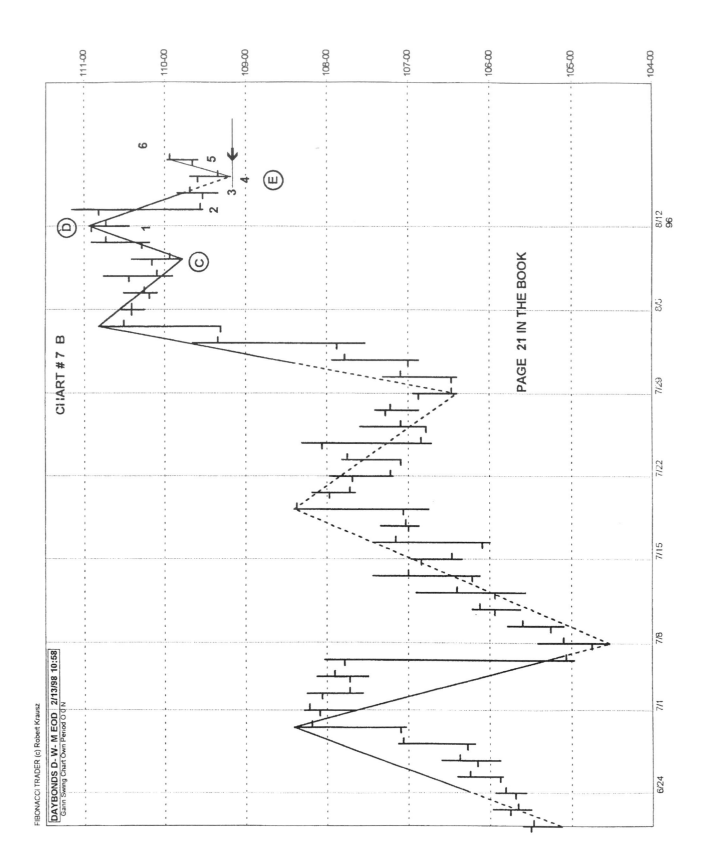

FIBONACCI TRADER (c) Robert Krausz

DAYBONDS D- W- M EOD   2/13/98 10:58
Gann Swing Chart Own Period O 0 N

CHART # 7 B

PAGE 21 IN THE BOOK

410

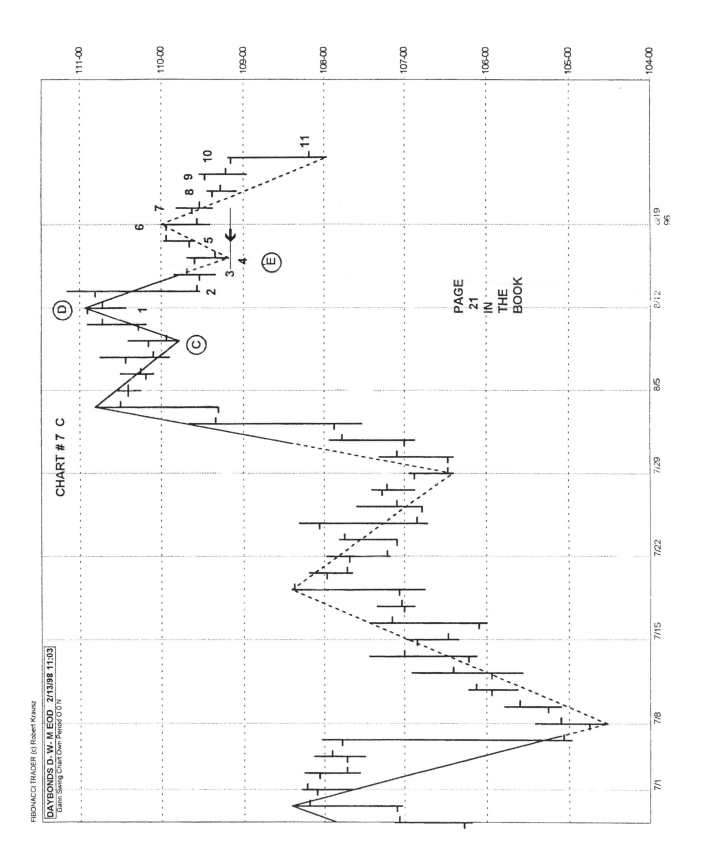

FIBONACCI TRADER (c) Robert Krausz

DAYBONDS D- W- M EOD 2/13/98 11:03
Gann Swing Chart Own Period O O N

CHART # 7 C

PAGE
21
IN
THE
BOOK

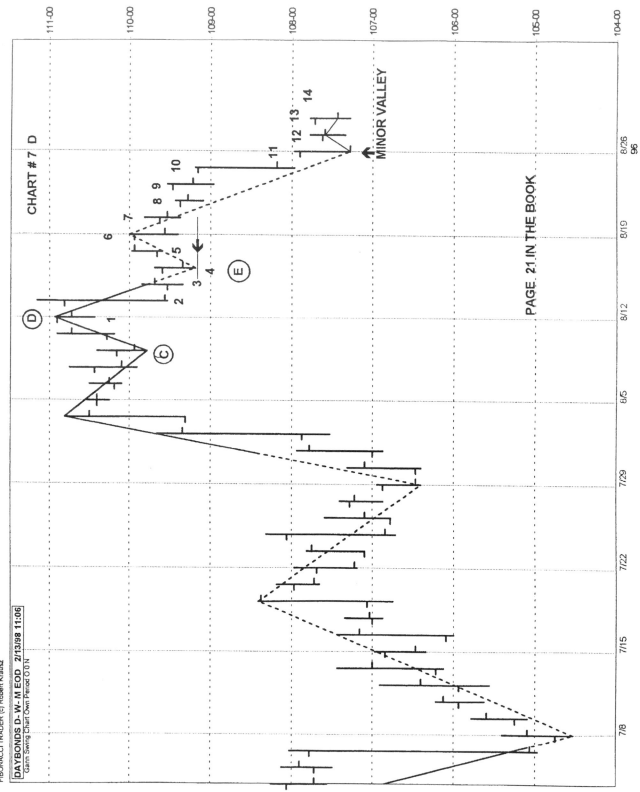

FIBONACCI TRADER (c) Robert Krausz

DAYBONDS D- W- M EOD 2/13/98 11:06
Gann Swing Chart Own Period O 0 N

CHART # 7 D

MINOR VALLEY

PAGE 21 IN THE BOOK

412

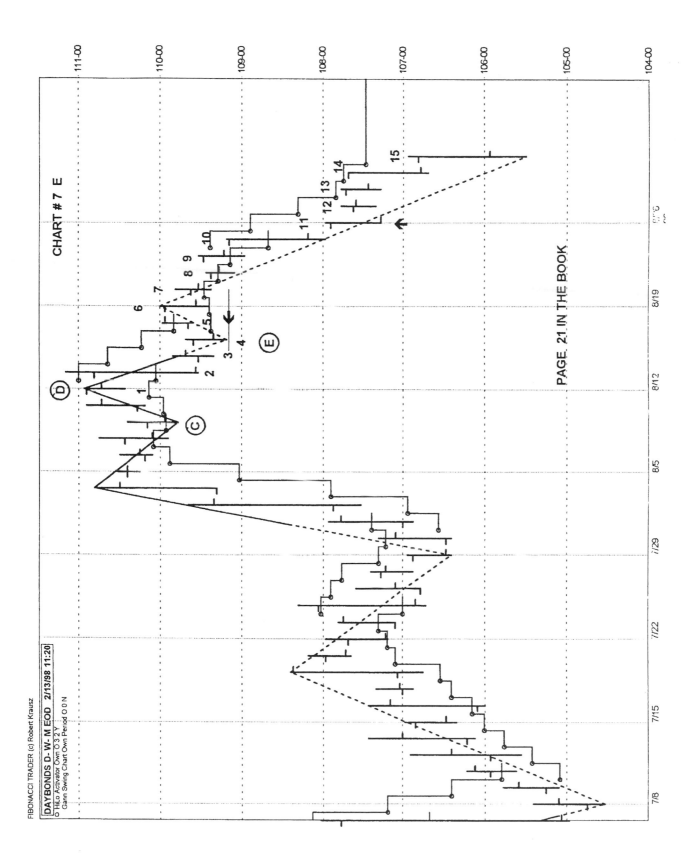

CHART # 7 E

PAGE 21 IN THE BOOK

FIBONACCI TRADER (c) Robert Krausz

DAYBONDS D- W- M EOD 2/13/98 11:20
O HiLo Activator Own O 3 2 Y
Gann Swing Chart Own Period O 0 N

413